Type Designers of the
Twentieth Century

Type Designers of the Twentieth Century

David Jury

BODLEIAN
LIBRARY
PUBLISHING

Contents

7	Preface
10	Introduction
27	William Morris and Nineteenth-century Perceptions of Technology
37	**PART ONE: Cold Metal Type**
43	Frederic Goudy
51	Bruce Rogers
61	Frederic Warde
69	Emery Walker
83	Edward Johnston
93	**PART TWO: Hot Metal Type**
101	Morris Fuller Benton
109	Rudolf Koch
117	Paul Renner
127	Oswald Cooper
133	William A. Dwiggins
141	Eric Gill
151	Harold Curwen
159	Stanley Morison
173	Jan van Krimpen
183	Hans Mardersteig
191	Robert H. Middleton
199	Georg Trump
207	A.M. Cassandre
215	Jan Tschichold
227	Berthold Wolpe
233	Roger Excoffon
243	**PART THREE: Phototypesetting**
253	Max Miedinger
257	Aldo Novarese
263	Hermann Zapf
271	Adrian Frutiger
277	Wim Crouwel
285	Bram de Does
293	Margaret Calvert
303	**PART FOUR: Digitization**
309	Matthew Carter
317	Gerard Unger
325	Erik Spiekermann
333	Neville Brody
343	Carol Twombly
349	Martin Majoor
357	Zuzana Licko
365	Jeremy Tankard
375	Tobias Frere-Jones
380	Chronology
385	Letterform Terminology
386	Glossary
390	Notes
408	Bibliography
412	Picture Credits
412	Index

Fontstand

Fonts Pricing Students Gift Cards Articles Blog iOS App Recommend Help

Download 1.3.0
Mac OS X 10.9 and newer
6.2 MB

One-click font rentals for desktop and web.

Fontstand is a Mac OS X app that allows you to try fonts for free or rent them by the month for desktop and web use for just a fraction of the regular price.

Choose from 1025 families from 43 foundries ›

▶ Introduction

Try fonts for free in any app
You can try fonts for free. They will be activated on your computer for 1 hour.

Rent fonts just for 10% of their price
You can rent fonts for 10% of their retail price per month and use them as you would any regular font.

Share fonts with co-workers
Share fonts with your team for just a fraction of the rental price.

Easy-to-use webfonts
Most of the fonts include also free, hosted, easy-to-set up webfonts.

Keep fonts forever
After you've rented a font for a total of 12 months, it will be yours to keep and use forever.

Production Type
17 families 190 fonts

Letters from Sweden
13 families 80 fonts

Emigre
101 families 520 fonts

Rosetta
24 families 186 fonts

Blackletra
8 families 58 fonts

CAST
16 families 196 fonts

Bold Monday
20 families 203 fonts

Commercial Type
26 families 311 fonts

OH no Type Co.
3 families 10 fonts

newlyn
6 families 69 fonts

TypeTogether
28 families 331 fonts

Retype
7 families 66 fonts

Storm Type Foundry
89 families 1082 fonts

Monokrom
7 families 28 fonts

Type Supply
6 families 57 fonts

Typotheque
139 families 1460 fonts

Typofonderie
10 families 93 fonts

Indian Type Foundry
76 families 445 fonts

Preface

The appearance of a letterform printed on the surface of a sheet of paper is the conclusion of an often long and convoluted process, with tensions between art, craft, technology and commerce rarely allowed to be far from the designer's mind. This book aims to provide an account of the elaborate and sometimes volatile process by which type was made; the ever-changing purposes for which it was designed; the identities and working processes of its creators and manufacturers; and, crucially, the changing occupations and expectations of those to whom it was sold – from printer to designer and, finally, the general public.

Without doubt, choosing just thirty-seven from the many hundreds of type designers who have made a significant contribution to type and typographic design during the twentieth century felt tawdry. The choice was determined by the need to explain what it meant to be a type designer in that tumultuous century; careers, working relationships, achievements and failures. Prodigiousness was not a consideration. A few designers included in this book created just one typeface, others a hundred or more, but in every case, their type has played an integral role in the culture it was designed to reveal.

The designers have been placed in order of birth. Most straddle two technological eras. Some straddle three. Matthew Carter and Hermann Zapf straddle all four.

A note about illustrations
Images of pre-digital type have been sourced from printed material – usually contemporaneous with the release of the typeface and where-ever possible from type specimens. Although every effort has been made to find printed samples that show a fount at its best, images will be affected by the variable standard of printing and the state of the substrate. Nevertheless, showing typefaces in their original and authentic form is preferable to using digital 'revived', 'refreshed' or 'renewed' equivalents.

Frontispiece: *Walbaum*, 24-point metal type that was cast on a Monotype Super Caster. Two 6-point leads (pronounced 'leds') can be seen between each line.

p. 4: A glass master (or 'matrix') on which a typeface is printed in negative form. This disc is from the Berthold Diatronic phototypesetting system, *c.*1979, and holds *Futura*.

Opposite: The website designed by Ondrej Jób for Fontstand, a 'one-click font rental' app that allows a designer to download and use fonts for a brief period or to rent them by the month. Fontstand was created by type designers Andrej Krátky and Peter Bil'ak, who are based in the Netherlands.

quod sub imperio Pharnacis fuerat:prouinciasq; populi romani a bar/
baris atq; inimicis regibus: interposito amicissimo rege muniuit. Eidē
tetrarchiā legibus gallograecorū:iure gentis & cognationis adiudicauit:
occupatam & possessam paucis ante annis a Deiotaro.Neq; tamē usq;
diutius moratus ē:q̄ necessitas urbanaeq; seditionū pati uidebat'. Rebus
felicissime celerrimeq; confectis:in italiam celerius ōiū opiniōe uenit.

CAII IVLII CAESARIS BELLI AFRICI OPII AVT HIR/
TII COMMENTARIVS QVINTVS.

Caesar itineribus iustis confectis nullo die intermisso
ad.xiiii.kal. ianuarii lilybeum peruenit.statimq; os/
tendit sese naues uelle conscendere:cum nō āplius
legionem tyronum haberet una:equitesq; uix sexcē/
tos. Tabernaculum secundum littus ipsū cōstituit:
ut prope fluctus uerberaret. Hoc eo consilio fecit:ne
quis morae quicq̄ fere speraret. & ut omnes in dies
horasq; parati essent. Incidit per id tempus:ut tempestates ad nauigā/
dum idoneas non haberet. Nihilo tamen minus in nauibus remiges
militesq; continere: & nullam praetermittere occasionem profectionis.
cum praesertim ab incolis eius prouinciae nunciaretur aduersariorum
copiae:equitatus infinitus : legiones regiae tres:leuis armaturae magna
uis:Scipionis decem:elephanti centum uiginti:classesq; esse cōplures.
tamen non deterrebatur animo:& spe confidebat. Interim indies & na/
ues longae adaugeri: & onerariae cōplures eodem concurrere: & legiones
tyronū conuenire. In his ueterana legio quinta:equitum ad duo milia
legionibus collectis sex: & equitum duobus milibus: ut quaeq; prima
legio uenerat: ī naues longas imponebatur:equites autem ī onerarias
ita maiorem partem nauium antecedere iussit. & insula petere aponia/
na:quae nō abē a lilybeo. Ibiq; commoratus bona paucorū uēdit publi/
cae. Deinde Allieno praetori qui siciliam optinebat de ōnibus rebus prae
cipit: & de reliquo exercitu celeriter imponendo. Datis mandatis con/
scendit ad.vi.kal. ianuarii & reliquas naues statim est consecutus. Ita
uento certo celeriq; nauigio uectus:post diem quartam cū longis pau
cis nauibus in conspectū africae uenit. Nā neq; onerariae reliquae praeter
paucas uento dispersae:atq; errabundae diuersa loca petierunt. clupeā
classe preteruehitur: deinde neapolim. complura praeterea castella &
oppida non longe a mari reliquit. Postq̄ adrumetum accessit: ubi prae/
sidium erat aduersariorū:cui praeerat.C.Considius:& a clupea secūdū

oram maritimam cum equitatu adrumeti.Cn.Piso cū mauris circiter
tribus milibus apparuit. Ibi paulisper Caesar ante portum cōmoratus:
dum reliquae naues conuenirent: exponit exercitum .Cuius numerus ī
praesentia fuit peditū tria milia:equitū centū quinquaginta. Castrisq;
ante oppidum positis:sine iniuria cuiusq; consedit. cohibetq; omnes
a praeda. Oppidani interim muros armatis cōplent. ante portā frequē
tes consident ad se defendendum. quorum numerus duarum legionū
intus erat. Caesar circum oppidum uectus natura loci perspecta: redit ī
castra. Non nemo culpae eius imprudētiaeq; assignabat:q̄ circum
loca gubernatoribus praefectisq; qd peterent:praeceperat:neq; ut more
ipsius consuetudo superioribus temporibus fuerat : tabellas signatas
dederat:ut ī tempore his perlectis locum certū peterent uniuersi.quod
minime Caesarem fefellerat. Nam neq; ullum portum terrae africae quō
classes decurrerēt:pro certo tutū ab hostium praesidio fore suspicabat'.
Sed fortuitu oblatam occasionem egressus aucupabatur . L. Plancus
interim legatus petit a Caesare: uti sibi daret facultatem cum Considio
de pace agendi:si posset aliqua ratione perduci ad sanitatem. Itaq; da
ta facultate litteras conscribit:& eas captiuo dat perferēdas ad oppidū
ad Considium. Quo simulatq; captiuus peruenisset : litterasq;(ut erat
mandatum)Considio porrigere coepisset:priusq̄ acciperet ille:unde sī̄t
istas? Tum captiuus:uenio a Caesare. Tunc Considius: Vnus est inquit
Scipio impator hoc tempore populi romani. Deinde in cōspectu suo
captiuum interfici iubet. Litterasq; nōdum perlectas:sicut erat signa/
tae:dat homini certo ad Scipionem perferēdas. Postq̄ una nocte & die
ad oppidum consumpta : neq; responsum a Considio dabat : neq; ei
reliquae copiae succurrebant:neq; equitatu abundabat : & ad oppidum
oppugnādum non satis copiarum habebat:& eas tyronum neq; primo
aduentu conuulnerari exercitum uolebat: & oppidi egregia munitio
difficilisq; ad oppugnādū erat ascensus: & nuntiabant auxilia magna
eq̄tatus oppidanis suppetias uenire:nō est uisa ratio ad oppugnādū
oppidum commorandi:ne dum in ea re Caesar est occupatus: circun
uentus a tergo ab equitatu hostium laboraret . Itaq; castra cū mouere
uellet:subito ex oppido erupit multitudo:atq; equitatus subsidio uno
tēpore eis casu succurrit:qui erat missus a Iuba ad stipēdiū accipiēdū.
Castraq; unde Caesar egressus iter facere coeperat:occupat. & eius agmē
extremum insequi coeperunt. Quae res cum animaduersa esset : subito
legionarii consistunt: & equites quanq̄ erant pauci: tamen cōtra tātam
multitudinem audacissime concurrunt. Accidit res incredibilis: ut eq̄
tes minus triginta galli maurorum equitum duo milia loco pellerent:

Quia noueram mores hominum; tum etiam pertentare te prorsus uolui, q̃ recte ista sentires. Sed omittamus haec iam tandem fili; atq; ad eam partem sermonis, ex qua egressi sumus, reuertamur.
B. F. Immo uero pater nec reuertamur: quid enim amplius nobiscum platanis illis? de iis enim loquebamur. Sed (si placet) ad Aetnam potius, de qua sermo haberi coeptus est, properemus.
B. P. Mihi uero pérplacet; ita tamen, ut ne festines: tibi enim ego omnes has pomeridianas horas dico. Sed quoniam me impellente nimium iam extra Aetnae terminos prouecti sumus, non cõmittam, ut te interpellem saepius; nisi quid erit, quod de ea ipsa te rogem. B. F. Sanè mons ipse situ, forma, magnitudine, feritate, incendiis mirus; demum tota sui qualitate ac specie longe conspicuus, et sibi uni par est. Ab aurora mare Ionium bibit; et Ca

tanam sustinet imo in pede: cum sole descendit in insulam, qua Tyrrhenum pelagus est; et quae Aeoliae appellantur: laterorsus, in septentriones uergenti Pelorus obiicitur, et Italiae angustiae sunt: contra reliqua insula súbiacet, tractúsque ii omnes, qui cum Lilyboeo in Africam protenduntur. Ipsa Aetna radices suas ferè in orbem deducit; nisi sicubi orientem, et meridiémuersus promisso cliuo paulisper extenditur: celebs degit; et nullius montis dignata coniugium caste intra suos terminos continetur. circumitur non minus, q̃. c. mil. pass. ascenditur ferè per uiginti, qua breuior uia. Imi colles, ac omnis radicum ambitus per oppida, et per uicos frequens inhabitatur; Baccho, Pallade, Cerere feraces terrae; armentorum omnis generis supra, q̃ credas, feracissimae. Hic amoenissima loca circunquaq: hic fluuii personantes: hic obstrepentes riui:

Introduction

At the beginning of the twentieth century, the focus of type designers was firmly on the fifteenth century – more specifically, on Renaissance Venice and two roman typefaces cut within twenty-six years of each other. The first was designed, cut and printed by Nicolas Jenson in 1470; the second designed and cut by Francesco Griffo for the printer and publisher Aldus Manutius in 1496.

Revered twentieth-century typefaces such as the *Doves Type*, *Goudy Oldstyle*, *Centaur* and *Lutetia* have their origins in Jenson's types, whilst *Garamond*, *Bembo*, *Times New Roman* and *Dante* have their origins in Griffo's types for Manutius's Aldine Press. All of these, and so many more, represent what are possibly the only products of the Italian Renaissance to have remained largely unchanged, not only in appearance but, more surprisingly, also in their production and use up to and including a considerable part of the twentieth century.

Jenson was born in Sommevoire, north-eastern France, in 1420. He had first-hand experience in fine metalworking and casting, and is thought to have been the director of the mint in Tours before travelling to Germany to learn about printing and then settling in Venice. It is assumed, therefore, that he cut his own types. In contrast, Manutius, born around 1450 into a wealthy family, was a scholar and a teacher before establishing the Aldine Press in his forties.

When Jenson arrived in Venice he knew how to print and how to make type.[1] In contrast, Manutius knew little about printing and probably even less about how type was made. He did, however, have a passion for books. He moved to Venice for the purpose of opening a printshop and brought with him two partners: a financial backer, Pierfrancesco Barbarigo, and a printer, Andrea Torresani, who had learned his printing skills from Jenson and who had acquired typographic material, including roman punches,[2] from Jenson's printshop. Possibly on the recommendation of Torresani,[3] Manutius commissioned Francesco Griffo from Bologna to cut his type.

Manutius will have owned copies of Jenson's books, and he certainly had the means to buy a fount of Jenson's acclaimed roman types,[4] or to arrange to have a close copy made for his own use (throughout northern Italy, many close imitations of Jenson's

Previous page: (left) Nicolas Jenson, Caesar's *Commentarii*, 1471. (right) Aldus Manutius, Pietro Bembo's *De Aetna*, 1496. Both Jenson and Manutius's type (the latter cut by Griffo) is approximately 16 point. Manutius popularized the smaller, octavo format.

Top: Nicolas Jenson's type, from his *De Praeparatio Evangelica*, by Eusebius, Venice, 1470.

Above: Aldus Manutius's type, cut by Griffo, from his *De Aetna* by Pietro Bembo, 1496. Both are approximately 16 point.

type had been already been cut). It can be assumed, therefore, that Manutius made a conscious decision that he not only wanted a typeface of his own, but that it should also be an improvement on Jenson's. Precisely how this was to be achieved, and the extent to which it was guided by Manutius or by Griffo, can only be speculated. Griffo was considered the 'most illustrious sculptor of Latin, Greek and Hebrew letters',[5] and as such was certainly capable of interpreting any instructions from Manutius, but he was also capable of creating a typeface that reflected ideas of his own.

It is not unusual for the identity of the creator of a typeface to be obscured by the convoluted way it came into existence. Who should receive the credit as 'designer' – the person who commissions and instructs, or the person who interprets and cuts the actual letters? This will be a recurring issue.

Early development
When Jenson set up his printing and publishing house in 1470, printing was still a new, exciting and innovative activity. Gutenberg had printed his 42-line Bible – the first Western book printed from moveable type – only fifteen years earlier in Mainz, Germany. Like Gutenberg, Jenson based the appearance of his type on the letterforms he admired and read in the handwritten books that preceded printing and which, no doubt, he had in his own collection.[6] For Gutenberg this had been blackletter, but for Jenson it was the humanist style of handwriting that was practised by scribes working in the vicinity of Venice and Padua.

Jenson used his roman types for all the books he printed between 1470 and 1473, but decided he needed a different type for the religious and legal texts that he planned to print and publish. For these he cut a rotunda typeface (a rounded style of blackletter), which he considered more appropriate for the subject matter. Jenson was a consummate businessman, and almost from the outset sold or perhaps leased copies of his celebrated roman type, in the form of founts cast from his matrices, to printers in Venice and across northern Italy. In this way Jenson was responsible for introducing the trade in type from about 1471.[7]

Some of the printers who bought Jenson's type would eventually sell or lease them to other printers. Attempts to record this spread of Jenson's types across Europe is, however, complicated by the fact that evidence of such transactions is generally limited to finding printed material that incorporates them. This is further complicated because the appearance of printed letterforms is affected by the varying levels of skill and/or working practices of printers, the deteriorating state of the type itself as it is used, and the necessity, eventually, of replacing individual worn, damaged or lost letters with locally created substitutes. Until very recently, with the combined use of a macro lens and digital technology, unequivocal identification had been all but impossible to establish.

Fortunately, matrices were made of copper. For this reason, coupled with their intrinsic value, many have survived and, indeed, can still be used today.[8] Also, there are examples of surviving metal type that go back to about 1580, so our knowledge of how early types were made is quite thorough. The process remained virtually unchanged and continued as a commercial practice into the twentieth century.

Perhaps less surprising is the fact that the appearance of printed letters has changed so little. Handwriting, when applied to correspondence, notes, receipts etc., is generally a compromise between letterforms that are quick and efficient to write and those that are easy to read.[9] When letterforms are created for printing they are designed solely to be read, with the result that, despite their close origins to handwriting, their appearance has culminated in a separate set of forms, each with a distinct identity that has come to represent its exemplar.

Much is made of Jenson's roman types being the result of his careful study of contemporary humanistic handwritten texts, but they are also a fabricated interpretation, a process formalized by the technical demands of their making. Unlike handwriting, in which variations of each letter are accepted, only one version of each letter is normally required in a given fount. These are then adjusted to enable each letter to fit evenly but comfortably alongside every other letter.

Some twenty years after the appearance of Jenson's type, Manutius commissioned Francesco Griffo to cut his roman type. The result, although deeply indebted to Jenson, also demonstrated a shift towards a more prudent, more rational set of letters. Griffo stayed close to Jenson when cutting the lowercase – with the exception of the cross bar of the 'e', which he made horizontal. His lowercase is fractionally narrower and the x-height is slightly larger, while the contrast between thick and thin lines has been marginally increased. A clear and significant divergence, however, can be seen when comparing capitals. Griffo's capitals are shorter than the ascenders. This distinct

Top: Handwritten blackletter from a composite manuscript, 12th–14th centuries.

Above: Handwritten manuscript (scribe: Ciriaco, d'Ancona) in Carolingian minuscule, 1436. Carolingian is the direct ancestor of most modern-day typefaces.

12 Type Designers of the Twentieth Century

design decision was to provide a more even textual colour and therefore, a smoother reading experience. Equally importantly, Griffo also chose to adhere more closely to roman stone-cut models for his capitals.[10]

All of these subtle adjustments moved Griffo's type further away from the handwritten sources that marked Jenson's type, and signalled the beginning of what was to be a continuing tendency in the design of type all the way through to, and including, the twentieth century. It was gradual at first – it was not until Robert Estienne, in Paris in 1530, started printing books using a type designed in the new 'Aldine fashion' that European typography experienced 'a new epoch'.[11] It then suddenly gained momentum in the second half of the eighteenth century – first in Birmingham, with John Baskerville's types (cut by John Handy), then in Paris, with Pierre-Simon Fournier and Firmin Didot, and culminating in Parma, Italy, with Giambattista Bodoni, who designed and cut his types during the final decades of the 1700s. Their distinctive flat, unbracketed serifs, the extreme contrast between thick and thin strokes, and their sharp, geometric construction, were magnificently displayed in Bodoni's *Manuale Tipografico*, published posthumously in 1818 and whose influence would remain potent until the end of the nineteenth century. After a brief hiatus, lasting about thirty years, Griffo's type returned once more to become the focus of type design in the twentieth century.

The 'hiatus' was created by William Morris, with the types he designed for books printed at his Kelmscott Press between 1891 and 1896. His enormous influence on type and typographic design dominated the first two decades of the twentieth century.

Since his days as a student at Oxford, Morris had cultivated a passion for medieval texts which led to his determination to master the arts of illumination, calligraphy and gilding. The

Below: Robert Granjon's *Civilité* of 1557 is an inventive typeface designed to mimic a style of handwriting used in France for business transactions. Technically *Civilité* is highly sophisticated and includes some fifty alternate characters and ligatures as well as many additional flourishes.

adherence of Jenson's type to the handwritten letter meant that, in Morris's much-heralded opinion at the time, Jenson had created 'the best and clearest' typeface ever conceived.[12] In contrast, and to emphasize the point, he thought that Griffo's types for Manutius marked the beginning of a descent that culminated in the 'sweltering hideousness' of Bodoni's types. Here is Morris's comment, in which he also provides a succinct, personal summary of type design from Jenson to his present day:

> The sweltering hideousness of the Bodoni letter, the most illegible type that was ever cut, with its preposterous thicks and thins, has been mostly relegated to works that do not profess anything but the baldest utilitarianism (though why even utilitarianism should use illegible types, I fail to see), and Caslon's letter, and the somewhat wiry, but in its way, elegant old-faced type cut in our own days, has largely taken its place. It is rather unlucky, however, that a somewhat low standard of excellence has been accepted for the design of modern roman type at its best, the comparatively poor and wiry letter of Plantin, and the Elzeviers, having served for the model, rather than the generous and logical designs of the fifteenth-century Venetian printers, at the head of whom stands Nicolas Jenson … [13]

Stanley Morison, influential writer as well as typographic and type designer, who was appointed in 1922 as advisor to the Monotype Corporation, profoundly disagreed with Morris regarding the types cut by Griffo for Manutius's Aldine Press. Far from marking the beginning of the end of fine printing in Italy, as Morris believed, Morison was convinced of its superiority: 'I wish to pull down the mighty [Jenson] from his seat and to exalt the humble Aldus'.[14] He argued that it was from Griffo that the finest typefaces – *Garamond, Granjon, Caslon, Baskerville, Fournier* – had flowed. When he initially voiced this opinion, the general consensus was against him. The most authoritative book at the time, Daniel B. Updike's two-volume *Printing Types, their History*

Right: *Monotype Bembo,* cut by the Monotype Corporation under the direction of Stanley Morison, and the Monotype Drawing Office, released in 1929. An alternative 'R' with a more tucked-in leg for body text was also available.

ABCDEFGHIJKLMNO
PQRSTUVWXYZabcd
defghijklmnopqrstuvwx
yz1234567890?!&

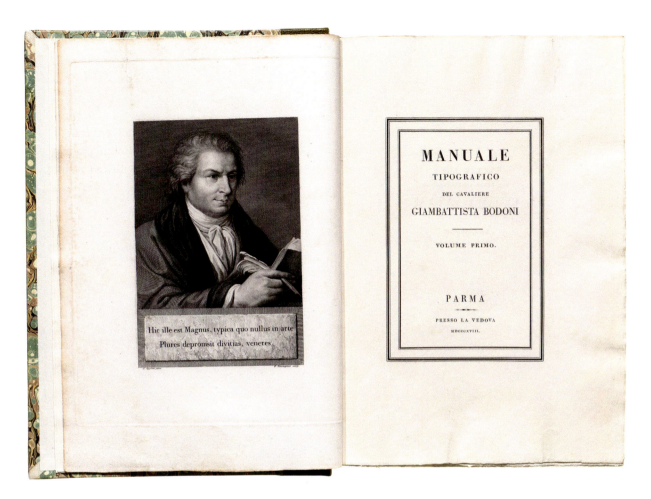

Form and Use, published in 1922, supported Morris's argument in stating that 'the Aldine type [was] distinctly inferior to Jenson's'.[15] However, between the book's first publication and an updated edition in 1937, Morison had initiated his groundbreaking array of twentieth-century type revivals at Monotype, culminating with the release of *Bembo* in 1929 – commonly referred to as the 'Aldine Roman'. In the new edition of his book Updike reversed his opinion, and so did much of the printing fraternity.

Apart from dismissing the prevailing scholarly opinion in regard to the history of typography – something he likely relished – Morison brought aesthetic and practical issues to the fore, characterizing Griffo's type as being of 'better proportions' than Jenson's, with its smaller capitals, absence of slab-like serifs, horizontal stroke in the 'eye' of the 'e', and its consequent ability to produce a restful page. It also freed type designers from the tyranny of the pen and gave license to think instead of the present and of type as a discrete entity, that could and should respond to

Above: Giambattista Bodoni, frontispiece and title page of *Manuale Tipografico*, 1818 (published posthumously by his wife). Bodoni became the most admired of type designers and his printshop in Parma became a popular destination for wealthy aristocrats on the European Grand Tour who, naturally, bought books to add to their libraries back home.

The increased fatness in JOB-LETTER is an improvement, but is it not in many instances carried to an extreme? ABCDEFGHIJKLMNOP

Above right: Vincent Figgins, *Antique No 1*, from his *Specimen of Printing Types*, 1837.

the necessities of the materials and the technologies with which it was both created and used.

Nevertheless, the roman lowercase letters we use today have essentially the same framework as those cut by Jenson in 1470. Considering that it is virtually the earliest-known roman ever designed, Jenson's type is rightly viewed as being one of the most significant contributors to the history of typography and Western culture.

Display type

Display types were created to meet the demands of commercial competition. This competition also encouraged a substantial growth in what the print trade had previously described as 'jobbing printing' – an entirely unpredictable array of work that might include packaging material, hand-bills, and in-store placards, as well as a range of printed items required to support the administration of any large commercial organization such as headed notepaper, invoices, receipts, statements and calling cards.[16] The purpose of a display typeface was to attract attention by its distinctive appearance, even before the words they created were read. For this reason, the design of display types showed little respect for historic typographic precedence.

The first display or 'jobbing' typeface was designed, manufactured and released by Robert Thorne's Fann Street foundry in London in 1803. Thorne's typeface has flat, hair-line serifs associated with Bodoni's types. However, the contrast in line-width of Thorne's type was so exaggerated that the width of the thick stroke was almost half the capital's height. The effect was such that this style became known as *Fat Face* (a general term previously reserved for bolder faces) and was quickly copied by other foundries. Thorne is also credited with the design of the first *Egyptian* typeface (initially also called *Antique*, and a style that today is generically described as 'slab serif'), although the first dated example of this kind of typeface appeared in Vincent Figgins's *Specimen of Printing Types* in 1815.[17]

It was the *Specimen of Printing Types* that emphatically announced the arrival of the display typeface. As well as a *Fat Face* and an *Egyptian*, Figgins's groundbreaking first catalogue also included types that gave the illusion of three-dimensionality. His second specimen book, published in 1817, included *Tuscan* types (originally called *Ornamented* types), with their distinctive bifurcated serifs generally divided at the centre of the stem. Other foundries were quick to follow suit, making their own closely copied versions and adding italics.

Sans serif, the most significant category of display typeface, made a tentative, single-line appearance in William Caslon IV's specimen catalogue of *c*.1816.[18] While links between earlier display typefaces and the unrestricted work of signwriters of the time have been justly speculated,[19] the origin of sans serif was a conscious attempt to revive the spirit of the earliest stone-cut roman letterforms.[20] The same single line of sans serif letters reappeared in the specimen book of Caslon's successor, Blake Garnett, around 1819. It presumably created little interest, because neither this nor any other sans serif appeared again until both Figgins and William Thorowgood issued their own versions in 1832. (Figgins described it as *Sans Serif*, Thorowgood as *Grotesque*.) Despite being crudely drawn, the 'tremendous blackness'[21] of these sans serif types was a major asset to the jobbing printer.

Figgins's 1832 *Sans Serif* is displayed as an 8-line specimen (96 point: a 'line' being 12 points). In the following year a 20-line (240 point) specimen is shown, magnificently represented by a single character that fills the page. The enormous size of the letterforms offered a very different viewing experience. Being too large to be read they became images, causing their negative, internal forms ('counters') to become transformed into positive white shapes trapped within heavy black contours, whose bold twists and

Below left: Sans serif typeface, commonly described at the time as *Egyptian*, from William Caslon IV's type specimen book, *c*.1816.

Below: Robert Thorne's *Fat Face*, 1821. 'Fat Face' has become a generic term, but in Thorne's specimen book this type is described as *Twelve Line Pica Roman No. 2*.

turns combined to become dynamic yet elegant abstract forms. Type for display had become a possible source of expression – a new and alien function for the printer.

The large size of display faces was essential to their purpose, but casting large type created practical problems. The molten metal would frequently cool unevenly in the larger mould, resulting in a concave surface. Weight was another problem. A single 10-line bold 'W' could weigh a pound (454 grams), and so difficulties regarding delivery and storage of a 120-point fount cast in solid metal were considerable. Type founders experimented by casting letters onto arches to reduce weight and material costs. Meanwhile, the nature of jobbing work meant that printers would lease larger letterforms by the character to fellow printers.

Right: William Caslon's first type specimen sheet, dated 1734 (but actually issued 1738). Prior to the twentieth century the approximate size of a type was indicated by a name rather than a number: Great Primer (18 point) and Two Lines Great Primer (36 point); English (14 point); Pica (12 point); Small Pica (11 point); Long Primer (10 point).

By 1828 wood was being used as an alternative to metal from which to cut large letters, using a pantograph machine and router (see p. 86). The first catalogue of wood type was published in March 1828 by Darius Wells, who ran a jobbing printing company in New York. The cheapness of the material encouraged a more adventurous attitude to design and experiment, including two- or even three-colour characters. Low costs also meant that a printer would more likely make a purchase despite the fact that a fount might only be used rarely. Such developments encouraged both printers and their customers to begin thinking of type less as an esoteric 'black art' and more as a commonplace commodity.

The design of metal display types continued to be led by British and European type foundries until around 1860–70 when the direction of trade, which had once been entirely Britain and Europe (the 'old countries') to America (the 'new country'), became reversed. The cultural influence of the old countries would, nevertheless, remain a significant attraction deep into the twentieth century.

Buying and selling type

From around 1600, type founding was an established mode of business quite separate from printing.[22] Each type foundry had a stock of matrices, punches and a printed specimen sheet displaying all the types and sizes that were available. Many would have bought their matrices and punches as and when they became available from various sources. Because there was no consistency of measurement between type founders, this

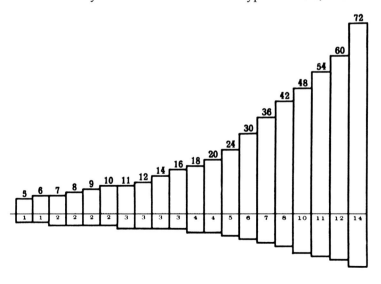

Left: The position of the baseline (or 'point line') in relation to body size, from a Stephenson Blake specimen book, 1915. The top numbers indicate the size of type, the numbers below the baseline indicate (in points) the space allocated to descenders. The effect on the proportions of letters was crude – for example the space allocated to descenders in 7-point type is the same as that in 10-point type. The diagram also demonstrates the priority given to ascenders over descenders in regard to readability.

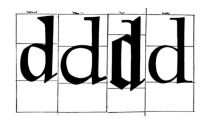

Above top: Frederic Goudy's *Medieval, Village No. 2, Goudy Text,* and *Goethe* do not share a common baseline. Adapted from an illustration in Goudy's *Typologia,* 1940.

Above bottom: *Goudy Oldstyle Light,* 1915. Frederic Goudy was critical of the American Type Foundry's enforced position of the baseline which he argued left insufficient space for descenders. The 'p' and 'q' are the worst affected. The lower bowl of the 'g' (and the vertex of the 'y') can be lifted to utilize part of the space above the baseline and so minimize its disruptive influence. This can not be done with 'p' and 'q'.

meant that great care had to be taken by a subsequent purchaser of types to ensure that what they were buying was capable of being used alongside those already owned. As late as 1755 John Smith complained in his book, *Printer's Grammar,* that, 'It ought to be made law, that each of the different bodies of letter should *always* be cast to *the same height, depth and line*; by letter Founders of the same place, *at least*' [Smith's italics].

By the time Smith wrote *Printer's Grammar,* the establishment of standard measurements of type was already a major talking point. The need for reform was all the more urgent because the significance of the industry to national prestige was beginning to be recognized. William Caslon I, punchcutter and type founder in London, had revived broader interest in type with his first Latin typeface: roman and italic, cut and cast in 12 point. It was first used by the publisher William Bowyer in 1725 and displayed on the Caslon foundry's specimen sheet in 1734. The commercial success and popularity of *Caslon* stung other type foundries in the UK and abroad into reassessing their stock, as seemingly every printer felt obliged to buy at least several pounds of *Caslon* type. Large quantities were also taken to North America by emigrant printers, so much so that *Caslon* dominated eighteenth-century American colonial printing. Following the successes of Caslon's type foundry, ambitious enterprises were established elsewhere – the most distinguished being in the Netherlands, where the printer Joh. Enschedé employed the punchcutter Joan Michael Fleischman and began manufacturing type in 1743. In France, Pierre-Simon Fournier took over the running of the Le Bé type foundry in around 1739.

The aspirational spirit, commercial success and subsequent national significance of these and other type founding companies transformed not only commercial but also cultural perceptions of type, typography and printing. Fournier realized that the ad-hoc way in which type was being made was counter-productive to the industry as a whole and that a standardization of elemental measurement should be established. In 1737 he published his *Tables des proportions des differens caractères de l'imprimerie,* in which a standard point system of measurement of type was proposed.[23] It failed, in part because of unforeseen changes in other measurement standards but also because of the inalienable interests of type manufacturers themselves. Most type founders were not concerned about a commonality of measurement because they knew that the 'problem' worked in their favour;

printers were forced to return to the same type foundry when they needed a new or replacement typeface. This also meant there was nothing in the method of creating a typeface to restrict any aspect of its style, shape or detail.

Improvements in communication, especially the growing network of roads, gave rise to stagecoach services which by the 1780s had sharply reduced travel times between Paris and the provincial cities. As a result, trade within France greatly expanded and printers were able to look further afield for new founts of type. In 1775 François Didot established a type foundry as an adjunct to his already highly respected printing, publishing and bookselling activities in Paris.

It was around this time that Didot devised a point system based on official subdivisions of the French 'foot', and in the course of the nineteenth century other type foundries felt obliged to fall into line in a bid to attract sales from new customers. The Didot system spread across France, and then the Continent and beyond.

All of this was ignored by type foundries in Britain but in America, where the number of type foundries was growing expeditiously, the need for regularity in typographic measurement was becoming increasingly evident. In 1886 the twenty-four members of the United States Type Founders Association formally adopted a point system as standard, based on that used by the largest and oldest foundry in the country: Mackellar, Smiths & Jordan in Philadelphia. Despite complaints that the MS&J system bore no relation to either the English or the French systems of measurement, it was nevertheless quickly adopted. This was due in large part to the creation of the American Type Founders Company (ATF) in 1892, with the amalgamation of twenty-three previously independent foundries. The first essential task was to make the hundreds of inherited typefaces fit a single, regularlized system of measurement in order to make all ATF typefaces compatible. Within a decade the importance of transatlantic trade caused the American point system to be adopted by type foundries in Britain.

The adoption of a standard method of measurement not only affected the manufacture of type, it also had a major influence on type design. Once it had become possible for type from one foundry to be placed alongside type from another, it became obvious that the letterforms themselves when printed together should align – meaning that they had to share a 'common' or 'standard' baseline. The 1915 specimen book of the Sheffield-based Stephenson Blake foundry included a diagram (see p. 19) showing the permanent position of the baseline for all standard sizes of type. The imposition of an immovable baseline was, of course, a severe restriction for type designers and some complained bitterly, especially during the 1920s and 1930s when revivals of renowned 'old style' types, such as *Garamond* and *Janson*, had to have their generous and rather elegant descenders truncated to fit the system. Frederic Goudy in the US was a particularly outspoken critic, and *Goudy Oldstyle*, which he designed for ATF in 1915, was a notable victim of its adverse effects. However, when Goudy designed and made his own typefaces independently at the Village Press and Letter Foundery – with no fixed baseline – they could of course, never be combined; a constraint Goudy was presumably content to acknowledge.

With the introduction in the US and then Britain of mechanized typesetting machines just before 1900, such as the Linotype and Monotype, type effectively became a machine part – if a printer bought Monotype typesetting equipment, they had no choice but to use Monotype typefaces. Monotype and Linotype quickly realized that the quality of their typefaces was critical to the sales of their typesetting machines, and so the continuous development of new types (and the revival of old types) became an imperative to commercial success. It was this, together with blatant plagiarism practiced by many type foundries, that was the prime cause for the enormous increase in the number of typefaces designed during the twentieth century. In his book *A Visual History of Type* (2018), Paul McNeil includes sixty-nine significant typefaces from the period 1450 to 1900, and over 300 between 1900 and 1999.

When the revolutionary technology of phototypesetting became commercially viable shortly after the Second World War, the typefaces that these machines used were negative images stored on film. The internal working of each maker's machine was different and so, once more, the typefaces available were limited to those in the machine-maker's library. Phototypesetting advanced quickly and new typefaces were developed that utilized the technology's unique lack of physical restriction. However, as each manufacturer's new and improved machine was launched the buyer was required to repurchase their favoured typefaces each time – a lucrative strategy for the manufacturer.

Proprietary type systems tying typefaces to specific manufacturers came to an end with the arrival of digital technology – or more specifically, PostScript, a software which allowed typefaces to be designed and sold independently of the manufacture of the systems on which they were created. When PostScript was included in the Apple LaserWriter in 1985, the desktop revolution was unleashed. A purchaser (designers having by now replaced printers as the predominant customer) could buy a typeface from, for example, Monotype, Adobe, Dutch Type

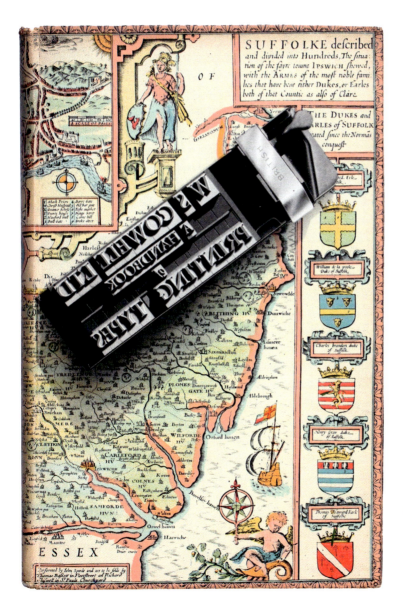

Left: *A Handbook of Types,* a book intended to promote the design prowess of renowned UK printing company W.S. Cowell, and designed in-house by John Lewis, 1948. The shadow 'points' to Ipswich, the location of the company.

Library or any of the numerous independent type designers, in the knowledge that it would load and work perfectly, regardless of which computer was used.

The change in the type founder's market, from printer to designer, is central to the narrative of twentieth-century type, transforming its use and appearance. At the beginning of the twentieth century the type founder's customer was still the printing establishment, but the jobbing printer's ability to respond to the increasingly sophisticated demands of their customers was, for the most part, inadequate, and advertising agencies moved in to fill the void. From the beginning of the century, J. Walter Thompson in the US, Mather & Crowther in the UK and other advertising agencies were employing writers and artists to create advertisements for their clients, and by 1910 they offered a broad range of services, including copywriting, layout and design, trademark development and rudimentary market research. A sound knowledge of typography and high levels of craftsmanship – the hallmarks of the jobbing printer – were no longer sufficient. Yet the printing fraternity could not, or was unwilling to, respond to these changing needs, despite conspicuous warnings in the trade's own press, such as this from New York in 1900: 'The intelligent job printer will never permit himself to forget that printing is allied to advertising, and that almost all of the printing he does depends in some way upon its success as an advertisement or as an advertising medium.'[24]

By the 1920s, strategic advertising campaigns had become a standard procedure. These were co-ordinated by the creative department within advertising agencies, staffed by art-school educated 'creatives'. The ability of advertising agencies to provide every aspect of their client's promotional requirements had progressed far beyond the capabilities of most jobbing printing establishments, leaving them to fight for the less sophisticated demands of local businesses who could not, as yet, afford full and integrated advertising services.

The printer's most lucrative and probably most demanding client was by now more likely to be the studio manager or art director of an advertising agency's creative department, or one of the growing number of independent designers of print (in the US, the American Institute of Graphic Arts had been established in 1914). In this way, while the purchaser of type remained the printer, the actual decision-making concerning which type the printer should buy was inexorably moving towards the designer.

The pressure on printers to have an extensive range of sizes and weights of the most requested typefaces was becoming unavoidable. The first half of the twentieth century was a painful and protracted period of transition for the printing industry, as it lost the ability to control the appearance of what it printed with the subsequent loss of cultural influence.[25]

Realizing this, type foundries began to adjust how they promoted their types. Unlike the print industry, there was less reluctance within type foundries to recruit designers to work on the premises, and many set up in-house design studios not only to design type but also to take responsibility for the design of promotional material. The Nebiolo foundry in Turin and Fonderie Olive in Paris, significantly both prodigious creators of display typefaces, produced exceptional promotional material showing type as a means of visual expression that was aimed at the designer. As well as often being beautifully designed – some of the best examples of twentieth-century graphic design are, indeed, type specimens – such material often included technical information about type to aid the designer in their liaison with a sometimes truculent printer.

These changes were also the reason type foundries began commissioning the design of type from 'outsiders' – renowned artists and designers – and then promoted the fact and sometimes even used the artist's name for the name of the typeface. In this way the personality of the designer, as well as their reputation, was projected onto the typeface. For some this was a controversial development, highlighting what they perceived as the degradation of a service by turning it into a celebrity spectacle. Nevertheless, the necessity of linking type and typographic design with a broader cultural milieu had become fundamental to its purpose.

Above: A. M. Cassandre, *Peignot*, in a type specimen published by Deberny & Peignot, Paris, *c*.1937. This booklet is designed for the independent typographer and graphic designer. Compare this with the specimen sheet produced by William Caslon in 1734 (p. 18), which was designed to meet the more prosaic needs of the printer.

William Morris and Nineteenth-century Perceptions of Technology

In the decade leading up to 1900, the popular press was regularly reporting momentous inventions and entertaining its readers with predictions of what radical wonders technology was going to bring in the next hundred years. The *fin de siècle* was the age of invention: 'Never before have men so ardently studied the secrets of nature and turned the knowledge thus acquired to practical account. We have become so accustomed to hearing of new inventions that nowadays they hardly surprise us.'[1] Steam had enabled the development of automotive transport and mass production, and now electronic technological miracles such as the telegraph and telephone were transforming national and international communications and media.

But advances in technology did not come without anguish. Automated machines were packed into huge factories where conditions for employees were compared to Biblical descriptions of Hell. Numerous groups, often affiliated to religious or socio-political organizations, such as The Ancoats Brotherhood in Manchester, were established specifically for the benefit of the men and women who worked in the 'Satanic' mills and factories. Such associations provided weekly concerts, dances, children's entertainments and 'enlightenment programmes' of lectures on, for example, Goethe, John Everett Millais, George Stephenson, or life in England 600 years ago. William Morris was a regular speaker.[2]

Technological advancement arrived late to printing, but by the final decades of the nineteenth century important changes to processes and working practices were taking place. The growing newspaper industry, where speed was intrinsic to success, had led the way with powered printing presses. As early as 1814 *The Times* printing house bought in a steam-driven cylinder press, and during the next eighty-five years a succession of ever faster and more efficient printing presses was installed.

Nevertheless, apart from newspaper and magazine publishers, a high percentage of nineteenth-century printing – be it an edition of 500 books or fifty jam jar labels – was achieved by hand, using one of several simple but excellent new iron presses introduced around and shortly after 1800. The first of these, the Stanhope, invented by Charles Earl Stanhope, reduced the manual force required by the printer while delivering increased

Opposite: A steam-driven, eight-cylinder revolving printing machine, 1878. The eight men are employed to feed paper into the press.

downward pressure to a printing area double the previous size. This was followed by the Columbian Press in North America in around 1813, and the Albion Press in England in around 1820. Both were used for smaller scale newspaper, book and jobbing printing for much of the nineteenth century, and thereafter mainly for proofing and then by private presses in the twentieth century.

Despite the eventual development of compact powered cylinder presses, hand-presses remained in use by most printing establishments throughout the nineteenth century and beyond. For the jobbing printer, the introduction of the treadle press (from 1840) provided automation of a limited kind but with the advantage of requiring just one person, who was able to print on to a range of papers. It also provided excellent registration, which encouraged the letterpress printer to introduce a second or even third colour.

Early fully automated printing presses worked most efficiently when smooth, harder papers – made with wood pulp and alum-rosin size[3] – were used, together with thinner inks. Speed had many benefits quite apart from improved profit margins. Improved efficiency reduced the wholesale price of books, magazines and newspapers, leading to improved levels of literacy which, in turn, created an increased demand for printed material. Between 1880 and 1900 the book trade quadrupled its production.[4]

Improved literacy enabled print to become the first mass-communication medium. The commercial and cultural influence of printing was hailed in 1877 when the Caxton Quadricentennial Celebration, which remains the largest exhibition ever mounted concerning the history of printing, was assembled in London. Its 472-page catalogue listed, sometimes with descriptive bibliographical notes, a total of 4,734 exhibited items.[5] Importantly, the exhibition not only included books but also examples of historic tools and wooden presses, as well as the latest printing presses, typesetting and type founding equipment. It was, in effect, a showcase for the printing industry.

Given William Caxton's influence in popularizing medieval literature, it is surprising that William Morris played no part in the exhibition's lengthy planning; he was certainly friends with many of those responsible, and his knowledge of Caxton, as well as medieval art, crafts and culture, was well known. In fact, the last book Morris published before he set up his own Kelmscott

Press was a private edition of Caxton's translation and printing of *The Saga of Gunnlaug the Worm-Tongue* (1899), for which Morris used a nineteenth-century facsimile of one of Caxton's types. Once his Kelmscott Press was established, five of Morris's fifty-three books to be printed were of Caxton-translated texts,[6] and all of these appeared in the first two years of the press's existence. (Morris's three-volume *The Golden Legend*, one of the Caxton translations, was intended to be his first Kelmscott Press book but this was delayed and so Morris's own, slim volume, *The Story of the Glittering Plain*, was published first.)

Morris had long held the desire to design and print his own books, an ambition no doubt fuelled by his close association over a long period with the renowned Chiswick Press in London.[7] His editing of the *Oxford and Cambridge Magazine* in his twenties had brought him into contact with one of the era's leading British printers, Charles Whittingham, then the owner of the Chiswick Press. When Morris later decided to publish his own writing it was natural that he would return to the Press, where he was able to watch his manuscript transformed into printed form as the type was hand-set, composed, locked up and transferred to the printing press. Morris was invited (or, more likely, his presence was impossible to resist) to study this process and discuss the finer points of typographic composition. Morris's ubiety within the Chiswick Press is significant in itself because it was rare for anyone from outside the print trade to be permitted to enter, let alone linger, as Morris frequently did, inside the composing room – more remarkable still, to be heeded when offering an opinion to the compositor. His assured demeanour meant that, despite his limited knowledge, he was accustomed to talking to Charles T. Jacobi, the press manager, and his staff on equal terms. Without doubt, Morris learned a huge amount from these discussions.

It was the Chiswick Press that printed *The Century Guild Hobby Horse*.[8] First published in 1884 and edited by Morris's close friend Arthur H. Mackmurdo, the journal was important in

Below: William Morris, *Golden*, 1891. The punches were cut by Edward Prince.

A B C D E F G H I J K L M N O P Q R S T U V W X Y Z Æ Œ & Qu fi ff fl ffi ffl
a b c d e f g h i j k l m n o p q r s t u v w x y z
1 2 3 4 5 6 7 8 9 0   ⁋   é è ê ë ö

ABCDEFGHIJKLMNOPQRSTUV
WXYZ & abcdefghijklmnopqrstu
vwxyz æ œ fi ff fl ffi ffl 1 2 3 4 5 6 7 8 9 0

Above: William Morris, *Troy*, 1892. The punches were cut by Edward Prince.

demonstrating that commercial printing need not inevitably mean feeble print on limp, lifeless paper. The extraordinary quality of the Chiswick Press's printing, the sound choice of paper and the finishing of *The Century Guild Hobby Horse* was reflected in the high cost of each issue. Nevertheless, it established itself as the harbinger of interest in the Arts and Crafts movement, and indeed, foreshadowed many of Morris's precepts concerning the design of print.

Significantly, the journal was designed under the guidance of Emery Walker, an acquaintance and close neighbour of Morris. Walker took full advantage of recent technical innovations available to the printing trade: especially that of photogravure to reproduce art and illustrations, achieved while not diminishing the sense of craft or craftsmanship by their use. In 1888 he was persuaded to deliver a lecture to the Arts and Crafts Exhibition Society on typography, in which he used close-up photographs of fifteenth-century printed letters by Johannes Gutenberg, Nicolas Jenson, Günther Zainer, Leonardo Bruni Aretino and others. Until this point, it had not occurred to Morris that 'printing' could venture beyond the type, paper and presswork accessible via the commercial printer at that time. It was Walker's pragmatic explanation and close-up photographs that compelled Morris, by now in his fifties, to design his *Golden* type and establish the Kelmscott Press in order to print and publish his own writing and books by the authors he loved most.[9]

Morris and Walker became close friends, no doubt helped by their mutual connection with the Chiswick Press and the Arts and Crafts Exhibition Society, as well as sharing a passion for typography and printing history. Morris bought a London-built Hopkinson & Cope Improved Albion Press and initially intended to make his own ink, but Walker found a German ink manufacturer, Gebrüder Jänecke in Hanover, whose ink had the high level of viscosity Morris was seeking. The density of the ink provided the results Morris wanted, but the printers he had employed found it difficult and time-consuming to roll out in order to achieve an evenly transferred distribution across the type. The density of the ink, together with the coating of size on the hand-made paper, severely delayed delivery of the finished sheets to the binders because they took such a long time to dry.

Morris designed three typefaces, all with Walker in close attendance. The first was *Golden* (1890), named after what had been intended to be the first Kelmscott book, *The Golden Legend*. It was based on the type cut by Nicolas Jenson and used for his printing of Pliny's *Historia Naturalis* in 1476.[10] The procedure by which *Golden* was designed, hand-cut and manufactured was repeated in 1892 when Morris decided he also needed a 'rather more gothic' typeface. This was called *Troy* (a rotunda – a rounded style of blackletter), which was cut at 18 point. Morris's third typeface was *Chaucer* (c.1893), effectively a 12-point version of *Troy*. Morris wrote that, when drawing *Golden*, he aimed to achieve letters that were 'pure in form',[11] meaning they had none of the conceits he so disliked in the popular types at the time, the most notable being an overt contrast of thick and thin strokes and compressed ('condensed') form.

Though a fervent calligrapher, Morris had no experience of designing type. To help him, Walker devised a method by which Morris could achieve his goal using photography, itself still a relatively new technology. Apparently with no qualms, Morris used enlarged photographs taken by Walker of Jenson's type which he traced and amended to his liking. Morris's final drawings were then photographed and reproduced at the required reduced size (approximately 13 point). These and Morris's drawings were then passed to the esteemed punchcutter Edward Prince, another invaluable contact provided by Walker. Later, Walker himself and then other twentieth-century type designers would repeat this same process. Nor was Morris unduly concerned about the making of the matrices and casting the type, as this was passed to the Fann Street Foundry, owned by his friend Talbot Baines Reed (who had played a major role in the organization of the Caxton quadricentennial exhibition).

A recently retired master printer, William Bowden, was employed by Morris to manage the daily activities of the press. Bowden also took responsibility for composition, all of which was done by hand. This was by no means unusual – the handsetting of type was still standard procedure in the 1890s, and for smaller jobs would remain so deep into the twentieth century. The numerous decorative initials designed and drawn

Following pages: William Morris, *The Works of Geoffrey Chaucer*, 1896. The text is set in *Chaucer*, Morris's third and final typeface which is, essentially, a 12-point version of the 18-point *Troy*.

the works of Geoffrey Chaucer now newly imprinted

HERE BEGINNETH THE TALES OF CANTERBURY AND FIRST THE PROLOGUE THEREOF

HAN THAT Aprille with his shoures soote
The droghte of March hath perced to the roote,
And bathed every veyne in swich licour,
Of which vertu engendred is the flour;
Whan Zephirus eek with his swete breeth
Inspired hath in every holt and heeth
The tendre croppes, and the yonge sonne
Hath in the Ram his halfe cours yronne,
And smale fowles maken melodye,
That slepen al the nyght with open eye,
So priketh hem nature in hir corages;
Thanne longen folk to goon on pilgrimages,
And palmeres for to seken straunge strondes,
To ferne halwes, kowthe in sondry londes;
And specially, from every shires ende
Of Engelond, to Caunterbury they wende,
The hooly blisful martir for to seke,
That hem hath holpen whan that they were seeke.

BIFIL that in that seson on a day,
In Southwerk at the Tabard as I lay,
Redy to wenden on my pilgrymage
To Caunterbury with ful devout corage,
At nyght were come into that hostelrye
Wel nyne and twenty in a compaignye,
Of sondry folk, by aventure yfalle
In felaweshipe, and pilgrimes were they alle,
That toward Caunterbury wolden ryde.

in Indian ink by Morris and others were photographically transferred to wooden blocks and then engraved by William Harcourt Hooper.[12] Illustrative material, of which Edward Burne-Jones and Walter Crane were major contributors, underwent a similar process.

The impact of the Kelmscott Press's first book, *The Story of the Glittering Plain* in 1891, was immediate and international. Five years later the general opinion was that the Kelmscott Press, and in particular its edition of *Chaucer* (completed weeks before Morris's death in 1896), represented the best example of printing since Johannes Gutenberg's 42-line Bible.

The opinion within the print trade was somewhat different. Any sense of awe was tempered by the extraordinary circumstances of *Chaucer*'s making. The fact that Morris was working to please himself rather than a customer, and that his printers were alone, working in a quiet space, could take as long as was necessary and had a plentiful supply of the best paper and inks, emphasized the fact that the *modus operandi* of the Kelmscott Press had little in common with conditions in the trade printer's high-street premises. Plus, it rankled the trade that Morris was not a *bona fide* printer; to them he was a self-trained enthusiast, an outsider – effectively an 'amateur' – and, perhaps worst of all, he had demonstrated that the printing press and its environs were no longer the sole preserve of the print trade.

However, nothing Morris achieved was a threat to the trade printer's livelihood. For most, life continued exactly as it had before. There were a few commercial printing establishments, most notably Bernard Newdigate's Arden Press, who aimed to uphold Morris's ideology. More significantly, a number of private presses were set up in the wake of Kelmscott that contributed to the development of type and typographic design, notably the work of St John Hornby's Ashendene Press in 1895, the Doves Press established by Walker and T. J. Cobden-Sanderson in 1900, and the Golden Cockerel Press in 1920, for whom Eric Gill later designed the *Golden Cockerel Roman* in 1931. But Morris's most important legacy was his inspirational influence on the following generation of 'outsiders', working independently of the printing establishment like himself, to take up the call for a print revival. They included (among others) Edward Johnston and Eric Gill in Britain; Will Bradley, Frederic Goudy, Bruce Rogers and Will Dwiggins in America; and Rudolf Koch in Germany.

It was Morris's anarchic defiance of the status quo as much as his return to the values of craftsmanship and quality materials that caught the attention and imagination of this disparate group of type designers and typographers; they recognized by his example that print and typography could be an occupation in which an individuality of vision could not only thrive but was a necessity for success. Morris's books were certainly admired for their weighty hand-made presence, but it was the cavalier display of affectations and idiosyncrasies that truly electrified so many twentieth-century type designers. Kelmscott Press books were unique, and indeed remain to this day some of the most distinctive books ever to be printed.

The Print Revivalists did not emulate the appearance of Morris's books, or if they did the affectation was brief – in fact, many would come to criticize the design of his type and of his books. But what stayed with all who saw Morris's work was the alluring and provocative demonstration of typography as a personal vision. In achieving this Morris made typography newly attractive, and the idea of becoming a 'typographer' a worthy vocation.

PART ONE
Cold Metal Type

Introduction

The term 'cold metal type' is used to distinguish between foundry type (always cold when handled) and typecast 'in-house' on Monotype, Linotype, Intertype or Ludlow machines (potentially still warm when handled). Foundry, or cold metal type, was cast from harder metals at a higher temperature and required more pressure to cast the type than is possible with in-house casters. It was therefore harder, sharper and longer lasting if handled correctly, and would be redistributed (or 'dissed') back into its case after use. At some point, probably with the invention of phototypesetting in the mid 1950s, some people began referring to any metal type as being 'hot', and anything set photographically as being 'cold'. For the purpose of this book cold metal type refers to type designed and cut by hand and manufactured by a foundry for hand composition.

The methods used to cut and cast type in the twentieth century were exactly the same as those described in the earliest surviving records and, as far as we know, are identical to those used by Gutenberg in the fifteenth century. But while the physical act of cutting punches had not changed, the structure and working methods of the type industry that grew at pace around the punchcutter's craft was transformed, especially in the nineteenth and twentieth centuries.

To all intents and purposes, punchcutters were (until William Morris) the type designers of their age. They would precisely engrave each letterform onto the end of a short steel rod which would then be heated and dipped in water to harden ('temper') the steel so that it could be struck ('punched') into a softer metal, usually copper, which was then realigned to form a precise matrix. The finished matrix would then be slotted in a hand-held mould into which molten metal was poured using a small ladle. The molten metal would set within seconds, the hand mould was then opened and the cast metal letter released. A mould cast one size of type only.

The cutting of a letterform was achieved with the aid of a magnifying glass and the use of fine files to cut the metal away from each letterform. Gravers were used to gouge hollows to create the internal shapes ('counters') into the face of the punch. Alternatively, counters could be created using a counter-punch, which was made in the same way as a punch.

Previous page: Hand-setting foundry type in a busy UK newspaper printing office, c.1930s. Working as a typesetter required several attributes; chiefly a level of education sufficient to enable speedy and accurate composition of type and the manual dexterity to aid this. An interest in type and how it worked would make the task more interesting.

To the right of the photograph type is being hand-set using adjustable composing sticks. The set type is then passed to the compositors on the left. The compositors are working around imposing 'stones' (usually a marble or granite slab). 'Imposition' is the arrangement of the texts into pages and then into signatures or sections (usually of four, eight or sixteen pages) of a given document.

In a smaller 'jobbing' print shop the compositor would have what was commonly called 'an eye for design'; a valuable asset before the rise of the professional typographic designer (though less important in a newspaper printing shop). A compositor working in a specialist book printing office would hope to have a quieter, more orderly working environment.

In the sixteenth century punchcutters generally supplied printers with matrices from which the printer could cast their own type. During the next 200 years printers slowly eliminated the founding side of their activities, presumably preferring the convenience of buying type ready-cast from a type founder. This was certainly to the type founder's advantage – as the printer's type became damaged or worn, they would return to the foundry where they were able to buy precise replicas cast from the same matrices. A foundry that had amassed a collection of matrices, of typefaces comprising various sizes, could cast type for innumerable printers from the same matrices for decades. By 1800 it was unusual for a foundry to be owned by a punchcutter.

At the beginning of the twentieth century most type foundries were using pantograph machines (see pp. 86–7) to cut type, and demand for the punchcutter's skills virtually disappeared. The few remaining practitioners were, however, held in the highest regard for their unprecedented knowledge of type and typography and outstanding craftsmanship. Some designers were eager, and considered it a privilege, to work alongside the punchcutter in order to learn in intricate detail about spacing, alignment, balance of weight and optical or 'non-linear' scaling. This was knowledge the punchcutter had gained from the exacting process of cutting every character of a typeface in every point size required.

Giambattista Bodoni, printer and prodigious punchcutter, wrote:

> Not many people would think that the number of the matrices for one Roman comes to one hundred and ninety-six, and one needs another one hundred and eighty-four for the Italics of the same width and typeface, to be interposed with roman type when necessary. So, to make an accomplished equipment of types, three hundred and eighty matrices are needed for one text.[1]

Bodoni's 350 matrices make up just one size of a typeface. Each different size of a typeface would require another 350 matrices. In the twentieth century, allowing for accented letters, continental consonants, vowels and punctuation, ligatures and just the elemental mathematic symbols, a single comprehensive font for book work could require as many as 500.

Attaining optical uniformity of weight and balance across all required sizes of a typeface ('non-linear' scaling) was one of the most challenging tasks for the punchcutter, but it was necessary

Top: A rare photograph of the punchcutter Edward Prince. In this photograph (probably posed) Prince appears to be striking a punch into a matrix. His modest house was also his place of work.

Above: A hand-cut steel punch and a copper (or similar softer metal) matrix.

Top: Composing room at the Oxford University Press, c.1950s.

Above: Using a composing stick to set metal type. The composer is adding spacing material cut specially for the task, between characters (kerning) to ensure they appear evenly spaced when printed.

to ensure that when different sizes of a typeface were used together the typeface remained visually unified in weight and style. Compensations generally require that smaller sizes are a little more open in the counters, larger in x-height, slightly heavier in stem weight, and wider in character width. The increased x-height results in shorter ascenders and descenders. In contrast, the larger sizes are relatively more enclosed in the counters, have a smaller x-height with longer ascenders and descenders, are lighter in stem weight, and are generally narrower in overall width.

This was an intuitive, largely non-verbal and primarily visual process. Writing in the 1950s, Harry Carter explained:

> The relation of small to large must be made evident not by uniformity but by skilful variations. Yet there must be a pattern letter in the reader's eye that is reproduced as well as possible in every one of a range of sizes. The punchcutter must see this letter in his mind's eye and cut it in all the necessary sizes with the right adaptation to scale. It must be a letter that is as suitable for large as for small types, handsome enough for the main line of a title-page and clear enough for a footnote. Many of our modern types fail at one or the other extreme: some in their large sizes are obviously mechanical enlargements, others have small sizes that are illegible.[2]

Punchcutting was a slow process. Renowned punchcutter Paul Koch said that 'on a good day' he might successfully cut three letters.[3] It was not uncommon for a punchcutter to be occupied for several years in the cutting of a single typeface required in roman and italic, and certainly if several sizes were also required. Intense familiarity with the letterforms came from repeated practice of cutting the forms until they became second nature to hand and eye. This was essential to the success in producing a typeface which appeared uniformly equable to the eye across all required sizes and all styles: roman, italic, small caps etc.

When typefaces began to be commissioned from designers, it was not at all uncommon for the punchcutter to be given just a single set of drawings by the designer, leaving them with the responsibility of making the necessary adjustments to form and weight distribution of each character to suit each required size of type. In deference to the punchcutter's knowledge and skills, many designers would provide drawings that were knowingly unfinished in order to give the punchcutter room for interpretation.

Not surprisingly, there were occasional disagreements about accuracy or interpretation between designer and punchcutter. These could be costly as well as embarrassing. Even the best

twentieth-century punchcutters, for example Edward Prince in London, Charles Malin in Paris and Paul H. Rädisch in Haarlem, experienced occasional issues regarding interpretation. Having been contracted to do what was required the punchcutter might closely follow the forms in a drawing, only to be accused of following the drawings too precisely – of being too literal – or alternatively, not being precise enough. It was an activity fraught with almost impenetrable subtleties that could lead to misunderstandings, frustration and accusations of ineptitude on both sides. The details of who said or did what and when have often been lost – deliberately or otherwise – leaving an inadequate trail from which to decipher individual contributions. Requiring a true rendering of his drawings was the reason, for example, that Bruce Rogers chose to have his second typeface, *Centaur*, cut using a pantograph machine, having been disappointed by the punchcutter's interpretation of his previous typeface, *Montaigne*.

A great deal of the work done by punchcutters over the centuries remains unidentified. Prince and Malin were fortunate in their association with the private presses, whose adherence to the values of the Arts and Crafts movement being a cooperative activity meant that they received generous credit for their work. Others, for instance those working in the bowels of a major type foundry, were often rarely if ever even mentioned.[4]

Prince has been described as: 'Never ebullient or extrovert, but rather shy and humble, [he] represented craftsmanship at its highest and most spiritual level'.[5] It would be fair to say that while some type designers shared the spiritual resolve characterized by Prince, there were many more who sought the spotlight and adulation.

Above: Letterpress printing continued well into the 1960s and the design of storage furniture reflected the development of new materials and production methods. Cornerstone became renowned for its range of precision engineered tools and furniture for the letterpress printer. This set of units includes an overhead lead rack; overhead furniture rack; a sliding random (a moveable 'sliding' work surface); typecase cabinet (holding twenty founts), plate storage cabinet and forme rack. Formica is much in evidence. (Photograph taken from a Cornerstone brochure, *c*.1960.)

THE DOOR IN THE WALL
AND OTHER STORIES

THE DOOR IN THE WALL

I

ONE CONFIDENTIAL EVENING, NOT three months ago, Lionel Wallace told me this story of the Door in the Wall. And at the time I thought that so far as he was concerned it was a true story.

He told it me with such a direct simplicity of conviction that I could not do otherwise than believe in him. But in the morning, in my own flat, I woke to a different atmosphere, and as I lay in bed and recalled the things he had told me, stripped of the glamour of his earnest slow voice, denuded of the focussed shaded table light, the shadowy atmosphere that wrapped about him and the pleasant bright things, the dessert and glasses and napery of the dinner we had shared, making them for the time a bright little world quite cut off from every-day realities, I saw it all as frankly incredible. "He was mystifying!" I said, and then: "How well he did it! . . . . . It isn't quite the thing I should have expected him, of all people, to do well."

Afterwards, as I sat up in bed and sipped my morning tea, I found myself trying to account for the flavour of reality that perplexed me in his impossible reminiscences, by supposing they did in some way suggest,

Frederic Goudy USA 1865–1947

Frederic Goudy was born in Bloomington, Illinois. His father owned a real-estate business. Having completed only two years of high school, and despite showing a talent for drawing and lettering, Goudy began working as a clerk in his father's company. In 1889, aged twenty-four, he struck out on his own, going to Minneapolis and then Springfield, Illinois, doing mundane work as an administrator. A year later, he moved to Chicago.

The 1890s was the decade when North America experienced a print phenomenon – the establishment of hundreds of independently designed, printed and published 'little magazines' – and Chicago was at the forefront of the movement. Goudy's intention was to become a commercial artist and printer. Influenced by the flurry of self-published little magazines he launched his own, *Modern Advertising*, in 1892, but as with many others its life was brief. William H. Bradley, who would become the leading graphic designer in America before the end of the decade, met Goudy when he was employed as a cashier during the day in a real-estate agency. When they next met, Goudy explained that he was setting up a small printing office called the Booklet Press with a friend (C. Lauren Hooper) and had received a commission from the publishers Stone & Kimball to design and print a book. Bradley offered Goudy the use of a couple of cases of *Caslon* type and a Golding press. The 'book' turned out to be the influential literary little magazine, *The Chap-Book*, whose first issue was published in 1894.

With this success – and 'inoculated with printers' ink'[1] – Goudy renamed his printing office the Camelot Press, in homage to William Morris. (Meanwhile, Bradley went on to design some of his most celebrated covers and posters for *The Chap-Book*.) However, running a commercial printing plant was too uncertain an undertaking, or perhaps not to Goudy's liking, because he sold his interest in the company in 1898 – and it failed just a few months later. There was, undoubtedly, a high demand for print during the 1890s, but there was not sufficient for all 360 printing companies in Chicago. However, Goudy had learned a great deal, made numerous contacts, and was now able to eke out a living as a freelance lettering artist – mainly for department stores – while experimenting with the design of typefaces. One of these was *Pabst*, designed in 1902. Three years later it was

Opposite: Frederic Goudy, opening spread showing the first chapter of *Door in the Wall*, by H. G. Wells, designed for the publisher Mitchell Kennerley, using his newly designed typeface *Kennerley*. Goudy also designed the decorative initials and head bands. Printed in a limited edition of 600 in New York, 1911.

Above: Frederic Goudy, roundel used on the title page of *The Alphabet and Elements of Lettering*, published by Mitchell Kennerley, New York, c.1926.

ABCDEFGHIJKLM
NOPQRSTUVWX
YZabcdefghijklmnopqrst
uvwxyz *The* and & of ÆŒ
£$₤([]-?.:;,!'1234567890

Above right: Frederic Goudy's *Pabst* is based on hand-lettering Goudy produced for the Pabst brewery in 1902. The following year ATF commissioned Goudy to draw an italic and matrices for both designs were cut by Robert Wiebking, retaining Goudy's drawn 'irregularities'. Wiebking would cut many of Goudy's types during the next two decades. ATF released *Pabst* c.1903, and numerous copies and variations followed.

released by the American Type Founders Company (ATF) and became a popular choice for adverting texts in America. A close copy was produced by Schriftguss AG in Germany who called it *Ohio* (and which, bizarrely, was used for the text of the Bauhaus manifesto in Weimar, 1919). Goudy's reputation enabled him to join the teaching staff at Chicago's new Frank Holme School of illustration as a lettering tutor.

In 1903 Goudy met Will Ransom and together they set up the Village Press. Ransom was twenty-five years old, Goudy thirty-eight. Ransom had served a printing apprenticeship and moved to Chicago to study at the Art Institute. They established the Village Press expressly to make beautiful books from the texts they most admired. Like the proprietors of other private presses, Goudy equipped it with a proprietary typeface: the *Village* type. Modelled on William Morris's *Golden* of 1891, and T.J. Cobden-Sanderson and Emery Walker's *Doves* of 1900, *Village* (not dissimilar to *Pabst*) was initially designed in 1903 for a clothing store who approved and paid for the drawings, but chose not to proceed. Later the same year Goudy reworked the design; it was used in their first book, *Printing*, a short essay by Morris and Walker originally published in 1893.[2]

The Village Press moved to Hingham, Massachusetts, in 1904, and then two years later to New York. New business connections were being established and personal reputations enhanced – but in January 1908 the building in which the Village Press was situated was partially destroyed by fire and Goudy lost his entire stock of printed books, work in progress, and type, and was forced to return to freelance lettering and design. Nevertheless, he was successful enough to be able to afford his first trip to Europe in 1909. Will Ransom, meanwhile, went on to build a commercial career in advertising typography and graphic design, and established the Screw Press to print limited edition books of contemporary poetry.

During that eventful first decade of the twentieth century, Goudy was one of America's pioneering independent commercial artists (along with Bradley and William A. Dwiggins). He also began designing bespoke typefaces for a variety of businesses, sometimes through the auspices of adverting agencies, including J. Walter Thompson, and sometimes through his own contacts. He effectively transferred the concept of the exclusive private press typeface to the world of commerce. Most important of these businesses was the book publisher Mitchell Kennerley who, in 1911, commissioned Goudy to design an edition of the H. G. Wells story *The Door in the Wall*. The trial pages were set in 18-point *Caslon Old Face*, but Goudy was not happy with the outcome. He offered to design a new type for the book and have matrices engraved at his own expense, on condition he retained ownership and was able sell the typeface to the trade. Kennerley agreed – this was to become a turning point in Goudy's career.

The *Kennerley* typeface, like *Village*, was in essence a fifteenth-century Venetian, but crucially it was not a revival of Nicolas Jenson's type – nor any other. It was an original typeface that also avoided the mannerisms of Art Nouveau, the contemporary style prevalent in America at that time. Pantographically cut by Robert Wiebking,[3] *Kennerley* was the moment when type design overtook lettering, general graphics and printing as Goudy's principal activity. He changed the name of his Village Press to The Village Press and Letter Foundery,

Below: Frederic Goudy, *Village*, the proprietary typeface of the Village Press. Excerpt taken from *Printing* by William Morris, the first book to be printed and bound by Goudy and Will Ransom, 1903.

which were the immediate predecessors of the true printed book, the invention of movable metal letters in the middle of the fifteenth century may justly be considered as the invention of the art of printing. And it is worth mention in passing that, as an example of fine typography, the earliest book printed with movable types, the Gutenberg, or "forty-two line Bible"

and published the first issue of *Typographica: A Quarterly Treating of Printing, Letter Design and Allied Arts*, exquisitely designed and printed in September of that year.[4] (His archaic – and to some, pretentious – spelling of 'foundery' came in for considerable criticism.) The first issue of *Typographica* contained an essay by Goudy entitled 'On Letter Design'. Set in *Kennerley*, it began:

> To attempt a revision of our letterforms as expressed in types is to set one's self a difficult task, requiring patient waiting for tangible results and recognition. There is to be met and resisted the possibility of ridicule, the accusation of egotism from the unthinking, of obstruction even, by those whose commercial instincts may be touched. We have reached the turning of the ways. If there is to be revision someone must lead. Letter design no longer lives as an artistic craft. To restore the craft to its original purity of intention and make it once more alive is to go back to the very foundations of typography.

Here, Goudy is criticizing type foundries for encouraging the design of types based on the latest artistic style, and for commissioning new types from artists (such as Otto Eckmann, George Auriol and Peter Behrens) rather than someone with a deep knowledge of lettering and its history. He was, in other words, arguing for a revival of traditional skills and Renaissance forms. Yet, in the same issue of *Typographica*, Goudy included an advertisement for a new service – in customized type design for the specific needs of specific companies: 'Mr. Frederic W. Goudy is prepared to design and cut for any Advertiser or Printer a distinctive typeface for his exclusive use, and solicits commissions of this character.' He makes the point that these new types would be 'simple, legible', but would also, of necessity, be 'distinctive'. The seemingly contradictory nature of Goudy's words and activities enabled his detractors to pour scorn on both his motives and his typefaces.

However, his typefaces proved extremely popular, especially within the advertising industry. Goudy, 'short, plump, pinkish and puckish',[5] was a popular figure within the print trade and his lectures, of which there were many, were hugely entertaining. His candid, practical outlook was in contrast to the unwavering erudition and scholarly airs of his critics, who accused Goudy of paying lip-service to the ideals of print revivalism and revered typographers such as William Morris and Daniel B. Updike, while fawning to the boorish demands of commerce. Some of this is true, but pomposity was rife, and to denigrate Goudy's typefaces because they were popular with advertising agencies, rather than the honourable world of books, was not so much pomposity as bigotry.

Goudy was aware of how galling, even provocative, his one-man type foundry appeared to some of his contemporaries (the recent merger of American foundries in 1892 to create the vast enterprise that was the American Type Founders Company had rocked the industry). But he undoubtedly also knew that his attitude towards type was itself cavalier, even irreverent, and he relished debunking the 'black art'. For example, when fellow typographer Bruce Rogers visited Goudy's home one day for lunch, Rogers, characteristically, was complaining he could not obtain capitals at a particular size or style for a title page. Goudy suggested he use one of his own typefaces, *Goudy Antique* – and immediately disappeared to his workshop where he engraved the required punches and struck the matrices in the intermediate size required, cast the types, and handed them to Rogers before he left. Rogers commented, 'some service', with a hint of sarcasm. Rogers had built a reputation predicated on the notion of type being an elusive, elite and sacrosanct art form. Goudy's 'service' demonstrated his disdain for such puffery. Nevertheless, and despite their strikingly different temperaments, Goudy and Rogers were to remain life-long friends.[6]

Following the success of *Kennerley*, Morris Fuller Benton, head of the design department at ATF, commissioned Goudy to create a typeface. The result was *Goudy Oldstyle*, visibly related to *Kennerley* but superior in quality and released in 1915. Important as *Kennerley* was, it was *Goudy Oldstyle* that sealed Goudy's reputation. It caught the popular trend in American printing for historicism, while also preserving more than a hint of Morris's *Golden* – and, of course, *Jenson*. The design is robust and yet open and light. It has short descenders (drawn under protest by Goudy) – particularly conspicuous on the 'p' and 'q' – to conform to ATF's 'common (base) line' (see p. 21).

Goudy Oldstyle is a handsome typeface, and bears comparison with the best types in Europe at the time (Sjoerd Hendrik de Roos's *Zilver*, for example, was designed the same year), especially when seen as Goudy chose to print it. He decided to accept a fee of $1,500 rather than royalties, a decision he later had reason to regret because *Goudy Oldstyle* proved so successful for ATF

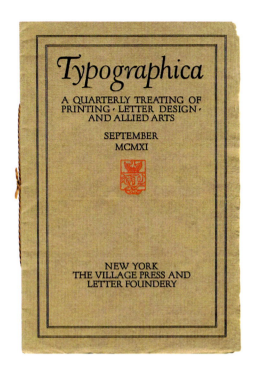

Above: Frederic Goudy, the first issue of *Typographica*, published 1911. The title is hand-lettered, everything else is set in *Kennerley*.

A B C D E F G H I J
K L M N O P Q R S T
U V W X Y Z &
a b c d e f g h i j k l m n
o p q r s t u v w x y z
æ 1 2 3 4 5 6 7 8 9 0 œ

that Benton expanded the typeface into a large family of variant weights – all designed in-house. ATF even issued a special supplement to its 1923 specimen book devoted solely to *Goudy Oldstyle*. However, the qualities that made it unique also limited its application; while hugely popular for the setting of text in advertising, it was only used once for the text of a book.

During the 1920s Goudy began to harbour visions of being able to carry out every aspect of type making, from drawing designs to cutting and even casting the type in his own studio (no doubt influenced by the commercial success, and his loss, regarding *Goudy Oldstyle*.) It was fate, however, that forced him to take this final step. Having moved the workshop to Marlborough-on-Hudson, New York, he received a commission in 1927 to furnish a private type for exclusive use of the journal, *Woman's Home Companion*. As he had done many times before, he expected to complete the designs and pass them to Robert Weibking who would cut the matrices. Goudy completed his drawings, but the day he was to deliver them in Chicago, he was told that Weibking had died.

As a result, Goudy, now aged sixty, decided his Village Press and Letter Foundery must, at last, become a *real* foundry. Goudy was unable to obtain a pantograph from one of the main matrix manufacturers or type foundries, and he so bought one intended for general commercial engraving with a rotary cutting tool used for watch cases and jewellery. Once again Goudy demonstrated

Above right: Sjoerd Hendrik de Roos, *Zilver*, designed exclusively for Jean François van Royen and his private press, De Zilverdistel, 1915.

not only his ingenuity but also a complete lack of pretension in his adaptation of non-specialist equipment to the making of type. Goudy taught himself how to use the pantograph, and began to make patterns, grind cutting tools and cast type, making his Village Foundery a complete 'start-to-finish', one-man type-making operation. He used his own publications – the journals *Typographica* and *Ars Typographica*, and the books *The Alphabet* and *The Elements of Lettering*, as well as numerous articles for the trade – to promote the fact.

In 1920 he was appointed as art consultant to Lanston Monotype (the name of the American Monotype company – the English company dropped 'Lanston' in 1931), and held the position until he died. In 1927 the Continental Type Founders Association added his typefaces to its library. Yet despite all of this, plus the medals, awards and laurels he received, his teaching, lectures and copious writing (his erudite *The Alphabet: Fifteen Interpretative Designs*, 1918, for example, is an excellent account of the history of his profession), Goudy always thought himself an outsider. And, indeed he was. The sneering of his prominent scholar-peers surely intended this to be the case, even if the popularity of his typefaces, some 123 in number,[7] meant they had to temper their views in public.

Goudy argued that there was nothing mysterious about the art of typography, everything was knowable and solvable – all that was required was determined ingenuity and hard work.

Below: Detail from an ATF type specimen eulogizing the 'type family' using Frederic Goudy's *Goudy Old Style*.

GOUDY TYPES in their shapes have a close affinity with the classic roman letters of early Venetian printers. The ancient models are enlivened by increased contrast of main and minor lines, and by more acute serifs. These modernizations increase the effectiveness for present day uses and give a free, flowing quality which is one of the chief reasons for the popularity of the Goudy types. The light shines through each character, establishing unusual clearness in mass effects. Goudy types are for all purposes and give dignity with strength to every piece of printing

"Bombed but Unbeaten"

EXCERPTS FROM
THE WAR COMMENTARY OF
BEATRICE L. WARDE

PRINTED FOR FRIENDS OF FREEDOM
BY THE TYPOPHILES : NEW YORK : 1941

Bruce Rogers USA 1870 – 1957

Bruce Rogers was born in Linnwood, Indiana, and went to Purdue University in Lafayette to study art. After graduation in 1890 he had several jobs, one of which was as a newspaper artist at the Indianapolis News which required him to draw letterforms as well as to illustrate. His interest in the design of books was stimulated by the sight of the Kelmscott Press's *Poems by the Way*, bought direct from William Morris by Rogers's friend, J. M. Bowles. He was the publisher of a quarterly magazine called *Modern Art*, one of the first in America to advance the aims of the Arts and Crafts movement.

Rogers later wrote about his first sight of a Kelmscott Press book:

Joe Bowles (to whom I owe most in those formative years) showed me a Kelmscott Press book in the '*Golden* type'. I tried to think I liked the type, but it was really the paper and the impression and the rich black ink that fascinated both of us. I, at least, had never seen an old well-printed book, and I doubt if Joe had, though he was years ahead of the times in all matters of art, as known and practised in the mid-west of that period.[1]

Rogers worked with Bowles on *Modern Art*. When it was taken over by the Louis Prang printing and publishing company in 1895, Bowles and Rogers moved to Boston. It was at this point that Rogers became type conscious (as opposed to letter conscious). In an exhibition of books held at the Boston Public Library he saw a copy of Nicolas Jenson's printing of *De praeparatione evangelica* by Eusebius of 1470. Rogers enquired about its owner and discovered that the book had been loaned by William G. Shillaber, a well-known collector in Boston who generously invited Rogers to examine it and take photographs. Rogers would later visit the Harvard College Library to view a page from Jenson's *Vitae XII Caesarum* by Suetonius of 1471, specifically to photograph Jenson's capitals. Having seen the original Jenson-printed types, Rogers began to lose interest in Morris.

As soon as he arrived in Boston Rogers had begun working as a freelance designer, and among his clients was the Riverside Press, a division of the company Houghton, Mifflin & Company. Within the year he was appointed by George H. Mifflin to join the company as a full-time designer at the Riverside Press (taking the place of Daniel B. Updike, who left in 1893 to establish his

Opposite: Bruce Rogers, title page from *Bombed But Unbeaten*, written by Beatrice Warde and published by The Typophiles, New York, 1941. The title is set in *Koch Antiqua* and all else set in *Centaur*. The frontispiece is a portrait of Warde by Eric Gill.

own Merrymount Press). Today, it is difficult to comprehend the significance of the position Mifflin offered to Rogers. Typographic design – or 'layout design' as the printer might call it – was an integral part of the compositor's responsibility and, as such, zealously guarded. Indeed, Rogers's lack of formal print training would normally have barred him from even entering a printing premises. Mifflin's support, no doubt, ensured a degree of protection for Rogers, but life in the noise and general brouhaha of the shop floor was sometimes difficult, made worse by his youthful vulnerability and shy demeanour.

In 1900 Rogers persuaded the company of the benefits of setting up a separate print division for the exclusive production of fine books for the collector. This gave Rogers a degree of independence and a place of calm in which to work. During the next twelve remarkable years Rogers established a reputation as the foremost book designer in the world, an extraordinary level of success that became a catalyst for the universal acceptance of the designer's role in the production of print, and of book design in particular.

Apparently produced with little thought for time or expense, Rogers was able to provide the forty-seven books he designed, many comprising multiple volumes, with a level of personal and detailed attention rarely possible within the maelstrom of a commercial printing company. As his confidence grew he began to experiment, mixing types and then designing special characters and decorative motifs for specific purposes. At one point he produced a modified *Caslon* by rubbing down the face of the letter to produce a slightly darker (emboldened) face and then rubbing down the sides to provide a tighter fit. The fount would later be released by Houghton Mifflin as *Riverside Caslon*; essentially a 12-point lowercase combined with 10-point capitals.

In 1901 the company agreed to Rogers designing a new typeface for a forthcoming folio edition, in three volumes, of *The Essays of Montaigne*, from which the typeface was named. He 'blithely set to work' (his own words), drawing from photographs he had previously taken of Nicolas Jenson's edition of Eusebius's *De praeparatione evangelica* of 1470.[2] Jenson's type, arguably the first true roman (earlier proto-roman types retained a distinct blackletter appearance) received a great deal of attention at the turn of the twentieth century, caused largely by William Morris's claims for its exceptional qualities and the success of his Jenson-inspired *Golden* type. Almost a decade later, in 1900, Emery

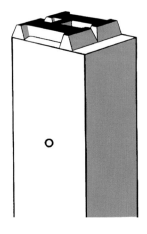

Above: The bevelled angle on which the face of a letter sits provides strength and durability during printing. It also means that if the face is 'rubbed down' the letter will print bolder.

Walker's equally impressive and much acclaimed *Doves* type was produced from the same source.

On the advice of Joseph W. Phinney, head of the Boston branch of the American Type Founders Company (ATF), Rogers passed his drawings to John Cumming, by general consent the best American punchcutter at that time. However, in his own written account, Rogers described his frustration at the results:

> The first proofs of the type were faintly disappointing to me, even in the excitement of seeing my drawings transmitted to metal. For Cumming worked almost free-hand, with only occasional measurements, and had not preserved either Jenson's letter or my adaptation of it. But Mr Mifflin was delighted with the new type, and

Above: Bruce Rogers, *The Compleat Angler*, written by Izaak Walton and published by the Riverside Press in 1909. The text is set in *Riverside Caslon*.

after several of the least successful letters were re-cut I decided it would have to do – for the time being, at least – until I could have another try for my ideal type.[3]

Following the death of Henry O. Houghton in 1906, the company's support of the Riverside Press's limited editions began to wane. Rogers left the company in 1912 and began working as a freelance typographic designer in New York. One of his clients was Henry Watson Kent (1866–1948), secretary of the Metropolitan Museum of Art. Kent was of particular interest to Rogers because he had inaugurated and was now director of the Museum Press – effectively 'a private press operating in a public capacity'.[4] The quality of workmanship demonstrated by the press was impressive, as was the quantity produced. Kent had established the *Bulletin* in 1905, a journal which began as a quarterly and then became a monthly publication with a print-run rising to around 16,000. He also set up an editorial department to support it. As well as the *Bulletin*, the press also produced museum books and numerous individual printing projects whose design was often commissioned from New York's independent designers, including Rogers; the Museum Press earned a formidable reputation for both its design and fine production values.

In 1914 Rogers showed Kent some drawings of a second attempt at his 'ideal type', something he had begun around 1909 while still at Houghton Mifflin. Kent relished the idea of having a proprietary typeface for his Museum Press and, presumably, also recognized the potential of the typeface as an institutional identity – and so agreed to support its completion on agreement of proprietary rights of the capitals.[5] An initial set of 14-point titling capitals was produced and used by the museum later the same year. Meanwhile, Rogers continued to expand the fount to include other sizes and lowercase. It still did not have a name. At the same time, Rogers was planning an edition of a short prose work by the French poet Maurice de Guérin, to be titled *The Centaur*. A new translation had been written and arrangements made for it to be printed by Carl Rollins's Montague Press. The new Museum Press fount was used, and was named *Centaur*.

Like *Montaigne*, *Centaur* was based on Jenson's *De praeparatione evangelica* of 1470, but this time Rogers hoped

Opposite: Bruce Rogers, *Monotype Centaur*, 1929.

54 Type Designers of the Twentieth Century

If it is worth printing then it deserves to be set in a good type...
Monotype* Centaur, Series 252,

[SHOWN HERE IN 72 AND (BELOW) 36 POINT]

ABcDEG HJjKklm NPQqR! TUVXxYZz134689

is one of the greatest type faces of our day. *Here is its fine italic, based on Arrighi's cursive.* The display matrices (14 PT up) may be hired by the day at little cost.

* *Registered Trade Mark of* THE MONOTYPE CORPORATION LIMITED   *Reg. Office:* 55-56 Lincolns Inn Fields, London, w.c.2
Head Office and Works: Salfords, Redhill, Surrey (Redhill 4641, *five lines*)

that the use of the new pantographic engraving machine would avoid the misinterpretations made by Cumming with his earlier type. The matrices were engraved by Robert Wiebking in Chicago, commissioned on Frederic Goudy's recommendation, and then privately cast by Barnhart Brothers & Spindler,[6] also in Chicago. (By then they were nominally owned by ATF, but ATF had no involvement in the making of *Centaur* at all.) The result was a much closer approximation to the original *Jenson* than the *Montaigne* type had been. But it was not a facsimile either. Rogers had amended details of several letters, and Wiebking also made a number of subtle alterations, for practical reasons. It has been claimed that with *Centaur* Rogers produced a more refined interpretation of Jenson's letters, when compared with those made by Morris (*Golden*) and Walker (*Doves*). But, crucially, the book Rogers used as a model – Jenson's *De praeparatione evangelica* – was printed in 1470 using crisp, newly made type, requiring less pressure than for printing *Historia naturalis* six years later, the model used by Morris and Walker.

In letterpress printing, applying the correct pressure is critical: too light and the type will look thin and grey, too heavy and the ink will spread causing the type to appear enboldened. Similar effects are caused by under- or over-inking. Arguably, Jenson's *Eusebius* is a cleaner and more accurate example of his type than his Pliny printed six years later, when the type was possibly becoming a little worn and thus required a little more pressure in order to obtain a distinct image. Rogers's *Centaur*, therefore, was not so much a 'refinement' of Jenson, as some have suggested, but simply an accurate interpretation of Jenson's type at its best. Perhaps he also captured something of the essential origins of Jenson's type. This is how Rogers described the process he undertook:

> When portions of the clearest page in my copy were enlarged to about five times the original size I was at once struck by the pen-like characteristics of the lowercase letters; so with a flat pen cut to the weight of the heavier lines, I wrote over the print as rapidly as I could, thus preserving the proportions at least, of Jenson's own characters. [These were then] touched up somewhat with pen and brush; and these, with capitals drawn with a pointed pen over photographs of the originals, served as models for the first cutting of the Centaur type.[7]

This led Rogers to surmise that, 'when Jenson embarked in his printing business at Venice and needed a model for his lowercase letters, he selected what seemed to him the finest humanistic writing at hand and copied it as faithfully as possible with a graver and punch'.

The Centaur was designed by Rogers, hand-set by Rogers's wife Anna, printed by Carl P. Rollins at his Montague Press, and published in an edition of 135 copies in 1915. The typeface received high praise but its commercial use in publishing, the main purpose for which it was designed, was limited because it was only available for hand-setting. (By this time Monotype and Linotype's mechanized typesetting systems already dominated the publishing industries.) In late 1927 Rogers was approached by American Monotype to have *Centaur* re-cut for mechanical composition and Rogers agreed. American Monotype started the process of producing *Centaur* by making three trial cuttings, but the drawings and proofs of these cuttings were then transferred to Monotype's English company at the insistence of Rogers.[8]

This decision may have been influenced by the close affection Rogers had for England, having worked there in 1916 at the invitation of Emery Walker to set up the Mall Press in London (in the tradition of Kelsmscott and Doves). It had not been a particularly happy adventure. Wartime conditions, the bitterly cold winter, and having been left to his own devices by Walker, made the experience less than ideal,[9] although the resultant book – and sole Mall Press publication – Albrecht Durer's *Of the Just Shaping of Letters*, was Rogers's only book to be printed (mostly) by his own hands and is now much sought-after.

While in London Rogers was invited by Sidney Cockerell – formerly William Morris's secretary at the Kelmscott Press, business partner with Walker and, since 1908, director of the Fitzwilliam Museum in Cambridge – to advise Cambridge University Press on its typography. As a result of Rogers's critical report, Stanley Morison was recruited as 'typographical adviser' to the Press together with a newly appointed printer, Walter Lewis. Shortly afterwards, Morison would also become typographic consultant to Monotype and, by this time, was a friend and frequent correspondent of Rogers.

All of this was, no doubt, a factor in Rogers insisting that *Centaur* be re-cut in England, but there were other more prosaic reasons for him accepting the approach from Monotype. In the promotional brochure later published by Monotype he wrote:

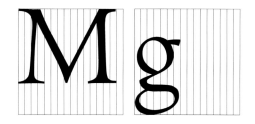

Above: Typefaces created for the Monotype composing machine were designed with character widths expressed in increments of one 18th of an em. Above is a *Centaur* cap 'M' superimposed on an 18-unit wide em square. 'M' occupies 17 units, the 'g' occupies 7 units.

> I naturally turned to the 'Monotype' method of composition and casting, on account of the satisfaction I have had in the past with results obtained by this method. Its flexibility, combined with its great range of sizes, has enabled me to produce work that would be difficult even for the hand-compositor, and which could not, so far as I am aware, have been done successfully by any other system of machine composition.

The 'flexibility' to which Rogers alludes included the ability with the Monotype system to kern letters (letterforms with overhanging parts such as the 'f') and to make amendments after casting, including fine adjustments to word spacing. Neither was possible with Monotype's rival, Linotype.

All composition machines required the type designer to take account of technical limits specific to that system. With Monotype, the challenge was that all letters had to fit snugly into a system of eighteen fixed-width units. Rogers made other, essentially aesthetic, changes too, most noticeable being that the entire *Centaur* fount is lighter, finer and more delicate than either of his two previous versions. In all, Rogers spent a year in England supervising the cutting of the typeface in seventeen sizes, requesting numerous revisions. Much later Rogers confided that he considered only the 16-point Monotype *Centaur* to be truly successful.[10] Rogers's reputation for truculent perfectionism was, doubtlessly, enhanced.

The italic that accompanied Monotype's *Centaur* was designed by Frederic Warde. Warde had been 'assistant' to Rogers[11] at the Mount Vernon Press, owned by the printer William Edwin Rudge, who employed Rogers as a book designer. This period, from 1920 to 1936, was Rogers's most productive and remunerative time, working three days a week designing books for Rudge, as well as being typographic adviser and designer of books for Harvard University Press while also acting as typographic adviser to Lanston Monotype in the US.

Rogers sought a mixture of humanity and exactitude in his work. However, 'exactitude' for Rogers was not concerned with achieving a measurable precision or uniformity, but, rather, it was in finding an arrangement that, ironically, allowed inexactness to play a part: 'Don't try to "design" every page of type throughout a book, or work it over too carefully after the style is chosen; leave something to accident, so long as it is not a glaring defect … There is entirely too much stress nowadays put on uniformity in composition.' Rogers considered the contemporary preference for 'everything squared up and tidy'[12] to be the result of laziness or ignorance – 'a mechanical faculty' – enforced supposedly by a lack of time or the curiosity necessary in order to seek something more appropriate, interesting or even surprising to convey.

In 1929 Rogers was commissioned to design *The Lectern Bible* by Oxford University Press. When it was completed in 1935, Rogers explained that he wanted it to appear as if he 'was accustomed to knocking off large folios daily, or at least weekly, as mere routine work'. The aim of the prodigious effort that went into the design of *The Lectern Bible*,[13] including a specially designed 22-point *Centaur*, with shortened ascenders and descenders, was simply to make each page exude amenity, candour and 'rightness'.

New type, first use, proof any

POOR POLL

I saw it all, Polly, how when you had called for sop
and your good friend the cook came and fill'd up your pan
you yerk'd it out deftly by beakfuls scattering it
away far as you might upon the sunny lawn
then summon'd with loud cry the little garden birds
to take their feast. Quickly came they flustering around
Ruddock & Merle & Finch squabbling among themselves
nor gave you thanks nor heed while you sat silently
watching, and I beside you in perplexity
lost in the maze of all mystery and all knowledge
felt how deep lieth the fount of man's benevolence
if a bird can share it and take pleasure in it.

If you, my bird, I thought, had a philosophy
it might be a sounder scheme than what our moralists
propound: because thou, Poll, livest in the darkness
which human Reason searching from outside would pierce,
but, being of so feeble a candle-power, can only
show up to view the cloud that it illuminates.

Thus reason'd I: then marvell'd how you can adapt
your wild bird-mood to endure your tame environment
the domesticities of English household life
and your small brass-wire cabin, who shouldst live on wing
harrying the tropical branch-flowering wilderness:
Yet Nature gave a gift of easy mimicry
whereby you have come to win uncanny sympathies
and morsell'd utterance of our Germanic talk
as schoolmasters in Greek will flaunt their hackney'd tags

φωνᾶντα συνετοῖσιν   κτῆμα ἐς ἀεί
ἡ γλῶσσ' ὀμώμοχ', ἡ δὲ φρὴν ἀνώμοτος

tho' you with a better ear copy us more perfectly
nor without connotation as when you call'd for sop
all with that stumpy wooden tongue and vicious beak
that dry whistling shrieking tearing cutting pincer
now eagerly subservient to your cautious claws
exploring all varieties of attitude
in irrepressible blind groping for escape
—a very figure and image of man's soul on earth
the almighty cosmic Will fidgeting in a trap—
in your quenchless unknown desire for the unknown life
of which some homely British sailor robb'd you, alas!
'Tis all that doth your silly thoughts so busy keep
the while you sit moping like Patience on a perch.

"—Wie viele Tag' und Nächte bist du geblieben!
    La possa delle gambe posta in tregue—"
the impeccable spruceness of your grey-feather'd pôll
a model in hairdressing for the dandiest old Duke
enough to qualify you for the House of Lords
or the Athenaeum Club, to poke among the nobs
great intellectual nobs and literary nobs
scientific nobs and Bishops ex officio;
nor lack you simulation of profoundest wisdom
such as men's features oft acquire in very old age
by mere cooling of passion and decay of muscle
by faint renunciation even of untold regrets;
who seeing themselves a picture of that which man should-be
learn almost what it were to be what they are-not.

But you can never ha[ve]
conciously to renounce
your threescore years
as any mumping monk
in peace that, poor Pol[l]
merely because you lac[k]
by Understanding. W[…]

C'est la seule diff[érence]
Ah! your pale sedenta[ry]
exchange it for one cr[…]
one blind furious tuss[…]
who would throttle yo[u]
shreds unintelligible of[…]
    dans la profonde[…]
Why ask? You cann[ot]
that you mischanged [?]
'twas that British sail[or]
Εἴθ' ὤφελ' Ἀργοῦς
I'd hold embargoes on[…]
I am writing verses[…]
absolument incapa[ble]
Tu, Polle, nescis
Alas! Iambic, scazon
Spondee or choriamb,
my well-continued fa[…]
wherein so many stra[…]
on the secure bedrock
not but that when I
in critical attention le[…]

Frederic Warde USA 1870–1957

Frederic Warde was born in Wells, Minnesota. He had a predilection for laying false trails about his personal history, especially regarding his early years. He was also notorious for being difficult, if not impossible, to work with, which meant that after his death his reputation quickly deteriorated. Unlike his close colleague and mentor Bruce Rogers, he inspired few fond anecdotes, only reminiscences ranging from bewilderment to the vehemently hateful. That he was once heralded as one of the pre-eminent American typographers of the interwar years was, unfortunately, forgotten.

When his father died in 1903, he and his mother moved away from Wells. While she eventually settled in San Diego, Frederic's activities remain obscure. However, there are signs that he had some involvement or at least an interest in the graphic arts before he enlisted in 1917, joining the air service flying school. A few days before armistice was declared in 1918, and while still in a training camp on Long Island, Warde met his future wife, the eighteen-year-old Beatrice Becker.

Beatrice's mother, writer and reviewer May Lamberton Becker, used her connections to help get Warde a job working as an editor for Macmillan & Co. Then, after a brief spell at the McHugh advertising agency and a longer spell at the Van Patten advertising agency, where he rose to production manager, Warde joined the prestigious printing company William Edwin Rudge in 1920 – where he found himself working in close proximity to Bruce Rogers.

This renowned printing company was based in Mount Vernon, New York. The building had been a glass factory during the war, but Rudge transformed the mundane one-story building into a two-story half-timbered imitation of a Tudor mansion. Warde arrived knowing almost nothing about typography – he was just one of the many eager 'apprentices', as Rudge liked to call his young, fresh out-of-college graduates. Warde's job was to learn everything about the Monotype typesetting and casting system, which required him to spend three months at the Monotype headquarters in Philadelphia. On his return he had overall responsibility for production of Rudge Monotype work. To gain an understanding of what typographic subtleties were demanded of the Monotype system, Warde was given a working space alongside Rogers.

Opposite: The first proof of Robert Bridges's *The Tapestry*, and the first use of Frederic Warde's *Arrighi* typeface. The note, top left, was written by Warde. The roman capitals were also designed by Warde and were used again to accompany *Vicenza*. Printed at the Fanfare Press, 1926.

Warde is often described as having been an assistant to Rogers, and this is certainly how Warde would prefer to describe his position at Rudge. The far more humdrum business of coaxing the complex Monotype machines to perform did not suit Warde's disposition, and anecdotal accounts suggest his results were poor. In view of the lack of evidence of any genuine training in design, or of typography specifically, it is likely that Warde was out of his depth for much of his time at Rudge. Melvin Loos, who would later become superintendent of printing at Rudge, explained that Warde's layouts, though 'beautiful', did not work in practice and required the compositors to make adjustments.[1] Warde countered such accusations by complaining to the management that his work was being sabotaged. Such tensions inside printing establishments between the young typographic designer and experienced compositor are legion. The reputation established by the young Warde for impetuous and narcissist behaviour is, however, difficult to ignore. More surprising is the fact that Warde appeared to encourage such opinions.

Below: Ludovico degli Arrighi, *Trissino: La Poetica*, printed using Arrighi's italic type, 1529.

A tacit knowledge of metal type remained a significant part of what it meant to be a typographer, not only in the interwar years but well into the 1960s. Warde, being responsible for the company's Monotype output, had access to composition and print room activities, but all the signs are that he preferred the ambiance of the design studio to the noise and clammer of the print room. If he confided in Rogers, he would have found a sympathetic ear. It is also likely his presence in the composing room was unwelcome. Instructing a compositor who, understandably, deeply resented being told how to do their job, could be an onerous task requiring, quite apart from a knowledge of the compositor's jealously guarded working process, a mature standard of diplomacy. Unfortunately, diplomacy was not one of Warde's attributes.

After just one year, Warde was keen to leave 'Mount Vermin', as he called it. Princeton University in New Jersey was looking for a new director to take charge of their prestigious university press, and Henry Lewis Bullen at ATF, and probably Rogers, wrote glowing recommendations on Warde's behalf. After two days of interviews, tours and deliberation, Warde was offered the job. News of his prestigious new position must have been received by the printing staff at Rudge with incredulity quickly followed, no doubt, by a sense of relief.

It was at Princeton University Press that Warde established his reputation as a designer of fine books, as well as for driving his pressmen beyond distraction with demands they could not fathom. Anecdotes abound of profligacy: a letterhead that had to be re-set eleven times; ephemera printed on extravagantly expensive paper; damaging a printing press by throwing his hat into the machine when the operator refused to obey his order to stop a run. Nevertheless, the quality of the Press's output did improve and Warde, no longer in the shadow of Rogers, was making himself noticed – despite the press authorities refusing his request to include his name in the books he designed: 'They don't want any person here who will be bigger than the press [they] think it is a dreadful thing that Rudge permits Rogers to put his name on work'.[2]

When Stanley Morison made his first trip to America in 1924, the extensive library at ATF and its archivist Henry Lewis Bullen were on his agenda. At that time Beatrice Warde was Bullen's assistant, and when he told her the news, Beatrice wrote and invited Morison to stay at their house. She also suggested that he might include a visit to Princeton University Press, where she explained her husband was director of printing. The invitation was accepted.

At some stage during Morison's brief stay at the Warde's home, a discussion took place regarding a collaboration on the design and publication of *The Tapestry*, a book of poems by Robert Bridges,[3] who was Britain's poet laureate at that time and whose work Morison admired. Bridges himself took a keen interest in typography, and his wife Monica had published an influential book, *A New Handwriting for Teachers*,[4] in 1898, influenced by Italian Renaissance writing. It was appropriate, therefore, that it was to the Italian Renaissance that Morison and Warde looked for inspiration and a model for a bespoke typeface for *The Tapestry*. The answer, certainly in Morison's mind, was the chancery cursive type of the printer Ludovico degli Arrighi, also known as Vicentino. Morison had already obtained a copy of Arrighi's *Coryciana* (a book of poems by various people in honour of the scholar Janus Corycius), published in 1524.[5]

> But to me heard afar
>   it was starry music
> Angels' song, comforting
>   as the comfort of Christ
> When he spake tenderly
>   to his sorrowful flock:
> The old words came to me
>   by the riches of time
> Mellow'd and transfigured
>   as I stood on the hill
> Heark'ning in the aspect
>   of th' eternal silence.

Right: Frederic Warde, *Arrighi,* from *The Tapestry* by Robert Bridges, 1926.

CRITO

A SOCRATIC DIALOGUE

BY PLATO

Translated by Henry Cary

Before Morison's return to England, he suggested that Frederic and Beatrice should join him there. Arrangements were made and on arrival in England, Frederic lost no time in departing for Europe. With the discussed bespoke cursive typeface in mind, he 'discovered a thoroughly good punchcutter of the most surprising ability. His work is excellent'.[6] Whether Warde really did 'discover' Charles Plumet or had been directed to him by Morison is not known. Presumably after discussing the matter with Morison, Warde returned to deliver the commission to Plumet whose task it was to cut a fount that replicated Arrighi's original as faithfully as possible. From this point onwards, Warde dealt with all the details concerning the cutting and manufacture of the type. Most importantly, he also paid the bill.

Plumet's version was more regular than Arrighi's original, which contains delicately shifting angles, spacing and alignments. It was also a little lighter, although, as always, this could depend on paper, ink and printing pressure. Warde also designed a set of accompanying roman (not cursive) capitals, to be used in the same manner as Arrighi had done. (These same roman capitals were also used to accompany *Vicenza*, see image above.)

The printing of *The Tapestry* took place in November 1926, 'over a week and a night'[7] at the recently established Fanfare Press, at that time operating from a basement at 41 Bedford Square, London. The amount of *Arrighi* type available was small and so turnover was tight. Type from the previous evening's work had to be dissed and the next pages set during the day to be printed on a Harild proofing press. Printing was done by Warde and the company print manager, Ernst Ingham, after the printing staff had gone home – late into the night initially, until the neighbours complained.[8]

Above left: Frederic Warde, *Vicenza*, accompanied by a set of idiosyncratic roman capital letters also designed by Warde. From the title page of *Crito: A Socratic Dialogue* by Plato, printed by Hans Mardersteig at the Officina Bodoni and published by Warde's own imprint, The Pleiad, 1926.

Warde then designed a revised version of his own *Arrighi* type in 1926, which he named *Vicenza*. The principal new feature was a more conventional (straighter) treatment of the ascenders now with backward facing serifs, while retaining the extravagant sweep of *Arrighi*'s descenders.

Based primarily in Paris at this time, Warde was working with gratifying success, designing books printed by (among others) Hans Mardersteig at the Officina Bodoni in Switzerland (the first showing of *Vicenza* was in Mardersteig's edition of Plato's *Crito*) and under Jan van Krimpen's careful eye at Joh. Enschedé en Zonen, in Haarlem. All of Warde's ambitions had, finally, come to fruition, causing links with Morison to become increasingly superfluous – a situation exacerbated by emerging disagreements regarding 'ownership' of *Arrighi*.

Having fallen in love with Europe, Warde, characteristically, now decided it had lost its lustre and returned in triumphant mood to New York in October 1927. Bruce Rogers, who was in talks with Monotype concerning his typeface *Centaur*, was keen to meet up with Warde. The inspiration for *Centaur* had been Nicolas Jenson's type of 1470, which predated the advent of italic – but Monotype were insisting that if they were to go ahead with *Centaur*, it must include an italic. Rogers, unwilling to undertake this task himself, contacted Morison about using *Arrighi* to partner *Centaur*.[9] This was a *faux-pas* of major proportions, at least as far as Warde was concerned. Warde wrote to Rogers:

> I have received Morison's letter about your request for use of some of 'my' *Arrighi* type. I say 'MY' in order to make it clear that the punches, matrices and type are, and have been from the beginning, entirely mine and fully paid for. The idea was mine … all Morison did was to provide encouragement and useful criticisms while the punches were being cut.

Rogers immediately redirected his request to Warde who, surely with an immeasurable sense of validation, readily agreed.

It was, however, a large and demanding task. A complete set of inclined capitals (not included in either of Warde's previous versions) had to be designed from scratch; the lowercase required an enlarged x-height to match *Centaur* – meaning shorter ascenders and descenders – and a number of new characters, including a set of lining numerals required for the American market. The serifs used on *Vicenza*'s ascenders were

MONOTYPE*
CENTAUR
Roman & *Italic* in

all sizes from 6 to 48 pt., roman to 72 pt. Designed by BRUCE ROGERS; a masterly re-statement of JENSON's 1470 roman. Exclusive to THE MONOTYPE CORPORATION LTD. Reg. Office: 55-56 Lincolns Inn Fields, London, W.C.2 Head Office and Works: Salfords, Redhill, Surrey.   [*REGISTERED TRADE MARK

bdefghjkmopqrsuvyz
ABCDEGJMNQ
RSTUVWXYZ&

BDGHIJKM

PQSVWYZ

employed once more, but this time less sloped. Warde was not a draughtsman and struggled to provide the visual means to describe with sufficient precision his intentions, but the women in the Monotype drawing office provided, as they had done on numerous other occasions, sensitive interpretations. Perhaps on this occasion Warde appreciated the expertise on offer – he was surprisingly amicable in his dealings with Monotype, generally approving their work and revisions without prevarication. The fact that all negotiations were carried out by post to and from New York probably also helped. Rogers was certainly pleased. He described Warde's third and final version of *Arrighi* (called *Centaur Italic* by Monotype for obvious reasons) as 'one of the finest and most legible cursive letters ever produced'.

Above: Frederic Warde's *Arrighi*, which was redrawn for Monotype to work alongside Rogers's *Centaur* and renamed *Centaur Italic*, 1929. The italic capitals designed for Monotype, although much tauter, have retained some of the singular characteristics of the earlier capitals Warde designed for Robert Bridges's *The Tapestry* (see p. 60).

GOETHES
DRAMATISCHE
DICHTUNGEN
BAND II

GROSSHERZOG WILHELM
ERNST AUSGABE

Emery Walker GREAT BRITAIN 1871–1933

Emery Walker was born in Paddington, London. His parents had moved from Norfolk to London where his father worked as a coach builder. In 1864, when his father's eyesight failed, twelve-year-old Emery left school and found various jobs to help support the family. In 1872 the artist Henry Dawson, perhaps recognizing an innate talent, suggested Emery work for his own son Alfred, who had just set up a typographic etching company with its office in central London and workshop in Chiswick. Walker joined the following year.

The company made engraved plates for reproducing line illustrations and photogravure, and later halftones. Dawson had also patented a process he called 'typographic etching', which involved coating a metal plate with wax into which metal type could be pressed. This process allowed type and line drawing to be combined on the same plate – ideal for the printing of maps, something in which the company would later specialize. Walker stayed for ten years and then, after a brief period working in his brother-in-law's gallery selling prints, he was able to borrow £500 and join forces with Walter Boutall to form Walker & Boutall, 'Automatic and Photographic Engravers'. Boutall retired in 1900 and the company became Walker & Cockerell (with Sidney Cockerell). From 1904 onwards the company would remain Walker Ltd. His letterhead lists the company's services as 'Process Engraver (Photogravure, Halftone, Line and Typographic Etching). Photographer of Works of Art, Map Constructor and engraver, Copperplate printer and Collotype Printer.' This was a remarkable achievement for a self-educated man.

The Walker's family house was on Hammersmith Terrace, and he would walk past William Morris's Kelmscott House each day on his way to work. Walker and Morris met for the first time at a socialist meeting around 1883–4 and Morris invited Walker to visit him at Kelmscott House, after which they became close friends.

The Arts and Crafts Exhibition Society mounted its first exhibition in 1888. As part of a programme of events to run alongside the exhibition, lectures were arranged on various related crafts. William Morris, accustomed to public speaking, readily agreed to talk on textiles. Walker was asked to talk on printing, but was an inexperienced and reluctant speaker. It was

Opposite: Emery Walker, *Goethes Dramatische Dichtungen Band II*. From the Grossherzog Wilhelm Ernst series of books published by Insel Verlag, initiated *c*.1904. The lettering is probably hand-drawn, and the designer is unknown.

only when his friend, the bookbinder T. J. Cobden-Sanderson, overcame his own reluctance to take part that Walker finally agreed. To accompany his talk he made a set of photographic lantern slides at his photo-engraving company, some of the images having been taken from books loaned to him by Morris.

On the evening of his talk, Walker was indeed nervous but his deep understanding of his subject and down to earth explanation caused Oscar Wilde, reporting for the *Pall Mall Gazette*, to describe Walker as having 'the keen artistic instinct that comes out of actually working in the art of which he spoke'. For example, here is Walker advocating the need for the close setting of words:

> The spacing [between words] should follow the lines of good masonry or brickwork as nearly as possible, that is, the 'whites' should not come, one over the other, but rather thus [shows slide]. Compositors as a rule begin with a 'middle' space and increase the spaces in size rather than reduce them [when justifying a line]. This practice has a tendency to make ugly 'rivers' through the page; a great disfigurement.[1]

However, it was the power of images that took the audience by surprise. Walker's slides were a revelation – and an epiphany for Morris. By showing enlargements not only of pages but also of individual printed characters, Walker provided his audience with an entirely new perception of print and a powerful insight into the type designer's craft. By showing in close-up the impact and subsequent impression of metal letters and transference of ink when they come into contact with paper, Walker made the reciprocity of press, ink, paper and type manifest. Morris had quietly harboured the idea of setting up a press of his own for several years. Talking to Walker on the way home that evening, he said, 'Let's make a new fount of type'.[2]

More fifteenth-century books from Morris's library were delivered to Walker's office, but this time to obtain enlarged photographs for Morris's own purpose.[3] Realizing that there was still so much more he needed to know about paper, inks, printing presses, punchcutting, type founding and much else, Morris offered Walker a partnership in what was to become the Kelmscott Press. Walker turned down the offer, perhaps because of lack of funds to commit to the venture, or perhaps he was intimidated by Morris who made it clear at the outset that everything would have to be done his way. Nevertheless, Walker became a partner in everything but name, visiting Morris daily

Conrad Sweynheym and Arnold Pannartz introduced printing into Italy, setting up a press at Subiaco in 1465. Their type, though considered fundamentally Gothic, shows the

to play a crucial role in enabling Morris's ambition to design his own typeface and establish his own press. Morris's first book from the Kelmscott Press appeared in 1891, printed using his first typeface: *Golden*.

The quality of Morris's Kelmscott Press work was immediately recognized and heralded, both in Britain and elsewhere, and Walker's close association in its establishment (emphasized by Morris's generous praise) caused others wishing to set up their own private press to seek him out. The Ashendene Press, founded in 1895 by C.H.St. John Hornby,[4] was one of the first. Hornby was a partner in W.H.Smith, the highly successful national newspaper vendor and library service. Inspired by Morris, he set up the Ashendene Press in a summer house in his garden as a private pastime, albeit with a permanent pressman and compositor on site. He also sourced the same paper and ink used by Morris, and used *Fell* types. This private diversion became more serious when he moved the press to a purpose-built, two-story building in Chelsea in 1903. He met Sydney Cockerell (at that time Walker's business partner), who suggested that Hornby's press should have its own bespoke typeface. When told the cost would be £100, Hornby replied 'is that all?' and passed the process over to Walker & Cockerell.

In his possession, Walker had photographs he had taken for Morris of a pre-Jenson, semi-roman type devised and printed in 1464 by Konrad Sweynheym from Mainz and Arnold Pannartz from Cologne, who set up their press in the Benedictine monastery of St Scholastica at Subiaco, Italy. Morris had been planning a typeface to follow *Golden*, and Walker had a photograph of Morris's drawings. Writing later, Cockerell explained that Morris had rejected the typeface, although not before having a trial cutting of the lowercase made [5] – something not mentioned by Cockerell:

Above: *Subiaco* from St. John Hornby's Ashendene Press; four lines from *A Book of Songs and Poems* from the *Old Testament and the Apocrypha*, 1904.

...it went no further. Recalling this experiment, [following the meeting with Hornby] I sought out the photograph of Morris's designs. After consultation with Emery Walker and Robert Proctor [of the British Museum] Hornby came to the conclusion that he could do no better than to take up what Morris had abandoned; so he instructed the firm of Walker & Cockerell to go ahead. Well, within a year the *Subiaco* type was designed and cut. Hornby's bill for it was exactly £100.[6]

The design of *Subiaco* is credited to Walker. It is significantly different to the initial drawings done by Morris, and closer to Pannartz and Sweinheim's original. Hornby subsequently used *Subiaco* for almost all Ashendene books for the next twenty-three years.[7]

Subiaco is of medium weight, cut at 18 point (a size known as 'great primer') but with generous ascenders and descenders. It is rather narrow in the lowercase and close-set, as emphasized by the unusual ligaturing of 't' with 'a', 'i', and 'u' besides 'ct' and the usual standard ligatures. There is no record of what drawings Edward Prince worked from when cutting *Subiaco* – he resisted any request to 'interpret', preferring always to work from precise drawings – but they were probably the work of Percy Tiffin who worked for Walker and who had made the drawings for the *Doves* type some three years earlier.

The Doves Press was established in 1900 by Walker and Cobden-Sanderson. They had known each other for some ten years, both had been close friends and neighbours of Morris (who had died in 1896) and, in different ways, been closely involved with the daily workings of the Kelmscott Press. Cobden-Sanderson's Doves Bindery was set up in 1893 just across the road from Morris's press, and he now wanted to set up a press of his own and offered Walker a partnership. Walker agreed. Later he wrote:

> Mr Cobden-Sanderson asked me if I would join him in starting a press on the lines of the Kelmscott Press. We were great friends and after premising that having just paid out a partner I was unable to put any cash into the venture I agreed. He told me that neither had he any capital but that his wife (a daughter of Richard Cobden, the Free Trader) could supply as much as would be required. We tacitly agreed.

From the outset it was implicit that the Doves Press would have its own proprietary typeface. In fact, for both partners this seems to have been a primary motivation in setting up the venture. They were keen to follow Morris's example and agreed

Emery Walker's *Subiaco* designed for St. John Hornby's Ashendene Press, here used in a spread from Dante, 1909. Admiration by Hornby of the Doves Press is clear.

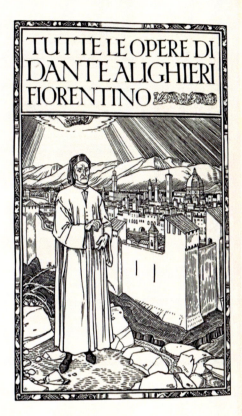

QUI COMINCIA IL LIBRO DELLA VITA NUOVA DI DANTE. CAPITOLO PRIMO.

IN QUELLA PARTE del libro della mia memoria, dinanzi alla quale poco si potrebbe leggere, si trova una rubrica, la quale dice: Incipit Vita Nova. Sotto la quale rubrica io trovo scritte le parole, le quali è mio intendimento d'assemprare in questo libello, e se non tutte, almeno la loro sentenza. Nove fiate già, appresso al mio nascimento, era tornato lo cielo della luce quasi ad un medesimo punto, quanto alla sua propria girazione, quando alli miei occhi apparve prima la gloriosa donna della mia mente, la quale fu chiamata da molti Beatrice, i quali non sapeano che si chiamare. Ella era già in questa vita stata tanto, che nel suo tempo lo cielo stellato era mosso verso la parte d'oriente delle dodici parti l'una d'un grado: sì che quasi dal principio del suo anno nono apparve a me, ed io la vidi quasi alla fine del mio nono anno. Ella apparvemi vestita di nobilissimo colore, umile ed onesto, sanguigno, cinta ed ornata alla guisa che alla sua giovanissima etade si convenia. In quel punto dico veracemente che lo spirito della vita, lo quale dimora nella segretissima camera del cuore, cominciò a tremare sì fortemente, che apparìa ne' menomi polsi orribilmente; & tremando disse queste parole: Ecce Deus fortior me, qui veniens dominabitur mihi. In quel punto lo spirito animale, il quale dimora nell' alta camera, nella quale tutti li spiriti sensitivi portano le loro percezioni, si cominciò a maravigliare molto, & parlando spezialmente allo spirito del viso, disse queste parole: Apparuit iam beatitudo vestra. In quel punto lo spirito naturale, il quale dimora in quella parte, ove si ministra lo nutrimento nostro, cominciò a piangere, & piangendo disse queste parole: Heu miser! quia frequenter impeditus ero deinceps. D'allora innanzi dico ch' Amore signoreggiò l'anima mia, la quale fu sì tosto a lui disposata, e cominciò a prendere sopra me tanta sicurtade e tanta signoria, per la virtù che gli dava la mia imaginazione, che mi convenia fare compiutamente tutti i suoi piaceri. Egli mi comandava molte volte, che io cercassi per vedere quest'angiola giovanissima: ond' io nella mia puerizia molte fiate l'andai cercando, e vedeala di sì nobili e laudabili portamenti, che certo di lei si potea dire quella parola del poeta Omero: Ella non pare figliuola d'uomo mortale, ma di Dio. Ed avvegna che la sua immagine, la quale continuamente meco stava, fosse baldanza d'amore a signoreggiarmi, tuttavia era di sì nobile virtù, che nulla volta sofferse, che Amore mi reggesse senza il fedele consiglio della ragione in quelle cose, là dove cotal consiglio fosse utile a udire. E però che soprastare

that Pliny's *Historia Naturalis* printed by Jenson, and Aretinus's *Historia del Popolo Fiorentino* printed by Jacobus Rubeus (both produced in Venice in 1476) should be the basis upon which their own *Doves* type should be designed. Walker already had detailed photographs taken from both books at Morris's request ten years earlier, and these were now to be utilized once more.[8] They agreed that Morris's *Golden* was too dark – the result, in Walker's view, of not taking account of Jenson's 'over-inked' printing, which 'gave an imperfect view of the type. The true shapes had to be extracted so to speak'.[9]

Percy Tiffin was nominated to provide the drawings, an exacting task which took about six months working from photographs and involved providing a number of variations from which Walker and Cobden-Sanderson would comment and advise. Approved drawings were then photographed, reduced to the required size (approximately 16 point) and analysed once more and further adjustments made. By June 1899 the process was complete, and a set of same-size photographs of all Tiffin's drawn letters was given to Prince (essentially the same working sequence devised for Morris's *Golden* type.)

The Latin alphabet used by fifteenth-century Venetian printers did not have a 'J', 'U' 'W' or a 'j' or 'w', and so Tiffin was required to design these himself. Moreover, the capital 'Y' in both Jenson's and Rubeus's types was considered unsuitable and so again Tiffin had to create an alternative. There is an assumption that Tiffin had little opportunity or indeed any need for interpretation, and that because of this his contribution has been considered of nominal importance. Yet 'extricating' (to use Walker's apt description) the original form from heavily printed pages required fine and discriminating judgement as well as an intimate knowledge and appreciation of type and printing.

While the beauty of the *Doves* type owes a great deal to Jenson and Rubeus, and to the drawings of Tiffin, the part played by Prince should not be underestimated either. At this time his reputation and craft skills as a punchcutter were at their zenith. He had cut Morris's *Golden* (1890), *Troy* (1891–2) and *Chaucer* (1892) to international acclaim, and after the *Doves* type (when aged fifty-four) he would go on to cut type for the Ashendene, Eragny, Essex House and Vale presses (UK), Merrymount Press (US), Cranach Press (Germany), Zilverdistel Press (the Netherlands) and others. For the Doves Press he hand-cut approximately 100 punches. The time taken to cut each punch

Opposite: Emery Walker and T.J. Cobden-Sanderson, The Doves Press Bible, 1905. The text is shown slightly reduced. The design, and especially the arrangement of Edward Johnston's calligraphy, was left to Cobden-Sanderson. Walker disapproved of the extended capital 'I' reaching the bottom of the page.

IN THE BEGINNING

GOD CREATED THE HEAVEN AND THE EARTH. ⁋ AND THE EARTH WAS WITHOUT FORM, AND VOID; AND DARKNESS WAS UPON THE FACE OF THE DEEP, & THE SPIRIT OF GOD MOVED UPON THE FACE OF THE WATERS. ⁋ And God said, Let there be light: & there was light. And God saw the light, that it was good: & God divided the light from the darkness. And God called the light Day, and the darkness he called Night. And the evening and the morning were the first day. ⁋ And God said, Let there be a firmament in the midst of the waters, & let it divide the waters from the waters. And God made the firmament, and divided the waters which were under the firmament from the waters which were above the firmament: & it was so. And God called the firmament Heaven. And the evening & the morning were the second day. ⁋ And God said, Let the waters under the heaven be gathered together unto one place, and let the dry land appear: and it was so. And God called the dry land Earth; and the gathering together of the waters called he Seas: and God saw that it was good. And God said, Let the earth bring forth grass, the herb yielding seed, and the fruit tree yielding fruit after his kind, whose seed is in itself, upon the earth: & it was so. And the earth brought forth grass, & herb yielding seed after his kind, & the tree yielding fruit, whose seed was in itself, after his kind: and God saw that it was good. And the evening & the morning were the third day. ⁋ And God said, Let there be lights in the firmament of the heaven to divide the day from the night; and let them be for signs, and for seasons, and for days, & years: and let them be for lights in the firmament of the heaven to give light upon the earth: & it was so. And God made two great lights; the greater light to rule the day, and the lesser light to rule the night: he made the stars also. And God set them in the firmament of the heaven to give light upon the earth, and to rule over the day and over the night, & to divide the light from the darkness: and God saw that it was good. And the evening and the morning were the fourth day. ⁋ And God said, Let the waters bring forth abundantly the moving creature that hath life, and fowl that may fly above the earth in the open firmament of heaven. And God created great whales, & every living creature that moveth, which the waters brought forth abundantly, after their kind, & every winged fowl after his kind: & God saw that it was good. And God blessed them, saying, Be fruitful, & multiply, and fill the waters in the seas, and let fowl multiply in the earth. And the evening & the morning were the fifth day. ⁋ And God said, Let the earth bring forth the living creature after his kind, cattle, and creeping thing, and beast of the earth after his kind: and it was so. And God made the beast of the earth after his kind, and cattle after their kind, and every thing that creepeth upon the

varied depending on the complexity of the letter, but generally averaged one per day. Varying time required can be judged by his charges. Most letters were 10 shillings, and most punctuation half that. Ligatures were 15 shillings and a 'Qu' cost £1. (£1 in 1900 was roughly the value of £130 today.) The *Doves* type was cast by machine by Miller & Richard in Edinburgh.

Doves Press books were unadorned. They had no illustrations, and just one typeface in one size, one weight, and no italics. Similarly, all binding and covers were essentially the same – plain white vellum with the title printed in gold, but only on the spine. As Ruari MacLean has remarked, 'The pages of the Doves Press books were the most devastating criticism ever made of Morris's work at the Kelmscott Press'.[10] The only internal embellishments were the exceptionally beautiful titles and initials added by master calligraphers Edward Johnston and Graily Hewitt. Walker might advise, but the final design of all Doves Press books was the responsibility of Cobden-Sanderson. (In all there were forty publications printed between 1900 and 1917, including the five-volume *King James Bible*.) Cobden-Sanderson described his books as 'beautiful in their beautiful simplicity'. He was the person in the press room reading proofs, checking and assessing every printed sheet, and instructing Johnston and Hewitt. In contrast, Walker was happy to delegate responsibility, and so having appointed John H. Mason as chief compositor (previously at the Ballantyne Press, where the Vale Press books were printed) and two excellent pressmen – Harry Gage-Cole (previously at Kelmscott Press) and Albert Lewis – he simply expected them to deliver the standard of work of which he knew they were capable. This was something Cobden-Sanderson could not understand, let alone condone.

The partnership worked well enough until around 1907–8, when sales began to fall. There was a sense that the press had run its course. The Doves Bible, considered one of the greatest achievements in book-making, was completed in 1905, and perhaps collectors were beginning to experience a sense of déjà vu as they unwrapped the latest offering from the press. Francis Meynell put it more bluntly: 'lovely, impeccable, taut and silky ... but they are in series a little automatic, a little boring,'[11] and, of course, all the texts were available elsewhere. Walker thought the press should close but Cobden-Sanderson disagreed, suggesting that his son might take over from him. Then, to Walker's surprise and indignation, ownership of the *Doves* type became an issue,

Above: Emery Walker and T.J. Cobden-Sanderson, Cover and spine of the Doves Press *The Tragicall Historie Of Hamlet*, 1909. The covers of all Doves Press books were identical, showing the title printed in gold on the spine only.

Ham. Let me see. Alas poore Yoricke, I knew him, Horatio, a fellow of infinite iest, of most excellent fancie, hee hath bore mee on his backe a thousand times, and now how abhorred in my imagination it is: my gorge rises at it. Heere hung those lyppes that I haue kist I knowe not howe oft, where be your gibes now? your gamboles, your songs, your flashes of merriment, that were wont to set the table on a roare, not one now to mocke your owne grinning, quite chopfalne. Now get you to my Ladies table,

with Cobden-Sanderson refusing to hand it over (as the legal agreement stated he should). Later, between 1916–17, Cobden-Sanderson took the matter into his own hands and threw the type, punches and matrices into the Thames.[12] A lengthy court-case ensued, ending with an out-of-court settlement.

Earlier, in 1904 and happier times, Count Harry Kessler had travelled to England to meet Walker, who introduced him to Edward Johnston, Eric Gill and others. Kessler was the son of a Hamburg banker and had a substantial private income. The reason for Kessler's visit was that, as well as being the honorary chairman of the Arts and Crafts Museum in Weimar and a co-editor of the journal *Pan*, Kessler also had strong links with the publishing house Insel Verlag. He invited Walker to design the *Grossherzog Wilhelm Ernst* series of books in conjunction with Insel Verlag (where August Kippenberg was co-director). This series, with Walker acting affectively as art director, included calligraphic title pages designed by Johnston and by Gill, and had a marked influence on German book design, not least for the fact that Walker used roman rather than blackletter type (clearly with the internationally minded Kessler's support). In 1913 Kessler decided to set up his own private press, named the Cranach Press after the street name in Weimar, and once more called on Walker for advice and assistance. John H. Mason (as compositor) and Harry Gage-Cole (as printer) were both engaged on Walker's recommendation, and Kessler requested that a proprietary roman typeface be designed.

The *Cranach Jenson* roman was produced efficiently, and its

Above: Emery Walker and T. J. Cobden-Sanderson, *Doves,* from Shakespeare's *The tragicall historie of Hamlet, Prince of Denmarke,* printed in 1909. Shown at approximately actual size; 16 point. (See also p. 73.)

Emery Walker   77

design is credited to Walker. There appears to be no record of the process of its making.[13] F. C. Avis, in his book *Edward Philip Prince*, describes the *Cranach* type as 'a magnificent latter-day Venetian, completely in the style of the *Doves*, with which it suffers no adverse comparison. Similarity between the two types is great'.[14] There was certainly sufficient similarity to have caused consternation for Cobden-Sanderson.[15] Much later, in 1923, when asked to write a report for the court case against the widow of his former partner (Cobden-Sanderson died in September 1922), Walker explained that 'When I heard that Mr Sanderson had put the type in the Thames, having the original models [drawings] I tried to get it recut, and although I have done all I could to make a good copy there are many differences visible to an expert'.

The fact that Walker had the original drawings for the *Doves* type is important. He admitted that he 'tried' to have copies cut (meaning copies were cut, though unsatisfactorily, presumably by Prince) after he had heard of Cobden-Sanderson's criminal actions in 1916–17. But it is possible that he attempted this when Cobden-Sanderson first refused him access to the originals (1908–9). If so, the *Cranach Jenson* could have included many, all, or, of course, none of the *Doves* letters re-cut by Prince. John Dreyfus noted that his own 'careful scrutiny of the original drawings for the *Doves Roman* reveals … two alternative designs for 's' and 'y', as well as the numeral '2' which were used only for the Cranach Press roman and not for the Doves Press.'[16] Regardless of how the *Cranach Jenson* type came into being, Kessler was pleased with the outcome and decided he now wanted an italic with which to accompany it.

No other private press had, until now, had an italic. This was, in part, down to cost, but more significantly it was because the typefaces chosen for revival were generally from the fifteenth century, when italics were designed to stand and function quite separate from their roman counterparts. This meant that when Kessler asked for an italic to accompany his *Cranach Jenson* there was no appropriate model to follow, and the extent of Walker's understanding of calligraphy – a significant part of italic type design – was left somewhat exposed. He chose to base the italic on calligraphy by Giovanni Antonio Tagliente in Venice, c.1525 (it would be the inspiration for Monotype's *Bembo* italic in 1928).[17] The decision left major issues of proportion involving x-height, ascenders and descenders as well as width to be redesigned. As well as having to make amendments for faulty presswork, neither

Opposite: Edward Johnston's *Cranach Italic* used by Harry Kessler for Rainer Maria Rilke's *Duineser Elegien*, printed by the Cranach Press and published by The Hogarth Press in an edition of of 230. Kessler designed the book; Eric Gill designed and cut the wood-engraved initials, 1931.

THE EIGHTH ELEGY

Dumb creatures gaze with their whole vision out
Into infinity. our eyes alone
Would seem to be inverted, and like snares
Set all around them, compassing their free
Passage. what lies beyond, for us is only
Intelligible through the mask of beasts,
For in his early years we take the child,
Turn him about, and, so compelling him
Make him look backwards at all conformation,
Not over space, that in the glance of beasts
Dwells so profound. exempt from thought of death!
That's seen by us alone; the freeborn beast
Keeps his perdition evermore behind him,
And God before him; when he goes, he goes
Into eternity, like springs of water.
But never for a single day have we
Clear space before us, space wherein the flowers
Spring endlessly. the world, and still the world,
Never a nowhere, blank, without negation;
Pure space, surveillance-free, in which to breathe,

DIE ACHTE ELEGIE

Rudolf Kassner zugeeignet

Mit allen augen sieht die kreatur
Das offene. nur unsre augen sind
Wie umgekehrt und ganz um sie gestellt
Als fallen, rings um ihren freien ausgang.
Was draussen ist, wir wissens aus des tiers
Antlitz allein; denn schon das frühe kind
Wenden wir um und zwingens, dass es rückwärts
Gestaltung sehe, nicht das offne, das
Im tiergesicht so tief ist. frei von tod.
Ihn sehen wir allein; das freie tier
Hat seinen untergang stets hinter sich
Und vor sich Gott, und wenn es geht, so gehts
In ewigkeit, so wie die brunnen gehen.
Wir haben nie, nicht einen einzigen tag,
Den reinen raum vor uns, in den die blumen
Unendlich aufgehn. immer ist es welt
Und niemals nirgends ohne nicht:
Das reine, unüberwachte, das man atmet und
Unendlich weiss und nicht begehrt. als kind

Walker or Tiffin fully appreciated the pen-formed transitions from one stroke to the next – a factor essential to the flowing anatomy required of an italic letter.

Nevertheless, Tiffin's drawings, produced under Walker's close supervision, were sent to Prince who duly cut the punches. This time the results were not well received. Kessler, unsure how to go about correcting the issues, turned to the calligrapher Edward Johnston who was already working on two typefaces for the Cranach Press (a semi-blackletter which would be used to great effect in the Cranach Press's *Hamlet*, and a Greek). Johnston was reluctant, but Kessler eventually persuaded him to meet with Prince and himself on 16 July 1912. Crucially, Walker, who was still effectively responsible for the making of the italic, was not present.

Initially, only five or six characters were identified as unsatisfactory but such scrutiny inevitably led to others coming under criticism. Before the end of the meeting it was decided that the only way forward was to redraw the whole fount. Kessler sent a letter to Walker informing him of this and of the decision to commission Johnston to do the work. A week later, Walker received a letter from Prince expressing his doubts about the new arrangement – and especially the involvement of Johnston. Eager to ensure that his close and long-lasting working relationship with Walker was not put in jeopardy, he made it clear that he thought that if Kessler had simply met Walker and himself to discuss his concerns, the outcome would have been far better. Walker's response was diplomatic as always, though he was clearly hurt. In answer to Kessler's letter he wrote to say he was concerned that the new arrangements might weaken the coherence of the fount and give it a 'jobbing' (laissez-faire) character.[18] Nevertheless, he agreed to do all that he could to make the new arrangement work and assured Kessler that Prince would do the same. As expected, long delays ensued but Johnston eventually provided the drawings and Prince was able to recut the italic.

It was an ignoble outcome for Walker – perhaps part of the reason for Johnston's reluctance to accept the commission in the first place – but Johnston did not fare any better. His italic proved to be an unsuitable companion to the *Cranach Jenson*; it was too narrow and lacked sufficient weight. The outbreak of the First World War in 1914 interrupted its first printing; the Cranach Press would not open again until 1924, with Johnston's italic waiting a further two years before it was used – and rarely seen again.

By the 1920s Walker was in his seventies, his company Emery Walker Ltd. was still active, and he remained an eminently respected figure; he was often referred to as 'the spiritual Father of the Revival of Fine Printing'.[19] Significantly, Walker (more so than Morris) bridged the generation gap and was feted by those such as Stanley Morison, Bruce Rogers, Francis Meynell and Oliver Simon. Like Walker, they saw the future of fine printing being in the commercial sector with a skilled and knowledgeable workforce using modern print technology. In 1925, Oliver Simon chose to 'sign off' his fourth and final issue of *The Fleuron* as its editor with engraved portraits of the two inspirational figures of the print revival movement: Emery Walker and Bruce Rogers.

PARADISE LOST
THE AUTHOR
JOHN MILTON

OF MANS FIRST DISOBEDIENCE,
AND THE FRUIT
OF THAT FORBIDDEN TREE,
WHOSE MORTAL TAST
BROUGHT DEATH INTO THE
WORLD, AND ALL OUR WOE,
With loss of Eden, till one greater Man
Restore us, and regain the blissful Seat,
Sing Heav'nly Muse, that on the secret top
Of Oreb, or of Sinai, didst inspire
That Shepherd, who first taught the chosen Seed,
In the Beginning how the Heav'ns and Earth
Rose out of Chaos: Or if Sion Hill
Delight thee more, and Siloa's Brook that flow'd
Fast by the Oracle of God; I thence
Invoke thy aid to my adventrous Song,
That with no middle flight intends to soar
Above th' Aonian Mount, while it pursues
Things unattempted yet in Prose or Rhime.
And chiefly Thou O Spirit, that dost prefer
Before all Temples th' upright heart and pure,

Edward Johnston GREAT BRITAIN 1872–1944

Edward Johnston was born in San José de Mayo, Uruguay, where his father, an officer in the 3rd Dragoon Guards, was stationed at the time. The family returned to Edinburgh in 1875, but with his father seeking work and his mother ill, Johnston was raised by an aunt and educated entirely at home. His mother died in 1891.

Johnston began working for an uncle as an office clerk before going to Edinburgh University to study medicine, but gave up due to health issues of his own.[1] He began to cultivate a deep interest in calligraphy and read Edward F. Strange's *Alphabets: A Manual of Lettering*, published in 1896. Through family friends he came to know the architect William Harrison Cowlishaw, a keen amateur calligrapher whose illuminated letters had been the subject of an article published in *The Artist*. Cowlishaw promised to introduce him to Emery Walker, known to Johnston for his work with William Morris, if he were to travel to London.

Taking up Cowlishaw's invitation, Johnston duly arrived in London in 1898, aged twenty-six. Cowlishaw was true to his word; within hours Johnston had met Walker and later the same day he was introduced to the architect W.R. Lethaby, who had very recently been appointed head of the newly formed Central School of Arts and Crafts.[2] Lethaby explained that he was thinking of starting a calligraphy class and offered Johnston the job of teaching it. The classes began in 1899. Cobden-Sanderson, Eric Gill, Harold Curwen, John H. Mason, Noel Rooke and Graily Hewitt (who took over Johnston's classes in 1911) were among those who attended. Later the same year he began teaching at Camberwell School of Art, and two years after that at the Royal College of Art (RCA). Lethaby also encouraged Johnston to contribute to a series of books he was editing called *The Artistic Crafts Series of Technical Handbooks*. Johnston's book, *Writing & Illuminating & Lettering*, published in 1906 and 'written without a superfluous flourish',[3] became enormously influential and was translated into German a few years later by Anna Simons, one of Johnston's pupils at the RCA.

The Central School of Arts and Crafts embodied the values of the Arts and Crafts movement, values which now formed the bedrock of Johnston's own beliefs. From 1900 Johnston lodged in a three-room flat in Holborn, close to the school and the British Museum. He was joined by his pupil, Eric Gill, who began

Opposite: Wood-engraved letters closely copied from Edward Johnston's calligraphy and printed red, here shown in the opening page of the Doves Press' *Paradise Lost*, 1902.

attending his class in 1901 and was in thrall to Johnston. Johnston married in 1903 and by 1905 had moved to Hammersmith Terrace. This neighbourhood had become a hub for the Arts and Crafts movement; it was where Morris's Kelmscott Press had been housed and where the Doves Press was currently flourishing. His landlord and (by now) friend, Emery Walker, was the director of his own process engraving company, and a co-partner of the Doves Press with T.J. Cobden-Sanderson who also lived just a few doors away. Although quietly spoken, Johnston thrived on the intellectual milieu in which he sought to live, and his teaching abilities were not merely inspiring but life-changing. His classes at the Central School took place on Monday evenings, 'from 7 until 9.30 in the Embroidery Room'. Eric Gill, some ten years younger, recalls the sensation he felt at the first of Johnston's classes:

> I won't say I owe everything I know about lettering to him ... but I owe everything to the foundation that he laid. And his influence was much more than that of a teacher of lettering. He profoundly altered the whole course of my life and my ways of thinking ... It will have to be sufficient to say that the first time I saw him writing, and saw the writing that came as he wrote, I had that thrill and tremble of the heart which otherwise I can only remember having had when ...
>
>   I first heard the plain chant of the church ... I did not know that such beauties could exist.[4]

Above right: Edward Johnston's block-letters, from his book *Writing & Illuminating & Lettering*, 1906. One of a series called *The Artistic Crafts Series of Technical Handbooks*, edited by W.R. Lethaby.

Johnson gave up his classes at the Central in 1912, prompted by the insistence of student assessment – a constant menace within art education. The same issue had already been the cause of Lethaby's departure.

In 1900, Cobden-Sanderson, who had his Doves Bindery close by, had embarked on establishing the Doves Press with Emery Walker. Considering calligraphy to be a prerequisite of good type design, he had attended Johnston's classes. For his part, Johnston was deeply impressed by Cobden-Sanderson's essay, *The Ideal Book or Book Beautiful*, which he had read in manuscript form. This would be the fourth book to be printed by the Doves Press, published in early 1901.

The first major undertaking of the Doves Press, far larger than all four preceding books together, was *Paradise Lost*. From the outset Cobden-Sanderson wanted to incorporate Johnston's calligraphy, and they began their collaboration in March 1901. The first idea was that Johnston should design a two-line 'heading' – the book's title – on the opening page of the work, and a single initial for the opening of each of the ten volumes (this would eventually grow to twelve volumes). A trial opening page was printed and copies were sent to Johnston on which to try out ideas.

The first word in the first volume was 'Of' and Cobden-Sanderson was not happy with the idea of a large hand-drawn red 'O' next to a far smaller printed black 'f', and so he suggested the initial should become a double initial: 'OF'. Johnston tried alternatives, including drawing the 'f' inside the 'O', but eventually agreed with Cobden-Sanderson's straightforward solution. The page was re-set and printed, incorporating space to accommodate Johnston's 'OF'. Then dozens more variations in design of the title and author were attempted by Johnston, including different styles of letters and over-lapping letters such as the 'R' and the 'A', and the 'O' and the 'F'. Eventually, 'PARADISE LOST' became one line followed by two more lines to accommodate 'THE AUTHOR' and 'JOHN MILTON'. The design was far more Cobden-Sanderson's than Johnston's, although there were enumerable adjustments, some fine, others less so, that Johnston made to enable the design to work so eloquently. In typical style, one of the later notes from Cobden-Sanderson to Johnston ends: 'Also I want you to design it as the enclosed pattern, which I am now sure is the best: the down strokes of the P and F line the design & O is written outside … I wish you to be so very kind as to think this over.'[5]

ACT I SCENE I
LINES 1-13

SAXONIS GRAMMATICI
HISTORIAE LIBER TERTIUS

HORVENDILLUS ET FENGO, QVORUM PATER GERVEN DILLUS JUTORUM PRAEFECTUS EXTITERAT, EIDEM A RORICO, IN JUTIAE PRAESIDIUM SURROGANTUR. AT HORVENDILLUS TRIENNIO TYRANNIDE GESTA, PER SUMMAM RERUM GLORIAM PIRATICAE INCUBUERAT, CUM REX NORVAGIAE COLLERUS OPERUM EJUS AC FAMAE MAGNITUDINEM EMULATUS, DECORUM SIBI FORE EXISTIMAVIT SI TAM LATE PATENTEM PIRATAE FULGOREM SUPERIOR ARMIS OBSCURARE QVIVISSET.

CUJUS CLASSEM varia fretum navigatione scrutatus offendit. Insula erat medio sita pelago, quam piratae collatis utrinque secus navigiis obtinebant. Invitabat duces jucunda littorum species. Hortabatur exterior locorum amoenitas interiora nemorum verna perspicere, lustratisque saltibus secretam sylvarum indaginem pererrare: ubi forte Collerum Horvendillumque invicem sine arbitris obvios incessus reddidit. Tunc Horvendillus prior regem percontari nisus, quo pugnae genere decernere libeat, praestantissimum affirmans, quod paucissimorum viribus ederetur. Duellum siquidem ad capessendam fortitudinis palmam omni certaminis genere efficacius fore, quod propria virtute subnixum, alienae manus opem excluderet. Tam fortem juvenis sententiam admirans Collerus: cum mihi, inquit, pugnae delectum permiseris, maxime utendum judico, quae tumultuationis expers duorum operam capit. Sane et audacior et victoriae promptior aestimatur. In hoc communis nobis sententia est, hoc ultro judicio convenimus. At quoniam exitus in dubio manet, invicem humanitati deferendum est, nec adeo ingeniis indulgendum, ut extrema negligantur officia. Odium in animis est; adsit tamen pietas, quae rigori demum opportuna succedat. Nam etsi mentium nos discrimina separant, naturae tamen jura conciliant. Horum quippe consortio jungimur, quantuscunque animos livor dissociet. Haec itaque pietatis nobis conditio sit, ut victum victor inferiis prosequatur. His enim suprema humanitatis officia inesse constat, quae nemo pius abhorruit. Utraque acies id munus, rigore deposito, concorditer exequatur: Facessat post fatum livor simultasque funere sopiatur. Absit nobis tantae

THE TRAGICALL HISTORIE OF

Enter Barnardo, and Francisco, two Centinels.

Barnardo }
Francisco } Nay answere me.

WHOSE there?
Stand and unfolde your selfe.
Bar. Long live the King.
Fran. Barnardo.
Bar. Hee.
Fran. You come most carefully upon your houre.
Bar. Tis now strooke twelfe, get thee to bed Francisco.
Fran. For this reliefe much thanks, tis bitter cold,
And I am sick at hart.
Bar. Have you had quiet guard?
Fran. Not a mouse stirring.
Bar. Well, good night:
If you doe meete Horatio and Marcellus,
The rivalls of my watch, bid them make hast.

4

HAMLET PRINCE OF DENMARKE

Enter Horatio, and Marcellus.

Fran. I thinke I heare them, stand ho, who is there?
Hora. Friends to this ground.
Mar. And Leedgemen to the Dane.
Fran. Give you good night.
Mar. O, farwell honest souldier, who hath reliev'd you?
Fran. Barnardo hath my place; give you good night.
Exit Francisco.
Mar. Holla, Barnardo.
Bar. Say, what is Horatio there?
Hora. A peece of him.
Bar. Welcome Horatio, welcome good Marcellus.
Hora. What, has this thing appear'd againe to night?
Bar. I have seene nothing.
Mar. Horatio saies tis but our fantasie,
And will not let beliefe take holde of him,
Touching this dreaded sight twice seene of us,
Therefore I have intreated him along
With us to watch the minuts of this night,
That if againe this apparision come,
He may approove our eyes and speake to it.
Hora. Tush, tush, twill not appeare.
Bar. Sit downe a while,
And let us once againe assaile your eares,
That are so fortified against our story,
What we have two nights seene.
Hora. Well, sit we downe,

ACT I SCENE I
LINES 14-33

ENGLISH TRANSLATION OF THE EXTRACTS FROM SAXO GRAMMATICUS BY OLIVER ELTON 1894

At this time Horwendil and Feng, whose father Gerwendil had been governor of the Jutes, were appointed in his place by Rorik to defend Jutland. But Horwendil held the monarchy for three years, and then, to win the height of glory, devoted himself to roving. Then Koll, King of Norway, in rivalry of his great deeds and renown, deemed it would be a handsome deed if by his greater strength in arms he could bedim the far-famed glory of the rover; and, cruising about the sea, he watched for Horwendil's fleet and came up with it. There was an island lying in the middle of the sea, which each of the ships up on either side, was holding. The captains were tempted by the pleasant look of the beach, and the comeliness of the shores led them to look through the interior of the springtide woods, to go through the glades, and roam over the sequestered forests. It was here that the advance of Koll and Horwendil brought them face to face without any witness. Then Horwendil endeavoured to address the king first, asking him in what way it was his pleasure to fight, and declaring that one best which needed the courage of as few as possible. For, said he, the duel was the surest of all modes of combat for winning the meed of bravery, because it relied only upon native courage, and excluded all help from the hand of another. Koll marvelled at so brave a judgment

5

Above: Harry Kessler, Cranach Press, *Hamlet*, set in Edward Johnston's *Kessler Blackletter* typeface, with wood engravings by Edward Gordon Craig, 1928.

ABCDEFGHIJKLMNOPQRSTUV WXYZ abcdefghijklmnopqrstuvwxyz

Above: John H. Mason, *Imprint Old Style*, in collaboration with Frank Pierpoint and the Monotype drawing office led by Fritz Steltzer, 1913.

Walker and Cobden-Sanderson, having realized how much time the three lines and double initial of the first page was taking Johnston to complete, decided that asking him to write it out 300 times was impractical. The solution was to have a precise wood engraving made from his calligraphy. Johnston agreed, but this still left him with a further eleven initials to hand-letter 300 times. At Johnston's suggestion Graily Hewitt, one of his ex-students, was recruited to help. Completion of *Paradise Lost* was delayed but no one seemed unduly concerned. It was clear that Cobden-Sanderson had produced his ideal book – the perfect example of what he had described in *The Ideal Book or Book Beautiful* – and even taking into account the magnificent Doves Bible, whose fifth and final volume was completed in 1905, *Paradise Lost* was never bettered.

In 1912, aged forty, Johnston left London to live in Ditchling, a village to the south of the capital, to join Eric Gill who had established a small craft community there in 1907. It was here that Johnston enjoyed his most creative period. Gill had left London to attain greater isolation and nurture a growing spiritual involvement in living from the land. But as Johnston and Gill's lives became ever-more intertwined, their circle of friends and clients increased.

One of these was Count Harry Kessler, honorary chairman of the Arts and Crafts Museum in Weimar and consultant to the prestigious German publisher Insel Verlag. He commissioned Emery Walker to act as designer of the *Grossherzog Wilhelm Ernst* series of books, and Walker engaged Johnston and Gill to design the title pages. From around 1909 Kessler began a protracted period setting up his own private Cranach Press. A roman face, very similar to the *Doves* type, was designed by Walker and then Kessler decided he wanted an italic to accompany it. This was also given to Walker but the result was not successful, and the task was passed to Johnston.

The circumstances and outcome of the *Cranach Italic* are described in the chapter on Emery Walker.

At that time, in 1912, Johnston was already working on another typeface for Kessler, a semi-blackletter type. (A Greek face

The Imprint

Johnston was also working on at this time for Kessler was never used). The blackletter was based on type used by Peter Schoeffer in 1472 for Gratiani's *Decretum*. Kessler had studied a copy of the book in the British Museum, and was enthusiastic not only about the design of its type but also its arrangement on the page. Johnston's capitals, however, were modelled on *Subiaco*, an early semi-roman type devised and printed by Arnold Pannartz and Konrad Sweinheim in 1465, at Subiaco, Italy. The progress of Johnston's design went smoothly, as did the punchcutting by Edward Prince; three sizes were cut – 18, 12, and 10 point – and cast by Shanks & Company later the same year.

The First World War, and then Kessler's subsequent ill health, impeded his work with the Cranach Press. *Hamlet*, the book for which he wanted to use Johnston's blackletter typeface (usually referred to as *Hamlet Type*, or *Kessler Blackletter*) would be the last, published in 1930. It is, however, Kessler's masterpiece. Its design and printing were undertaken by Kessler with the close collaboration of the theatre director and designer Edward Gordon Craig, who produced the distinctive wood-engraved illustrations. Kessler arranged the 12-point text and 10-point glosses around Craig's wood engravings in the manner he had admired in Schoeffer's book of Gratiani's *Decretum*.

A second crucial liaison for Johnston was with Gerard Meynell, director of the renowned Westminster Press, who met Johnston and Gill in Ditchling in late 1912.[6] Earlier that same year, the exhibition of the Arts and Crafts Exhibition Society had been both a commercial and critical failure, and disaffected members – whose call for a commercial arm for the Society had been rejected – were now seeking an alternative means of promoting a more progressive attitude towards design.

Meynell decided to establish a journal, *The Imprint*, the aim of which was to spearhead improved printing standards by aspiring to apply the values of the Arts and Crafts movement to modern industrial printing technology. Johnston clearly supported the idea because he contributed an article, 'Decoration and its Uses', and became a co-editor along with his previous fellow tutors at the Central School of Arts and Crafts: John H. Mason and Ernest Jackson, and Meynell himself. Johnston also hand-lettered the journal's masthead and Mason, previously head compositor at the Doves Press, designed its typeface *Imprint Old Style*[7] in close collaboration with Monotype (specifically Frank Pierpont, manager of the Monotype Works, and Fritz Steltzer, head of the

Above: Edward Johnston, masthead for the journal *The Imprint*, 1913.

Monotype drawing office). This was the first notable typeface to be designed for mechanical composition. It was cut by Monotype who, in agreement with *The Imprint*'s editors, then made the face commercially available. Only nine issues of *The Imprint* were published, all during 1913, but it established a new and significant way of thinking about design for print that would supersede the Arts and Crafts movement.

The same year, Frank Pick, the young, dynamic commercial manager of the Underground Electric Railways Company of London (UERL), set in motion events that would lead to the design of a proprietary sans serif – 'block letter' – for the company. Pick wanted a distinctive typeface for use on London Underground poster work, and it was Harold Curwen, director of the Curwen Press, who suggested he consider a sans serif. Curwen had already designed a 'monoline' sans serif and would certainly have talked enthusiastically about the potential of such a typeface. It is not known if Pick ever saw Curwen's typeface, but he did attempt to draw a set of 'block letters' himself using a ruler and compass.[8] Although this convinced him that Curwen's advice was correct, he realized that he could not design it himself. He then met Gerard Meynell to ask who might design such a face, and Meynell suggested Johnston. Meynell organized and attended an initial meeting with Pick and Johnston; what precisely was discussed or what conclusions were reached were not recorded.

Recent events at the time will have had an influence on Pick, Curwen and Meynell. The failure of the 1912 exhibition of the Arts and Crafts Exhibition Society had been a shock, and there was a genuine sense that British design was out of touch with public expectations. This was vividly demonstrated when, in March 1915, an exhibition of German products was held at the Goldsmiths' Hall, London. Comments made by the art critic of *The Times* reflect the anxieties of many younger designers at that time:

> Finely printed books, not quite as good as the very best British, but showing their influence in every letter, are produced and sold in Germany far cheaper than in England. Mr Edward Johnston, known only to specialists in England, has influenced the whole German artistic typography, and his lettering, or lettering very like his, may be seen upon the cigarette boxes of an enterprising German industrialist.

This exhibition prompted Gerald Meynell, with others who were concerned that British design was falling behind in terms

Above left: Edward Johnston, a lithographic print of a preliminary drawing for the *Underground Alphabet*, 1916.

Above right: *Granby*, designed by the Stephenson-Blake type foundry, Sheffield, and used extensively by London Underground, c.1930.

of both quality and efficiency, to form the Design & Industries Association (DIA). Members included Lethaby, Curwen, Mason, Cowlishaw, Hewitt and Pick – all close associates of Johnston. The council of the DIA immediately reprinted Lethaby's opening article from the first issue of *The Imprint* – 'Art and Workmanship' – and an exhibition was mounted at the Whitechapel Gallery, London, in November 1915. Work by Johnston and Gill was included. In this way, Johnston and Gill, both of whom would doubtlessly refuse to call themselves reformists, became associated with the modernist aspirations espoused by the DIA. It was in the midst of such circumstances that on 16 June 1915 Johnston, this time with Eric Gill also in attendance,[9] would meet Frank Pick once more and the *Underground Type* was formally commissioned. Pick's only stipulation was that it must be a 'block letter monostroke'.[10]

Johnston was, of course, primed for Pick's request. While critical of 'ordinary heavy block letters … so commonly used', he had also written and spoken about the possibilities of a finely proportioned 'equal stroke' (monoline) block letter in *Writing & Illuminating & Lettering* (see p. 76) and advocated the Trajan model – the roman capitals in an inscription at the base of Trajan's Column, Rome, AD 113 – as being the most readable, having the 'utmost simplicity, distinctiveness and proportion'.[11]

Johnston set out with the understanding that his alphabet would be printed on sheets from which the letters, one inch high, could be traced and transferred to poster artwork. It was only later that the alphabet was adopted for directional signing.

Beginning around 1922, the type foundry Stephenson Blake in Sheffield cut the wood letters for poster work in sizes 6-line (72 point) to 36-line (432 point).[12] Johnston had earlier resisted the idea of mechanically producing his letters, but by 1914 he was working on typefaces for Kessler and so, presumably, was no longer perturbed by the knowledge that his letters were being manufactured. From 1930, London Underground used Stephenson Blake's *Granby*, a typeface designed in-house by the foundry for mechanical composition. *Granby* is close enough to Johnston's original to encourage speculation that it was the result of a discreet request from Pick, or at least produced with his agreement, since litigation did not occur.

The 'bull's eye' logo – a red rondel with a bar through it, initially carrying the word 'Underground' – was designed by Johnston in 1919. Variations of the original lettering were later commissioned for other parts of London Transport, such as a 'compressed type' for the destination signs on buses in 1919, and a bolder, titling version for printed matter in 1929. Both were drawn by Charles Pickering to notes provided by Johnston.[13] Pick retired in May 1940.

PART TWO
Hot Metal Type

Introduction

Mechanical typesetting became available during the final two decades of the nineteenth century, with the independently developed inventions of the Monotype and Linotype machines. Both combined typesetting via a keyboard, physically similar to a typewriter, and a type casting unit that utilized brass matrices and molten metal – hence the term 'hot metal type casting'.

Throughout the nineteenth century, attempts had been made to mechanize typesetting operations; the first patent for a composing machine had been registered in 1825. Early versions used a keyboard arrangement connected to existing foundry-cast metal type which had to be pre-loaded into the machine. Then, at the press of a key, the type characters dropped from their storage channels into position as required. *The Times* newspaper in London had one of the more successful machines of this kind: a Kastenbein, installed in 1872. In the US during the 1880s, Ottmar Mergenthaler and Tolbert Lanston both devised composing machines – the Linotype and the Monotype. Two very different solutions, they both incorporated the production of type from brass matrices made possible by the fact that molten metal becomes solid within a second or two of casting.

The Linotype arrived first. Mergenthaler (1854–1899) was a German immigrant working as a mechanic in Baltimore. His typecasting machine cast a 'line-o-type' as a single solid piece, called a 'slug'. When the operator keyed in a line of text the machine released the corresponding brass matrices, which dropped into position in the correct order along with the required word spaces. Once a complete line of matrices was in place, it was justified by the use of inter-word wedges and then set in molten metal as one piece. After the slug was made, the brass matrices and space wedges were returned to their channels ready to be reused. A Linotype caster was first installed by the *New York Tribune* in 1886, and by 1900 Linotypes had replaced hand-setting in virtually every newspaper office in America and in many parts of Europe.

The Monotype was introduced by Lanston (1844–1913) in 1889. The system was divided into two parts: the Monotype keyboard and the Monotype caster. Text was typed and as each key was pressed it was recorded as a perforation; holes were punched into a narrow roll of paper. The keyboard was also used to record

Previous page: Type casting at Oxford University Press, *c*.1950s. The Monotype caster cast loose type using information conveyed by a series of holes punched into paper tape. The holes were generated by an operator as he pressed the keys on a keyboard while typing the text. The tape could be stored and reused for casting of subsequent editions, making Monotype a popular system for book work. Newspaper production preferred the more robust and easier to handle Linotype system.
 Monotype allowed for small amendments, corrections and additional complex work by hand (with the aid of tweezers) after the bulk of the text had been set by the machine. This was not possible with the Linotype typecaster, but both systems produced perfectly aligned text with all spaces in each line exactly the same width.

information concerning line length, indents etc. The perforated paper role was then transferred to the Monotype caster. The caster would 'read' the perforations as characters and spaces and, using matrices, cast these from molten metal and drop them into position as individual characters in lines. This made corrections or fine adjustments within text at a later stage easy, because individual characters or spaces could be substituted by hand, an activity that also maintained a welcome link with craft-associated skills of the past. With Linotype, the whole line (slug) containing the mistake would have to be re-set on the machine.

Both the Lanston Monotype Corporation and the Linotype Company provided 'types similar in appearance to ordinary types and of commercial character'.[1] Initially, typefaces were seen as little more than fodder for the caster with no pretence made towards originality – and there was little incentive when type patents proved so hopelessly inadequate. The first typeface offered by Monotype was *Modern* (c.1901). It was very similar to a typeface cut by Richard Austin for the type foundry Miller & Richard in Edinburgh, which in turn owed its origins to the eighteenth-century designs of John Baskerville in Birmingham and Pierre-Simon Fournier in Paris. Close copies of Austin's types had been a popular choice for printing of every kind for much of the nineteenth century.[2]

When Monotype and Linotype realized that the range and quality of typefaces available for use with their machines was a factor in the printer's decision concerning which system to buy, both companies embarked on a programme of development and design of typefaces, historic and contemporary in origin, to match commercial demands. For larger printing enterprises, the advantages of mechanized typesetting were considerable. The machines increased the output of a re-trained compositor threefold, and the time-consuming task of dissing (dispersing type back to their cases) was obviated because the used type was simply recycled via the 'hellbox' and re-melted. In this way, type was created anew for every job.

Each typecasting machine needed a set of matrices, and it quickly became apparent that the use of hand-cut punches to make the required vast quantities of matrices was inadequate. Despite being made from hardened steel, punches could break and the hand-cutting of a precise replacement was all but impossible. Fortunately, a mechanical punchcutting device had been developed by Linn Boyd Benton (father of Morris Fuller

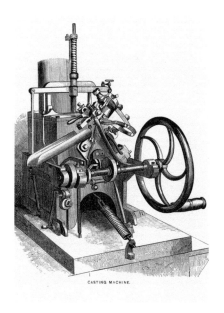

Above: The Bruce pivotal type caster, the first commercially successful typecasting machine, patented in the US, 1838.

Above: The pantograph was the first device designed for making a copy with the crucial added ability to change the size of an image. It was invented by Chistoph Scheiner, a German astronomer in Italy, in about 1603, but he did not publish an account of his invention until 1631. This image is taken from a later Italian edition: *Prattica del parallelogrammo da disegnare,* published in Bologna in 1653.

Benton) in the US, and brought into mass production in 1885. Benton's invention, the pantograph, was an essential factor in the success of both Linotype and Monotype.

The pantograph required an operator to trace around the outline of a large letter, called a pattern, cut from a sheet of brass. Adjacently connected, a small sharp, fast-rotating cutting tool cut away steel from a precisely positioned blank punch to eventually recreate a precise replica of the pattern. With simple adjustments to its settings the pantograph could cut a letter within a given range of point sizes from the same pattern. Three or four patterns of each letter were needed to capture the necessary adjustments to weight distribution and form required in the nonlinear scaling of a full range of point sizes.[3] Settings built into the pantograph enabled the operator to interpolate the required sizes between those of the standard size pattens.

Mechanical punchcutting brought the art of punchcutting by hand to an end, but it also changed the nature of the working process for the type designer. As Beatrice Warde later explained:

> In hand cutting, the punch can be called the only original work of art in the whole process of making type. It is that single and unique object by which one can obtain as many as 500 matrices, each matrix being capable of forming millions of types. But in machine cutting the unique object is the drawing, from which any number of patterns can be made, each pattern serving for any number of punches of the letter.[4]

The fact that the pantograph saved time and money in the design as well as the manufacture of type emboldened foundries to commission artists and designers working in fields other than type design. Such designers would generally be asked to provide a single fount of letters, representing an 'average' size. The necessary adjustments to the form of each letter (to take account of adjustments in size, the input of spatial side-bearing values, and the addition of missing accented letters and punctation such as essential monetary and mathematical symbols) were achieved by the in-house drawing offices established by Monotype, Linotype and most other larger type foundries.

Many designers were only too pleased to have the expertise of the drawing office take on this demanding (and to some, tedious) and time-consuming work, but there were a few who took great offence at the adjustments made by those they accused of having an 'engineer's mentality', if not by profession then in attitude

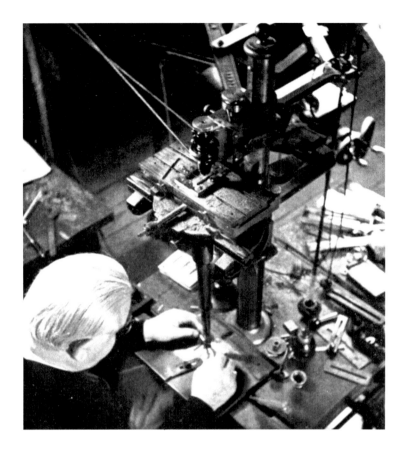

Left: Frederic Goudy photographed using a pantograph machine, to illustrate an article for *Advertising and Selling* magazine (published May 1939). The piece was titled: 'Type: Frederic W. Goudy Here Demonstrates the Design of One of Advertising's Oldest Devices, a Type Face'. To cut a type matrix, the hand-held tracer is guided along the outlines of the sunken metal pattern while a small, fast-rotating router precisely duplicates each movement, engraving a matrix at the required size.

and approach. A criticism often levelled at the drawing office was its inability or reluctance to retain, for example, the subtle curve of a stroke and then to recognize and accept that a curve on the next letter might be fractionally (and intentionally) different. Daniel B. Updike put it succinctly when he wrote, quoting an unnamed source: '"A type too ideal in its perfection is not an ideal type". The eye becomes tired when each character is absolutely perfect. Thus the good effect of the type in mass depends somewhat upon the variations in, and consequent "movement" of its integral parts.'[5]

The tendency, especially when working within a tightly knit group, to 'correct' what might be perceived as minor imperfections was certainly real. This was especially so when the head of such a group demonstrated frustration at having to take what was perceived to be poor quality design and turn it into a workable type, in the sure knowledge that it would be the 'incompetent' designer who received the plaudits should the drawing office succeed.

Of course, some designers were far from incompetent. Frederic Goudy famously fought with both Monotype (in America) and the American Type Founders Company (ATF). Of these experiences Goudy said:

> Drawings like mine which were made free-hand, were not the sort usually worked from at the Monotype Company, so there was a constant fight to see that the workmen did not 'correct' what seemed to them to be bad drawing on my part. If I intentionally gave a letter an incline of one degree, they straightened it up. My serifs, which had a definite shape, were changed to meet their own ideas…[6]

Eric Gill, Jan van Krimpen and Bruce Rogers all had running battles with the Monotype drawing office in London. In all these cases the distinguished results must speak for themselves. However, the triumphant tenor struck by these designers in the description of their apparently heroic exploits 'fighting the machine' must have infuriated the drawing office workers who, of course, were advised that it would be inappropriate (meaning commercially detrimental) for them to publicly contradict their 'star' designers.

Monotype and Linotype machines quickly and grievously affected hundreds of smaller independent type foundries. Previously agreed price-scales were broken as companies attempted to stave off bankruptcy, but the resulting price wars drove many to ruin anyway. Amalgamations were a logical alternative, the most spectacular of which was the establishment of the ATF in 1892 with its head office in New York.

In the newspaper printing industry and book printing houses, the effect of the mechanization of typesetting on hand-compositors was also devastating. Mergenthaler's Linotype machine could do the work of seven or eight men. Its rapid deployment replaced thousands of highly skilled compositors, which resulted in strikes and violence wherever mechanized typesetting machines were being installed. However, by reducing the production costs this new technology also caused a huge increase in the production of graphic material which, over time, created thousands of new jobs. As a result, many hand-compositors were able to re-train as keyboard operators.

Great effort was made to establish the status of the 'machine compositor' as a step-up from the hand-compositor. It was emphasized that these needed to be better educated and better trained in order to deal with the technical aspects of a complicated system. In this way, both Linotype and Monotype successfully gained the support of machine compositors by creating 'an elite of workers within the trade'.[7]

Meanwhile, very little changed for the hand-compositor employed in thousands of smaller jobbing printers. When small amounts of text were required it remained far easier, quicker and cheaper to do such work by hand in-house using foundry (cold metal) type. A jobbing printer was likely to hand-set items such as price lists, timetables, catalogues, handbills and the like, as well as shorter amounts of textual matter, because such material was not compatible with the advantages of mechanized typesetting machines. Hand-composition would, therefore, remain a required and sought-after skill up until and including the 1950s and, consequently, there remained a commercially viable demand for foundry type.

While Monotype and Linotype dominated the field, others were able to find lucrative niche markets for alternative systems. The most successful of these was the Ludlow Typograph, manufactured by the Ludlow Typograph Company, founded in 1906 in Chicago by the machine's inventor, Washington Irving Ludlow. The Typograph was a compact machine used in the setting of advertisements, posters, pamphlets and other smaller jobs. It also became a standard fixture in newspaper and magazine printing shops, as well as larger jobbing printers across the world.[8] The Typograph produced metal slugs that could be used alongside Linotype slugs, or with Monotype or foundry type. But while Monotype and Linotype operators worked from a keyboard and set type mechanically, Ludlow material was always set by hand. The operator composed their text by placing matrices (not type) into a lockable hand-held stick, similar in appearance to the standard compositor's type stick, which was slid into the Ludlow caster from which a slug was produced. Ease, speed, variety and flexibility were the major selling points of the Ludlow system but, like Linotype and Monotype, the company also needed to offer its customers a good range of (mostly display) typefaces.

A TYPOGRAPHIC TRIUMPH

The CLASSIC CLOISTER FAMILY

*With
Appropriate Decorative
Material*

AMERICAN TYPE FOUNDERS COMPANY

LARGEST AND MOST PROGRESSIVE TYPE FOUNDRY IN THE WORLD

Morris Fuller Benton USA 1872–1948

Morris Fuller Benton's father, Linn Boyd Benton, was an exceptional engineer and the director of the type founding company Benton, Gove & Co. When Gove died in 1882 and the company became Benton, Waldo & Company, Linn was already well known within the printing industry, due in large part to his innovative inventions – such as a multiple mould for casting leads and slugs, a typesetting machine with automatic justification,[1] and, in 1884, the first version of a pantograph machine invented for engraving steel punches. (Benton received a patent for the latter's third version in 1885.) *The Inland Printer* in September 1886 described Benton as 'an intelligent, entertaining, unostentatious gentleman, a mechanical genius of whom [Milwaukee] has every right to feel proud'.

His son Morris began learning to set type at age eleven in the composing room of his father's newspaper, the *Milwaukee Daily News*, and then Linn helped Morris set up his own press in the family's home on Wells Street in Milwaukee. Here, Morris designed and printed admittance tickets for children's music classes, tickets for neighbourhood shows, receipts for work he did for his father, as well as modest little books of riddles.

In September 1892, at the age of twenty, Morris left Milwaukee for Cornell University in Ithaca, New York. He was older than most of his fellow students, due to childhood illnesses. It was not Morris's intention that he follow his father into the type founding business – only later did he decide to study mechanical engineering, no doubt recognizing that he, like his father, had a natural ability for it. However, Morris's best grades at Cornell were in mechanical drawing.

The year Morris left home for university, his father was embroiled in a business merger of massive proportions. Many American type foundries, including Benton, Waldo & Co., had found it increasingly difficult to survive since the mid-1870s because, simply, there were too many of them. Mechanized manufacturing processes enabled new foundries to be established, some by unscrupulous entrepreneurs who simply sold copies of their rivals' types surreptitiously made by electro-duplication.[2] Another problem was the arrival of the Linotype (c.1886) and Monotype (c.1897) casting machines. There was a huge number of local newspapers in the US, all of whom had relied

Opposite: Morris Fuller Benton's, *Cloister*, c.1913, in an undated type specimen published by the American Type Founders (ATF) claiming to be the 'originator of the family idea in type design'. *Cloister* was cast on the 'art line' rather than ATF's standardised 'common line' to allow more space for descenders. *Cloister* became very popular and both Monotype and Linotype made almost identical versions.

on local foundries to provide supplies at short notice. But once a Linotype machine had been installed, the services provided by the foundry were no longer required. Type foundries began the undignified practice of undercutting each other, resulting in bitter recriminations and reprisals. It became apparent to Linn Boyd Benton and several other foundry owners that there was no choice other than to consolidate, and so a merger was organized. Linn had been party to such discussions from their beginning in 1878, and when the oldest and largest type foundry – MacKellar, Smiths & Jordan (with assets of six million dollars) – agreed to join, success was all but guaranteed. In 1892 there were twenty-three foundries who joined forces; within a year those estimated to be loss-making enterprises had been closed, leaving just fourteen,[3] one of which was Benton, Waldo & Co. The American Type Founders Company (ATF) was born.

For the first few turbulent months after the merger, the Bentons remained in Milwaukee, but it soon became evident that Linn's expertise and experience were required in New York where the new company had established its head office. Lynn moved his foundry to New York in 1894, leaving his business partner, Waldo, in Milwaukee to manage a sales office.

A few months after Morris graduated from Cornell, he became his father's assistant at ATF. In 1897 he married and moved into an apartment on Staten Island, ten blocks from where his parents then lived. Each morning, Morris and his father would meet and take the ferry to New York City. At that time the foundry was on the southern-most tip of Manhattan. Initially, Morris used his engineering skills to design equipment and machinery but he also, gradually, began to learn about typefaces. Much of this was achieved while undertaking his first, but hugely significant assignment at ATF. Taking over from Joseph W. Phinney, who had already spent four years on it, the task was to apply a standard system of measurement to the numerous typefaces that ATF had acquired from the twenty-three type foundries in the merger. It was an immense and complex undertaking, made much worse not only by the enormous amount of unscrupulous electro-duplicating that had taken place but also by the fact that the standard point system of measurement had only recently been adopted by some foundries, meaning that much of the type and matrices ATF inherited had been manufactured according to various and now redundant systems. In particular, baseline alignment had to be standardized (sometimes referred to as the

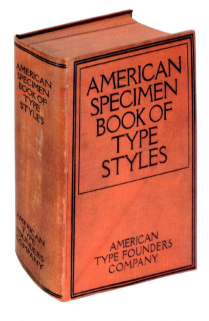

Above: The American Type Founders' substantial catalogue, *American Specimen Book of Type Styles*, 1912.

'common line') to ensure that all of the ATF typefaces could be used alongside each other.[4]

A vexing issue was duplication. Every type foundry tended to make its own version of a proven popular typeface and yet, for legal reasons, each would have subtle differences – between characters, or overall weight or width, as well as the placement of the baseline. It was Benton's job to research the origins of the typeface in question and look for the original version or the one they had that functioned best. While exasperating, all of this also provided a comprehensive introduction to type, typography and typographers and, having established order to the vast ATF library of types (the 1912 ATF catalogue of typefaces contained over 1,096 pages), Morris Benton was appointed as ATF's chief type designer in 1900.

The term 'designer' is significant. Until this point, a type foundry employed a staff punchcutter, not a staff designer – exemplary examples being Hermann Ihlenburg at MacKellar, Smiths & Jordan (Philadelphia), P. H. Rädisch at Joh. Enschedé en Zonen (Haarlem), and Charles E. Heyer at Barnhart Brothers & Spindler (Chicago). Morris was able to design without the intervention of a punchcutter because the pantographic engraving machine, invented by his father in 1884, was able to cut punches mechanically from a brass pattern created directly from his drawings. The designer now had more independence and the process, potentially, was far quicker.

Robert W. Nelson was elected as president of ATF in 1901 and it was only then that the company finally began to function as a single institution, achieved by his insistence that all branches do business under the ATF name instead of retaining their former identity. He also 'foresaw that the future of the type industry depended on a never-ceasing succession of new typefaces of a new order of type design, now known as publicity type – type which is adapted as well for text pages as for display pages'.[5] Morris Benton's role as 'designer' was therefore considered crucial, and during the next thirty-seven years he was responsible for the creation of more typefaces than any other American type designer by far.

However, one of the earliest new typefaces to be released by ATF was *Century*, designed by his father, Linn, in collaboration with Theodore Low De Vinne (also, no doubt, with Morris closely following proceedings). It was also the first project for which Linn cut punches using his own punchcutting machine in the new

CENTURY EXPANDED

HIS CENTURY EXPANDED FACE was planned to make a more readable type than the thin and gray-faced old-style letter in which most books had been printed for many years. The thin lines of this Century face were made of a perceptible thickness, the serifs were shortened,

CENTURY BROAD-FACE

HE CENTURY BROAD-FACE was made by the De Vinne Press for service on books to be set in a broad measure, which do not require a compression of letters for the saving of space. It retains the thickened hair-line, the short serif, and all the characters of the face de-

Above: Theodore Low De Vinne and Linn Boyd Benton's *Century Expanded* is the same typeface as *Century Roman* produced two years earlier but with additional characters (hence 'expanded'). *Century Broad-Face* is a wider (hence 'broader') version of *Century Expanded*. ATF regularly caused confusion by the naming of their typefaces. From *The Types of the De Vinne Press*, 1907.

ATF offices in New York.[6] De Vinne, typographic scholar and the renowned printer of *The Century Magazine*, was dissatisfied with the *Caslon*-derivative types his press was currently using to print the magazine. He described the situation:

> In the bewildering variety of faces devised during this century, one peculiarity, the sharp hair-line (a fashion introduced by Bodoni and Didot in imitation of the delicate lines of the copperplate printer) has never been changed. When printing was done on wet paper, against an elastic blanket, the hair-line was necessarily thickened by its impress against the yielding paper ... But when the new method began ... of printing on dry and smooth paper against an elastic surface, the hair-lines were not thickened at all ... From the reader's point of view, the general effect of the print was relatively mean and wiry, grey and feeble'.[7]

De Vinne decided that the solution was to maintain the width of the thicker lines, but to thicken the hairlines and enlarge the x-height. He described the typeface on which he modelled the new typeface as 'some Scotch roman of the middle 1800s'[8] – a reference to a transitional face, *Scotch Roman*, so called because of its association with the foundry Miller & Richard Company in Edinburgh, reputedly cut by Richard Austin prior to 1822. Linn made enlarged drawings of each character and adjusted them to De Vinne's specifications. The result, called *Century Roman*, appeared in the November 1895 issue of *The Century Magazine*. Its enhanced vertical stress suited the narrow double columns in which it was set, but it was also criticized for being 'over refined, with every trace of character squeezed out of it'.[9] Shortly after *Century Roman* had made its debut De Vinne collaborated once more with Linn, this time with Morris alongside, to design a wider (or 'broader') version called *Century Broad Face*, with the intention that it should suit longer line-lengths required of standard bookwork. In the process, Linn refined his punchcutting machine[10] and became head of ATF's general manufacturing department in 1903, whilst Morris became head of type design.

The projects Morris focused on first were the two *Century* typefaces, but especially *Century Broad Face* that he had seen his father working on. With advice from his father, Morris designed

Top: Morris Fuller Benton, *Century Bold Condensed*, 1909.

Above: Morris Fuller Benton, *Century Oldstyle*, from 1909.

Right: Morris Fuller Benton, *Clearface*, designed for early readers, 1907.

a revised version which was called *Century No 2* and included it in the 1901 ATF *Desk Book*. Two years later the same typeface was shown as *Century Expanded* and accompanied with italics in a comprehensive range of sizes in ATF's *Specimen Book of American Line Type Faces*.

In 1905 Morris's bold version of *Century Expanded* – called *Century Bold* – and a *Century Bold Italic* were also released. The word 'expanded' was now omitted, although both were clearly intended as a companion to *Century Expanded*. Similarly, *Century Bold Condensed* was released in 1909 and became one of the most popular headline typefaces for American newspapers and magazines. The commercial success of the *Century* family was probably the impetus for the development of *Century Oldstyle*. Yet, despite having the same Scottish roots as *Century Expanded*, *Century Oldstyle* is not strictly part of the same family (the upper serifs of ascending lowercase letters – 'd', 'b', 'k', etc. – were slanted and the caps 'Caslonized'),[11] and it was almost certainly given the *Century* name for marketing reasons. It did not have the same level of success.

In the 1912 ATF catalogue, the range of *Century* types alone now filled sixty-four pages and, as a result, came to be regarded as the world's first coordinated type 'family'– meaning a group of varying types ('siblings') closely related to a 'parent', but in bolder, lighter, extended or condensed versions. This was not an entirely original concept; both Pierre-Simon Fournier in his *Manuel Typographique* (1764–6), and Giambattista Bodoni in his *Manuale Tipografico* (1818), offered many variations of the same typeface. Nevertheless, at the turn of the twentieth century printers generally had very little variety of weight of typeface from which to choose. According to Beatrice Warde, once Henry Lewis Bullen's assistant at ATF's famous library, it was Bullen himself who invented the concept of the type family).[12] However, it is generally agreed that it was Morris's handling of *Century* and then *Cheltenham*, another hugely successful ATF typeface with at least ten variations by 1913, by which the concept of the type family took a firm hold.

By 1915 Morris's children were aged thirteen and seventeen, and since their early childhoods he had become acutely aware of issues concerning legibility and the specific needs of younger readers. Morris became mindful of the legibility studies undertaken by Louis Émile Javal, published in 1879, when his father and De Vinne had discussed Javal's findings[13] and taken

Century Schoolbook

Above: Morris Fuller Benton, *Century Schoolbook,* from 1920.

Morris Fuller Benton

them into account while designing *Century Roman*. Morris had also read the recent results of investigations into legibility undertaken by the British Association for the Advancement of Science, titled 'Report on the School-books Upon Eyesight', which argued that there was justification for the design of a type with the specific needs of young readers in mind.

Early readers generally break words down into constituent parts or even individual letters. Javal, who had demonstrated the importance of whole-word recognition in efficient adult reading, was clearly taken into account in the report, as it explained that 'the best type for isolated letters is not necessarily the best for word-wholes'. More recently, Morris had been involved in both the preliminary stages and the final evaluations of a legibility study published in 1912 by Barbara E. Roethlein of Clark University, Massachusetts.[14] Also, between 1905 and 1907, he had collaborated with his father on the creation of a typeface designed for maximum legibility that was called *Clearface*. This was around the same time he was also working on *Century Oldstyle*, and with which *Clearface* has much in common. As a result, when the schoolbook publisher Ginn & Company approached Morris to design a typeface specifically for its younger readers, in 1915, he was well prepared.

The resultant *Century Schoolbook* was first advertised in 1920 in ATF's *Supplement No. 2*, but its adoption for use in children's books, an understandably conservative market, was negligible; complaints at the time that it was too dark seem unjustified and immaterial. Slowly, *Century Schoolbook* began to appear in general use, but it was not until the 1940s that it became popular and it was only then that it also became a common sight in children's books. Copies were made by rival foundries, including Linotype, but the most successful version was Robert H. Middleton's *Century Modern* for Ludlow in 1964. By 1965 *Century Schoolbook* was 'the most widely used member of the [Century] family ... available on all composing machines as well as foundry type'.[15]

Earlier, when Morris was eagerly reorganizing the thousands of founts that now belonged to ATF, he came across *Taylor Gothic*.[16] 'Gothic' was the commonly used contemporary American word for 'sans serif'. *Taylor Gothic* had been designed by Phinney for Charles H. Taylor of the *Boston Globe* newspaper in around 1897. Morris is credited as designing a refined version of this, called *Globe Gothic*, to which he then added three different widths followed by a bold version.[17] At some stage in *Globe Gothic's* development, Morris began work on what would become the ultimate American gothic

Top: *Akzedenz Grotesk Medium*, published by H. Berthold, 1898.

Above: Joseph W. Phinney and Morris Fuller Benton, *Globe Gothic Bold*, c.1900. This typeface was originally called *Taylor Gothic*, which in turn was a refinement of *Quentell*, produced by Central Type Foundry in 1895.

ABCDEFGHIJKLMNOPQR STUVWXYZabcdefghijklm nopqrstuvwxyz 12345678 ⅛ ¼ ⅜ ½ ⅝ ¾ ⅞

typeface, and what McGrew called 'the patriarch of modern American gothics',[18] *Franklin Gothic*.

Designed in 1902 but not released until 1905, *Franklin Gothic* was named in honour of the prolific American printer, Benjamin Franklin. *Franklin Gothic* is a heavy face but with a sensitive modulation in the width of line, most notable at the junctions of rounds with uprights. Subtle allegiances to roman letters are also perceivable, but overall the dominant sense is one of power and energy. Its immediate success encouraged the development of alternative weights and widths, but instead of retaining the *Franklin Gothic* name these variants were called *Alternate Gothic*, 1903 (condensed and lighter in weight), *Lightline Gothic*, 1908 (lighter but less condensed than *Alternate Gothic*), and *News Gothic*, 1908. A medium weight version of *Lightline Gothic* followed.

The influx of new, more geometric, sans serif typefaces in America from Europe during the 1920s caused *Franklin Gothic* to be overshadowed, despite ATF's aggressive promotion. European types were sold simply as single-type families (for example, *Futura Light*, *Futura Medium* and *Futura Bold*), rather than the confusing Benton habit of changing the names.

It was not until interest in the mechanistic European sans serifs fell away after the Second World War that awareness of Benton's *Franklin Gothic* family returned. It was now lauded as the embodiment of the American spirit – resilient and powerful, perfect for a triumphant post-war America. Naturally, the name helped, with '*Franklin Gothic*' being uniquely American in every respect. It was these characteristics that persuaded Ivan Chermayeff to choose to go back to Benton's original *Franklin Gothic* for the logo of the Museum of Modern Art in New York in 1964.

The Museum of Modern Art

Above: Morris Fuller Benton, *Franklin Gothic*, released 1904–5.

Left: Ivan Chermayeff & Tom Geismar adopted the original Morris Fuller Benton's *Franklin Gothic no. 2* for the logo of the Museum of Modern Art, New York, in 1964. (*Franklin Gothic no. 2* has slightly shorter descenders than *Franklin Gothic*.)

GROBE

KABEL

KURSIV

Rudolf Koch GERMANY 1876–1934

Rudolf Koch was born in Nuremberg. His father was a sculptor who also worked as a security guard at the Bavarian Arts and Crafts Museum. He died when Koch was aged ten, and the pension received by the family was meagre. At the age of sixteen Koch was taken in by a family friend as an apprentice metalworker in a factory in Hanau. Koch attended evening drawing classes after his eleven-hour working day, several days a week, but found this all but impossible to sustain. It did, however, make him realize that he had no intention of spending the rest of his life as a metalworker.

Koch returned to Nuremberg before his apprenticeship had been completed to begin attending the School of Arts and Crafts, with the intention of becoming a drawing teacher. Unfortunately, an administrative mistake thwarted this ambition, forcing Koch to take alternative jobs, one of which was with a lithography company in Leipzig as a draughtsman. In 1898, now aged twenty-two, he got a job as a designer at Wezel und Naumann, a book binding company in Leipzig; during that year he lived for a few months in London where he worked for the publisher Raphael Tuck & Sons. In 1902 he decided to strike out as a freelance designer. During this and his previous period as a book cover designer, Koch had been working in the fashionable Jugendstil (Art Nouveau) style. Looking back, Koch took no pride in the work he had done: 'May God forgive me for the things I produced in those days', he wrote in 1922.

Nevertheless, it had been a period during which he learned a great deal about the practicalities of design and printing, as well as its history and culture. Magazines such as *Jugend*, *Die Insel* and *Pan* provided Koch with an insight into the work of artists, writers and designers from outside Germany. The calligraphic roots of William Morris's type designs, Edward Johnston's and Eric Gill's work for the publisher Insel Verlag, and Johnston's book *Writing & Illuminating & Lettering* all made a deep impression on Koch, and provided stimulus for the 'gothic or roman' argument being discussed at great length in Germany. German publishers and other businesses had felt for some time that the use of blackletter was an impediment in selling German products abroad. They argued that a simpler, roman style was required, and Morris's types, especially *Troy*, designed in 1892, seemed to

Opposite: Rudolf Koch, *Grobe Kabel Kursiv*, on the cover of an eight-page type specimen designed and immaculately printed by the print studio at the Klingspor foundry, 1930.

offer a way forward. In designing *Troy* Morris had said 'I designed a black-letter type which I think I may claim to be as readable as a Roman one, and to say the truth I prefer it to the Roman'.[1]

Troy had been the model for *Satanick*, a typeface drawn and manufactured by the American Type Founders Company and released in 1900. Perhaps to the surprise of many at ATF, *Satanick* sold particularly well in Germany – so well, in fact, that some German foundries quickly released their own versions, such as *Morris–Gotisch*, *Archiv* and *Unical*, and added light, heavy and open versions.

In 1905 Klingspor,[2] a recently established type foundry in Offenbach near Frankfurt, with its own excellent printing facilities (and whose printing has not been bettered), published an essay by Gustav Kuhl in which he argued that while blackletter was the appropriate letter-form with which to express German culture, roman was easier to read. The answer, he suggested, was an amalgam of the two. Klingspor had recently released two typefaces which it was claimed addressed this issue: Otto Eckmann's *Eckmannschrift* and Peter Behren's *Behren Antiqua* – although it was 'Art Nouveau' rather than roman or blackletter that both typefaces reflected, especially the former. These typefaces brought a helpful notoriety to the young and ambitious Klingspor foundry, but both quickly and deservedly lost favour.

The debate concerning blackletter in German culture had been present for centuries, but it also became a political issue during the first three decades of the twentieth century. In the sixteenth century blackletter was in use all over northern Europe, although roman type spread from Italy and found centres of innovative design in France, Belgium and the Netherlands. By the eighteenth century, blackletter type had become restricted to Germany, although it maintained a stubborn presence in Scandinavian countries. It was during the nineteenth century, with the influence of the industrial revolution and the spirit of Enlightenment, that some German publishers began to use roman type. Jakob Grimm (collector of German folk tales with his brother Wilhelm) was a leading exponent of the view that the use of blackletter was damaging the international reputation of German books. He argued that blackletter types in current use were 'malformed and ugly', giving German books a 'barbaric' appearance in comparison with those of other countries. He also made the point that learning both blackletter and roman letterforms doubled the reading effort of children.[3] During the

Top: Rudolf Koch, *Frühling*, 1914.

Middle: Rudolf Koch, *Maximilian*. The almost incomprehensible capitals were completed c.1914, the lowercase was completed about three years later.

Above: Rudolf Koch, *Deutsche Schrift Bold*, (also commonly called *Koch Schrift*), 1910.

first two decades of the twentieth century, increased pressure was applied. German calligrapher Rudolf von Larisch claimed in several publications that German printing oppressed its readers, overloading them with the 'horrific complexity' and 'sameness of letters … No reform can help in this situation of need; something new must replace the old'.[4] The broader argument by those supporting the acceptance of roman types was that their use signalled an outward-looking, progressive Germany. Karl Klingspor argued strenuously for maintaining blackletter, albeit in a refreshed and more vital form. It was a view he would retain through the political storms in which the issue became enmeshed during the 1930s and 1940s.

In the autumn of 1905 Klingspor placed an advertisement in *Kunst und Dekoration* for a position at their foundry. Koch applied with no expectation of being successful, but his commercial experience, appreciation of William Morris's types and their influence, together with evidence of his exceptional calligraphic skills, earned him the position. This appointment also led to an offer of a part-time post teaching lettering at the Offenbach Technical Institute. His facility with the pen was also put to use at Klingspor where he began designing types. Karl Klingspor became a life-long friend of Koch, who remained with the company until his death and designed only one typeface for another foundry: the *Deutsche Anzeigenschrift* family for Stempel between 1923 and 1934 (Stempel had a controlling interest in Klingspor, from 1918). Later, Koch wrote the following in answer to a rival foundry who tried to lure him away: 'If I have produced a useful type design, it is large measure due to the proprietor of the Klingspor foundry, whose advisory role in each task I have undertaken for the company has amounted to a collaboration. My relationship with Klingspor goes far beyond a question of business, and I will never seek another'.[5]

Below left: Rudolf Koch, *Koch Antiqua*, 1922.

Below: Rudolf Koch, *Wallau*, showing the romanized capitals, 1930.

Koch's first typeface for Klingspor was the *Halbfette* (bold) *Deutsche-Schrift*, a blackletter issued in 1910. A condensed version followed in 1913 and a medium in 1918. It was an immediate success, and established Koch's position at Klingspor and his reputation nationally; *Deutsche-Schrift* was also popularly known as *Koch-Schrift*. In 1914 the delicate *Frühling* was released, a light, traditional blackletter. Later the same year Koch began work on *Maximilian*, the first blackletter for which he drew matching roman capitals. Though magnificent in their graphic presence, Koch realized that the complexity of blackletter capitals made them all but illegible, especially when removed from their far simpler companion lowercase. With Karl Klingspor's encouragement, Koch had been experimenting by combining blackletter lowercase with 'romanized' capitals which, even for German readers, provided a more comfortable and efficient reading experience. He also designed a decorative in-line set of *Maximilian* capitals which was released in 1914.

Work on a *Maximilian* lowercase was in progress but abruptly halted when, in 1915, Koch was called up for war service, despite being aged forty and having four children. It was a heinous experience, first at the French and then the Russian fronts, and included seven months in an army hospital in Offenbach during 1916 before being sent back to the front. Ill health finally brought his war service to an end in 1917. He recuperated by immersing himself in the work left unfinished before the war, which

Above: Rudolf Koch, *Jessen Schrift*, c.1925–6.

Right: Rudolf Koch, *Neuland*, 1923.

resulted in *Maximilian* being released later the same year. Koch's most productive period at Klingspor was about to begin.

Koch's first roman typeface was *Koch Antiqua*. Supremely elegant, it was better known in Europe as *Locarno* and as *Eve* in America. It was issued in 1922; a less successful italic appeared the following year, and a bold roman, incorporating a number of changes, in 1924. It began as a lettering exercise Koch had drawn at the Offenbach school in 1921. Karl Klingspor saw it and encouraged him to develop it into a typeface. The Klingspor Press introduced the type in a special printing of Alfred Lichtwark's *Der Sammler* (The Collector) and from which a sample page was tipped into issue 5 of the typographical journal *The Fleuron*. Koch used *Koch Antiqua* when commissioned by George Macy to design *Grimm's Fairy Tales* for his Limited Editions Club (New York). It was printed by the Klingspor Press in 1931, and included hand-coloured woodcut illustrations by Fritz Kredel.

Koch Antiqua is a highly individual design with many unusual characteristics – tapering of the vertical strokes, unconventional widths, and an unorthodox lowercase 'g' and number '2'. It was certainly not a natural choice for bookwork, but Koch demonstrated that a lack of respect for convention could, on occasion, provide a wholly appropriate solution; something he would repeat to great effect on many occasions. *Koch Antiqua* became very popular in the 1920s, especially in America where it was often used to express elegance and exclusivity. ATF engaged Willard Sniffin to design a very close imitation which they called *Rivoli*.

Between 1924 and 1926 Koch worked on the magnificent *Wilhelm Klingspor Schrift* (p. 96), considered to be the summit of his blackletter types. Koch then designed a far simpler blackletter with romanized capitals called *Peter Jessen Schrift* (Jessen was a major figure in nineteenth-century German book arts). It was designed for a splendid edition of *The Four Gospels*, printed at the Klingspor Press in 1926. This was followed by an even simpler blackletter, *Wallau* (Heinrich Wallau was a late nineteenth-century printer and typographer in Mainz), for which Koch designed two sets of capitals, blackletter and romanized. However, by the mid-1920s the market for blackletter types, even less complicated versions by Koch, had become virtually limited to Germany alone. But even here blackletter was falling out of favour, a situation exacerbated by the Bauhaus, which argued for elemental letterforms capable of expunging national boundaries.

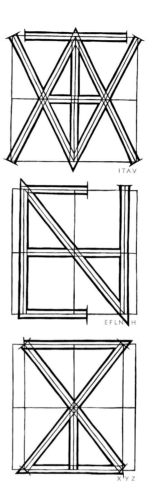

Above: Diagram purporting to show the elemental structure of *Kabel*, from a type specimen booklet printed and published by the Klingspor foundry, 1927.

Sans serif – the antithesis of blackletter – was the proposed solution. Designer and Bauhaus teacher Herbert Bayer's *Universal* typeface, though never put into production, was used to good effect on Walter Gropius's new Bauhaus building in Dessau, as well as on Bauhaus posters and correspondence. Meanwhile Paul Renner was working on *Futura* for the Bauer type foundry and made no secret of its development, giving public lectures and explaining the ideology behind it in print.

Bauer, just a few miles away in Frankfurt, was the Klingspor type foundry's local rival and Karl Klingspor knew he needed a response to *Futura*. Koch had generously been given a free hand in the design of *Neuland*, a sans serif of sorts but a highly idiosyncratic typeface cut directly into metal by Koch himself. Its popularity surprised everyone at the foundry except, perhaps, Koch. Now Karl Klinspor asked Koch to design a *Futura*-esque typeface: a typeface that would appear to contradict everything Koch stood for and on which his international reputation had been forged. Yet Koch recounted later: 'The task of creating a type with a pair of compasses and a straight edge had always attracted me'.[6] This statement seems hardly credible until it is realized that Koch was an admirer of Edward Johnston, and he must surely have compared his own position to Johnston's when, some ten years earlier, Johnston had willingly accepted the challenge of designing the elemental *Underground Alphabet* letters. Koch, though proud of his popular nickname 'der Schreiber', must have rationalized the task as being something from which he could learn and, once committed, would complete to the best of his ability.

The result was *Kabel*, a clever name that implies communication, connectivity and the energy-carrying wires of a modern city. The success of *Kabel* led to an in-line companion, *Zeppelin* (1929), and

ABCDEFGHIJKLMNO
PQRSTUVWXYZÀÅÉÎ
abcdefghijklmnopq
rstuvwxyzàåéîõøü&

Right: Rudolf Koch, *Kabel Light*, 1927.

the variegated and vibrant *Prisma* (1928–31) which took *Kabel*'s modernist attributes still further. While *Kabel* is predominately geometric, it also has divergences that (as with Johnston's *Underground Alphabet*) reveal Koch's unwavering humanist sensibility and his fascination for pen and ink. The light version was the first to appear, in 1927.

Klingspor published a superb 32-page booklet displaying all the sizes of *Kabel Light* from 6 to 84 point, which included diagrams purporting to show the construction of the typeface. The impression is of a typeface conceived within a strictly regulated modular structure. However, the viewer will quickly deduce that the squares in which each capital letter appears are not a controlling element. Instead, each character has been visually, not geometrically, constructed.[7] In other words, there is nothing formulaic about *Kabel*'s elegant capitals. The lowercase, as is so often the case with sans serif types, is less successful. A number of characters, especially 'm', appear unnecessarily narrow alongside the round counters of the 'o', 'b', 'd', 'p' and 'q'. When the medium weight was released it maintained these erroneous characteristics; however, adjustments were made in the bold version. *Kabel*'s original 'e' is distinctive – in fact too distinctive for what purports to be a 'geometric' face – and an alternative straight bar version was included (along with an alternative 'a', 'g' and 'W') in a later version named *Neu-Kabel*. *Kabel* has, indeed, been favourably compared with Johnston's *Underground Alphabet*, with which it shares some similarities, most obvious being its diamond tittles.

Above: Rudolf Koch, *Prisma*, derived from *Kabel* (spelt *Cable* for British and American markets). *Kabel* is used for the 'addresses', in this specimen. Designed and printed at Klingspor, 1927.

BAUERSCHE GIESSEREI

FUTURA

FRANKFURT AM MAIN

1.

Paul Renner GERMANY 1878–1956

Paul Renner was born in Wernigerode, a town in the Harz district of central Germany. The family, including five brothers, lived in a vicarage, his father being an evangelical theologian who went on to become court chaplain to the Earl of Stolbert in Wernigerode. Renner's mother died when he was young, and later Renner was critical of his father for 'taking [childish] foolishness far too seriously … attempts to scrub their little souls clean too severely; so the bloom of uninhibitedness and security is wholly destroyed'.[1]

From the age of eleven Renner attended a Gymnasium. These state schools had a distinctly conservative outlook – 'citadels of humanistic learning and philosophical idealism' – and included Ancient Greek, Latin, ethics and social sciences.[2] A mistrust of industrialization and modern technology permeated Renner's schooling. He described his outlook at the turn of the century as being 'in an artificial world that stood alongside the real one [feeling] disgusted by all politics; machines, factories, economy, progress'.[3] On leaving school Renner's response was to enrol at the Berlin Academy of Fine Arts. He completed his art education at the Art Academy in Munich in 1899.

During the next few years Renner made his living as an artist. He married in 1904 and in 1906, the year his daughter was born, he spent a year at the Debschitz Scule in Munich, a newly established school of applied art in which students were taught in workshops to design for manufacture. One of the specialized areas of study was Grafik, described at the time as 'drawing, illustration, graphic art for printing, book decoration and typography'.

In October 1907 Renner attended the inaugural meeting of the Deutscher Werkbund, a state-sponsored organization founded by politicians, artists and industrialists to encourage the integration of traditional crafts and industrial mass-production techniques in order to put Germany on a competitive footing with Britain and the United States. Renner had been deeply impressed by the work and ideas of William Morris and the Arts and Crafts movement, and so he followed the activities of the Werbund closely and in 1910 became a member.

It was also in 1907 that Renner met the publisher Georg Müller through a mutual friend. As a test, Müller gave Renner a strip of

Opposite: Paul Renner, *Futura*, on the cover of an elaborate type specimen folder published by the Bauer type foundry, 1927.

card corresponding to the spine of a book and asked him to create a design for it. Renner's solution delighted Müller so much that, from that point onwards, Renner was given copious amounts of work – initially designing covers, usually leather bound, but over time progressing to the design of every aspect of Georg Müller Verlag's books.[4]

Taking control of typographic layout in this way was not considered to be the responsibility of the book designer, but Renner believed that every book should be designed as a harmonious whole. In this he took his lead from the private presses in England, especially Emery Walker's and T. J. Cobden–Sanderson's Doves Press. The restraint that Renner admired in English private press printing corresponded with his own preference for formal austerity. Novelty was to be rejected. He complained that book designers too often wasted their time in search of originality that amounted to feckless differentiation and self-aggrandisement, a futile enterprise that Renner felt was:

> ... conducted at the edges of the still permissible, of the still possible, instead of a search for the perfectly beautiful, which is never tiresome: because only that which we consider as absolutely perfect and valid for all time – the wholly original expression of our time and personality – is that which we will always change with us and our times, without us having to bother about it.[5]

The books published by Müller before the First World War were mostly designed using blackletter types, although Renner generally chose roman types for texts written by non-German authors. (He had a particular liking for the classic typefaces held at the Enschedé type foundry in the Netherlands.) All Müller books were, essentially, luxury items created using hand-set type, high-quality papers and traditional binding materials. However, a new industrial era was emerging in Germany, and Renner, aware of the dwindling book-buying middle class, had to seek out ways of being able to maintain standards while, at the same time, reducing costs. He compared the merits and costs involved in machine- and hand-binding as well as the quality of various papers in a bid to find a satisfactory way of utilizing mass-production technologies. This was in line with the kind of functionality that had been extolled by the German Werkbund, and the result, perhaps inevitably, was a new and more austere aesthetic. 'Functionality' became equated with a pared-down, often modular-inspired simplicity. Decoration, meanwhile, was considered deceitful, its purpose being merely to conceal or distract.

Renner resisted this polarization of views, stressing instead the need for new mechanized advances to be utilized with an imaginative sensibility. To achieve this, Renner and others argued that the traditional method of training printers 'on the job' within the industry environment must be replaced by a system enabling them to be educated in schools, where tasks could be devised that explored the creative potential of new technology. Renner put these ideas into practice in 1911 when, together with illustrator and designer Emil Preetorius, he established a privately funded school with students paying a monthly fee of 45 marks. It was housed in a new building owned by a printing company with whom Renner regularly worked on Georg Müller Verlag projects. The close proximity of a genuine commercial printing enterprise was intended to provide the students with the practical knowledge and experience required while he, Preetorius and others taught drawing, typography and design history. The success of this endeavour led to the offer of a new teaching position, this time with the Münchner Schule für Illustration und Buchgewerbe (Munich School for Illustration and Book Trade) which had merged with the school Renner had attended as a student, the Debschitz Schule. It was renamed Münchner Lehrwerkastäten (Munich Teaching Workshops) and Renner became a co-director.[6]

The timing of this undertaking was unfortunate. Just a few months later, in June 1914, the First World War broke out, and between January 1915 and the autumn of 1917 Renner found himself occupied as an Oberleutnant in charge of a recruiting office and later training field-artillery men in the 'laws of gunnery', which meant he only had Saturdays left to teach. When his five-year teaching contract expired, shortly after the end of the war, Renner left.

Georg Müller died in 1917. Renner felt little affinity with the company's new owners, so his links with them dissipated. In the years immediately following the war Germany experienced a period of huge inflation, creating political unrest and social instability. Renner and his family (now with three children) moved away from Munich while he continued to work for several publishing houses, including the German Publishing Association (DVA).

Renner would certainly have watched developments at the Bauhaus in Weimar since its inception in 1919. Its director

Walter Gropius had made a number of public statements and there had been considerable interest in the press, not all of it complimentary. But by 1923, and after various changes of staff, the Bauhaus had established its abiding identity – the unification of art and technology, consolidated by an exhibition of student work that generated international prestige for the school. Perhaps watching the social and commercial consequences of Gropius's school renewed Renner's interest in the potential of education to affect genuine change. In 1925 he was offered a teaching role at the Frankfurter Kunstschule (Frankfurt School of Art). This forward-thinking institution was led by Fritz Wichert under whose stewardship the school was collaborating with the architect Ernst May (appointed as Frankfurt's city planner in the same year) on a programme of civic design.

Although Renner taught typography at the Frankfurter Kunstschule for barely a year, his involvement there was significant. He contributed a sans serif typeface for public signage that was appropriate to the functionalist style of architecture being designed by May. When Wichert saw it, he christened it *Futura* (Future). The genesis of this typeface had been a visit by Jakob Hegner, publisher and director of the Hellerauer Printing Company, to Renner's studio in the summer of 1924.

Renner's reputation as a typographer had been elevated by his book *Typografie als Kunst* (Typography as Art), published in 1922. Set in blackletter type, this 176-page book provided a detailed

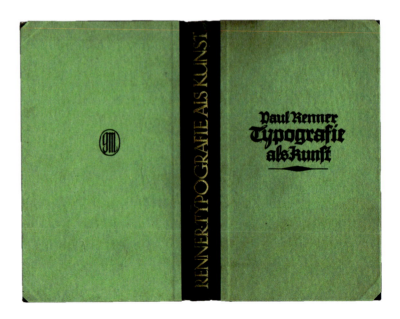

Right: Paul Renner, *Typografie als Kunst* (Typography as Art), published by Georg Müller Verlag, 1922.

examination of typography, including its historical development, before offering a set of rules on its make-up and use. After seeing examples of Renner's work, Hegner proposed that he should 'design a typeface of our time'. This was a suggestion Hegner had made to other designers with no response, but Renner took Hegner's suggestion seriously. In the following days Renner sketched several typefaces, each displayed as a sentence: 'die Schrift unserer Zeit' (The Typeface of our Time). One was chosen and sent to Hegner who was encouraging, and particularly impressed by the distinctive 'ft' ligature. Renner then drew the whole alphabet on blue graphpaper and sent it to Hegner. Thus, by the autumn of 1924, the first incarnation of Renner's typeface – containing a number of rather idiosyncratic characters – was completed.

Hegner, however, did not respond to the drawings, and after several months had passed Renner asked for their return. They were then sent to Heinrich Jost, artistic advisor of the Bauer type foundry and a former pupil. Jost showed Renner's drawings to Georg Hartmann, director of the Bauer type foundry, who was enthusiastic and eager to proceed. A collaborative scheme was immediately drawn up and the cutting of a trial size begun before the end of 1924. By the time Renner began teaching at the Frankfurter Kunstschule (he became a full-time member of staff in July 1925) and was involved with the architect Ernst May's city plans, *Futura* had already been in development for some twelve months.

The brief time that Renner was at the Frankfurter Kunstschule (he left early in 1926) was a stimulating period. He became close friends with Ferdinand Kramer, an architect and designer of unit furniture who had studied briefly at the Bauhaus and was now working in May's offices. As a result of their close liaison a set of 'geometric capitals', drawn on graph-paper in 1925 for the city planning office, has been credited both to Kramer or Renner at various times. Kramer used a set of geometric capitals on the fascia of his family's hat shop in Frankfurt that are very similar to *Futura* capitals. However, when a photograph of the shop front was shown in the journal *Das Neue Frankfurt* in 1927, the fascia lettering was credited to Renner.

Futura's lengthy four-year gestation period was due to Renner's perfectionism and Georg Hartmann agreeing that its development should proceed without harassment – despite the fact that he must have known that other type foundries were developing versions of *Futura* of their own. They could do this because of the attention caused by the use of the early version of *Futura* by the city of Frankfurt, and because Renner himself delivered a number of well-publicized lectures on *Futura's* development. He even used Bauer's trial cuts in the design of the invitations. As a result, rival geometric sans serif typefaces were released before or at roughly the same time as *Futura*: Jakob Erbar's *Erbar Grotesk* (Ludwig & Mayer) in 1926, Rudolf Koch's *Kabel* (Klingspor) in 1927, Wilhelm Pischner's *Neuzeit Grotesk* and Hans Möhring's *Elegant Grotesk* (both Stempel) in 1928. *Futura* was released in late 1927.

Between 1925 and the eventual release of *Futura*, Renner worked closely with Heinrich Jost at the Bauer type foundry, refining each character in detail – included the decision to abandon some of the more radical, 'wilfully bizarre' early alternative lowercase charaters.[7] Renner based the proportions of *Futura's* capitals on the circle, triangle and square, with the 'E', 'F', 'L', 'T' and 'P' being half-square in width. However, *Futura* is not truly geometric in its detail, neither is it truly monoline (as is, for example, Theo van Doesburg's experiental all uppercase alphabet in 1919 and Herbert Bayer's all lowercase *Universal Alphabet*, 1925, though neither was never put into production). Renner later recalled, 'In contrast to the fashionable Constructivists, I did not want to glorify the compass as a tool',[8] and so a great deal of sensitive modulation was introduced to ensure that *Futura* maintained its geometric orthodoxy while retaining equilibrium of weight and balance. This meant that circles were subtly adjusted to be become ovals and stroke widths intricately modified. *Futura*, therefore, is constructed of finely adjusted lines designed to make it appear monoline while enhancing legibility. These almost infinite adjustments help to give *Futura* an even, 'pearly grey' texture (Renner's description) when set on the page, as Renner later explained: 'No letter should be darker than the others, and there should be no spots [black or white] anywhere within the body of a letter'.[9]

Such painstaking refinements are contrary to the mechanical simplicity suggested by the geometric ornaments released by Bauer, without Renner's involvement, to accompany *Futura* and which helped establish an indelible if erroneous link between *Futura* and the Bauhaus. This was exacerbated by the artist and Bauhaus teacher Wassily Kandinski's theory linking primary colours to elemental form (circle–blue, square–red and triangle–

Top: Theo van Doesburg's *Geometric Alphabet* using rectangles only and based on a 5 × 5 grid, 1919. Doesburg was a founding member of the De Stijl Group.

Above: Herbert Bayer, *Universal Alphabet*, commissioned by Walter Gropius for The Bauhaus, 1925.

yellow), which was widely reported and incorporated by others into Bauhaus publicity. Consequently, when Renner explained that *Futura* was based on elemental forms such as the circle, square and triangle (he was talking about the geometric proportions intrinsic to classical roman capitals), this once again falsely linked *Futura* to Bauhaus theory.

Renner's close study of the classic roman capitals and the transference of their elemental proportions to his sans serif typeface suggests unanimity with Edward Johnston's alphabet for the London Underground in 1916. Renner never visited Britain, although his close colleague Heinrich Jost did, taking part in a group excursion to London in 1925 specifically to assess the state of British design for print.[10] The translation of Johnston's *Writing & Illuminating & Lettering* by his pupil Anna Simons in 1910 made him an influential figure in German typographic circles, augmented by his work for the respected German publisher Insel Verlag. Nevertheless, Renner claimed to have been unaware of Johnston's sans serif prior to *Futura*'s release.

The strict geometric structure Renner had applied to *Futura*'s capitals was continued in the design of its lowercase letters. He explained: 'I consciously suppressed and eradicated all those subtle qualities that creep into the design of their own accord when the form is developed from writing'.[11] Calligraphy had played an important role in Renner's design of books, so eradicating all trace of handwriting in *Futura*'s lowercase letters was not a

Left: Paul Renner, *Futura*, 1927.

decision Renner could have taken without anguish. Its effect was that the lowercase took on the same static, detached form that predominates in the capitals. Renner, aware of the consequences, wrote: 'There is no flow from one to the other. The movement, the vigour these letters receive is through their simple appearance, the crystalline clarity of the forms.'[12] Not surprisingly, a slanted font rather than italic was designed to accompany the roman. Renner would later admit that his attempt to deny the written dynamic in, for example, the 'n', 'm' and 'r' had not been entirely successful, and modifications followed. Other subtle aspects of handwriting that Renner allowed to creep in included the additional option of non-lining numerals, and the making of the lowercase ascenders slightly taller than the capitals to reduce the omnipresence of capitals on the printed page (particularly acute in German texts).

When first released, *Futura* was available in three weights: light, medium and bold. *Futura Black*, a rather incongruent stencil-form display typeface, appeared in 1929. In 1930 slanted (or 'oblique') versions to accompany the three original weights were released, along with a new semi-bold and a semi-bold slanted. In the following years Bauer closely monitored *Futura's* performance, and their response to trade demands meant that many variations were produced, including an elegant inline version in 1931. It is reasonable to assume that Renner did not supply master drawings for each size of type to be cut by Bauer, and his involvement in the design and development of some of the later variations was probably minimal.

The upsurge in the quality of sans serif typefaces in the 1920s raised the form from its previous utilitarian status – limited to railway timetables and headlines – to something approaching equality with serifed romans. What is more, typographers now saw them as having personalities of their own, despite the term

INDUSTRIE
PROBLEM

Right: Paul Renner, *Futura Black*, 1929, and *Futura Inline*, 1931.

'mechanical' having been applied to all and sundry.

Renner worked on other typefaces, most notably *Renner-Grotesk*. It was designed in 1936 with the Stempel type foundry, but was then taken over and developed by Bauer with whom its forms became less modular and eventually began to hint at the suggestion of a pen, emphasized by its true italic accompaniment. When it was eventually released in 1952–3 (its development was stalled for the duration of the Second World War), Bauer called it *Steile Futura*, shamelessly renamed to connect it with the extraordinary success of Renner's *Futura* family.

Below left: Paul Renner, *Futura*, a single leaf from the specimen folder published by Bauersche Gießerei, Frankfurt, 1927.

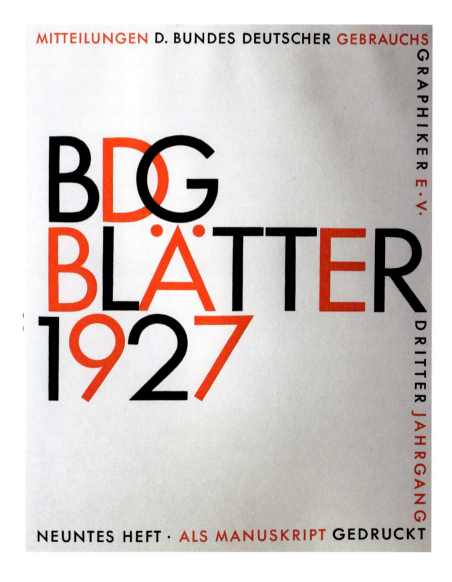

VIGNETTEN nach Zeichnung erster Reklamekünstler: J. Klinger-Wien, K. Sigrist-Stuttgart, C.H. Meyer-Leipzig u.a.

UTENSILIEN Winkelhaken · Setzschiffe · Schrift- und Formenregale · Format- und Unterlagstege · Schließzeuge usw.

MASCHINEN aller Art für Buchdruckerei und Buchbinderei

Schriftguss A.-G.
vorm. Brüder Butter, Dresden

Nr. 1915 8/10 Cicero

National

Nr. 1916 10/12 Cicero

Dessau

Nr. 1917 12/15 Cicero

Busch

Nr. 1918 16/20 Cicero

Luft

See

Nr. 1919 20/25 Cicero
Nr. 1920 24/30 Cicero
Nr. 1921 32/40 Cicero
Nr. 1922 40/50 Cicero

Die fette Cooper
liefern wir bis 40/50 Cicero Größe als

Plakat-
Holzschrift!

Oswald Cooper USA 1879–1940

Oswald Cooper was born in Mount Gilead, Ohio. The family later moved to Coffeyville, Kansas, where, at the age of sixteen, Cooper became an apprentice in a printing shop. During this time he took several correspondence courses established by the Frank Holme School of Illustration in Chicago. On completion of his apprenticeship, at the age of twenty-one, Cooper moved to Chicago to attend classes in person. His goal was to become 'a famous illustrator', but he quickly discovered that beyond the entry level course his talents were insufficient. Nevertheless, meeting the other students and seeing what else was going on he realized that there were other options, and he eventually began attending the lettering classes run by Frederic Goudy.

Goudy befriended Cooper and helped him to earn his tuition fees by assigning him jobs setting type for correspondence course booklets. Cooper was later appointed as a lettering teacher, and when Frank Holme became ill, Cooper and his wife took over the administration of the school. The pay was negligible but he enjoyed his work and the friends he made – in particular Will Dwiggins, cartoonist Harry Hirschfield and Goudy himself. Cooper also met Fred Bertsch, a flamboyant and energetic entrepreneur who ran an art service agency close to the Frank Holme School. Bertsch was a consummate salesman while Cooper was rather reticent, even retiring in character. In 1904, when his business partner left, Bertsch persuaded Cooper to become his new partner. They were opposites in every sense but became close friends, and their company, Bertsch & Cooper, would become hugely successful.

Having set themselves up in the Athenaeum Building in Chicago, in August 1905 a brief note appeared in *The Inland Printer* under the heading 'The Artist and the Typographer', describing Bertsch as the artist and admirer of William Morris and Walter Crane, while Cooper was the typographer, 'who holds before his mental vision as worthy of all imitation the merits of Bradley, Goudy and Goodhue. The combined efforts of these two enthusiasts produce many beautiful things'. Bertsch was the likely author of this puffery.

The intention was to establish a full-service design and type shop, including typesetting, layout, copywriting and design. Opening a type shop was expensive, so Bertsch & Cooper

Opposite: Oswald Cooper, *Cooper Black*, one of several elaborate fold-out pages from a 48-page type specimen, published by the Schriftguss A.G. vorm. Brüder Butter foundry, Dresden, 1926. (Under license from Barnhart Brothers & Spindler.)

ABCDEFGHIJKLMNOPR
STUVWXYZ abcdefghijklm
nopqrstuvwxyz 1234567890?

established their initial reputation through hand-lettering for small local jobs and later for larger national campaigns. Cooper concentrated on lettering and design, while Bertsch's primary responsibility (despite previously describing himself as the artist) was to find customers and bring in the work. By 1914, ten years after the partnership began, the firm had become the full-service shop they intended and was attracting major national clients such as the Packard Motor Car Company and Anheuser-Busch Breweries.

The 'full service' meant that as well as designing, illustrating, hand-rendering lettering and writing copy, Bertsch & Cooper also acquired founts of type and a proofing press, and hired compositors and a type department manager. In addition, a fixed studio camera was bought and a darkroom built. With these facilities, artwork in the form of illustration, hand-lettering and hand-set texts could be photographed and reduced or enlarged to the required size, then brought together and pasted into position as 'finished artwork'. In this way, a full pre-press service was on offer and the company could maintain complete creative control. On final approval by Cooper and the client, the artwork with full instructions would be passed to a commercial printer. When Bertsch retired in 1924, Bertch & Cooper employed more than fifty people and was the largest design and production agency in the Midwest.

Cooper had no aspiration to be a type designer – and, indeed, his first typeface was manufactured without his knowledge. He regularly created customized lettering to be used in advertisements for Bertsch & Cooper's clients, and the lettering he drew for the Packard Motor Car Company caught Morris Fuller Benton's attention at ATF. The advertisement was it attributed to any artist or agency, and so Benton innocently ordered the face to be redrawn, cut and founded. It was released in 1913 and named *Packard*. To his credit, when he learned that Cooper was the designer of the original lettering, Benton paid him a fee and attributed the design to him. *Packard Bold* followed in 1916, again

Below: James Pryde (Brothers Beggarstaff) cover for *The Poster*, a monthly magazine, February 1899.

Above right: Oswald Cooper, *Packard*, drawn in-house at ATF, 1913.

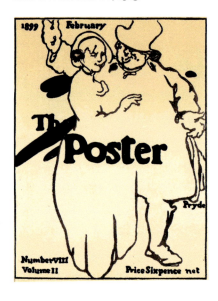

128   Type Designers of the Twentieth Century

drawn in-house at ATF. To retain the original hand-drawn quality of Cooper's lettering, Benton gave the characters irregular edges and provided several alternative characters and ligatures.

As Cooper's eminence grew, the Bertsch & Cooper partnership prospered. Bertsch was aware that the company was not only dependent upon Cooper's abilities, but also on people knowing of Cooper's ability, and so he was never slow to promote Cooper's talent. He once described Cooper as the 'Michelangelo of lettering'; what the diffident Cooper thought of this is easy to imagine. When Cooper was approached by Barnhart Brothers & Spindler Foundry (BB&S), then America's second largest type foundry after ATF, and asked to design a typeface, he initially turned down the commission. His field of expertise was hand-lettering and he knew enough about type to know they were very different activites. But Bertsch persuaded him that a typeface bearing his name would be of huge benefit to the company, and so Cooper relented.

BB&S knew what Cooper was capable of and made it clear from the outset that they wanted an original display typeface, not a revival. Their sales manager, Richard N. McArthur, stated that the company would 'not revive the letter styles of the old masters, but ... encourage our own modern artists, and try to add some contribution in our time'.[1] It is likely they had something in mind – perhaps Cooper's hand-lettering on Bertsch & Cooper's company labels, for example – as a point of departure. This lettering is remarkably similar to the Cooper family that would develop.

Left: Oswald Cooper, two-colour printed label with hand-drawn lettering c.1914, several years prior to the production of *Cooper* for the Barnhart Brothers & Spindler Foundry.

Above: Oswald Cooper, *Cooper Black*, released by Barnhart Brothers & Spindler, 1922.

Strangely, considering the earlier statement about avoiding revivals, BB&S initially called Cooper's typeface *Cooper Old Style*. Cooper disapproved, for the simple reason that there was nothing at all 'Old Style' about it – in fact, its major attribute was that it did not really resemble any style apart, perhaps, from a faint hint of the lettering devised by the Brothers Beggarstaff (the poster work of this British artistic partnership, comprising James Pryde and William Nicholson, was popular in North America from around 1895). The name was shortened to *Cooper* on its release in 1918. Its distinctive features, such as the rounded serifs, laid-backward 'f' and the back-facing 'o', gave *Cooper* a memorable appearance whose characteristics were enhanced by *Cooper Black* which appeared in 1922. This was intended to be a bold version, but the result was so bold that McArthur famously named it *Cooper Black* and marketed it with all the zeal he could muster, describing it as 'the selling type supreme [making] big advertisements out of little ones'. Cooper, who was also an excellent copywriter, was heard describing *Cooper Black* as being 'for far-sighted printers with near-sighted customers'. Because of its novelty, the face caused consternation in more conservative circles which, no doubt, was precisely what McArthur had hoped for: 'The trend was on – the advertising world accepted the *Black* in a thorough-going way and the orders rolled up in a volume never before known for any typeface'.[2] When other members of the *Cooper* type family followed in quick succession, it became known as the 'black blitz'.

The remainder of the *Cooper* family were: *Cooper Italic* (1924), *Cooper Hilite* (1925), *Cooper Black Italic* and *Cooper Black Condensed* (both 1926). A little later, just as *Cooper Fullface* was about to be released, BB&S's production was taken over by ATF,[3] who decided to call the typeface *Cooper Modern*.[4] The term 'modern' was used to highlight the typeface's elemental similarity to *Bodoni*. Cooper, annoyed at such a vacuous association, wrote (stating the blatantly obvious) that *Cooper Modern* 'differs from *Bodoni* in that its serifs are rounded and its main stems drawn freely, with the suggestion of curve in almost every line'. The name was changed back to *Cooper Fullface*.

Goudy Stout, designed for the Continental Type Founders Association[5] by Frederic Goudy in 1939, is remarkably similar. Goudy later said it was the sort of typeface he didn't care for (perhaps a comment influenced by poor sales), and only cut one size (24 point). In contrast, *Cooper Fullface*, even without an italic, was exceptionally popular and considered by many to be Cooper's most innovative typeface.[6]

Type designers were often required to write a few lines for specimen sheets and leaflets, produced for marketing purposes to describe the potential uses of the typeface they had designed. Cooper wrote this about *Cooper Fullface* (and even managed to mention *Bodoni*): 'This style, lately revived by the practitioners of the "modernistic" typography, had created a demand for display letters that comport well with it – letters that reflect the sparkling contrasts of *Bodoni*, and that carry weight to meet the needs of advertisers. *Cooper Fullface* is such a letter.' It was completed and released in 1929.

The phenomenal success of the *Cooper* family during the late 1920s enabled BB&S to lure Cooper away from Bertsch & Cooper in 1927 to spend five days a week for one year developing new types (Bertsch had retired, but the company was mature enough by this time to withstand Cooper's temporary absence). Sadly, it was a disaster. He considered the work he was assigned to be mere frippery, while the expected pace allowed no time for introspection. He was given an advertising headline cut from a newspaper and asked to use it to design an alphabet, which he did, disclaiming all credit. The typeface was named *Boul Mich*, after Michigan Boulevard, a street in Chicago where many of the city's advertising agencies were located. *Pompeian Cursive* was not released. *Dietz Text* was based on original drawings made by August Dietz but not suitable for making patterns. Cooper spent two months re-drawing them in readiness for matrix cutting.

BB&S was struggling for survival at this time and no doubt pinned its hopes on another '*Cooper*' to help get them out of their financial mess. When ATF took over the company in 1933 the premises were closed, and their substantial casting operation moved to Jersey City. Cooper, meanwhile, was grateful to get back to his drawing board at Bertsch & Cooper.

Above: Oswald Cooper, *Cooper Fullface* (also known as *Cooper Modern*) released by Barnhart Brothers & Spindler, 1929.

Oswald Cooper

BOOK PAGES IN ELECTRA

THE AUTHOR'S PROLOGUE

144

mon Gargantua and his fol
of the land if it were necess
agreed with the council and
tions, dispatching Basque,
the following letter.

XXXIX *The Tenor of the
Wrote to Gargantua.*

The enthusiasm with wh
studies would prevent me fr
your philosophic repose ha
allies I always trusted disap
age. But since destiny wills t
those I most relied on, I mu
back to defend the people a
trusted to you by right of na
are unavailing abroad if the
home, so study and consult
they be applied fittingly and in good season.

I intend to appease rather than provoke, to defend rather than assault; I do not seek to conquer new lands but rather to preserve my faithful subjects and hereditary dominions which Picrochole has invaded without rhyme or reason, and which he oppresses day by day with a fury intolerable to freeborn spirits.

Hail, o most valiant and illustrious drinkers! Your health, my precious pox-ridden comrades! To you alone, I dedicate my writings. Suffer me, therefore to draw your attention to a dialogue of Plato's called *The Banquet*.

In this work, Alcibiades, praising his master Socrates (undoubtedly the prince of philosophers) happens, among other things, to liken him to sileni.

Sileni, in the days of yore, were small boxes such as you may see nowadays at your apothecary's. They were named for Silenus, foster-father to Bacchus. The outside of these boxes bore gay, fantastically painted figures of harpies, satyrs, bridled geese, hares with gigantic horns, saddled ducks, winged goats in flight, harts in harness and many other droll fancies. They were pleasurably devised

Above and left: These two pages from Rabelais' *Gargantua and Pantagruel*, now newly translated into English by Jacques Le Clercq and with decorations by W. A. Dwiggins, published by The Limited Editions Club for its seventh series. The text is in 12 point Electra.

Printed in U.S.A. 312.25.1-A-Q-5X

William A. Dwiggins USA 1880–1956

William Addison Dwiggins was born in Martinsville, Ohio, as the son of a doctor. Little is recorded of Dwiggins's early life but, judging by his lively wit and good humour, it can be assumed his childhood was a happy one. At the age of nineteen he went to Chicago to study at the Frank Holme School of Illustration. Here Dwiggins met Frederic Goudy, fifteen years his senior, who was teaching lettering and decoration and who would be a major influence. But there were other teachers who made an impact, such as John McCutcheon, Pulitzer prize-winning cartoonist; the Leyendecker brothers, cover artists for the *Saturday Evening Post, Vogue, Vanity Fair* and other national magazines; W. W. Denslow, illustrator of the recently published *The Wonderful Wizard of Oz*; and Frank Holme himself, an eminent newspaper sketch artist. The most conspicuous characteristic of Dwiggins himself was the range and distinguished quality of his skills; he was, above all, the consummate designer.

In 1903 Dwiggins moved to Cambridge Ohio with his wife Mabel and set up his own press, the Guernsey Shop, but struggled to generate sufficient work. When Goudy and his wife Bertha moved to Hingham, a suburb of Boston, to establish the Village Press, they invited Will and Mabel to join them. Here Dwiggins worked on book design and illustration, enjoying the work and the company and especially New England – so much so, that when Goudy moved his press once more, this time to New York in early 1905, Dwiggins decided to stay in Boston.

For the next two years Dwiggins struggled. Commissions were infrequent, and he was forced to think about alternative ideas of how to establish a career. These included collaborating with his art school friend John W. Reed to establish a publishing venture they called Reed and Dwiggins. Before this there had been The Ridge Shop, a private press which the two friends had briefly operated with Oswald Cooper, another school friend, in Park Ridge, Illinois. Nothing came of these ventures (both Reed and Cooper were already establishing successful careers independently) and Dwiggins, having begun to take advertising work, returned to Cambridge, Ohio.[1]

During the time Dwiggins was working at Goudy's Village Press he had met Daniel B. Updike, owner of the Merrymount Press, which was renowned for its fine printing. In the spring

Opposite: William A. Dwiggins, back cover of a 12-page type specimen displaying *Electra*, published by Linotype, c.1935.

of 1906 Dwiggins decided to approach Updike for work. By chance, his timing was perfect. Updike had been employing Thomas Maitland Cleland for most of the design work he required, but there had recently been disagreements over the nature of the work or fees. After a hesitant start, Dwiggins began to receive a regular flow of commissioned work from Updike. Within twelve months Updike was inundating Dwiggins; he received over fifty commissions – including lettering, illustrations, ornaments, borders, end papers and title pages – in 1907 alone.

Updike was an exceptional printer and a scholarly typographer,[2] who had set out in 1893 to 'to do common work uncommonly well',[3] although later much of his work was for a blossoming private collectors' market and limited-editions clubs. For this work he depended on the services of designers such as Cleland, Dwiggins and, later, Rudolph Ruzicka, to bring individual character to each of his books as well as solving a broad range of more mundane tasks that he or his compositors were unable or unwilling to do. Without doubt, Updike's love of classical design (the antithesis of William Morris, Goudy and, initially, Dwiggins himself) began to influence Dwiggins's views, who found a way of merging Updike's preference for a rather dry formality with his own more playful use of colour and abstract forms to create a design that was more his own. Theirs was a productive and mutually beneficial partnership.

The two became good friends,[4] although Updike remained the mentor; he even orchestrated a trip to Europe for Will and Mabel in 1908 (with special attention given to Rome). On their return, family issues caused a delay to their arrival in Boston. Due to their extended absence demand for his attention was now intense, not only from Updike but also numerous advertising commitments. Dwiggins had always suffered from stomach problems and this pressure of work brought on renewed ailments, establishing a pattern of overwork followed by physical breakdown. Dwiggins would learn how to live with such pressures but never lost the feeling of being 'handicapped by the clock and calendar – twenty-four hours a day was not long enough'.[5]

During the next fourteen years, although always busy, Dwiggins became increasingly dissatisfied. The work he did for the Merrymount Press was, naturally, eclipsed by Updike himself, while working for the advertising industry was becoming tedious, and its brief useful life-span frustrating. Then, in 1922, he was

Above: William A. Dwiggins, one of hundreds of small commissions received from Daniel B. Updike. This required Dwiggins to add a date to a Thomas Bewick woodcut.

diagnosed with adult-onset diabetes (commonly a fatal disease at that time). It is likely that it was this event that prompted Dwiggins to turn his back on advertising in order to 'make every day count'. Insulin, invented soon after his diagnosis, no doubt saved his life.

In 1923 Dwiggins was introduced to Alfred A. Knopf, the eminent New York publisher, by Frederic G. Melcher,[6] editor of *Publishers' Weekly*. Knopf took great pride in his books and employed the very best in production, with the expectation that every Knopf book would be treasured as much for its design as it was for its prose. He paid special attention to paper stock, typography, layout, bindings, endpapers and jackets.

Dwiggins had previously written a scathing 'exposé' concerning the shoddy standards employed by many publishers, and it seems likely that this had been seen by Knopf.[7] They had much in common and, in fact, became life-long friends with Dwiggins eventually designing over 300 books for Knopf's publishing company. Over the next few years Dwiggins also began working for a number of other high profile, fine press publishers, and before the end of the 1920s his reputation was soaring. Regular clients included George Macy's Limited Editions Club (for whom Dwiggins effectively became art director), the Chicago Lakeside Press, and Random House. Prime examples of Dwiggins's celebrated books designed for these publishers are, respectively, *Tartarin of Tarascon* (1930), *Tales of Edgar Allan Poe* (1930), and *The Time Machine* (1931). Although designed almost simultaneously, each of these three books offers a visualization that is unique to its subject. It was at the height of this success that Dwiggins was approached by Harry L. Gage of the Mergenthaler Linotype Company.

The drawing of letterforms had been a constant occupation for Dwiggins since his student days. In his seminal book, *Layout in Advertising*, published in 1928 – his valediction to a profession he had only recently left – he criticized the design of contemporary sans serifs, especially the capitals, writing: 'Gothic types are indispensable, but there are no good Gothic capitals. The type founders would do a service if they will provide a Gothic of good design'. The book, and this statement in particular, caught the eye of Gage who wrote to Dwiggins in early 1929 to ask, 'What do you mean by "good design?" And having defined it would you like to illustrate it?

And if so would you like to see it cut?' Attached to his letter was an advertisement for the Norddeutscher Lloyd shipping line, set in *Futura*.

In his reply to Gage, Dwiggins conceded that more recent sans serif typefaces (released since the publication of *Layout in Advertising*) were, indeed, 'fine in the capitals [but] bum in the lowercase', and admitted that he was not sure if it were even possible to design a good lowercase sans serif, but that he would like to try. At the age of forty-nine, Dwiggins became a type designer.

Dwiggins's answer to his own criticism was *Metroblack*. Its production was remarkably swift. Dwiggins drew the letterforms and it was released by Linotype later the same year (1929). *Metrolite* then *Metromedium* followed, both designed in-house at Linotype, under Dwiggins's supervision. His early humanistic predilection held sway, making the capitals closer to Eric Gill's *Gill Sans* than Paul Renner's *Futura*, and the lowercase suggestive of a traditional rather than the truly geometric appearance achieved by Renner. In addition, Linotype made serious misjudgements with their additional weights. *Metrolite* was designed to the same width as *Metroblack*, which gave it a 'sprawling' appearance and then, with *Metromedium* – possibly in an attempt to remedy the issue created with *Metrolite* – they over-reduced the width.[8] Dwiggins rarely used it.

Bauer opened a sales office in New York in 1927 and *Futura* became available in North America the following year. In 1929, the year *Metro* was launched, *Futura* was used in a landmark redesign of *Vanity Fair* and sales of Renner's typeface took off. As a result, sales of *Metro* – despite being the best of the American geometric sans serifs designed after *Futura* – suffered badly. Nevertheless, Linotype were sufficiently impressed by Dwiggins to offer him a contract. This was effectively a retaining fee plus payment for the designs he supplied, and a guarantee to make punches and matrices of any trial design he provided. (A similar arrangement had been offered to Will Bradley by ATF in 1904.) Dwiggins's association with Linotype would last twenty-seven years, resulting in twelve typeface designs, of which five were released to the trade.

Both Dwiggins and Linotype were initially preoccupied with ongoing projects, and it was not until several years later that Dwiggins's second typeface began to take form; it was 1935 when it was finally released. Called *Electra*, it was designed for

Above: William A. Dwiggins, *Metroblack* and *Metrolite* were released c.1929. *Metroblack No. 2* and *Metrolite No. 2* were released three years later following revisions by Linotype.

abcdefghijklm nopqrstuvwxyz

extended reading. In describing the salient features of *Electra* in the specimen book, *Emblems and Electra*, Dwiggins equates its forms to those created by a pen when writing quickly. It provided an easy reading experience or, as Dwiggins described it, *Electra* 'moves along the line nicely', helped by its characteristic flatter top curves. It has distinctive modern features and yet retains fluidity. Sebastian Carter described it as 'a kind of calligraphic modern face'.[9]

In all his dealings with Linotype, Dwiggins worked with C.H. Griffiths, who had started at Linotype in 1906 as a salesman and worked his way up to assistant manager, before taking responsibility for typographic development around the time he met Dwiggins. They got on extremely well, corresponded constantly, and were aware of Stanley Morison's theory – extolled in issue 5 of *The Fleuron* – that the appropriate support for roman type was a sloped roman rather than an italic. (This was later rescinded by Morison). Following suit, *Electra* was accompanied by a sloped roman with no concessions offered to traditional cursive forms. On its release the response was hostile and Dwiggins was asked to quickly design an 'alternative'– cursive – italic, which was named *Electra Cursive* and released in 1940. *Electra* became a popular book face in America, but in Britain only four sizes of the roman with its original sloped italic were available; when the Second World War broke out production was stopped and so it was barely seen at all.

Dwiggins's third and best-known typeface is *Caledonia*, a book typeface released in 1938, whose appearance grew out of his liking for the sturdier version of the Didone style faces that were developed by Scottish foundries in the early nineteenth century. He also nurtured an affection for a type cut by William Martin in around 1790–92, called *Bulmer*; commissioned and used by William Bulmer's Shakespeare Press in London.

At the beginning of the twentieth century, the New York type foundry A.D. Farmer had released a transitional face which they

Above left: William A. Dwiggins, *Electra*, 1935.

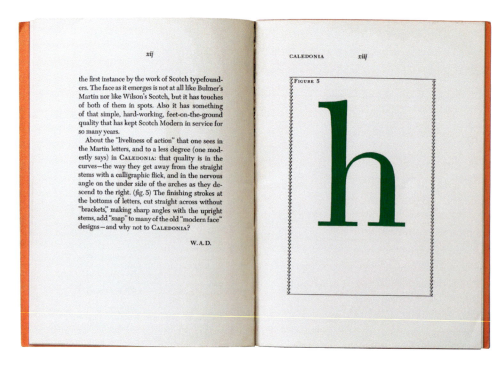

called *Scotch Roman*, based on a typeface cut for Miller & Company in Edinburgh (known as Miller & Richard from 1832). Whether the A.D. Farmer foundry had an arrangement with Miller & Richard or whether they opportunistically made their own electrotype matrices from imported types is not known.[10] In 1903 Linotype released its own version of *Scotch Roman* and in the same year Monotype in Philadelphia released *Scotch Roman Series 36*, which was revised and much improved in 1920.

At the time that Dwiggins's *Caledonia* (the Roman name for Scotland) was being designed, Monotype's *Scotch Roman* was probably the best current reproduction of the Miller & Company type. Nevertheless, Linotype's own version of *Scotch Roman* had remained a regular choice for book work until the 1930s. But following the subsequent appearance of numerous revivals of classic typefaces (for example, Monotype's excellent *Garamond*, *Bembo* and *Ehrhardt*), *Scotch Roman* had declined in popularity. The main criticism from typographers was its excessively heavy capitals in comparison with its lowercase, which gave the face an uneven tone on the page. It was generally considered a dependable but anonymous workhorse; Dwiggins described Linotype's *Scotch Roman* as 'wooden heaviness'. Griffiths decided that it was the right time to refresh this popular typeface and asked Dwiggins to explore ways of addressing its deficiencies.

Above right: William A. Dwiggins, booklet published by Linotype, to promote *Caledonia*, 1938. The serifs are slightly bracketed (curved) in all of the capital letters but not all lowercase – the feet of the 'h' being a good example.

An amalgamation of the best features of *Baskerville*, *Bodoni* and *Didot* with *Scotch Roman* were attempted, but all Dwiggins's efforts led him back to Martin's *Bulmer*. It was when *Bulmer* was applied to the basic structure of *Scotch Roman* that one of the most admired American book types was produced: *Caledonia* was released in 1938; *Caledonia Bold* was added two years later.

Caledonia's capitals are slightly shorter than the lowercase ascenders, providing a perfectly even colour across a page of text. It has a vertical stress with a generous, but not over-large, x-height. The stroke contrast remains pronounced but the thins are sufficient to hold up even at the smallest sizes. In a letter to Griffiths, Dwiggins described *Caledonia* as having

> that simple, hard-working, feet-on-the-ground quality that has kept *Scotch Roman* in service for so many years. About the 'liveliness of action' that one sees in the Martin letters, and to a less degree (one modestly says) in *Caledonia*: that quality is in the curves – the way they get away from the straight stems with a calligraphic flick, and in the nervous angle on the underside of the arches as they descend to the right.

Caledonia was designed to 'supply a color and style that will do what [Linotype] *Garamond* should have done ... a fluid molten face – suave, and running along like melted lead'.[11]

The redirection of resources at Linotype during the Second World War, and then the onset of photocomposition, hindered the release of a number of typefaces that Dwiggins designed during the 1940s. *Eldorado*, *Falcon*, *Charter*, *Arcadia*, *Stuyvesant*, *Tippecanoe* and *Hingham* were all abandoned at the 'experimental' stage. Sadly, only *Eldorado* was released during his lifetime (c.1953).

Dwiggins's entertaining and knowingly homespun writing style was an asset throughout his career and very much his own. He employed his wit to guard against pomposity, but also to promote change. Throughout his life, Dwiggins concocted comic fake documents and prodded the establishment in a myriad of ways, inventing colourful personalities to serve as noms de plumes. Dwiggins wanted everything he did to be amusing and to appear effortless. A good typeface, he once said, was 'simply a line of letters so full of energy that it can't wait to reach the end of the measure'.

Eldorado

Above: William A. Dwiggins, *Eldorado*, 1953.

Below: *Bulmer*, ATF, 1923. Morris Benton adapted *Bulmer* from a face cut by William Martin c.1790–92.

ABCDEFGHIJKLMNOPQRSTUVW abcdefghijklmnopqrstuvwx

REGISTERED

MONOTYPE

TRADE MK.

GILL SANS

Light & Normal Bold &

Twenty-four different series, some ranging from 5 to 72 pt., make this the ideal 'family' for large-scale typeface standardizations.

Condensed Bold ,, Bold Extra ,,

Extra Bold, Ultra Bold

CAMEO TITLINGS

ABC DEFG

TITLINGS, OUTLINE, SHADOW, ETC., ETC.

HKM g QRS

The Monotype Corporation Ltd. Reg. Office: 55-56 Lincolns Inn Fields London, W.C.2. *Head Office & Works:* Salfords, near Redhill, Surrey

Eric Gill GREAT BRITAIN 1882–1940

Eric Gill was the son of a non-conformist minister, one of thirteen children. He was born in Brighton in 1882, but brought up in Chichester where the family moved when his father converted to Anglicanism and became a curate in the Church of England. The move was significant for Gill who felt an immediate affinity with Chichester's old stone walls, historic market and medieval cathedral.[1]

Gill attended the Technical Art School in Chichester and learned the rudiments of drawing. At the age of seventeen his interest in architecture and lettering led to him being apprenticed to W.H. Caroë, a prosperous architectural firm in London specializing in church buildings. Here Gill acquired the drawing skills of a draughtsman, where explanation rather than expression was required. It was also here that Gill first became aware that the status of the architect was dependant on the skill of hundreds of craftsmen, and in particular the stone and wood carvers, whose rich and multifarious contribution was all too often erroneously attributed to the architect.

Seeking an alternative to the 'wage slavery' of the architect's office, Gill decided that, instead of studying architecture in the evenings, he would attend classes in masonry at the Westminster Technical School and then lettering at the Central School of Arts and Crafts; both schools specialized in practical, hands-on instruction in materials and methods. His teacher at the Central School was Edward Johnston. Ten years his senior, Johnston immediately became a hugely influential figure in Gill's life.

Johnston was not only a consummate calligrapher, but also an exceptionally eloquent and persuasive proponent of the Arts and Crafts movement. For Gill, Johnston's unwavering integrity in his approach to work was as influential as his skills as a calligrapher. He taught that the poverty of modern type was chiefly due to the loss of its ties to writing, which was, he argued, its origin and first principle. Gill was captivated by watching letters 'flow firm but free' from Johnston's hand, and described attending Johnston's classes 'as though a secret of heaven were being revealed'.[2]

Nevertheless, Gill was able to resist falling entirely under his mentor's influence. Johnston's personality, philosophy and teaching were apt to turn pupils into disciples, who were then inclined to seek escape from contemporary life and all aspects of

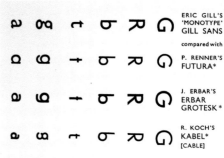

Opposite and above: Eric Gill, *Gill Sans*. Monotype diligently promoted Gill's sans serif. This example is a small – approximately A6 – card printed both sides. It not only shows many of the reincarnations of the *Gill Sans* family, it also confidently provides comparison of *Gill Sans* with its chief rivals. Undated.

mass production. The fact that lettering, and particularly type design, was reproduced or manufactured by machines – 'symbols of all that the true scribe must abhor, or, at least distrust' – meant that both Gill and Johnston would over time, relent, adjust and learn to utilize 'complex mechanisms' for their own means.[3]

From around 1903 Gill proudly called himself a 'workman', with a 'workman's rights, the right to design what he made; and a workman's duties; the duty to design what was to be made and to make what he had designed'.[4] Although he was meticulous about recording hours worked, and in great demand for all his working life, his financial state was always precarious, in large part because he charged so little. Yet when disputes occurred, they inevitably concerned money – despite Gill never being overly attached to worldly wealth or personal reputation. But he was adamant that the dignity of his practice must be reflected in the manner of remuneration, without rancour or question, and absolutely on time.

Although his links to Morris and the Arts and Crafts movement were important, Gill's sympathies were more radical, distinctly more anarchic than Morris's Marxist socialism, and so he stood apart from the Arts and Crafts movement (with the exception of his involvement with the Golden Cockerel Press). However, Gill also stood apart from the machinations of the Design and Industries Association (DIA), which sought to utilize industrial processes to design and make products more efficiently and cheaply. Later, when he found good reason to give succour to industrial production, Gill nevertheless continued to pour scorn on automation in his lectures, essays, books and letters to the press.

Gill and his brother Max shared Johnston's rooms for several years. Then, when Gill married, he eventually moved to Hammersmith in 1904 to be in close proximity to the Doves Press, T. J. Compden-Sanderson and Emery Walker, as well as Johnston who had moved there the previous year. Gill set himself up as a letter-cutter. Architects were quick to appreciate and patronize a craftsman who understood their requirements, saving them time and money by relieving them of the necessity of providing the scale drawings required by 'trade' letter-cutters. Gill soon had more work than he could personally handle, and so he began to employ assistants.[5] This was in large part due to the increasing variety of work undertaken – not only cutting inscriptions, tombstones and commemorative plaques, but also painting lettering on shop fascias, notably W. H. Smith's in the Rue de Rivoli in Paris in 1903. In 1906 he drew examples of lettering for plates in Johnston's *Writing & Illuminating & Lettering* and, in 1909, five of the sixteen plates for Johnston's working supplement to that book, *Manuscript and Inscription Letters*.

Walker introduced him to new opportunities and personalities, notably Count Harry Kessler, consultant to the prestigious German publisher Insel Verlag who, through Walker, commissioned Gill (and Johnston) to design title pages for the *Grossherzog Wilhelm Ernst* series of books. The titles were hand-drawn and then printed via line blocks. Gill found this process, by which his penmanship was photographically scaled down, morally repulsive. He argued that it was intrinsically dishonest, allowing errors and second thoughts to be disguised while the reduction of scale falsely suggested the artist was endowed with miraculous skills in drawing detail. Instead, Gill turned to engraving in wood, and with growing mastery of the material created artwork at the original scale to be transferred directly onto paper without the 'trickery' of photographic intervention.

By 1907, Gill's Hammersmith studio was too small and he decided to strike out and move to Ditchling, a Sussex village to the south of London. Johnston and his family would join him there in 1912. Gill's move[6] also marked the beginning of a number of major sculpture commissions – leading in 1913 to his carving of the *Stations of the Cross* in Westminster Abbey, completed in 1918, and later his work *Prospero and Ariel* (from Shakespeare's *The Tempest*) for the BBC on Broadcasting House, London. These works brought Gill national fame as an artist, comparable with renowned contemporary sculptors such as Jacob Epstein and Henri Gaudier-Brzeska. (It was such work that prevented Gill having more than an advisory role in the design of the *Underground Alphabet* with Johnston.) But Gill was never interested in being part of the art world, his goal lay in the 'little revolution', as he described his work: 'I was reuniting what should never have been separated: the artist as man of imagination and the artist as workman'.[7] 'I never was a serious artist as serious art was understood by that world. I was the son of a nonconformist parson, the grandson of a missionary. Life was more than art.'[8]

Gill's association with Hilary Pepler was an important factor in igniting his interest in the wider aspects of printing and typography. Pepler had moved to Ditchling in 1915, where

THE
FOUR GOSPELS OF THE LORD JESUS CHRIST
ACCORDING TO THE AUTHORIZED
VERSION OF KING JAMES I
WITH DECORATIONS BY ERIC GILL
PRINTED AND PUBLISHED AT THE
GOLDEN COCKEREL PRESS
MCMXXXI

Above: Title page from *The Four Gospels*, featuring *Golden Cockerel* type (14 point, and 24- and 36-point titling) and wood engraving by Eric Gill. Set and printed by Robert Gibbings, 1931.

he founded the St Dominic's Press with the intention of printing books 'about crafts which machinery threatened with extinction'.[9] It was an association which ended acrimoniously (over money) but proved an invaluable preparation for Gill's later partnership with Robert Gibbings and the Golden Cockerel Press, as well as with Stanley Morison, typographic consultant to the Monotype Corporation.

The Golden Cockerel Press was founded by Harold (Hal) Taylor, his wife and two of her female friends in 1920, having been directly inspired by Elizabeth Yeats's Cuala Press.[10] Gibbings and his wife Moira took over the press in 1924 (Taylor had been ill and died of tuberculosis in 1925). Gibbings was taught how to wood-engrave by Noel Rooke, one of Johnston's earliest students, and was one of ten founder members of the Society of Wood Engravers in 1920. During the period 1924 to 1933, when he directed the Golden Cockerel Press, Gibbings was responsible for printing and publishing seventy-two limited edition books, many of outstanding quality. Of these, his most ambitious projects were all conceived and designed in close collaboration with Gill; *The Four Gospels* in 1931, richly illustrated by Gill, is the outstanding achievement of the Golden Cockerel Press.

Prior to *The Four Gospels*, Golden Cockerel books were set by hand using *Caslon Old Style* type, cast in London by H. W. Caslon & Company. Gibbings inherited the type from Taylor for whom it had seemed an inevitable choice; it was the type used by renowned commercial houses such as the Chiswick Press (for whom the typeface had been revived in the 1840s), and it was for R. & R. Clark of Edinburgh that Monotype cut their version in 1916. Critically, it had also been the type of choice for private presses without proprietary typefaces such as the Cuala Press and Pepler's St Dominic Press.

Gibbings made the foundry-cast *Caslon Old Style* appear darker by taking great care not only with the close and even spacing of the type but also with its inking. He explained in 1927 how best to integrate type with wood engravings:

> Type when properly printed requires a nicely adjusted quantity of ink per square inch: a fraction too much, and it fills up; a fraction too little, and it prints grey. It must be obvious that a block set amongst type must, for success, approximate to the texture of the type, otherwise one or the other must suffer in printing. But even if the area of the actual printing surface conforms to that of the type, there is need that the unit of texture should in some degree

approach the unit of the texture of type ... One might almost suggest that it would be a good rule only to use gravers of a size which might conceivably have been used for engraving the type, but that is perhaps a little severe.[11]

As their collaboration and friendship deepened, both Gill and Gibbings recognized that to achieve perfect harmony between text and illustration it would be necessary for the press to have a proprietary typeface robust enough to match Gill's wood engravings. Gill, clearly relishing the idea, immediately began work on the *Golden Cockerel* type in 1925. Around the same time, Morison had also persuaded Gill to supply drawings for a new typeface for the Monotype Corporation and although he knew that the *Golden Cockerel* type was to be made by the Caslon foundry, he was happy to provide Gill with technical advice (knowing, of course, that such help would also aid the progress of Gill's work for Monotype).

At one point, Gill wrote to Morison regarding the *Golden Cockerel* type, explaining, 'I am at a loss how to proceed. I have made drawings to a large scale but how am I to tell what they'll look like small?' The letters were required at 18 point.[12] Morison arranged to have Gill's drawings photographically reduced, from which Gill made the necessary adjustments and then had these re-photographed – a process that continued until the desired results were achieved. Photographic enlargements of 18-point *Caslon Old Style* were also made for Gill to study. By now Gill was clearly reconciled to the use of the same photomechanical processes he had vehemently rejected some fifteen years earlier.

When it was decided to have additional capitals made – titling founts at 24 and at 36 point – they simply enlarged the drawings made for the 18 point. The result was unsatisfactory. Gill had to adjust the drawings by reducing the weight of the horizontals in proportion to that of the verticals in order to retrieve the lost elegance of the design. A lowercase italic was also designed, but was not ready in time for *The Four Gospels*. Gill did not make capitals or numerals for the italic, preferring to follow the example of early printers of italic types by combining the 'sloped miniscules' with roman capitals.[13]

The Golden Cockerel typeface was designed by Eric Gill for printing limited editions on hand-made paper Cast in 14 and 18 point: 24 and 36 point Capitals only

Left: Sample setting using Eric Gill's 18-point *Golden Cockerel* lowercase type (shown approximately actual size), 1931. The edition includes sixty-five wood engravings completed by Gill in just ten months.

Eric Gill

The Golden Cockerel type was completed under the supervision of the Caslon foundry's chief punchcutter, J. Collinge, in December 1929. It was first used for *The Four Gospels*, which was printed in an edition of 500 (including twelve on vellum) and finished in 1931. It was a huge success, both financially and critically, and comparable to the Doves Bible as one of the greatest achievements of twentieth-century books.

Gill's *Golden Cockerel* type appears larger than its 18 point would suggest. However, its rather majestic character – a quality enhanced by generous fitting (a judgement made by Collinge) – somewhat undermines Gill's stated intention that it should be 'a heavy closely massed type'.[14] However, if printed with the necessary gusto to ensure the larger areas of the sixty-five wood engravings (four being full-page) presented as a solid black, the *Golden Cockerel* type was able to retain its elegance while exuding a powerful presence.

The convoluted progress of Gill's *Perpetua* (those 'drawings for new types' mentioned by Morison, earlier), which ran almost in parallel with the development of the *Golden Cockerel* type, was a reflection of Morison's own evolving typographic theories – and political machinations within Monotype – rather than Gill's inexperience. For these reasons, *Perpetua* is discussed in the chapter on Morison.

In May 1925 Gill also began experimenting with the design of 'simple block letters' for the Army & Navy Stores, 'for them to use for all their notices and signs'.[15] Nothing came of this project, but in October the following year, when asked by Douglas Cleverdon,[16] then a young bookseller in Bristol, to paint the name of his bookshop on its fascia, Gill drew some alphabets which included a block letter for him to consider. A few weeks later Morison was staying with Cleverdon who showed him the drawn alphabets; Morison immediately realized the potential of Gill's block letter.

German type foundries had released, or were about to release, a number of geometric sans serifs: *Erbar* by Jakob Erbar from 1922, and *Kabel* by Rudolf Koch and *Futura* by Paul Renner, both 1927.[17] Morison, all too aware that Monotype needed a new sans serif of its own, commissioned Gill who quickly supplied drawings of a complete upper- and lowercase alphabet. Its design owed much to Johnston's *Underground Alphabet* (although there are also many differences), as well as to Frank H. Pierpont and Fritz Steltzer's craftsmanship and manufacturing acumen in Monotype's

Above: Eric Gill, the fascia sign for Douglas Cleverdon's bookshop at 18 Charlotte Street, Bristol, using a 'block letter', the precursor of Gill Sans. It was completed in the autumn of 1926 and seen by Stanley Morison the following summer.

ABCDEFGHIJKLMNOPQ
RSTUVWXYZ abcdefg
hijklmnopqrstuvwxyz

ABCDEFGHIJKLMNOPQ
RSTUVWXYZ abcdefgh
ijklmnopqrstuvwxyz

drawing office. *Gill Sans Titling* was released in 1928, and initially promoted as being ideal for advertising and display use. It was the first of Gill's typefaces to be released by Monotype. *Perpetua*, despite having begun its development three years earlier, would not be finished for another three years.

Gill Sans capitals are beautifully balanced, taut but full of life (for example, the way the tale of the cap 'R' curves away before turning down and away from the stem), and perform exceptionally well in all-caps settings as well as alongside the lowercase – which has several surprises. The two-story 'g', with its geometric structure based on a circle and an oval, is beautiful though strikingly unorthodox for a sans serif, as is the triangular top of the 't'. The proportions of *Gill Sans* are close to *Perpetua*, and both are accompanied by a hybrid italic: a sloped roman but with distinct calligraphic touches, the spur on the 'p' for example.

Initially, Monotype described *Gill Sans* as a display face. Despite this, and possibly to Morison's surprise though less so to Gill, *Gill Sans* also became a popular text face for certain books and magazines. The Netherlands and Britain were among the countries that adopted *Gill Sans* for administration material – notably the LNER railway company, owners of the Flying Scotsman locomotive; the British Post Office; and the Dutch PTT (postal services). When *Gill Sans* proved successful, Monotype produced a broad range of derivatives, including light, bold, condensed and bold varieties; *Shadowline, Inline, Cameo* and *Cameo Ruled* versions; and the most extreme of all, *Gill Sans Ultra Bold*, also known as *Kayo* (and which Gill playfully called 'Double Elephants'). Gill's apparent amenable reaction to the boorish

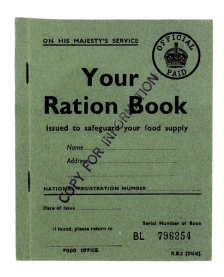

Top: Comparing Edward Johnston's *Underground Alphabet* (top row) 1916, with Eric Gill's *Gill Sans*, 1928.

Above: *Gill Sans* was a common sight on British government documents during the Second World War.

demands of market forces enamoured him to Monotype, who paid him a retainer to act as advisor. Elsewhere he described *Kayo* as 'an ugly typeface for an ugly profession'[18] (the 'ugly profession' presumably being advertising). In the circumstances, it is surprising that Gill designed just one other typeface with Monotype: *Solus*. It was designed and cut in 1929 for the Empire Marketing Board, but never used.

When his youngest daughter, Joanna, married René Hague in 1930 Gill established a printshop for his new son-in-law which was called Hague & Gill. The same year Gill designed a proprietary typeface for it called *Joanna* (owing a clear debt to *Solus*),[19] which was cut and manufactured by the Caslon foundry in two sizes.

Joanna was first used for Gill's *Essay on Typography*, published in 1931 – making Gill the author, type designer, typographer and, without doubt, close collaborator with Hague on its printing. The

Below: Eric Gill, *An Essay on Typography*, written by Gill, designed and printed by Hague & Gill using Gill's *Joanna*, 1931.

sparse design of the book, especially when considered alongside Gill's deep involvement with the Golden Cockerel Press at this time, might be surprising, but Gill was keen to establish that Hague & Gill was 'a public press' whose aim was to achieve 'a good reasonable commonplace and therefore pleasant standard of excellence'.[20] While the text pages are set in *Joanna*, the dust jacket is set in *Gill Sans*. This gives emphasis to the close relationship between these types (Martin Majoor has described *Joanna* as 'a sort of *Gill Sans Avec*').[21] When printing commenced on *Essay on Typography* Gill had only designed the roman *Joanna*; the italic came later.

Gill's approach to the design of the text was more akin to a scribe than a compositor. If at the end of a line a word did not fit he would begin it in one size type and complete it in another – the kind of liberties to be found in handwritten medieval manuscripts. The result, though ranged left, has a disconcerting, *almost* justified appearance. In the *Joanna* typeface itself however, there is 'a master of letterforms engaged upon a pleasurable task for his own delight'.[22]

Despite Gill's proclaimed intent of Hague & Gill being a 'public press', its high standards reached the notice of George Macy in New York – who commissioned them to design and print Laurence Sterne's *A Sentimental Journey* for his Limited Editions Club in 1934 (published 1936), and for which Gill designed a typeface called *Bunyan*. (Unfortunately, he was not commissioned to provide the illustrations.) *Bunyan* was Gill's last roman. After his death in 1940 the design was bought by Linotype from his widow, Mary, and the punches, patterns and matrices from his son-in-law René Hague. Walter Tracy, head of Linotype England's type department from 1948 to 1978, then adapted the face for machine-setting and designed an italic using unfinished sketches left by Gill. Linotype released the typeface in 1953 and called it *Pilgrim*, which they promoted, with justification, as being a rival to *Perpetua*.

In 1937, recession-hit Hague & Gill was acquired by the publisher J.M. Dent & Sons (including the rights to *Joanna*). In the same year, Dent commissioned Monotype to produce a machine-set version of *Joanna* for Dent's exclusive use. Dent later agreed to a general release of *Joanna*, and Monotype added it to its typeface library.

Below: Eric Gill, *Bunyan*, from the title page of Laurence Sterne's book. It was printed by Hague & Gill in 1934 and published by the Limited Editions Club in 1936.

A Sentimental Journey

Eric Gill 149

30 POINT

ABCDEFGHIJ
KLMNOPQR
STUVWXYZ
&1234567890

36 POINT

ABCDEFGH
IJKLMNOP
QRSTUVW
XYZ&
1234567890

Harold Curwen GREAT BRITAIN 1885–1949

The modest family-run printing company John Curwen & Sons Limited was established in 1863 in Plaistow, East London. John Curwen's great-grandson, Harold Curwen, joined the company in 1908 aged twenty-two. Harold's preparation for his role in the family printing firm had been carefully planned. He went to Abbotsholme in Derbyshire, a new, forward-thinking school, with a curriculum designed to reflect the ethos of the Arts and Crafts movement. It even had a printing press and two sizes of the newly popular *Caslon Old Face*.

Imbued with the ideals of John Ruskin and William Morris, Curwen spent several years in various departments of the company before joining in a full-time capacity. Part of this training was a year spent in Leipzig with Oscar Brandstetter, the music printing company (a significant part of John Curwen & Sons had always been the printing and publishing of sheet music). Awareness in England of forward-looking German print design had been growing since the turn of the century, and Oscar Brandstetter itself was well equipped with new typesetting machines and rotary presses. More importantly for Curwen, the city of Leipzig had become a focal-point within the printing fraternity for the harnessing of craft and moral issues, as espoused by Ruskin and Morris, to new and much improved printing technologies.

One of the companies that attracted Curwen's attention was Insel Verlag ('Island Publishing House'). This company had been set up in 1899 by the editors of *Die Insel*, a short-lived literary journal edited and designed with the ideals of the Arts and Crafts movement to the fore. However, the enterprise was in a fragile state when Anton Kippenberg joined in 1905. He stabilized the company by initiating the production of affordable classic texts while maintaining remarkably high production values. The design of these books – simple, elegant, and illustrated by artists such as Eric Gill, Rudolf Koch and Emil Preetorius – caused Curwen to realize that the care and high technical quality of private presses, such as the Doves Press, could be applied to mass production.[1] Suitably inspired, Curwen returned to London and attended Johnston's calligraphy classes (from June 1908) at the Central School of Arts and Crafts, one evening a week for almost a year. Curwen became a director of John Curwen & Sons in 1911,

Opposite: Harold Curwen's *Curwen Sanserif Titling,* from the Curwen Press Miscellany, 1931.

and when his father, Spedding Curwen, retired in 1913 he took over the business.

At a time when the advertising industry was growing in size and influence, Harold Curwen guided the Curwen Press to become one of a small group of London-based printing companies that was intent on maintaining control of the design of their printed material. Francis Meynell with Stanley Morison at Burns & Oates and then the Pelican Press, Bernard Newdigate at the Arden Press, and Gerard Meynell (cousin of Francis Meynell) at the Westminster Press, were the most prominent of those who were offering what at the time was called 'style' and today we call 'design'. Significantly, the printing of books was not their primary preoccupation. For these companies the social purpose of 'ordinary commerce' was recognized, and they relished the creative and varied technical demands inherent in such work. This is not to say that they did not also quietly covet the idea of printing books, but Francis Meynell explained the allure of 'jobbing' work in this way: 'The [Pelican] Press set itself from its beginning to do good printing for the daily, not the exceptional, purpose. [Such work] satisfied my need as a typographic zealot and propagandist to influence typography generally.'[2]

Apart from this modest number of rather exceptional companies, the printing industry did not have the expertise to deal adequately with the new commercial opportunities. More significantly, it was also unwilling to seek out the expertise. Within a printing house the appearance of print – its design – on the page was the responsibility of the foreman compositor. But the ability to fulfil this task was hampered by the nature of their training, which was primarily a rule-governed process based on a long-standing and, indeed, esteemed tradition of bookwork.

Outside the printing industry, however, the design of print (including typography) was becoming a profession in its own right, a process conducted by people educated at art school or university who called themselves 'applied artists' or 'commercial artists', and who were employed in the art departments of advertising agencies or were working independently. Harold Curwen's intention (one shared by cousins Gerard and Francis Meynell and others) was to harness creative endeavour with craftsmanship in the service of commerce. The ramifications of this did not result in anything resembling a coordinated movement, but certainly like-minded developments did occur, led by groups in England,

Europe (especially Germany) and America. The eventual outcomes differed, sometimes radically, but intentions were generally described as being a 'revival of print' and those participating as Print Revivalists.[3] From the outset, Harold Curwen was a leading exponent.

Despite the print revivalists' natural affinity with historic precedents, their work could result in unfamiliar, even innovative outcomes. This was demonstrated by Harold Curwen's – *Curwen Sanserif* – which initially comprised capitals only and was designed around 1911–12.[4] What induced Curwen to design a sans serif is not recorded, but Johnston, a talismanic figure for the revivalists, had anticipated a block letter design in his book, *Writing & Illuminating & Lettering* in 1906: 'It is quite possible to make a beautiful and characteristic alphabet of equal stroke letters, on the lines of the so-called "Block Letter" but properly proportioned.' Three years later in a lecture, significantly on signwriting, Johnston advocated that the roman (Trajan) carved letters were the most readable, having the 'utmost simplicity, distinctiveness and proportion',[5] and could be used as a model for a block letter. Curwen's primary purpose in designing his sans serif was, most likely, to provide his company with a proprietary typeface for the growing opportunities in display work.

Harold Curwen and Gerard Meynell were friendly rivals, so friendly in fact that their companies would share exhibition stands. As two of the most prestigious printing companies in London, both knew Frank Pick, the dynamic young publicity officer (and from 1912 commercial manager) for the Underground

CURWEN SANSERIF TYPE
DESIGNED BY HAROLD CURWEN

THIS IS SET IN CABLE
DESIGNED BY RUDOLPH KOCH. CUT BY KLINGSPOR

THIS IS GILL SANS
CUT BY THE LANSTON MONOTYPE CORPORATION

Left: Harold Curwen, *Curwen Sanserif Titling* compares favourably with Rudolf Koch's *Cable* (or *Kabel*) and Eric Gill's *Gill Sans*. From the *Curwen Press Miscellany*, 1931.

Electric Railways company of London (UERL). Pick was aware that UERL posters needed to be distinctive enough to stand out from the plethora of other advertising material that filled the Underground stations. Harold Curwen advised that he use a sans serif typeface.[6] The circumstances in which this discussion took place are not known, nor is it known if Curwen showed Pick his own sans serif design. Notwithstanding, Pick attempted to draw such a typeface himself,[7] failed, and then approached Gerard Meynell, who suggested that Edward Johnston be offered the task. (Meynell was already printing posters for Pick, and so even if Meynell knew of Curwen's sans serif design he would not want to risk losing a lucrative client and such prestigous work to the Curwen Printing Company.)

   Although *Curwen Sanserif* was modestly introduced on several jobbing projects (it was used for display lines in a catalogue for Crittall, a manufacturer of metal windows, and printed from line blocks made from the original drawn letters), it was not cut and manufactured as metal type until 1928. The reason for this long delay is unknown, but it is easy to imagine the self-effacing Curwen thinking it inappropriate to bring out a typeface with the same purpose ahead of one that he knew was being designed by Edward Johnston for Frank Pick. Some fifteen years later, with Ludwig & Mayer's *Erbar* having been designed in 1922 by Jakob Erbar, and Paul Renner's *Futura* having recently been released,

CURWEN SANSERIF

24 POINT

After the prime necessities of life nothing is more precious to us than books. The art of Typography, their creator, renders a signal service to society and lends it invaluable support, serving, as it does, to educate the citizen, to widen the field for the progress of sciences

Right: Harold Curwen's *Curwen Sanserif*, 24-point lowercase, from the *Curwen Press Miscellany* (actual size), 1931.

plus the launch of the much-anticipated *Gill Sans* imminent, Curwen finally felt comfortable about going ahead with the production of *Curwen Sanserif*.

The capitals of *Curwen Sanserif*, like Johnston's *Underground Alphabet* (completed in 1916, some four years later), follow the classical proportions of the roman inscriptional capital letters at the base of the Trajan column built in AD 113 (a plaster replica is in the British Museum). Curwen's crossed 'W', balanced on pointed feet, being a stand-out character. However, Curwen's reticence in getting his capitals cut and manufactured meant that, when it did eventually appear in 1928, the innovative nature of his achievement was lost. Even after its manufacture *Curwen Sanserif* was retained for sole use by the Curwen Press, and so it remained virtually unknown in comparison with the numerous other sans serifs that were manufactured in the decade following the international success of *Futura*.

More curiously, *Curwen Sanserif* was rarely used by Curwen either. He had designed his *Curwen Sanserif* capitals before taking over as director of Curwen Press and from 1913 onwards his time and energy were focused on establishing and building his company's reputation. It was not until around 1925 that Curwen returned to *Curwen Sanserif*. Motivated by its successful use in the Crittall catalogue, and perhaps encouraged by the successful launch of *Erbar* in 1922, he began designing a lowercase to accompany the caps he had designed twelve years earlier.

It is far more difficult to design a satisfactory set of lowercase letters than capitals when all lines must remain the same width. While capitals originated from letters cut into stone, the origin of lowercase letters is that of pen and ink on paper or similar, the natural result of which are lines that vary in thickness. The nineteenth-century type designers of heavy sans serifs revealed their efficacy by delicately varying line widths – especially the crossbars of the 'a' and 'e'. *Curwen Sanserif* however, remained a determinedly true monoline so varying the thickness of line was not an option. Curwen exacerbated the problem by giving them generous ascenders and descenders, leaving insufficient space for the x-height of many characters to function effectively. The result is little short of a disaster. The counters appear indistinct, especially in the 'a' and even the 'e', despite its 'opened' eye. Probably due to an awareness of its limitations, the lowercase was only cut at 24 point, while the caps were cut at 12, 18, 24, 30 and 36 point. Only one weight was cut.

The 1920s was the period when the Curwen Press was at its most influential, due in part to the prestige attached to the high profile projects brought to the company by Oliver Simon (who joined in 1920), but also to the care that Harold Curwen lavished on everything that passed through his presses, regardless of how modest the job might be. The attention given to the design and letterpress printing of bus and tube tickets –'the visiting cards of London Transport'[8]– is typical. This was a commission from Frank Pick and the London Passenger Transport Board. Trial designs using *Gill Sans* and *Cloister Bold* were made and numerous proofs pulled.[9] These most ephemeral of small items are prime examples of design and printing at its most utilitarian, yet distinctive and perfectly fit for purpose. At the same time the Curwen Press was attracting prestigious 'fine press' commissions from, for example, The Medici Society, The Limited Editions Club and Francis Meynell's Nonesuch Press, including his first publication, *Genesis*, with wood engravings by Paul Nash. Curwen insisted that there should be no caste division between the most prestigious of book printing projects and the most elemental jam label. As a result, Curwen's press was able to contribute with pride to every aspect, and at every level, of British society.

Harold Curwen and Oliver Simon were responsible for different, though overlapping, activities of the Curwen Press. Curwen was a printer with a strong sense of design, while Simon represented a new kind of designer – a 'typographer' – as well as being a mixture of patron and cultural impresario. His partnership with Stanley Morison in creating *The Fleuron*, each issue a substantial book published annually and certainly the most influential English typographical journal ever published, is testament to that. Indeed, with the final issue, published in 1930, the most intense period of discovery for the print revivalists effectively came to an end, leaving the 1930s to become a decade of consolidation. Simon would later design and edit the influential *Signature*, a journal of typography and graphic arts, and printed, of course, like *The Fleuron*, at the Curwen Press.

As is often the case, some of the most superlative examples of Curwen presswork were self-generated projects instigated by Simon and Curwen. *The Curwen Press Miscellany* (1931), *Curwen Type Specimen Book* (1931), the twice-yearly *Curwen Press Newsletter* (from 1931) and of course *The Fleuron* (issues 1 to 4)[10] are all typical, and remarkably fine examples. While there remained, of necessity, a commercial basis to the work in which Simon was engaged,

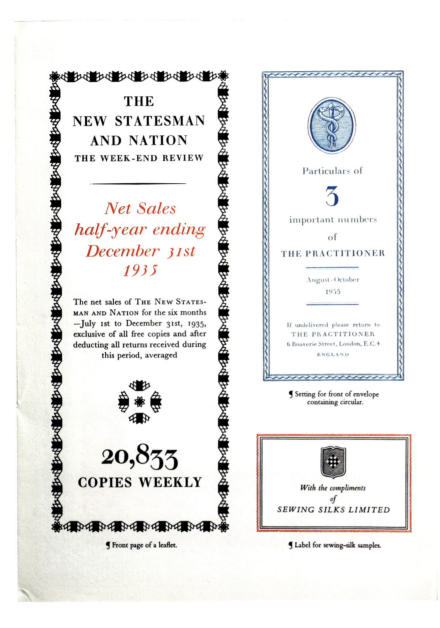

there was also a determined sense of cultural responsibility that (discreetly) went beyond profit and loss. Without doubt, Curwen concurred. The combination of these two dissimilar men with shared ideals made the Curwen Press a persuasive and wholly positive force for cultural change.

Curwen retired in 1940 shortly after the outbreak of the Second World War. Simon became director and stayed with the company until his death in 1956. The Curwen Press closed in 1984.

Above left: A page from *Curwen Press Newsletter* displaying recently printed ephemera, representing the small jobs ('jobbing') in which Harold Curwen took great pride.

Nº VII

FINAL NUMBER THE FLEURON CONTAINING

MODERN PRINTING IN THE NETHERLANDS BY J. VAN KRIMPEN

THE TYPOGRAPHICAL WORK OF ERIC GILL BY PAUL BEAUJON

THE TYPOGRAPHY OF THE 'NINETIES BY A. J. A. SYMONS

FIRST PRINCIPLES OF TYPOGRAPHY BY STANLEY MORISON

THOMAS MAITLAND CLELAND BY DANIEL BERKELEY UPDIKE

THE OFFICINA BODONI BY FRIEDRICH EWALD

FOOTNOTES TO BOOK PRODUCTION

NEW TYPE SPECIMENS INCLUDING

MISFORTUNES, by ROSE MACAULAY, a new short story, with three full page wood-engravings and vignette by Denis Tegetmeier: 16 pp. royal 8vo. in Bembo roman type.

THE PASSION OF SS. PERPETUA, FELICITY & SATURUS, newly translated by W. H. Shewring; with three newly-cut engravings by Eric Gill; 24 pp. crown quarto printed on Arches wove in the thirteen point of Mr. Gill's new Perpetua book-face.

THIS OUR BROTHER, by SYLVIA TOWNSEND WARNER. A short story hitherto unpublished; 20 pp. post 8vo. in Centaur; three illustrations by Sheila Dunn.

TWO LETTERS BY PETRARCH. Translated by A. F. Johnson of the British Museum. Composed in the Treyford type designed by Graily Hewitt for the with two collotypes after a MS. by Petrarch.

Stanley Morison GREAT BRITAIN 1889–1967

Stanley Morison was born in Wanstead, mid-way between London and Epping Forest, but spent most of his childhood and early adult years in London in a modest family terraced house, one of many built alongside a key railway artery in Harringay. His father, a travelling salesman, abandoned the family and Morison was compelled to earn money on leaving grammar school in 1903, aged fourteen. However, he retained 'an abundant sense of curiosity'[1] as a series of office jobs were supplemented by lunch-breaks and Saturdays spent at the British Museum and the bookshops that surrounded it.

A chance sighting in 1912 of a 'Printing Supplement' published by *The Times* would change his life. It contained a masterly survey titled 'The Story of Printing since Gutenberg' by A.W. Pollard, and articles on 'The Origin and Growth of the British Newspaper' and 'Fine Printing in Germany', probably written by Count Harry Kessler,[2] in which the work of Edward Johnston and Eric Gill for the Insel Verlag publishing house was given prominence. There was also a quarter-page advertisement for a new journal 'devoted to the printing and allied trades', called *The Imprint*.

The first issue of *The Imprint* appeared towards the end of January 1913. Morison, who at this time was working as a bank clerk and feeling desperately frustrated, would surely have empathized with W.R. Lethaby's words, 'Art is the humanity put into workmanship, the rest is slavery', from the journal's opening article, 'Art and Workmanship'. The final paragraph of the editorial requested 'the services of a young man of good education and preferably some experience of publishing and advertising'. Despite being notably unqualified on all counts, Morison was interviewed by Gerard Meynell, one of the journal's four editors and whose Westminster Press was its printer, and was offered the job. Morison joined as issue number two (17 February) was published.

It was an opportune moment to arrive. Meynell had persuaded Frank Pick, advertising manager of the London Underground, of the merits of a unifying 'block-letter' typeface on all stations, trains and printed matter, and recommended Johnston, one of the other four editors of *The Imprint*, to design it. John H. Mason, another editor, had designed the journal and collaborated with Monotype in the design of its typeface, *Imprint*. Until recently

Opposite: Stanley Morison, the protective dust jacket for *The Fleuron* no.7 and featuring Eric Gill's *Perpetua* and wood engraving.

he had been chief compositor at the Doves Press, and was now regularly travelling to Weimar, Germany, to work as compositor on Kessler's Cranach Press as well as maintaining his role as head of typography and printing at the Central School of Arts and Crafts. Indeed, outside pressures on its editors may well have contributed to the brief life of *The Imprint*, although financial issues are generally blamed for its closure. The ninth and final issue appeared in November, but by then Morison had already left. Meynell had recognized Morison's potential, as well as the doubtful future of *The Imprint*, and offered him a more stable position with the publisher Burns & Oates during the summer.

Gerard Meynell's uncle, Wilfred Meynell, was the managing director of Burns & Oates and in 1911 had given his son, Francis, then aged twenty, responsibility for book design. Gerard Meynell instinctively knew that Morison and Francis had much to gain from each other. Although Francis was two years younger he had two years' experience of designing for print, and so it was Morison who initially did most of the watching and learning. Through Francis, Morison met Eric Gill, Charles Jacobi of the Chiswick Press and Bernard Newdigate of the Arden Press, and discovered the work of American designers Will Bradley and Bruce Rogers. Morison realized early on that, although he 'still sought few opportunities to design books', he was 'more content to offer occasional suggestions to Francis whose talent as an inventor of interesting typographic display he increasingly admired'.[3]

During the First World War, Morison and Francis Meynell were conscientious objectors and both went to prison – Morison first, with Meynell providing the £5 bail. Meynell was released after a hunger strike, and Morison ended the war working for the government at the Finchley Tomato Farm.

Francis Meynell was a staunch supporter of women's suffrage and left Burns & Oates after an argument with his father on the subject. However, his stand brought the support of Mary Dodge, an American heiress who was largely financing the left-wing, anti-war weekly *The Herald*. Meynell set up the Pelican Press as part of *The Herald*'s printing facility, and used its printing equipment ostensibly to publish material supporting the socialist cause, although Meynell described the press as being preoccupied with: '"jobbing" printing: catalogues, posters, press advertisements, political manifestos'.[4] When the war ended in 1918 *The Herald* became a daily paper once more, and Meynell, now its assistant editor, found himself enmeshed in the travails of the paper's day-to-day business and asked Morison to take over as Designer of Printed Matter at the Pelican Press. Morison grasped the opportunity, and as he gained in confidence he struck up correspondence with, for example, Bruce Rogers (at this time working as an independent typographer in New York), and Daniel B. Updike at the Merrymount Press in Boston, Massachusetts. Morison exchanged examples of work with both and his reputation was growing when Meynell was forced to resign from *The Herald* (over allegations of Russian diamond smuggling, no less) and his enforced return to the Pelican Press meant that Morison had to seek employment elsewhere.

However, the war was over, change was in the air and Morison did not have to wait long for a new opportunity. It came courtesy of Walter Lewis, ten years older and an outstanding printer with already twenty-five years in the trade, mainly with the excellent Ballantyne Press (where a young John H. Mason had learned his trade) in Covent Garden, London. In 1919 Lewis met Charles Hobson who had set up an advertising agency in Manchester, and there they established the Cloister Press – both to serve Hobson's clients and any other customers simply seeking high quality printing that Lewis might attract. Hobson needed someone to take charge of 'design of printed matter' and Lewis, having already been impressed by Morison's work for the Pelican Press, recommended him. Hobson made an offer and Morison accepted, although he loathed having to leave London. He began in May 1921. Being in sole charge of design, he was able to order type (no doubt with Lewis's approval – one of the first being ATF *Garamond*, designed by Morris Fuller Benton) and develop his own style of grandiloquent copywriting. Also, and predictably, Morison began to seek reasons to utilize the small office in London that Hobson had rented at the beginning of 1922. Morison never gave his time exclusively to his employers.

It was at this time that Morison met Oliver Simon, who was employed doing a similar job for Harold Curwen's Curwen Press that Morison was doing for Hobson's Cloister Press – although Simon was considerably more congenial, convivial and, of necessity, proactive in seeking out new clients for Curwen. Together with Francis Meynell and the writer Holbrook Jackson, a nucleus of new talent with shared ambitions was taking form in London. Eric Humphries at Lund Humphries printers and publishers in Bradford, and Herbert Simon (brother of Oliver) at the Kynoch Press in Birmingham, were other notable, though unavoidably more detached supporters.⁵ Despite being very different in character, Morison and Simon were of a similar age, shared a passion for books, print and cricket, and happily complemented each other's strengths and weaknesses – so much so that, when Hobson's ambitious plans collapsed, Simon took over the Cloister Press London office and invited Morison to remain and work alongside him. (Walter Lewis, meanwhile, was appointed University Printer at the prestigious Cambridge University Press in May 1923.)

Shortly before the Cloister Press closed, Morison helped to bring the printing of *The Monotype Recorder*'s January/February issue of 1922 to the Cloister presses. *The Monotype Recorder* was the journal of the Monotype Corporation,⁶ and a prestigious commission to which Morison contributed two articles – one about the Cloister Press, the other about Monotype's recent recutting of *Caslon Old Face*. Morison was in his element. He had found the trenchant tone of voice for which his writing would become renowned and his true vocation: less typographic designer, more researcher and educationalist, though his intended audience was not the independent typographic designer – in whom he had little interest – but, rather, the print trade and, equally important, customers of the print trade.

Morison's purchase of *ATF Garamond* reflected his growing interest in revivalism – the creation of genuine historic types based on a detailed study of original punches, type and printed material – rather than the latent production of vaguely termed 'old face' or 'modern' designs previously on offer. (Monotype's first typeface, issued in 1896, was just such a generic design, called *Modern*.) Morison surmised that typographic quality was to be found by scouring the best of the past; historic typefaces, precisely recreated and optimized for machine composition, would be used in a studied, historically conscious manner. This approach to the study and practice of typography was given considerable momentum by the publication of Daniel B. Updike's two-volume *Printing Types* in 1922.

Morison's political acumen was demonstrated when, having been commissioned by Eric Humphries to design the next edition of the influential *Penrose Annual* of printing and graphic arts (printed and published by Lund Humphries), he chose to use Monotype's *Garamond*, a new typeface whose release, though imminent, was still in production. Morison ingratiated himself with Monotype by supplying original printed specimens of *Garamond* from the French printers, Imprimerie Nationale,[7] and established a regular correspondence with Monotype's Fritz Steltzer, head of the drawing office, which in turn led to Steltzer sending proofs to Morison for his opinion.[8]

All of this not only ensured Morison had the attention of Monotype's management but, equally important, aligned him with Lund Humphries, another major printing company and purchaser of Monotype material. When the development of *Garamond* fell behind schedule, Eric Humphries (primed, and arguing on Morison's behalf), along with a number of other printers, met with William Burch, Monotype's acting managing director, who finally told them that '*Garamond* would be cut, even if it ruined the Corporation'.[9]

In December 1922 the *Penrose Annual* was published and its designer, and Monotype's *Garamond*, received glowing reviews. The close association with Monotype that Morison had developed throughout 1922 was put on a permanent footing early in 1923 when he was formally appointed 'typographic advisor'.[10] (Monotype's rival, UK-based Linotype, had appointed George W. Jones[11] as its typographic advisor fifteen months previously.)

From this position, Morison established himself as the leading figure in the revival of historical typefaces by gaining the confidence of William Burch. But to help his cause he needed the support of prominent book house printers to convince the management at Monotype of the commercial value of his proposals; he also needed printers of the highest calibre to do credit to the types he planned. Walter Lewis, Eric Humphries, Harold Curwen, Herbert Simon and both Francis and Gerard Meynell were all hugely important allies in Morison's revival campaign.

Although he was now employed by Monotype, Morison maintained a base in the central London office that he shared with Oliver Simon and pursued a broad range of activities, all of which, in one form or another, reverberated to Monotype's advantage. Morison was appointed, at Lewis's recommendation, as typographic consultant to Cambridge University Press which, in 1924, printed his *Four Centuries of Fine Printing* in a limited folio edition of 400 copies. Together, Morison and Simon worked on a new typographical journal, *The Fleuron*, with Simon editing the first four issues between 1923 and 1925, which were printed at the Curwen Press. Morison then took over, editing three further

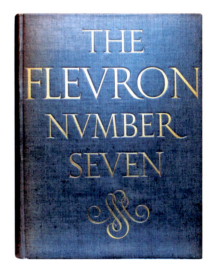

Above: Stanley Morison and Jan van Krimpen, cover of *The Fleuron*, no. 7, with debossed gold-blocked lettering on blue buckram, 1930.

and more extensive issues between 1926 and 1930, which were printed by Cambridge University Press. In its scholarly articles and effusive production, *The Fleuron* has never been surpassed. Monotype realized the value and influence their typographic advisor now wielded. And so did Morison.

However, Morison's influence was not universally appreciated at Monotype. Frank Hinman Pierpont, an American and 'an engineer of genius',[12] had built and ruled over the Salford works, based in the London borough of Newham, which included the drawing office and all aspects of type manufacture and, not unreasonably, considered it his domain. Before Morison's arrival he had established enviable standards and attained considerable success with the production of acclaimed revivals *Imprint* (based on Caslon's types) and *Plantin* – albeit with significant input by Fritz Steltzer, head of the type drawing office. Understandably, he found it difficult to comprehend the purpose of hiring Morison. Tensions between the two would remain until Pierpoint's retirement prior to the Second World War.

Morison, especially in his first few years, was sceptical of the working methods of the company's drawing office and its manufacturing processes (particularly the use of pantograph punchcutting machines), and was concerned that the separation of design from making was detrimental to a satisfactory outcome. These concerns found a sympathetic ear with Eric Gill, who Morison persuaded in 1924 to begin drawing a new typeface, at Morison's own expense, which would, eventually, be *Perpetua*.

Morison, again at his own expense (and so presumably without the knowledge of Monotype's management) then commissioned Charles Malin in Paris, one of a dwindling number of traditional punchcutters, to cut a fount of 14-point characters from Gill's drawings. Morison's intention was to provide Monotype with printed proofs taken from Malin's punches rather than Gill's drawings. Morison later explained his reasoning for this:

> As to a book type of the highest ambition, no reproduction direct from the drawing board had been as satisfactory as those made from type already existing, e.g. Bell's roman and italic. The difference between the drawn pattern and the engraved letter was crucial. Virtue went out with the hand-cutter when the mechanic came in with his pantograph and the rest of the gear.[13]

The progress of *Perpetua* became convoluted and highlighted Morison's lack of intimate, practical experience in type design,

Above: Stanley Morison, his initials placed within a floral scroll. From the final page of *Monotype Flower Decorations*, a specimen booklet published by Monotype, 1924. Note the use of asterisks.

as well as both his and Gill's lack of understanding or sympathy for the manufacturing processes at Monotype. Morison ensured a distance was maintained between Gill and Malin by acting as go-between (as Emery Walker had done between Johnston and Kessler). For Gill the idea of his drawings being passed to a fellow craftsman, rather than the Monotype drawing office, must surely have made his decision to work for Monotype more acceptable. By May 1926, Malin had cut the 14-point and then 12-point punches.

Gill responded positively to the smoke proofs, and by December Malin had cut the 24-point punches. This time, however, Gill was critical, describing the proofs as 'decent but very dull'.[14] This posed a problem for Morison because the Monotype Works had already begun work on *Perpetua* using characters cast from Malin's 12- and 14-point punches, by the type foundry Ribadeau Dumas in Paris, as their template. At this point, William Burch, Monotype's managing director, requested that Gill's original drawings, still in Malin's possession, be sent to him. What Burch thought of Morison's motives in arranging Malin's involvement in the process is not recorded (a record of Pierpont's opinion is unnecessary). Morison's position as typographic advisor at Monotype was, to say the least, under strain.

While *Perpetua* had been haltingly progressing, Gill had been quietly working on another, similar typeface for Gerard Meynell. This typeface advanced no further than drawings, and these were now offered to Monotype as a possible solution to some of *Perpetua's* issues. Monotype now had three alternative sets of characters: Gill's original drawings, proofs from Malin's punches and corresponding foundry type, and a set of drawings by Gill for Meynell. Trials commenced. In October 1927, all work stopped on the project and a meeting was called. It was decided to continue using the proofs taken from the punches cut by Malin, and that Gill should re-draw those characters deemed to require further attention. Monotype began work again on *Perpetua* in January 1928.

ABCDGHJKQRUVWXZ&
BCDGHJKMNQSVWXYZ&
abcdfghjkmnpqtuvwxyz
abcdefghjkmnpqrstuvwxyz

Left: Eric Gill, *Perpetua* accompanied by *Felicity*, c.1932.

The italic to accompany *Perpetua* was a little less convoluted, though no less controversial. In 'Towards an Ideal Italic', *The Fleuron*, no. 5, Morison argued that italics were originally intended for independent use and not for articulation of text set in roman. He contested that a sloped roman was less conspicuous in text than a standard italic and persuaded Gill (as Van Krimpen would be persuaded with *Romulus* and Dwiggins with *Electra*) to substitute a sloped (or 'slanted') roman for the cursive italic. Gill designed two sloped romans, for Meynell and Morison; both were trialled by Monotype and the Meynell version was chosen. When the much-delayed *Fleuron* issue no. 7 was published in November 1930, it tendered the launch of *Perpetua* with a magnificent type specimen and an article written by Paul Beaujon (Beatrice Warde's pseudonym) praising Eric Gill, Stanley Morison and Monotype. Malin's work was also praised: 'The punchcutter who produced the first version of *Perpetua* gave every advantage to the nervous delicacy of the design,' although, inexplicably (if the political machinations at Monotype are ignored) he was not mentioned by name. More surprisingly, Gill in his comments did not mention Malin either.

Only the first proof of the italic was shown because, even as *The Fleuron*, no. 7 was being distributed, revisions were still being made as Morison and Gill jousted over the design of several characters. Just as Gill must have thought this protracted saga was finally coming to a close, he was asked to produce a new set of drawings for *Perpetua* italic, this time with a greater incline, a little more flourish to some lowercase letters and several additional decorative capitals – in other words, more cursive. In 1932 *Perpetua* and *Felicity,* the name given to the italic, was finally released. Morison, in a letter written the same year to Van Krimpen, explained the situation like this:

> I may say that the sloped roman idea does not go down so well in this office as it does outside. The reason for this is that when the doctrine was applied to *Perpetua*, we did not give enough slope to it. When we added more slope, it seemed that the fount required a little more cursive in it. The result was rather a compromise.[15]

Times New Roman was the only typeface Morison actually designed. On 1 August 1929 he was asked by *The Times* to supply proposals for the improvement of the appearance of the newspaper. This request was the result of a visit by Edmund Hopkinson, acting advertising manager of *The Times*, who met with Burch to persuade Monotype to advertise in a new 'Printing Supplement' due to appear later that year. Morison also happened to be in the office, and when he heard Hopkinson explain, as an inducement, that *The Times* would look after the design and typesetting of Monotype's advert, he allegedly hit the table with his fist saying Monotype would do better to pay to keep *The Times* compositors away from their advertisement, and followed it with a lecture on the iniquities of the current state of *The Times*. Hopkinson, no doubt taken aback, was also impressed, and reported the incident to William Lints Smith, the general manager. Smith arranged a meeting with Morison and asked him to provide a 'proposal for improvement'.

The general state of English newspapers had been in decline for some time. Although presses were faster, the ink thinner and the paper courser, the types being employed were invariably the same 'modern' faces that had been introduced a hundred years previously. In America, significant changes had already been implemented. Linotype of New York had introduced *Ionic* in 1926 – plain, sturdy, with strong serifs and little contrast. Closely based on a design by William Page, whose own company had manufactured it as wood type in 1859, *Ionic* had been developed for use on Linotype machines by Chauncey H. Griffith, head of typographic development at Linotype, and adopted by many American newspapers. The first appearance of *Ionic* in Britain was on March 1930 with the redesign of the *Daily Herald*. It was an acclaimed success and Linotype produced several variations during the next few years: *Textype, Excelsior, Opticon, Paragon* and, best of all, *Corona* in 1941, to enable other newspapers to fall in line while maintaining a modicum of individuality. Before long, every foundry had its own version of *Ionic* in its specimen book. Morison, however, was not impressed and focused instead on book types.

Above left: *Ionic* no. 5 and *Bold Face* no. 2 (14-point versions). *Ionic*, whose origins lay in a typeface released by the Blake and Stevenson foundry c.1833, was one of a series of typefaces that Linotype called the 'Legibility Series', led by Chauncey H. Griffith. As well as *Ionic* (of which there were at least five versions) there was also *Ideal* (1928), *Excelsior* (1931), *Paragon* (1935), *Rex* (1939), *Corona* (1941), *Imperial* (1957) and *Aurora* (1960) among others. All are very similar but designed, supposedly, with modifications in response to evolving technical requirements. Linotype's 'Legibility Series' dominated newspapers worldwide for over thirty years; Morison's *Times New Roman* was a rare exception.

ABCDEFGHIJKLMNOPQ
ABCDEFGHIJKLMNOPQ
abcdefghijklmnopqrstuvwxyz
abcdefghijklmnopqrstuvwxyz

Above, top line: Monotype *Plantin*, generally attributed to Frank Hinman Pierpont and Fritz Steltzer at the Monotype works, released 1913.

Bottom line: *Times New Roman*, Stanley Morison, and Victor Lardent, 1932.

In November 1930 *Baskerville, Perpetua* and *Plantin* were all under consideration as possible candidates when Morison submitted a memorandum to *The Times* presenting work in progress. The outcome was an instruction to drop *Baskerville*, to prepare a thickened *Perpetua* (Morison had presented a version of Gill's 11-point *Perpetua* with shortened ascenders and descenders to fit onto the required 9-point body) and to use a 'modernized' version of Monotype's *Plantin*; this had sharper serifs and a further reduction of its thin strokes while maintaining the same character widths. Morison then dropped the *Perpetua* option to concentrate on adapting *Plantin*.[16] In his *Tally of Types* (1953) Morison wrote, in the third person: 'Finally it was decided to put in hand a new design to be excogitated by Morison ... He pencilled the original set of drawings and handed them to Victor Lardent, a graphic artist who specialized in lettering and worked in the publicity department of Printing House Square [*The Times*]'.

Walter Tracy and James Moran (separately) discussed the design's creation with Lardent in the 1960s. Both found that he had little memory of exactly what material he had been given from which to draw the typeface, but he told Moran that he remembered working 'from archive photographs of vintage type' which he thought were taken from a book printed by Christophe Plantin – but did not remember receiving any drawings by Morison.[17] The proportions of *Times New Roman* so closely align with Monotype's *Plantin* that it seems likely that Lardent was instructed to work to the same proportions, using photographic enlargements and perhaps copies of Monotype's own working drawings.[18] The 'archive photographs of vintage type' were probably a sixteenth-century source of Robert Granjon's type,[19] used by Morison to demonstrate anomalies in the 1905 *Index characterum* of the Plantin-Moretus Museum model that was employed by Pierpont when designing Monotype's *Plantin*.

Why did Morison approach Lardent rather than a proven expert type draughtsman, such as Fritz Steltzer at Monotype? Perhaps he feared his role as 'designer' might be undermined during the inevitable trials and critical scrutiny if drawn by Steltzer, who would be working, of course, under Pierpont's discretional eye. It has also been suggested that Morison did not begin with a clear vision of what he required and effectively had to feel his way towards the solution – again a process made more difficult if each volte-face is being publicly scrutinized. But another reason might have been that Morison was seeking a prominent and lasting role on *The Times*, and wanted to impress by embracing the newspaper's own pool of talent in the making of its own new typeface. Whatever the reason, Lardent's drawings were sent to the Monotype works where a great deal of trial manufacture was undertaken and many punches recut, probably due to the review and modification of its design, before the type was passed.[20] Interestingly – bearing in mind Morison's previous advocacy of sloped roman – the *Times New Roman Italic* was a 'true' (calligraphic) italic. Morison later wryly commented, 'I owe more to Didot than dogma'.[21] Having been delayed by initial opposition to Morison's proposed changing of the masthead from an inline blackletter to roman, *The Times* appeared in its new typographic guise on 3 October 1932 – to huge positive approval.

Its bold companion typeface was less successful. When designing *Times New Roman Bold*, Morison had the freedom to give the letters a little extra width to enable the internal spaces to balance with the thicker vertical strokes and to ensure harmonization with its counterpart standard weight. But for reasons unknown, Morison designed fifteen of the bold lowercase characters the same width, and eleven slightly narrower. The bold caps suffered the same fate – exacerbated by the fact that *Times New Roman* was already decidedly narrow. This might not have been such a problem if the amount of weight added to the characters had been modest, but *Times New Roman Bold* is, in fact, exceptionally bold. Unsurprisingly this, combined with its narrow width, gave it a distinctly vertical appearance, or as Walter Tracy described it, 'a harsh picket fence effect'.[22] It is conceivable that this was a misjudgement, but the fact that Morison also gave his lowercase bold version flat head serifs – a distinctive characteristic

abcdefghijk lmnopqrst uvwxyz

Above: Stanley Morison, *Times New Roman Bold*, with its distinctive 'picket fence effect' caused by the open counters being roughly the same width as the vertical stems.

of the modern *Ionic* newspaper typefaces commonly used by *The Times*'s competitors and much maligned by Morison – cannot be assuaged so easily. It had little in common with the bookish regular *Times New Roman*, and was used only briefly before being taken out of service. Was the cause for this a crisis of confidence? Or pressure from another quarter? Knowing what we know of Morison neither seem credible. Later bold versions by other hands, for example, Walter Tracy's *Europa* in 1974, have been more successful.

Meanwhile, the success and wholly positive impact of *Times New Roman* was exceptional, but it was assisted by other factors. The print-run of *The Times* was smaller than most British daily newspapers and so the presses did not have to run at full speed. More importantly, the quality of the paper was heavier and more opaque than any of its competitors. The importance for *Times New Roman* on the quality of the paper was demonstrated in 1956 when, for economic reasons, a lighter weight and more translucent paper was introduced, causing the text to appear weakened. Adjustments were made to the type to no avail, and the original paper was reintroduced.

The Times retained sole right to the use of the type for one year, and then Monotype was free to offer the face for general sale. Its immediate popularity was astonishing, commercially becoming the most successful typeface of the twentieth century, outselling its nearest rival at Monotype two to one. As with most newspapers, *The Times* used linecasters: Linotype 'slug' machines for much of the text setting, and Intertype 'slug' machines for headings, while Monotype machines were reserved for more complex tabular work or advertisement setting. As a result, although all the development work was done by Monotype, *Times New Roman* had to be adapted for setting on linecasters.

Until about 1950 Monotype called the face *The Times New Roman*, but since then it has been called *Times New Roman*. Linotype always called the face *Times Roman*. In the 1980s, Apple chose to license the Linotype catalogue while Microsoft licensed Monotype's, which is why the name of this typeface differs, depending on the choice of Mac or PC.

SPECTRUM

ROMAN

AND

ITALIC

Jan van Krimpen THE NETHERLANDS 1892–1958

Jan van Krimpen was the youngest of four children. He was born in Gouda, mid-way between Rotterdam and The Hague. His mother died when he was aged nine and his father, a wealthy grain merchant, died when he was seventeen. Van Krimpen studied drawing and other subjects at the Academy of Art at The Hague and intended to become an artist, but he discovered the German translated version by Anna Simons of Edward Johnston's *Writing & Illuminating & Lettering* and began to teach himself calligraphy. An example of his earliest lettering appeared in a new publication, *Der Witte Mier* (The White Ant), 'a magazine for friends of book and print', edited and published by the poet Jan Greshoff.

In 1912, the year that Sjoerd Hendrik de Roos's first typeface, *Hollandsche Mediaeval*, appeared, Van Krimpen finished his studies at the Art Academy. He was growing increasingly interested in the word – both written and printed – and subscribed to *The Imprint* (1913), the new English journal co-edited by Edward Johnston and others.[1] The editors' aim for *The Imprint* was to improve standards of design and craftsmanship within the commercial print sector, using modern printing technology. Prior to this in the Netherlands – and an early indicator of the renewed interest in well-designed and well-made books – was the establishment in 1910 of a small publishing company, De Zilverdistel (The Silver Thistle). It was the creation of two poets, Jan Greshoff, by now a friend of Van Krimpen, and P. N. van Eyck. When Greshoff left in 1913, Jean François van Royen joined De Zilverdistel and took the press in a rather different direction.

Van Royen was a lawyer, art lover and book collector who believed, like William Morris, that beautiful, harmonious and well-made products would contribute to the spiritual well-being of society. In a famous article written in 1912 he criticized the state printing office, whose publications he called, 'ugly, ugly, ugly – thrice ugly – ugly in typeface, ugly in typesetting and ugly in paper'.[2] Van Royen bought an Albion hand-press in 1914 and commissioned De Roos at Lettergieterij Amsterdam (Amsterdam Type Foundry) to design a proprietary typeface, requesting that it be based on the Doves Press type. At this point De Zilverdistel ceased to be a minor publishing concern and became the first private press in the Netherlands – and was critically scrutinized as such.

Opposite: Jan van Krimpen, *Spectrum*, on the cover of the type specimen published by Monotype (designed by Van Krimpen and Will Carter, and printed by Enschedé en Zonen), 1952.

It was not only the historic nature of Van Royen's books that was criticized, but also the very premise of a private press and the purpose of reverting to the use of a hand-press. A particularly venomous critic was the twenty-two year-old Van Krimpen. In 1914 he accused Van Royen of snobbery and, perhaps with *The Imprint* in mind, argued in favour of contemporary design that took advantage of more inclusive modern printing and production methods rather than the inherent exclusive nature of a private press. Although Van Krimpen generally praised *Hollandsche Mediaeval* and *Zilvertype* (*Zilvertype* was designed by Van Royen and Van Krimpen had used *Hollandsche Mediaeval* almost exclusively for a number of years),[3] De Roos wrote a sharp rejoinder a month later suggesting that 'the young Van Krimpen' needed to improve his knowledge of his subject before committing further opinions to print.[4] It was to be the beginning of a long-term rancorous, though not an entirely unfriendly, relationship.

In 1920 Van Royen became secretary-general of the Dutch Post, Telephone and Telegraph service (PTT) with responsibility for design administration, and introduced a transformational design policy that became a beacon for Dutch design worldwide. Nevertheless, he never gave up producing limited edition books for De Zilverdistel and later set up his own company, Kunera Press. Having seen and admired Van Krimpen's hand-lettering, Van Royen commissioned him in 1923 to design the lettering of two series of postage stamps celebrating Queen Wilhelmina's silver jubilee. The stamps were printed by the great printing house and type foundry Joh. Enschedé en Zonen, in Haarlem.

Enschedé was founded in 1703 and remained in the hands of the same family, adding a bookshop in 1724, a newspaper in 1737 and a type foundry in 1743. The renowned punchcutters J. M. Fleischman and J. F. Rosart both worked there in the eighteenth century, and the acquisition of Ploos van Amstel's type foundry in 1799 added to an already important collection of historic punches and types. The printing of bank notes and stamps had been the mainstay of Enschedé for centuries, having printed the very first Dutch banknote in 1814 and all Dutch postage stamps since 1866.

While the security printing side of the business was doing well in the early 1920s, the letterpress and book printing divisions were at a low ebb. Dr Johannes Enschedé, head of

Above: Jan van Krimpen, stamp design for the Dutch PTT, 1923.

the company, looked for a designer to help reestablish standards. He was impressed by Van Krimpen's calligraphic work on the recently released set of stamps, and they met towards the end of 1923 at the Laurens Janszoon Coster 500th anniversary celebrations (Coster is Haarlem's rival to Mainz's Johannes Gutenberg as the inventor of printing from moveable type).[5] Enschedé commissioned a typeface from Van Krimpen, which, when released two years later, was called *Lutetia*.

Left: Jan van Krimpen, *Lutetia*, second version with flat cross-bar of the e, c.1929.

Above: Jan van Krimpen, a comparison of some of the contentious *Lutetia* characters from the first version (left) with the second (right).

This was the perfect commission for Van Krimpen. He had a clear idea of the type he wanted to design, and promised Enschedé that he would begin work immediately. The sketches were accepted and Van Krimpen began drawing a full character set for the roman, which he finished towards the middle of 1924. Van Royden was curating the Dutch exhibition that would form part of the *Exposition Internationale des Arts Décoratifs et Industriels Modernes* in Paris, and when he saw Van Krimpen's new typeface he urged Enschedé to speed up its production so that it could be used on all the Dutch printed material. Van Krimpen swiftly drew the italic and punches were cut at 16 point but, unfortunately, Enschedé ran out of time and *Lutetia*, the Latin name for Paris, could only be used for the exhibition catalogue. Van Krimpen's calligraphic and typographic work was included in the exhibition and the new typeface was met with admiration. He was awarded a grand prix.

Despite having never designed a typeface before, Van Krimpen succeeded in making a refined set of drawings, with his knowledge largely acquired from the close reading of Edward Johnston's *Writing & Illuminating & Lettering* and the technicalities of type from L.A. Legros & J.C. Grant's *Typographic Printing Surfaces* (1916). However, the remarkable success of *Lutetia* and the speed of its production also surely owed something to the skill of P.H. Rädisch,

Right: Jan van Krimpen, *Romulus*, roman and sloped roman, Enschedé, 1931.

CORPS 16 NO. 6515   6,50 KG

DE HISTORIE VAN DE MENS WORDT VOOR
een niet gering deel bepaald door de ontwikkeling van ver-
schillende kundigheden, die het gevolg waren van zijn toe-

its punchcutter. The drawings which might have recorded the inherent development by design – all the inevitable adjustments causing forms to evolve – were not preserved, but there are significant differences between the initial sketches drawn by Van Krimpen and the final cuts made by Rädisch. Who instigated the modifications, or when they occurred, is not known.

   Rädisch was one of the last masters of a craft which became increasingly rare during the early decades of the twentieth century, as pantograph technology ('mechanical punchcutting') was installed in many of the major type foundries. Enschedé was one of the last foundries in western Europe where punchcutting remained a task undertaken by hand. Rädisch had learned his craft in Leipzig and at the German Reichdruckerie in Berlin. The collaboration between Van Krimpen and Rädisch, both in their early thirties, appeared amicable and harmonious. Yet Rädisch held strong views and his input in the design process of other type designer's work – for example, his four-and-a-half-year fight with the designer Sem Hartz over the development of his *Emergo* typeface – makes it clear that he could be remarkably stubborn. However, such impasses appear to have been avoided in his collaboration with Van Krimpen, so either they always agreed or had sufficient respect for each other to enable adjustments to be offered and incorporated amiably. Yet despite this remarkably successful working relationship – 'a team of unusual effectiveness',[6] each depending on the skills and best motives of the other – Van Krimpen quite pointedly never credited Rädisch by name, referring to him, for example, as 'the punchcutter of the House of Enschedé' or even as an 'auxiliary hand'.[7] Presumably Rädisch acquiesced, or felt it was beneath his dignity to broach the matter.

   The most astonishing aspect of Van Krimpen's first typeface was not so much the proficiency of its execution but, rather, its originality. *Lutetia* eschews pastiche or revivalism, indeed Van Krimpen was highly critical of the idea of reviving old type for contemporary use. Stanley Morison, who by now had successfully

Above left: Jan van Krimpen, *Romanée*, 1928. 16 point, shown approximately actual size.

ABCDEFGHIJKLMNOPQRSTUVWXYZ

established a programme of typographic revivalism at Monotype, might have been expected to sow doubt on such views but, instead, praised Van Krimpen in his review of the typeface in *The Fleuron*, no. 5 (1926), explaining that the 'exceedingly handsome' *Lutetia* was not derived from any historic predecessor or school, and that the designer had 'kept himself free from current English, German or American fashions'.

Nevertheless, there were several characters in *Lutetia* that were, by general opinion (including Morison's), out of proportion. For example, when the American printer Porter Garnett placed a large order for *Lutetia* in 1928–29 for his Laboratory Press (intending to use it for the text of his monumental Catalogue of the Frick Collection), he asked for a number of revisions. Most notable was the angled slope on the cross-bar of the 'e', the narrowing of several upper- and lowercase characters, especially the 'E', the shortening of the tail on the 'Q', and increasing the weight of the tittles and punctuation. Presumably Van Krimpen's agreement to make the requested changes was contingent on the sale. What he thought of Porter's judgement at the time was not recorded, but thirty years later he conceded that the changes did, indeed, improve the typeface.

Lutetia was easier to admire than to use. Oliver Simon, who met Van Krimpen in 1928, ordered *Lutetia* for the Curwen Press (UK) as did Daniel B. Updike for the Merrymount Press (US), although both rarely used it. The Grabhorn Press (US), renowned publishers of fine press limited edition books, was a more frequent user, although when they tried the 18 point for an edition of *Leaves of Grass* they decided that *Lutetia* was too delicate for Whitman's reverberant verse. *Lutetia* was original and refined, though unassertive. Nevertheless, it established Van Krimpen's reputation as a type designer, and the typefaces he created during the next twenty years – including (among others) *Romanée* and *Spectrum* – were held in high esteem, yet sales to the printing trade were never high.

Romanée was based on a roman typeface attributed to Christoffel van Dijck, printed in a type specimen book issued by Enschedé in 1768. Only the punches and matrices of the 16-point italic had survived. This project was instigated by Enschedé who hoped that the new roman would accompany a reissued Van Dijck italic. Photographs were taken and enlargements

PARLIAMENT
a small pathway runs
NEDERLAND
between the hedgerows
LA MADELEINE
immaculately cut and
ESPOSIZIONE
shaped to resemble the
GESCHICHTE
turrets of the big house

Top right: Jan van Krimpen, one of the four weights of a sans serif (or 'monoline effect') version of *Romulus* (12 point), 1931. Its development was curtailed by Enschedé.

Above: Jan van Krimpen, *Spectrum*, a page from the type specimen published by Monotype, designed by Van Krimpen and Will Carter, and printed by Enschedé en Zonen, c.1957.

made of the printed typeface. However, after closely studying the photographs, Van Krimpen chose to draw the characters freehand. The result, issued in 1928, was a distinct improvement on *Lutetia* – the capitals are particularly accomplished – although surprisingly, the tittles and punctuation are, again, too small. The roman was described by the reviewer in *The Fleuron*, no. 7, as 'distinguished [though] bland'. *Romanée* is better than that, although as a companion to Van Dijke's italics it was 'a distinct failure', as Van Krimpen himself admitted. A new italic was designed by Van Krimpen for *Romanée*, though, inexplicably, not until twenty-one years later.

Despite holding differing views, Van Krimpen and Morison became friends for life. Their mutual respect even influenced Van Krimpen's practical work, most notably with *Romulus* begun in 1932. (Beatrice Warde persuaded him to change the design's original name, *Epiphania*.) Van Krimpen, whose italic for *Lutetia* had been criticized for being too distinctive [8] – a polite way of saying that it lacked rapport or even compatibility with its roman counterpart – was persuaded by Morison's argument, that a simple 'sloped' (or slanted) roman was the natural accompaniment to a roman, rather than a traditional italic. This time his sloped 'italics' were criticized for being too close in appearance to the roman and the regularity of their slope wearisome. Both Morison and Van Krimpen later admitted their mistake. Van Krimpen went on to make drawings for a 'monoline effect' – meaning a sans serif – companion for *Romulus* in four weights, but having allowed trial 12-point punches to be cut and matrices struck Enschedé decided to terminate its progress.[9] However, the concept of designing a companion sans serif to function alongside a serif typeface – in effect creating what could have been the first comprehensive typographic 'family' – was to become hugely influential with the next generation of Dutch type designers.

Van Krimpen's *Haarlehammer*, completed in 1938, was a private typeface to be used in the printing of a Bible for an association of Dutch bibliophiles. His drawings were sent directly to Monotype to be cut but the impending threat of war in Europe caused the project to be abandoned, although Monotype would resurrect the typeface after the Second World War.

During the German occupation of the Netherlands, Van Klimpen was able to continue working on a second typeface intended for the composition of a Bible, this time from the

Utrecht Catholic publisher Het Spectrum. This was, effectively a more refined version of *Haarlehammer*, and a trial font was cut by Rädisch and cast at Enschedé in 14 point. Immediately after the war Van Klimpen passed specimens of his recent type designs to Morison via John Dreyfus (who would succeed Morison at Monotype ten years later).

However, the next five postwar years at Monotype were very difficult for all concerned, and Morison decided to focus on his work for *The Times* until Monotype was in a position to consider manufacturing new types again. During this time Het Spectrum had investigated the possibility of developing the commercial potential of their typeface, without success, and in 1950 decided to relinquish the rights to *Spectrum*, leaving Enschedé free to jointly develop the typeface with Monotype. What might have been expected to be a postwar celebratory cross-European project became a protracted and often bitter feud between Van Krimpen and the Monotype Corporation concerning, once again, the problem of adapting a freely designed foundry typeface to fit the Monotype matrix case.

The high regard in which Monotype was held was undoubtedly due in large part to its engineering prowess, and it was certainly an engineering ethos that permeated the drawing office. As discussed elsewhere (see chapters on Bruce Rogers, Eric Gill, Stanley Morison and Hans Mardersteig), tension could sometimes rise because of perceived differences of attitude as much as technical issues, but Van Krimpen's running battle with Monotype's drawing office was the most acrimonious by far. This is puzzling, because Van Krimpen already had first-hand experience of the Monotype drawing office from working on *Romulus* and *Haarlehammer*, and so he was fully aware of the potential pitfalls. Yet he entered the process apparently more determined than ever not to compromise. Perhaps the fact that the drawing office, as well as Van Krimpen, had examples of Rädisch's 14-point hand-cut foundry type – clearly demonstrating his ideal outcome – made it all the more difficult for Van Krimpen to accept any variation whatsoever in the Monotype version.

Frustration led him to write a memorandum which arrived at the Monotype offices in March 1956. This was not an act of momentary petulance – an earlier draft had been sent to Morison in August 1954. In it, he not only criticized the work of Monotype's drawing office but also the fundamentals of the matrix-case system upon which the Monotype Corporation's typesetting technology was built and functioned. He even attacked Morison's policy of recutting classic typefaces. In the circumstances, Morison's reply was exceptionally placatory: 'I do not believe that you mean that Monotype and foundry type are two essentially different things. I do not believe these differences are essential'.[10] *Spectrum* was finally released in 1957, and displayed in a particularly fine specimen booklet designed by Van Krimpen and Will Carter, and printed by Enschedé.

Van Krimpen's original position at Enschedé was as 'house designer', and as such he designed or oversaw the design of many books that were printed by Enschedé's print works. He began with the handsome and literate specimen books of the company's type holdings, and continued with many fine books whose publishers were attracted by Enschedé's and Van Krimpen's reputation. These included Francis Meynell's Nonesuch Press (London), Frederic Warde's Pleiade Press (Paris) and, later, Macy's Limited Editions Club (New York). With such people he was relaxed, charming and generous, as he always was with Morison. But as already noted, he could also be a tyrant. His colleague at Enschedé, Sem Hartz, who took over Van Krimpen's position when he died, explained:

> No typography outside the typography of the book existed for him, and all the busy doings of advertising, sales promotion and the like, he abhorred, as with the people and jargon connected with them. Unforgiving, he stood in the breach for what he thought was right. Lonely because of his unrelenting criticism of situations and persons, [he was] harsh and unforgiving.[11]

Although Van Krimpen did not become a director at Enschedé, a position he coveted, he was, nevertheless, always his own master. He accepted commissions from other publishers at will and, in later years, decided without consultation to limit his time in his office to the morning hours, leaving the afternoons to spend on his own private press work. This kind of presumptuous behaviour irritated some directors, which no doubt pleased Van Krimpen, who remained with Enschedé until the day he died of a stroke, aged sixty-six, on his way to work.

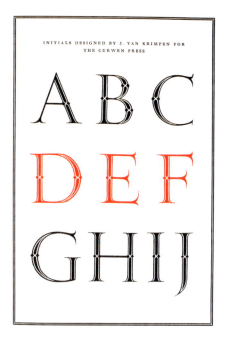

Above: Jan van Krimpen, a variation of *Lutetia* and a rare example of Krimpen's more decorative design work, commissioned by Oliver Simon at the Curwen Press. From the *Curwen Press Miscellany*, 1931.

«MONOTYPE»
DANTE
SERIES 592

WITH

DANTE TITLING
SERIES 612

THE MONOTYPE CORPORATION LTD.

Hans (Giovanni) Mardersteig GERMANY 1892–1977

Hans Mardersteig was born in Weimar, previously the home of Goethe, and J.S. Bach. During his childhood the city became a focal point for modern art under the influence of, amongst others, Count Harry Kessler, a family friend who later founded the Cranach Press, and Henry van de Velde who, in 1907, established the Grand-Ducal School of Arts and Crafts (later transformed by Walter Gropius into the Bauhaus). At university Mardersteig studied law to doctorate level (his father was a lawyer), but he also attended classes in art history which led to a fascination for fine-printed books.

Mardersteig's health was compromised by tuberculosis, and he consequently remained a civilian during the First World War. In 1917 he joined a highly respected book publishing house in Leipzig founded by literary historian Kurt Wolff, who was a publisher of Expressionist literature and launched the 'New Writing' series *Der Jüngste Tag* ('The Last Judgment') between 1913 and 1921.[1] Mardersteig and his friend the art historian Carl Georg Heise went to Wolff (who was only slightly older than Mardersteig and Heise), and proposed that he publish a new modern art and literary journal, *Genius*, with Mardersteig and Heise sharing editorial duties. Wolff agreed, with Mardersteig also taking responsibility for its design and overseeing production in Leipzig. Issued triannually between 1919 and 1921, *Genius* was a substantial and influential journal featuring original prints, many by Expressionist artists.

Mardersteig was forced to leave his editorial job with Wolff because the damp climate threatened his health. However, his work on *Genius* had brought him into contact with some of the best commercial printers. He became fascinated by the processes and materials but was often frustrated by the ultimate results – despite *Genius* gaining an enviable reputation for its production values. Having seen the books of the Doves Press through a bookbinder friend who had worked for T. J. Cobden-Sanderson, he came to the conclusion that if the highest standards of typography and printing were to be attained, he would have to establish his own press and take personal control of every aspect of production.

In 1921 Mardersteig moved to the opposite, southern side, of the Alps to help improve his health, and *Genius* ceased

Opposite: Hans Mardersteig, *Dante*, cover of a type specimen published by Monotype, 1957.

publication. Drawn by a love of Renaissance culture as well as the warmer climate, Mardersteig set up a private press at Montagnola near Lugano, Switzerland, and called it the Officina Bodoni. The name was in honour of the types he used. However, Mardersteig's type was not one of the early twentieth-century revivals from ATF or Monotype. Having studied these, Mardersteig concluded they lacked the subtleties, and therefore the essence, of the original. Astonishingly, he gained permission from the Italian government to arrange for new castings to be made from the renowned Italian printer Giambattista Bodoni's original matrices, which were stored in the museum at Parma where Bodoni had lived and worked. Mardersteig chose four founts from Bodoni's later work: 12-point *Cuneo*, 16-point *Catania*, 20-point *Casale* and a decorated italic. The Officina began publishing in 1923.

With Germany in the grip of political and economic instability, and the brouhaha created by the emergence of the Bauhaus, Mardersteig, now thirty years old, was quietly printing his first books in the peace and stability of Montagnola. His interest in Expressionism was over and, henceforth, he was concerned with the kind of restrained perfectionism for which he would become renowned. The Officina Bodoni was a place of bookbinding as well as printing on handmade papers and vellum; only gilding was outsourced. Editions were usually limited to about 200 (although early books far less), and never more than 500. It was an exclusive and elitist world and one which, in later years, even Mardersteig would come to consider rather remote. His style was simple to the point of austere, the only exception being an occasional small extravagance – perhaps a tiny decorative detail in the binding.

The cost of living in Switzerland was considerably lower than in Germany which certainly helped to make the press commercially viable, but more important by far was Mardersteig's use of Bodoni's original matrices – which attracted international attention in bibliographic circles. This, and his lack of compromise towards standards of scholarship, editing and production, assured the status of Officina Bodoni. The early work of the press consisted of a broad and multilingual selection of European classics and attracted a loyal group of patrons and customers, one of whom was Stanley Morison. He had recently become typography advisor to the Monotype Corporation and, from around 1925, was captivated by Mardersteig's press and particularly by the scholarly interest of its owner in Renaissance writing masters.

Frederic Warde, a young American typographic designer, had recently completed a small book of poems by the British poet laureate, Robert Bridges. This project had been undertaken in collaboration with Stanley Morison, and Warde's own typeface *Arrighi* (based on Ludovico Vicentino degli Arrighi's sixteenth-century script) had been used. Warde now wished to establish himself as a fine press typographer and publisher. He travelled to Montagnola to meet Mardersteig, his aim being to establish a working partnership – Warde designing and composing, Mardersteig printing and binding. Needless to say, Warde was hugely impressed by what he found, so much so that he encouraged Morison to consider transferring the printing of future editions of *The Fleuron* to Mardersteig's Officina. Warde wrote: 'Such Germans I have met, who are the prime movers in their typography and printing, are also splendid scholars and possess much sound aesthetic judgement'.[2]

Mardersteig was also impressed with Warde, and they formed a close working relationship. Their first project was to be *Operina*, a facsimile of Arrighi's writing books from 1522 and 1523, with an introduction by Morison set in Warde's *Arrighi* type.[3] Flush with confidence, Warde decided to set up his own imprint and his next collaborative book with Mardersteig was a slim (38-page) octavo volume – Plato's *Crito* – for which his variant of *Arrighi*, called *Vicenza*, was used for the first time (see p. 65). Mardersteig later recalled:

> Warde's intention was to establish a hand press and produce bibliophile editions for the few American collectors who had shown an interest ... We agreed that he should come with his new type and we should produce two books: he should do the composition and I was to look after the printing.[4]

Following these successes working with Warde, Mardersteig became a little less self-restrained and began using foundry types other than *Bodoni*, many bought from the Monotype

Bembo

Left: Hans Mardersteig, *Griffo*, cut by Charles Malin (shown reduced), 1929.

Above: *Bembo*, instigated by Stanley Morison, drawn and cut by Monotype and released 1928–29.

ABCDEFFGHIJKLMNOPRRSTUVW
abccdeeffgghhi1jjklmmnopqrrstuu
vwxyzæœ ff fi fl ? ! : ; - (✠ ℭ   h j p p p q y

Above right: Hans Mardersteig, *Zeno*, c.1937.

Corporation – no doubt encouraged by his growing collaboration and genuine friendship with Morison. Enthused by discussions with both Morison and Warde concerning the practicalities of type design and its manufacture, Mardersteig cautiously began to contemplate the possibility of designing a typeface of his own.

In 1927 the Officina moved to Verona. Mardersteig had helped Francesco Pastonchi, writer and bibliophile, with his plans to publish a series of classics which Mardersteig was to print; a typeface was designed by Eduardo Cotti for the purpose. Mardersteig took great interest in the progress of its design and put Cotti in touch with Morison at Monotype where *Pastonchi* was cut. Through Pastonchi, Mardersteig met Arnoldo Mondadori who was the organizer of a competition held in 1926 for the design and printing of an edition of the complete works of Italy's national poet Gabriele d'Annunzio – a monumental undertaking. Mondadori explained that if the Officina was to stand a chance of winning the competition, it would be necessary for Mardersteig to move the press to Italy. Mardersteig moved to Verona, and won the commission. 'Hans' Mardersteig became 'Giovanni' Mardersteig.

The scale of the commission, which took almost ten years to complete, was huge, comprising forty-nine volumes, all hand-set in *Bodoni*. A deluxe edition of 209 copies was printed on the Officina's hand press on imperial Japanese paper, and a further nine copies on parchment. The locked-up pages of type were then transferred to the Mondadori printing house, where a further 2,501 copies were printed on mechanized cylinder presses.

It was during the late 1920s, and whilst the d'Annunzio project was still occupying much of Mardersteig's time, that he began to be actively involved in the process of type design. It was a gradual initiation which started when he noticed that some of the delicate serifs were regularly breaking during the longer printing of the *d'Annunzio* volumes on Mondadori's cylinder presses. Replacements were needed but with minor amendments in an attempt to avoid further breaks. Mardersteig needed a skilled punchcutter to make them and, following the advice of Warde or Morison, he contacted Charles Malin in Paris. Malin's visits to the Officina became regular, encouraged by the allure of the workshop set up in Mardersteig's home.

Morison encouraged Mardersteig to take a close look at the typeface cut by Francesco Griffo for Aldus Manutius, who first used it for his book *De Aetna* in 1496. Morison had recently used the same model for Monotype's *Bembo* (see p. 14) but was disappointed by the result – accusing the Monotype drawing office of smoothing out ('correcting') the distinctive affectations in Griffo's original – and was interested to see what Malin might create from the same model (all, of course, at Mardersteig's expense). The result of Mardersteig and Malin's work, named *Griffo*, was completed in 1929 and was closer to the original than Monotype's *Bembo*. Nevertheless, there was a ten-year gap between the completion of the 16-point *Griffo* and its first appearance in an Officina Bodoni book, Mardersteig's hesitancy suggesting that he must have been uncertain of its merits. After the war some letters were revised and a 'second state' of *Griffo* was used in Rudolf Hagelstange's *Die Elemente*, 1950.

The first typeface that Mardersteig designed to appear in print was *Zeno*. It was begun at the beginning of the 1930s and was finally used in 1937. It was named after Verona's patron saint, whose story is the subject in the slim book in which it was first used. The model for *Zeno* was a formal (roman) script written by Ludovico Arrighi in 1520. Mardersteig was perhaps a little naive in choosing a handwritten text as a model; he quickly realized that, although Arrighi's characters might be similar, no two were exactly the same. Moreover, Arrighi's manuscript was archived in Berlin and could not be moved, so Mardersteig had to draw the letters – a hugely demanding process – and then pass them to Malin to use as a guide. The result is a strong but refined face with unforgivingly small 'a' and 'e' counters that required precise presswork to avoid black dots appearing across the page. Mardersteig carefully followed Malin's type-cutting process, which was completed in 1936 and put to use the following year. Other sizes were subsequently added to the range, all cut by Malin who made the necessary modifications to weight and proportions without recourse to new drawings. Two revisions were made and the definitive version appeared in a second printing of Montano's *San Zeno* in 1964. No italic was ever designed to partner the roman *Zeno*. During the protracted time it took to produce *Zeno*, Mardersteig designed his first typeface

A B C D E F G H I J K L M
N O P Q R S T U V W X Y Z
a b c d e f g h i j k l m n o
p q r s t u v w x y z æ œ fi
1 2 3 4 5 6 7 8 9 0
N O P Q R S T U V W X Y Z
a b c d e f g h i j k l m n

Above: Hans Mardersteig, *Fontana*, c.1936. The name was given by Monotype, who released it in 1961.

for Monotype, called *Zarotto*, in 1932. However, it was never released.

When the *d'Annunzio* edition was completed in 1935, Mardersteig worked for a year in Glasgow for the Cleartype Press, part of the substantial William Collins & Sons publishing company. He persuaded them that they should have a typeface of their own in order to distinguish themselves from other printers. He chose an eighteenth-century typeface of Scottish origin derived from Alexander Wilson of the Glasgow Letter Foundry. The new typeface was cut by Monotype for Collins's exclusive use, although Mardersteig was allowed to use it for a book he designed and printed for George Macy's Limited Editions Club. In 1961 it was agreed that Monotype could release it; they called it *Fontana*, a reference to the Collins famous fountain logo.

No doubt Mardersteig learned a great deal from these experiences and, after the war, was able to apply the knowledge gained in his last and far superior typeface: *Dante*. Between 1946 and 1952 Mardersteig worked in collaboration with Malin once again but, unlike his previous typefaces, *Dante* was in no sense a copy. If Mardersteig made drawings for Malin to work from, they have not been published.[5] Hans Schmoller explains: 'We can assume that because of his close understanding with Malin, and because the punchcutter interprets rather than slavishly copies a design, Mardersteig's drawings [if they ever existed] were less highly polished.'[6]

Although *Dante* had been conceived as a proprietary typeface, its commercial potential was immediately recognized by Morison who, with Mardersteig's agreement, made initial arrangements for Monotype to cut their version for machine composition. However, this was delayed until resources for matrix manufacture at Monotype were increased by the setting up of a new matrix department in the corporation's Frankfurt offices. The recutting and extension of the *Dante* type was finally planned to start in January 1955.

By this time, Morison was on the cusp of retiring and so the work was overseen by his successor, John Dreyfus, at the Monotype Corporation. Using Malin's original punches as a model, Monotype's drawing office was able to produce an exceptionally accurate interpretation of the typeface, despite the original being created without any of the character width and spacing restrictions imposed by machine-set technology. Much of this work was done in the Frankfurt factory. Production

ABCDEFG
HIJKLMN
OPQRST
UVWXYZ
abcdefghij
klmnopq
rstuvwxyz

«Monotype» DANTE has been designed for printers *by* a printer. Most printers know quite a lot about what is *required* of type, because they learn from technical experience in handling it just how it behaves under working conditions. But few printers are able to *design* a type, because they lack the ability to draw, and so remain inarticulate about what they know and what they need.

Dr. GIOVANNI MARDERSTEIG, the designer of «Monotype» DANTE, has forty years of experience as a printer in the course of which he has designed four other

moved to London when Monotype sought to enlarge the *Dante* family. Mardersteig resisted; without Malin, who died in 1955, Mardersteig had lost interest in designing type. However, with the gentle persuasion and enthusiasm of a then twenty-year-old Matthew Carter, Mardersteig eventually changed his mind. Monotype *Dante* was released in 1957.

Mardersteig first used his own, original version of *Dante* in 1955 to publish Boccaccio's *Trattatello in Laude di Dante*, after which the typeface was named. Mardersteig did not produce another typeface but other interests flourished. Since the end of the war he had been involved in setting up a commercial printing enterprise, the Stamperia Valdonega – the aim being that standards expected of his Officina Bodoni hand-press should be attained using mechanized, mass-production printing technology. He had assumed that the days of the private press were over but was happily proved wrong, and continued to work at the Officina Bodoni until 1977 and just a few days before his eighty-sixth birthday.

Above and left: Hans Mardersteig, Monotype's 10-point *Dante*, shown enlarged, 1952.

Robert Hunter Middleton USA 1896–1985

Robert H. Middleton was born near Glasgow in Scotland. When he was aged ten his family emigrated to America when his father became the manager of a coal mine in Alabama. Several years later, the family moved to Illinois. Middleton attended the Chicago Art Institute with the intention of becoming a painter. Here he met Ernst F. Detterer (1888–1947). Detterer, only eight years older than Middleton, had recently been appointed as a teacher to instigate a new curriculum in printing and calligraphy. He had travelled around Europe and attended Edward Johnston's classes at the Central School of Arts and Crafts in London. Detterer had a reputation as a serious scholar of letter forms and their history, but was also knowledgeable of contemporary designers and their work in Europe and America. Middleton was inexorably drawn to Detterer's classes, who would remain a hugely influential figure in Middleton's early career.

The Ludlow Typograph Company in Chicago commissioned Detterer to design a 'Venetian' typeface. Linotype and ATF were already developing similar typefaces following the popularity of Bruce Roger's *Centaur* type, published in 1914. All were using Nicolas Jenson's printing of *Eusebius* (1470) as their model, and Detterer followed their example. Like Rogers,[1] Detterer traced enlarged photographs to obtain outlines for the new type, but he was unable to provide the precise drawings Ludlow required. Middleton, on Detterer's recommendation, was hired to do the drawings (he was already drawing the italics under Detterer's supervision). The roman, initially named *Nicolas Jenson*, and first cast in 1923, was later named *Eusebius* to avoid confusion with the ATF and Linotype typefaces released earlier, which also used the Renaissance printer's name.

Middleton expanded *Eusebius* into a complete type family and credited its success to the generous mentoring of master engraver and punchcutter Robert Wiebking (1870–1927), who had previously cut Rogers's *Centaur*. In fact, Wiebking was also

Opposite: Robert H. Middleton, *Radiant*, designed between 1938 and 1941 for the Ludlow Typograph. This page, designed by Middleton, is from a '27 Chicago Designers' group booklet. Publication date unknown.

Below: Robert H. Middleton, *Eusebius*, 1924.

ABCDEFGHIJKLMNOPQRSTUVWXYZ
abcdefghijklmnopqrstuvwxyz   1234567890$

providing a similar service for Frederic Goudy. He introduced Middleton to Rogers who offered advice on the design of *Eusebius*, and they would remain close friends. Although *Eusebius* was considered to be a sound and faithful interpretation of Jenson's types, it never achieved wider acclaim because it was only available to users of the Ludlow Typograph system – not ideally suited for setting textual matter.

The Ludlow Typograph, commonly known as 'the Ludlow', was a common sight in most printing houses. In larger establishments it was used to set headlines which could then be placed within Linotype or Monotype text setting; smaller printers would use the Ludlow as an alternative to Monotype and Linotype machines to set smaller amounts of text. The Ludlow operator would pick brass moulds of each character from a Ludlow case and place them in the proprietary composing stick.[2] The line of moulds would then be locked in place and the composing stick clamped into the casting machine. Molten metal was then injected into the line of moulds to form a solid, single line of type (or 'slug') after which the moulds were returned to their case. The advantage of the Ludlow was that it was simple to use, meaning that training required was minimal, and importantly, it could cast up to 240-point type. In contrast, the Monotype Composition machine cast type up to 14-point, the Monotype Super Caster (available from 1928) to 72-point.

With the design of *Eusebius*, a refined textual face, Ludlow had hoped to persuade a new market – the fine press printer/publisher, a substantial market in the 1920s – to use the Ludlow in place of handset foundry type. Commercially this was naïve, but it was the design of *Eusebius* that enabled Middleton to build what would be a lifelong career at the Ludlow Typograph Company.

In November 1927 Douglas McMurtrie was appointed as director of typography by Ludlow. McMurtrie was a designer who had only recently taken up a post at the Cuneo Press where he planned advertising and undertook the design of fine press books, notably for the Chicago-based limited editions publisher Pascal Covici. He had also designed *Procopius*, a calligraphic sans serif typeface, but this was abandoned after a single use.[3] Prior to Cuneo, McMurtrie had also made a name for himself as a writer concerning printing history and design for the trade press, while his design work for Condé Nast and *The New Yorker* was well known. When he arrived at Ludlow, his instruction was effectively to do what he had been hired to do at Cuneo.

The appointment of McMurtrie followed a growing trend seen in major printing houses and type founding companies. Ludlow would certainly have been aware of the startling effect that the designer William A. Kittredge (1891–1945) had had on the Chicago-based Riverside Press (owned by R.R. Donnelley & Sons) in 1922. Kittredge had previously established a reputation for himself in advertising and book design in Boston, New York, and Philadelphia. When he arrived at the Riverside Press he was appointed as director of design and typography, a fact trumpeted with a direct-mail piece (designed by Kittredge) that attracted wide coverage in the print trade press.[4] Goudy, also Chicago-based, had been appointed 'art consultant' for Lanston Monotype USA in 1920, while further afield in Britain the designer and printer George W. Jones had joined Linotype in 1921 and Stanley Morison had joined Monotype in 1923.

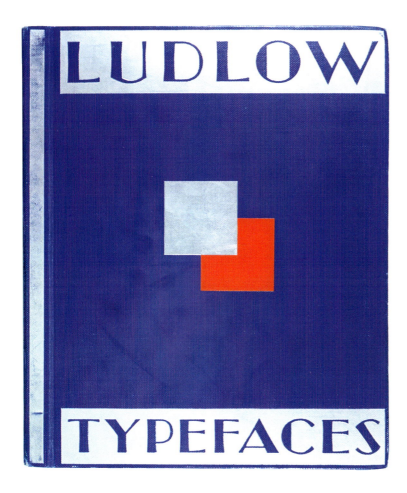

Left: Douglas McMurtrie, cover of Ludlow Typefaces, published in 1936, featuring McMurtrie's *Ultra-Modern*, designed in 1928. The cover of this ring binder is printed in red, blue and silver.

McMurtrie had been an advocate for revivalist typefaces; Middleton's *Eusebius* was a prime example. But in September 1927 he wrote an article titled 'Our Mediaeval Typography' for the *American Mercury*, in which he complained about the lack of originality in American typography. This about-face was probably linked to his involvement in the founding of the Continental Type Founders Association, a company set up in 1925 to import European types to America. Through this he discovered Russian and German experimental typography, and followed the debates concerning New Typography brought to the fore within a special edition of the journal *Typographische Mitteilungen*, (Typographic Communication) edited by Jan Tschichold in 1925. When McMurtrie entered the Ludlow Typograph Company in late 1927, America was still taking tentative steps towards Modernism. His appointment, therefore, was a radical decision (or perhaps the Ludlow management were not aware of McMurtrie's recent volte-face). Nevertheless, McMurtrie would provide Ludlow with

Below: Robert H. Middleton, *Stella*, 1929, and Robert Wiebking, *Ludlow Square Gothic*, c.1921. From a Ludlow type specimen booklet (undated) designed by Douglas McMurtrie.

the distinctive voice they had sought, through his writing and design work, over the next sixteen years.[5] The speedy release by Ludlow of McMurtrie's typeface, *Ultra-Modern*,[6] was an emphatic statement of their support for their new director of typography.

McMurtrie was flamboyant, arrogant, egotistical – and decidedly difficult to work with. The only person, it appears, who escaped his wrath was the ever modest, ever tactful Robert H. Middleton. Middleton was sceptical of McMurtrie's approval of modern typography but would later admit that he (like Goudy, Dwiggins, Cooper and others) thought that Americans would not accept the mechanical geometry of a typeface such as Paul Renner's *Futura*, especially since America already had several fine 'home-grown' sans serif faces, *Franklin Gothic* for example, from which they could choose. (Wiebking's *Ludlow Square Gothic* was based on *Franklin Gothic*.) Wisely, Middleton kept his opinions to himself and, in fact, he and McMurtrie appear to have built a strong and long-lasting working relationship founded, it seems, on a genuine respect for each other's complementary knowledge and skills.

McMurtrie only worked full-time for Ludlow from 1927 to 1931, but continued to work for the company on a consultative basis until his premature death in 1944. Shortly after 1931, Middleton's role became one of directing Ludlow's type development strategy and then he was formally made director of type design in 1933. McMurtrie took the title of director of advertising, principally writing copy and designing Ludlow's distinctive promotional material.

Inevitably, much of Middleton's time was spent providing Ludlow with versions of successful typefaces designed by other foundries. His first task, for example, was to provide a version of Oswald Cooper's hugely successful *Cooper Black* (1921), which was called *Ludlow Black* (1924). Middleton realized, with encouragement from Wiebking and Goudy, that Ludlow needed a type library broad enough to enable the company to compete with its larger rivals. This included new and original ideas as well as type based on rival's models. For much of Middleton's career he would be asked to design types that offered a blend of both – proven and popular design traits, but with sufficient originality to make it one of Ludlow's own. Middleton designed over 100 typefaces, all of them for Ludlow.

When *Kabel*, designed by Rudolf Koch, and then *Futura* appeared in America, Ludlow needed a response and so Middleton

48 POINT
MEDitation
36 POINT
CONGRatulate
30 POINT
THE WICK & CO.
Wm. B. Pollock Co.
24 POINT
THE W. B. LEWIS CO.
The Standard Slag Co.
18 POINT
HELLER BROS. LUMBER CO.
The Christ Mission Settlement
14 POINT
NORRIS BRAKE SERVICE COMPANY
Daughters of American National Council
12 POINT
THE YOUNGSTOWN SOCIETY FOR THE BLIND
Efficiency and speed the most important basis
10 POINT
EVERYTHING IN PRINTING–CARD TO CATALOGUE
If One Job You Do Is Better Than Another One—

Tempo Bold   Ludlow

Above: Robert H. Middleton, *Tempo Bold*, 1930.

immediately began the design of a sans type, but a sans serif that would express what he considered to be American, not German, modernity. The result was *Stellar*, an entirely unique design and not at all like *Futura*. Middleton chose to model *Stellar* on classical roman proportions, with moderately contrasting thick and thin strokes and subtly flaring lines designed to avoid it looking rigid or mechanical. Sales were poor, while the demand for *Futura* continued to grow. Predictably, Middleton was sent back to the drawing board and this time he designed *Tempo*. In its promotional brochure (1930), designed and written by McMurtrie, the roots of *Tempo* are made clear: '*Tempo* is a typeface of the impersonal character so highly esteemed by the proponents of the modern style'. Middleton resigned himself to the fact that *Futura* had to be the goal and so that is what he delivered. Morris Fuller Benton at ATF did the same and called it *Spartan*.

Middleton designed a more notable sans serif at around the same time, called *Record Gothic* (1927–28). It was not dissimilar to Benton's *News Gothic*, but like this, and Benton's earlier sans serifs, Middleton's *Record Gothic* was eclipsed by the new wave of geometric sans serifs. Ludlow appeared to have had little faith in *Record Gothic* from the outset. When released it was only made available in smaller sizes and a medium weight, and although demand slowly grew over the years (helped by McMurtrie regularly using it to good effect on Ludlow's promotional material) nothing was added until the 1950s, when American typographers rediscovered what could justifiably be called their own 'traditional American gothics'. Suddenly *Record Gothic* was in demand, and in 1956 Middleton extended the family to twenty variations of weights and widths, including extra condensed. (A helpful feature of sans serifs is that they are far more capable than serifed faces of undergoing severe modification without losing their identifying features.) *Record Gothic* became Ludlow's most successful typeface. Middleton retired in 1971.

The sole means by which the ever-modest Middleton chose to show and write about his work was through the '27 Chicago Designers' group. This was not an organization as such, but a self-selected group of designers who wished to design and publish a book annually to promote their field of activity. Each member would design four pages displaying their own work for the book, with one member assuming responsibility for the cover design, printing and distribution. It began as a modest, square-format, spiral bound booklet, the first appearing in 1936, and continued

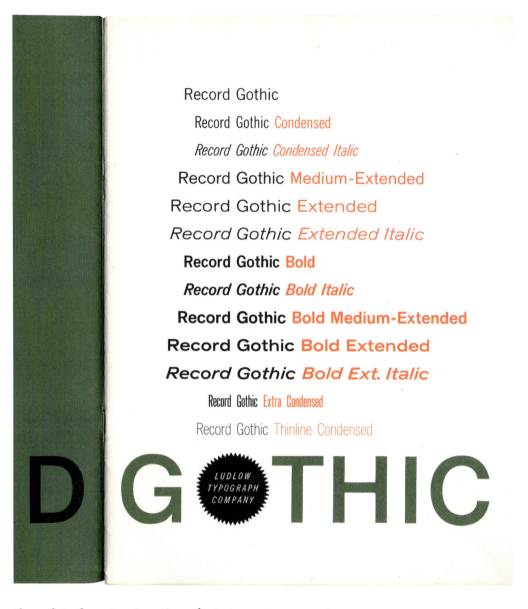

Above: Robert H. Middleton, the eventual extensive *Record Gothic* family, c.1956.

through to the 1960s. Over time, the '27' came to represent a Chicago school of design.[7]

Despite the rapid decline of letterpress printing in the 1960s, Ludlow continued in operation through to the mid-1980s, in part because its matrices could also be used by rubber stamp manufactures. In the early 1980s, the company claimed that 16,000 Ludlow Typographs were still in operation around the world. Nevertheless, the company closed before the end of that decade.

Continental Typefounders

CITY

COMPACT NORMAL   COMPACT BOLD

Georg Trump GERMANY 1896–1959

Georg Trump was born in Brettheim, in Baden-Württemberg where his family had long been farmers and brewers. At the age of sixteen he went to the School of Arts and Crafts at Stuttgart, but his studies were interrupted by the First World War. He joined the army and did not return home until 1919, decorated and having attained the rank of lieutenant.

Trump immediately returned to art school in Stuttgart where one of his teachers was the type designer F. H. Ernst Schneidler, who would later design *Schneidler Mediäval* in 1936 and *Legend* in 1937 for the Bauer type foundry.[1] Schneidler was head of the graphic department from 1920 to 1948, from which a 'Stuttgart School' of calligraphy emerged. As well as Trump, this included Rudo Spemann, Imre Reiner and Walter Brundi. The foundation of Schneidler's teaching was that lettering should not be studied separately from other graphic disciplines. Trump himself would continue to illustrate, often in the form of linocuts, throughout his life.

For almost all of his career Trump was involved in teaching, apart from the first three years following graduation when he lived in southern Italy designing ceramics. He returned to Germany in 1926 to establish a graphics department in the School of Arts and Crafts in Bielefeld in Westphalia. Trump's commitment by this time to New Typography and especially in its application to book design was demonstrated by his active involvement with 'neue Werbegestalter' (modern advertising designers), established in late 1927. Trump was a founding member of this short-lived but highly significant group of designers led by Kurt Schwitters, whose aim it was to further the ideas of New Typography within commercial art and provide a platform for progressive ideas. Other members[2] included Walter Dexel, Paul Schuitema, Jan Tschichold and Piet Zwart, who together organized approximately twenty-two exhibitions between March 1928 and July 1931.

It was an exhibition of Trump's students' work in 1928 at Pressa, a major international printing exhibition in Cologne, that caught the attention of Paul Renner, then director of the recently established Meisterschule für Deutschlands Buchdrucker (Advanced School of Book Printing) in Munich. He invited Trump to come and join him and Jan Tschichold to teach lettering and

Opposite: Georg Trump, *City*, cover of a type specimen published by Continental Typefounders for the American market, c.1931.

typography. Renner was finishing work on *Futura* for the Bauer foundry – a typeface which had already garnered a great deal of attention – while his reputation within the education sector was well established. Trump accepted.

During his initial period in Munich Trump began work on his first typeface, *City*, for the Berthold type foundry. The time and place of its development has led to *City* being aligned with the ideas of the neue Werbegestalter group and New Typography. Its geometric, slab serif structure and predominant right-angles encourage this idea, but it is a far more mature typeface than the 'elemental' letters that make up, for example, Bayer's *Universal*. *City* was released in 1930 and produced in three weights: light, medium and bold, each accompanied with an italic. Tschichold helped to popularize *City* by using it to good effect on the cover of his book *Typographische Gestaltung*. The following year Trump moved to Berlin to become the head of the Kunstgewerbeschule (School of Arts and Crafts). The early 1930s were politically turbulent times in Germany. In 1933 Hitler rose to power and Renner's *Futura* was suddenly considered 'un-German', with the result that he was dismissed from the Munich school (as was Tschichold). Renner was determined that a Nazi appointee should not take his place and so he personally asked Trump to be his successor, who accepted.[3] Perhaps *Trump Deutsch* (1935), a blackletter type and released by Berthold, was, in part, designed as a means of keeping the attention of the Nazi Party away from himself and the school. In the tumultuous circumstances it is remarkable he managed to design any typefaces at all, and yet during the mid-1930s Trump was able to establish what would be a lifelong association with the Weber type foundry in Stuttgart.

Above: Georg Trump, *Trump Deutsche*, 1936.

Below: Georg Trump, *Schadow-Antiqua Bold*, c.1937–38.

SCHADOW-ANTIQUA wurde im Jahre 1936 geschnitten nach Entwürfen von Professor Georg Trump

Type Designers of the Twentieth Century

At this time Weber was an emerging foundry, having grown from a small, local craft-based company at the beginning of the century into a modern and fully mechanized corporation with a national distribution network. Sole owner Emile Ratzky had died in 1928 and his son, Hermann, became Weber's technical manager, while Rudolf Görwitz, who had worked at the company since 1908, became a joint partner and was made its commercial manager. From 1935 until his retirement in 1959, it was Görwitz who was Trump's primary contact at Weber.

Schadow was the first typeface Trump designed for Weber; this would be expanded in the following years eventually to become Trump's second-largest type family. Like *City, Schadow* is a slab serif, but they have little else in common. *Schadow* is infinitely more sophisticated, more refined, and as such, considered to have the 'precision mixed with flair'[4] for which his work would become renowned.

At the outbreak of the Second World War, Trump was again called up to serve in the army, this time as the commander of a reserve battalion based at Füssen near the Austrian border. From there Trump continued drawing and correcting proofs, but under increasing difficulties. The Weber type foundry was remarkably lucky in that their premises remained intact even though much of Stuttgart suffered heavy bomb damage. This meant that, in the aftermath of war, the company was in the fortunate position of being one of very few foundries able to respond to an unprecedented demand for type.

In November 1945, only a few months after the fall of Germany, Trump visited Görwitz in Stuttgart and showed him, among other things, drawings he had made of a 'new Aldine roman'

Below left: Georg Trump, *Forum I* (left) and *Forum II*, 1948–52.

Below: Georg Trump, *Codex*, 1953.

('Aldine' being the name of Aldus Manutius's press). Neither was in a hurry. Trump was finishing work on an addition to *Schadow* – called *Schadow Antiqua Black* – while the Weber foundry was unable to manufacture type fast enough to meet current orders from printers who had lost all their type during the war. In correspondence with Trump (8 January 1946) Görwitz suggested, 'Regarding the new roman, I am not sure how its shapes should look. Similarities to the *Schadow* should be avoided by all means'. Görwitz also dismissed anything 'Bodoni-esk', but, clearly forgetting the drawings Trump had showed him a year earlier, he offered this: 'Could you delve into shapes of the old Aldine? Would it be possible to create something out of this that can address a lack of clear, open romans with unpretentious effect of contrast?' In other words, he reiterated, 'A plain, open roman'.[5]

The years immediately after the war were extremely difficult for Trump. He had been seriously wounded in the final days of the war. In addition to the pain and restrictions caused by his stomach wound, he returned to the Munich school to find that it had been practically destroyed by bombing in January 1944. Rebuilding when there were shortages of every kind was frustrating and slow. Nevertheless, Trump designed several typefaces, some of which suggest the lingering influence of Schneidler, his teacher in Stuttgart, including *Delphin*, in two weights (1951–55) with a warm and energetic italic, and *Codex* (1953), a rough, brush-formed script. These, and other types – for example, *Forum I and II* (1948–52), *Signum* and *Palomba* (both 1955) – were created during a relatively short period of enormous productivity. This was due in large part to Trump having resigned from his post at the Munich school in 1953 because of his fragile health condition.

For the Weber type foundry, the constraints caused by a shortage of raw materials after the war did not recede until around 1948. However, a shortage of staff – and punchcutters in particular – continued to be a problem. As a result, all of Weber's types since 1945 (including those by Trump) had been cut in Leipzig. Efforts to attract punchcutters to Stuttgart failed simply because of a basic lack of housing. It was not until 1949 that a punchcutting department was functioning once more at Weber, established by the arrival of renowned punchcutter Egon Graf from Leipzig.

In June 1947 Trump finished drawing the Aldine roman (called *Industria* at this point), but another two years elapsed during which Trump's other typefaces had been selling well, and so he felt this was an appropriate time to remind Görwitz again of his

'Aldine roman'. This time Trump not only sent photographs of his drawings, but also wrote a detailed commentary and a reminder that the foundry was falling behind its competitors:

> Weber has not published any new roman with medieval style, whereas the Bauer foundry as well as Stempel have both published new romans of this kind. Secondly, despite having these 'rival typefaces' we are still lacking a new modern typeface for books, at least as foundry type … I have strived to design a typeface which has a rather neutral appearance, which abstains from cheap fashion, which is rather economical in space, but yet expresses enough modernity to be considered a contemporary roman.[6]

Görwitz's apparent intransigence was due to the commercial success of his company in the postwar years. In fact, all German foundries were prioritizing production of existing typefaces simply to meet the high demand. However, by the 1950s the preference for roman over blackletter typefaces in Germany had become conspicuous. But it was Weber's commercial and critical success at the first DRUPA print fair, held in Düsseldorf in 1951, that finally caused Görwitz to look more seriously at the prospect of Trump's 'Aldine roman'. Trump's typefaces *Delphin*, *Forum II* and *Amati* had impressed visitors to Weber's exhibition stand, and Görwitz now realized that if his company was to maintain its position alongside its much larger rivals he needed to hold onto Trump and, more specifically, develop his new roman. Görwitz and Trump met at the beginning of 1952 to discuss Trump's typeface – now called *Mauritius*, a reference to one of the world's rarest stamps – and by April the regular weight was finished. Görwitz confidently began to expand his typecutting department to cope with the expected level of demand. Meanwhile, in France the Fonderie Olive published its new typeface *Vendôme*, while both Lettergieterij Amsterdam and Klingspor released new romans – all potential rivals to Trump's typeface.

In December 1952 it was agreed to put Trump's roman, now in two weights and accompanying italics, into production. But to Trump's surprise, Görwitz told him that to save time the type was to be machine cut, not hand-cut. Previously, Trump's drawings had been used as a model to be interpreted by the punchcutter, now he had to produce a set of drawings to a higher level of clarity and precision to serve as a pattern for exact mechanical replication.

Above: Georg Trump, *Amati*, 1951.

Rüfş Émpiré-dävh
HÌDŁØȘȚÅÑĞ
jg.2 MÛJÇK,bțç
ŽFÇ

Above: Georg Trump, drawing for *Trump Mediaeval Regular*, April 1952.

A significant added complication then arose. Görwitz approached Linotype and it was agreed that Trump's Aldine roman would be manufactured for use on their mechanical typesetting/casting machines. This was the first (and only) adaptation of a typeface for machine composition that Görwitz would undertake and Trump, like Görwitz, knew almost nothing about the manufacturing process of matrices. Trump's drawings were assessed at the Stempel foundry, who it had been agreed would oversee the adaptation of Trump's typeface on behalf of Linotype. Some adjustments were necessary in order to conform to the Linotype process, the most significant being that the italic had to be the same width as the roman. Hermann Zapf, who was artistic director at Stempel, provided Trump and Görwitz with helpful information concerning Linotype requirements. Trump understandably felt this level of prescription prohibitive and suggested to Görwitz that two versions of the italic should be made, one for mechanical composition and another for hand composition.

Trump resigned from his teaching post in 1953 due to his war wound. This gave him time to concentrate on design commitments and, by the end of January 1954, the first cut of Trump's 'Aldine' typeface was complete in 16 point. It was a little narrower than earlier versions to make it more economical – this may have been in response to advice from Zapf, whose own *Palatino*, released in 1949–50 by Stempel, had been so successful. Trump was happy to concede because the narrower roman enabled him to design a narrower and more natural calligraphic italic. Having been completely redrawn, the finished results were considered by all to be a huge success and the following month Trump's roman finally received its definitive name: *Trump Mediaeval*. It was Görwitz's idea to name it after its designer. Trump, feeling that his typeface embodied everything he had learned, was happy to accept the suggestion. For the Weber type foundry *Trump Mediaeval* proved to their rivals that it remained a major commercial and creative competitor.

Production did not go as smoothly as anticipated, due in large part to Görwitz's lack of knowledge regarding mechanical composing machines. The intention had always been that while *Trump Mediaeval* would be available with Linotype composing machines, it would also be manufactured by Weber as foundry type for hand composition. Because it was essential that the typeface be compatible, whether set mechanically or by hand, Zapf explained that the foundry version would have to be spaced according to Linotype's technical requirements and Görwitz – and Trump – had no choice but to agree. When two typesetting systems must coexist, the one with most restrictions inevitably imposes its limitations on the other.[7] *Trump Mediaeval* was finally released in 1954; the italic followed a year later. With roman and italic combined this is Trump's masterpiece; inventive yet traditional – original and natural.[8]

Bad Ditzenbach
Zentralverband

Left: Georg Trump, *Trump Mediaeval Regular*, 1954.

MOTS QUI CLAQUENT

A.M. Cassandre FRANCE 1901–1968

A.M. Cassandre (real name Adolphe Mouron) was born in Kharkov, Ukraine, which in 1901 was part of the Union of Soviet Socialist Republics (USSR). His father, Georges, came from an affluent French family in Bordeaux and moved to Kharkov to run a very successful business importing French wines. Adolphe was the youngest of five children. His childhood was split between Paris, where he was educated, and the family mansion at Kharkov where he spent his holidays. When the First World War broke out the Mouron family moved to Paris while Georges travelled back and forth hoping to keep his business viable, but in 1917 the Russian Revolution caused all ties with Ukraine to be abruptly ended.

On leaving school Adolphe decided he wanted to be an artist and began attending the Académie Julian in Montparnasse, a private college renowned for its liberal, congenial approach (this followed a brief and decidedly less pleasant experience at the more traditional École des Beaux-Arts). Although his father was happy to support him, Adolphe wanted to be self-sufficient and so he turned to poster design as a temporary means of supporting himself while studying. This was by no means uncommon, particularly in Paris where 'poster art' by celebrated artists such as Manet, Toulouse-Lautrec, Miro, Picasso, Bonnard etc. had proved hugely popular. Yet there remained a distaste in fine art circles, even at the more liberal Académie Julian, for artistic endeavour being applied to any form of mass communication media. It was deemed a shameful act – a sign of spiritual weakness that would ruin an artist's future reputation. Adolphe conceded and created the pseudonym 'Cassandre', preceded by his intitials.[1]

Cultural developments taking place in Germany during the early 1920s, even those emanating from the Bauhaus, were largely ignored in France, even within avant-garde circles. Neither people nor art travelled much, due in large part to anti-German sentiment which, understandably, remained resolute in France, as it did in Britain. Furthermore, France, unlike Germany, did not have the same urgent need to reconstruct. Paris was a major cultural centre before the First World War and remained one afterwards, attracting artists from all over Europe, Britain, America and, following the 1917 Revolution, from Russia.

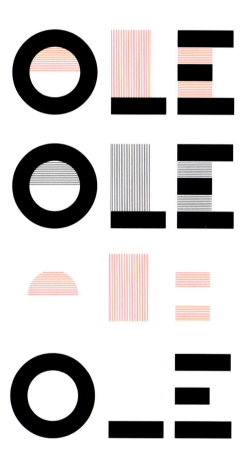

Opposite: A.M. Cassandre, *Bifur*, from *Arts et Métiers Graphiques* Paris, published by Deberny & Peignot, 1929.

Above: A.M. Cassandre, the constituent parts and print options offered by *Bifur*.

Memories of childhood holidays spent in Kharkov meant that Russian culture remained a strong influence on Cassandre, and the aesthetic style employed by young Russian designers who had recently arrived in Paris, such as Alexey Brodovitch, made a big impression. Brodovitch was unusual in that he did not consider himself an artist 'temporarily' working in the commercial maelstrom, but rather someone who was committed to the new popular medium of the streets, shops and theatre. Cassandre also began to consider the art of the poster and the magazine cover to be far more genuinely rooted in contemporary life than his easel painting could ever be. By definition, such graphic work also provided the opportunity to communicate directly and with a far larger and more diverse public. Seeing one of his first commissioned works, the poster *Au Bucheron* of 1923, transferred to vast billboards in central Paris must surely have dismissed any lingering doubts concerning the capacity of graphic communication.

Cassandre's friend, the sculptor Raymond Mason, wrote in 1966:

> Cassandre's initial instinct was the right one. He went out into the street. Look at his designs of thirty-five years ago! What makes them so fresh and bright?...Unquestionably it is because they were made to be viewed in broad daylight. They were conceived to take their place in the thick of life, in the joyous tumult of the street where they spoke to people.[2]

The poster for *Au Bûcheron* won the grand prize at the *Exposition Internationale des Arts Decoratifs et Industriels Modernes* in Paris in 1925. The prevailing style came to be called 'Art Deco', after the name of the exhibition. The exception was the more radical Soviet pavilion designed by the architect Konstantin Melnikov, with graphics and furniture designed by Alexander Rodchenko. Le Corbusier's pavillon, *de l'Esprit Nouveau* (New Spirit), included his diabolical *Plan Voisin* – a monumental scheme consisting of eighteen identical tower blocks in which the workers of Paris could be housed – while Rodchenko's dramatic printed designs used elemental blocks of red, grey and black, synchronized with

Below: A. M. Cassandre, *Bifur*, the two-part solid version. This is taken from the cover of a type specimen published by Continental Type-founders Association for the US market, c.1930. The technical challenges of using *Bifur* are inadvertently but clearly demonstrated – little wonder sales were minimal.

similarly constructed letter-forms. Cassandre was convinced that the design of type should follow the model of modern architecture – to simplify form in order to become more efficient – meaning (in theory) that it would also be easier to read.

At the exhibition Cassandre met Charles Peignot, director of the Paris-based Deberny & Peignot type foundry. It was the beginning of a lifelong association; they were of similar age, both ambitious and excited by the display of modernist ideology that surrounded them. Deberny & Peignot had been created just two years previously by the merger of G. Peignot et Fils and Laurent & Deberny foundries, and Peignot, keen that his company be perceived as a forward-looking and quintessentially French institution, was impressed by Cassandre's lettering on his poster for *Au Bûcheron*. German type foundries had dominated mainland Europe for decades and the New Typography movement, emanating primarily from the Bauhaus, had caught his attention. Peignot wanted to lift Deberny & Peignot and compete with its German rivals, and so he hired Maximilien Vox as director of

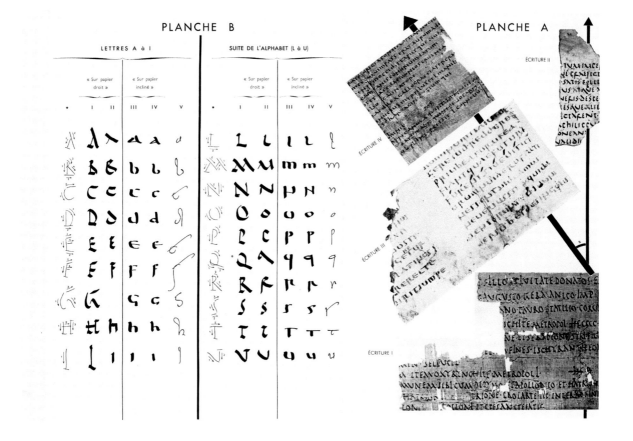

Below: Jean Mallon, 'The problem of the letter's evolution' in a fold-out page from *Arts et Métiers Graphiques*, purporting to show the evolution of roman capitals to lowercase Latin script, 1937.

typography[3] and commissioned Cassandre to design what he hoped would be the ultimate modern typeface.

Bifur was released in 1929. Geometric and modular, consisting of capitals only, its 'form is reduced to its simplest expression', and restores 'to letters everything that belongs to them and to them only'.[4] This description suggests a modern, pared-down typeface that might sit comfortably on a Le Corbusier building. The reality was quite different. Despite Cassandre's admiration for the crisp, immaculate lines of Le Corbusier's architecture, *Bifur* lurches back to a playful and more flamboyant Art Deco style of which Cassandre had previously been critical. Two versions of *Bifur* were released. The regular version included the fine parallel lines integrated with the solid forms that define each letterform, but the second, two-part version included a solid form instead of the fine lines, enabling the two parts that make up each character to be printed separately as two colours. (*Bifur* is from the French word *bifurquer*, to divide into two.) This offered huge potential for creative applications, but it also posed a genuine challenge for the compositor in its assemblage and the printer in its registration.

Bifur provided Deberny & Peignot with the attention Peignot so desperately sought, and gave Cassandre free rein to design a 32-page type specimen brochure (including a silver cover with cut-out) and featured it in his house magazine, *Arts et Métiers Graphiques*,[5] to demonstrate its versatility. Cassandre's design is a virtuoso performance, celebrating *Bifur*'s visual distinctiveness; it effectively comprises twenty-six individual and (especially in the two-part version) almost abstract forms. *Bifur*'s attraction is beyond doubt, in fact it is one of the most attractive (as in 'attention-grabbing') typefaces ever designed – as is the accompanying brochure in which Cassandre incorporated yellow, blue and orange acetate sheets. But Peignot discovered that *Bifur*'s unique individuality was also a problem; no photograph or illustration could compete alongside it. Peignot admitted, '*Bifur* may have been a manifesto, but it was not a brilliant financial operation'. In fact, sales were almost non-existent. Significantly, Peignot decided to buy the rights to Paul Renner's *Futura* (released the year before) from the Bauer foundry in German around this time for exclusive distribution in France, the French colonies and French-speaking countries – changing the name to *Europe*.

In 1930 Cassandre, Charles Loupot and Maurice Moyrand

founded Alliance Graphique, a design studio producing poster work, publishing, advertising and a broad range of 'jobbing' (graphic ephemera) printing. It was relatively short-lived, due to the accidental death of Moyrand in 1934, but it inspired several other independent graphic design studios to be established. In 1935 Cassandre published *Le spectacle est dans la rue* (The exhibition in the street), a collection of his work in a slim, elegant booklet designed with restraint, printed on a substantial paper and bound with a plastic comb. The following year the Museum of Modern Art, New York, mounted an exhibition of Cassandre's posters, establishing his international reputation as a graphic designer (MOMA preferred the term 'graphic artist') commissions for prestigious American magazine covers such as *Harper's Bazaar*[6] and advertising for the American Container Corporation and Ford Motor Company followed. Throughout this extraordinary period, and having learned from the severe practical limitations of *Bifur*, Cassandre was developing the idea of a pared-down typeface – but this time he was determined that it should function in textual setting as well as display. He had long been impressed by the findings of the French palaeographer Jean Mallon (edited versions were published in *Arts et Métiers Graphiques*) into the evolution of roman capitals to lowercase Latin script, and it was through Mallon that Cassandre discovered

There once lived, in a sequestered part of the county of Devonshire, one Mr. Godfrey Nickleby; a worthy gentleman, who, taking it into his head rather late in life that he must get married, and not being young enough or rich enough to aspire to the hand of a lady of fortune, had wedded an old flame out of mere attachment, who in her turn had taken him for the same reason.   Thus two people who cannot afford to play cards for money sometimes sit down to a quiet game for love.   Some ill-conditioned persons who sneer at the life matrimonial may perhaps suggest, in this place, that the good couple would be better likened to two principals in a sparring match, who, when fortune is low and backers scarce,

Left: A.M. Cassandre, *Peignot Medium*. The opening paragraph of Charles Dickens's *Nicholas Nickleby* set in 24 point, ostensibly to demonstrate Peignot's readability. From the *Peignot* type specimen booklet, 1937 (for the cover, see p. 25).

medieval half-uncial calligraphy – essentially an amalgam of upper- and lowercase characters – and a precedence for his ambition of a simplified but fully functional typeface.[7]

Peignot was sympathetic to Cassandre's intentions, but persuaded him to compromise by limiting the more experimental hybrid characters to the lowercase and to include a standard style set of capitals. Whatever Cassandre thought or said, it is likely that he relented with good grace because he named the resulting typeface *Peignot*. The final version, released in 1937, had fifteen standard and eleven hybrid lowercase characters. A major concession, intended to improve its range of application, was that all standard ascenders and descenders be retained. The lowercase characters are softer, having conspicuously rounded apexes (most notable on the 'v' and 'w', and 'm' and 'n').

It was launched with typical aplomb by Peignot in time for the *Exposition Internationale des Arts et Techniques dans la Vie Moderne* (International Exhibition of Arts and Techniques in Modern Life), and used for part of the signage system, invitations and the inaugural printed programme. This ambitious exhibition marked a high point for the Modern movement in France. Covering 250 acres, it had forty-five participating countries and attracted over thirty million visitors. Peignot was in charge of the Graphic Arts and Printing section and organized a display that explained

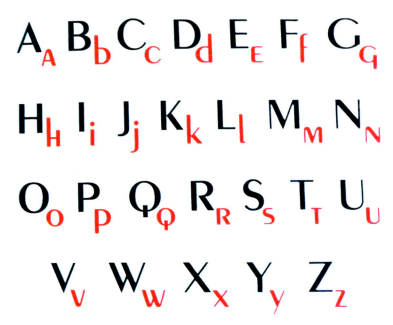

Right: A.M. Cassandre, *Peignot*, upper- and lowercase, from the *Peignot* type specimen booklet, 1937.

the origins and evolution of Cassandre's typeface, supported by a film made by Jean Mallon: *La Lettre*.

Peignot was made available in three weights, and although geometrically constructed it also had a distinctive contrast of thick and thin strokes and a pronounced vertical stress, caused in large part by its bold lines accentuating the uprights. Despite Cassandre's best intentions, Peignot is almost unreadable as continuous text. Unusually, the type specimen produced by Deberny & Peignot was not helpful either; the text was set justified and the inter-word and character spacing is conspicuously uneven. Not surprisingly, Peignot did not bring about the revolution in literacy that Cassandre had hoped for. In fact, it was criticized mercilessly, particularly in France. The journal *Le Courrier graphique* complained, 'Charles Peignot … is correct when he writes that a text in uppercase letters is less legible than in lowercase letters. [But with *Peignot*] a text that combines uppercase and lowercase letters is even less legible than a text in capital letters.'[8]

However, it was not only Cassandre's typeface that drew criticism – much of the exhibition in the French pavillion itself was roundly condemned. Texts, intended to inform, were 'overly detailed and over abundant'. Exhibits were precious and pedantic, their 'sickeningly facile juxtapositions' embarrassingly self-evident.[9] Although it was Peignot who attracted much of this criticism, Cassandre was profoundly affected by the failure of the exhibition and his own typeface. France and Modernism were to remain estranged.

During the Second World War, Cassandre served in the French army until the fall of France. With his design studio long abandoned, he survived by designing stage sets and costumes for the theatre. After the war, *Peignot* grew in popularity, although it was common for purchasers to order the capitals only. Nevertheless, interest was sufficient for the Paris-based Olive foundry to commission Roger Excoffon to design a version of their own (named *Chambord*) but with conventional lowercase characters. Cassandre continued working in the theatre and undertook projects with several famous French fashion houses, designing playing cards and scarves for Hermès and the renowned logo for Yves Saint Laurent. In his later years Cassandre suffered increasingly severe bouts of depression and, in 1968, committed suicide.

Above: A.M. Cassandre, logo design for Yves Saint Laurent, 1961.

Jan Tschichold GERMANY 1902–1974

Jan Tschichold (originally Johannes Tzschichhold) was born in Leipzig. His father was a professional signwriter, and so an appreciation of letterforms as well as a general love and esteem for drawing and painting was, for the young Jan, inevitable.

The city of Leipzig was a centre for printing excellence, and a focalpoint for the harnessing of technological advancement with the popular ideology advocated by William Morris and the Arts and Crafts movement. An exemplary example of this amalgam of ideas was the publishing house Insel Verlag who, under the guidance of Anton Kippenberg, launched the first twelve of a series of books called Insel Bücherei (Island Library) in 1912. Remarkably, two years later, about 150 titles had been printed and over a million copies sold. These slim, pocket-sized books, with their stiff boards – each covered in a different patterned paper and with the title printed separately as a label and attached to the cover – made a deep impression on the young Tschichold. Much later, his work for Penguin Books in England, most notably the celebrated King Penguin series, would take on an almost identical appearance.

Tschichold's initial ambition was to be an artist, but his cautious parents persuaded him to attend the Teacher Training College at Grimma, the idea being that he might become an instructor of drawing. A growing interest in calligraphy, typography and printing caused Tschichold to change direction and attend the Akademie für Künste und Buchgewerbe (Academy of Arts and Book Trade) in Leipzig where he was able to study calligraphy and lettering, in particular that of Edward Johnston and Rudolf von Larisch. He then studied at the School of Arts and Crafts in Dresden and was taught by Heinrich Wieynck, a renowned designer of typefaces – both roman and blackletter.

When Tschichold returned to Leipzig in 1921, he was appointed as an assistant to Walter Tiemann who was teaching evening lettering classes. During this time Tschichold also worked at Pöschel & Trepte (printers of the Insel Bücherei books), where he learned how to set type by hand and also found time to study the excellent collection of type specimen books and writing manuals at the Master Printer's Federation Library in Leipzig.

By 1923 Tschichold was practising what he described, erroneously, as 'the previously unknown profession of typographic designer'

Opposite: Jan Tschichold, working drawings for *Sabon*, the *Penrose Annual*, vol. 61, 1968.

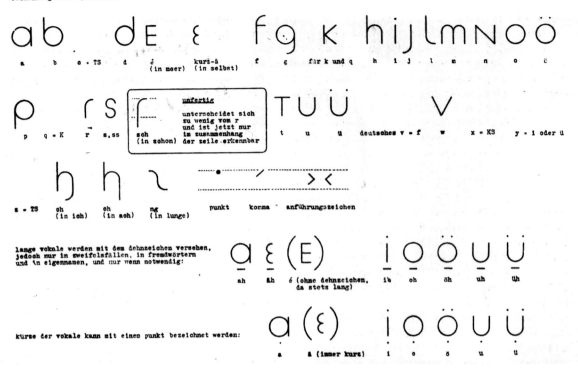

Above: Jan Tschichold's experimental *Universal Alphabet*, c.1929.

with the printing company Fischer & Wittig.[1] It was during the summer of that year that Tschichold travelled to Weimar to see the exhibition of student work produced at the Bauhaus, and his already growing interest in the socio-artistic ideas of the Russian Constructivists was ignited. Suddenly he considered that all his historic knowledge was merely a burden that he had to discard, and for the remainder of the decade he became a willing and eloquent propagandist for the New Typography movement.

The exhibition of 1923 caused the Bauhaus to be recognized far beyond Germany's borders; it was a new kind of art school where 'famous avant-garde painters such as Wassily Kandinsky and Paul Klee were combining forces with craftsmen and industrial designers under the direction of the architect, Walter Gropius'.[2] A little later, a series of groundbreaking books was published by the Bauhaus, notably Oskar Schlemmer's book on the theatre, *The Stage in the Bauhaus*, and László Moholy-Nagy's *Malerei, Photographie, Film* (Painting, Photography, Film). Both were released in 1925, and helped to further promote Bauhaus ideology.

At the height of his evangelizing efforts, Tschichold was offered guest editorship of the October 1925 issue of trade journal *Typographische Mitteilungen* by the German Printing Trade Union. That a print union was willing to provide a platform for a designer – and one with such radical ideas – says a great deal about the enlightened state and confidence of the German printing industry. Outside Germany's borders the print trade was, with a few notable exceptions, highly resistant to the growing influence of the independent typographer. It also reflects positively on the level of commitment to typographic design and interest in communication theory within Germany's print education system.

Despite, or perhaps even because of, the furore created by the views expressed in *Typographische Mitteilungen*, the educational division of the German printing trade union then agreed to publish Tschichold's *Die Neue Typographie* in 1928. This was a typographic design manual which firmly placed typographic practice in the context of literary and visual avant-garde culture, rather than a history of print. For example, Tschichold included the work of Cézanne, Kandinsky, Rodchenko, Man Ray and others, before tracing a path from the free-form textual arrangements of Stéphane Mallmarmé and Guillaume Apollinaire's 'calligrammes'. These, he argued, paved the way for a less conventional reading experience – 'liberating' the typographer from the traditional book form supported by illustrated work by the Futurists, Dadaists and De Stijl.

No concession is made to the printer's expectations of what a printing manual contained, nor any possible assumptions about the traditional structure and nature of standard working methods within the printing trade, despite his publisher being the print trade union. Tschichold explains in his introduction that the purpose of the manual is 'to stimulate … and make the printer aware of himself and the true nature of his work'.[3] As well as his experience working at Pöschel & Trepte and Fischer & Wittig, since 1926 Tschichold had been teaching typographic design and calligraphy at the Meisterschule für Deutschlands Buchdruker (Advanced School of Book Printing), whose director was Paul Renner – so he knew his audience well. However, his correspondence with, for example, Piet Zwart and El Lissitzky, makes it clear that Tschichold also had a readership beyond the printing fraternity in mind.[4]

Die Neue Typographie has a modest appearance – a small quarto format, flexible boards covered in fine black cloth, the title

DISTINGUISHED Government

printed in silver on the spine alone. The utilitarian appearance of the book continues inside with a text set in *Aurora*, an undistinguished sans serif type, its choice being 'limited [by] what the printer had available', although Tschichold also stated that the 'old anonymous sans serifs' were preferable to the new designs such as *Erbar* and *Kabel*, which he thought 'too individualistic'.[5] The combination of this typeface and a hard, high-white coated paper makes for an unpleasant reading experience. The content is organized into two parts of almost equal length. First is a historical and theoretical discussion concerning the 'Growth and Nature of the New Typography'. The second, 'Principal Typographic Categories', is divided into nineteen sub-sections, each dealing with a common 'jobbing' design subject – for example, the typographic symbol, the business letterhead and advertising matter. Magazine design and 'new book design' are also included. All topics are supported by reproductions of graphic work, which also include examples of bad work which Tschichold accompanies with a reasoned critique.

In *Die Neue Typographie* the typographer was urged to grasp an integral role alongside the fast-evolving progress of other communication media such as the telegraph, telephone, radio and film. Tschichold places the typographer beside the architect, engineer and scientist, while aligning the cultural value of the typographer's work with that of the artist, poet, author and film director. The typographer, Tschichold insisted, was now an influential, independent participant in the maelstrom of a fast-changing culture of communication. His authority as a renowned professional typographer, his deep understanding and appreciation of the expertise within the printing trade, to say nothing of his experience teaching at a school for printers, meant that he was by far the best and certainly most eloquent practitioner to explain the origins and purpose, theory and practice, of New Typography to a broader audience.

In contrast, and despite Gropius's intention that his school should actively bring about a reconciliation between artists and

Above right: Jan Tschichold, *Transito*, for Lettergieterij Amsterdam, 1931.

the industrial world, there was no meaningful attempt made to bring the technology of the commercial printer into the Bauhaus. In Weimar, the 'fully equipped print workshop' described in a Bauhaus prospectus was, in fact, more a printmaking workshop, and certainly provided nothing approaching the equivalent facilities of a commercial printing company – as were available at Renner's Meisterschule für Deutschlands Buchdruker.

Design for print was given improved facilities when the Bauhaus moved to Dessau in 1926. The newly constructed Bauhaus building, designed by Gropius, was the likely impetus for the design of a typeface to advance Bauhaus ideology as well as complement the modernity of the school's architecture. The task was offered to Herbert Bayer and the result was *Universal*, a typeface built on a geometric grid (see p. 122). Bayer's methodology aligned with Bauhaus strategy – make the underlying structure unambiguous, and clarity will prevail. These 'reformed' letterforms were lowercase only, sans serif and monoline, their formulation having meticulously stripped away the myriad subtle interventions 'complicating' typefaces cut by the craftsmen during the previous 450 years. As its name suggests, the intention of *Universal* was that it should be validated internationally.[6] Like other experimental 'elemental' typefaces designed at this time – for example, by Josef Albers, a fellow tutor and ex-Bauhaus student, and Van der Leck and Van Doesburg, the latter both founder members of De Stijl, and *Universal Alphabet*, Tschichold's own experimental attempt – Bayer's *Universal* was never put into production.[7]

It is curious that the Bauhaus itself did not generate a manufactured typeface. Indeed, the lack of engagement with the printing or type founding industries by its leading typographic exponents – particularly if compared with Tschichold's active

Left: Jan Tschichold, *Saskia*, Schelter & Giesecke, 1931.

Above: Jan Tschichold, *Zeus*, Schriftguss AG, 1931.

Jan Tschichold

and productive partnership with, for example, the printing trade union – was a major failing of the typographic teaching at the Bauhaus. However, through the distinctive design of printed matter, the Bauhaus did encourage type foundries to seriously consider the idea of a sans serif being capable of a broader application than merely headlines.

Between 1929 and 1931 Tschichold designed three typefaces, all of which were put into production and released in 1931. The first of these was *Transito*. The drawings were completed and sold to Lettergieterij Amsterdam in 1929.[8] Each character is constructed from discrete geometric forms that resemble the stencil letterforms. The rational forms and industrial application of stencilled lettering had made it an attractive concept for avant-garde designers since the 1910s. Tschichold was disappointed with the outcome of *Transito*. Lettergieterij Amsterdam had made amendments to his drawings (or 'sketches' as Tschichold later described them), but Tschichold also admitted that its design had been too hurried. Unfavourable comparisons to his former teaching colleague Paul Renner's *Futura Black*, released in 1929, did not help either – but although Tschichold's opinion of *Transito* was low, he considered it to be 'much better than the idiotic *Futura Black*'.[9]

The second, and far more interesting, typeface designed at this time was *Saskia*. This also has a stencil-like quality, but it can also justifiably be described as an 'italic' as well as a 'sans serif'. It was drawn in just one weight and manufactured by the Schelter & Giesecke foundry in Leipzig. *Zeus*, another hybrid, was Tschichold's third and commercially most successful of these three display faces. All had been created in a rush in order to alleviate financial problems and Tschichold regretted the results, later describing all three as 'superfluous'.[10]

Modernism was an optimistic movement; cultural receptivity to international developments allied to technological progress was key to its purpose. The seizure of power in January 1933 by the National Socialist Party changed everything. All centres of

Below: Jan Tschichold, *Ramses*, closely modelled on Georg Trump's *City*, 1935.

Below right: Jan Tschichold, *Uhertype Standard Grotesk*, closely modelled on Eric Gill's *Gill Sans*, c.1933.

ABCDEFG HIJKLMN

ABCDEFGHIJKLMNOP abcdefghijklmnopqrsßtuv

Modernism in Germany were forced to close or were taken over. The Bauhaus school was a prime target, as were proponents of New Typography. During the years running up to and into the Second World War, the sense of cultural isolation and desolation became absolute in Germany. Renner was forced to resign his teaching post at Munich, and many of those associated with the Bauhaus emigrated if they could. Modernism in Germany was extinguished with remarkable efficiency.

Ten days after the Nazis gained power, Tschichold was arrested in Munich and placed in 'protective custody'.[11] His contact with Russian designers and the presence of Soviet printed material in his flat was sufficient for him to be accused of collaboration with communists, but his close contact with the German printing trade union also gave rise to speculation about Tschichold's 'Bolshevik' leanings. Tschichold remained in detention for a further six weeks. With the help of his friend Hermann Kienzle, director of the Allgemeine Gewerbeschule (School of Arts and Crafts) in Basel, Switzerland, Tschichold emigrated with his wife and their four-year-old son to Riehen on the outskirts of Basel. The brutality of these experiences would have a profound effect on Tschichold's attitude to his work as a typographer.

Kienzle was able to offer some part-time teaching, and Tschichold found work with the print and publishing house of Benno Schwabe. More significantly, Tschichold was also engaged in the design of typefaces for a pioneering phototypesetting system still in development by Uhertype, a company based in Zurich. In 1932 the company built a second, much improved, prototype, and using type adapted by Deberny & Peignot Uhertype printed its first publicity brochure in 1932. Realizing the advantages of having a range of typefaces unique to their machine, Walter Cyliax, acting as a creative advisor to Uhertype, approached Tschichold in May 1933. (Cyliax was also a former student of Tschichold.) He explained that six typefaces were needed quickly: a sans serif, an Egyptian (slab serif) and an old-style serifed face, each to be accompanied with italics. The following month, while still based in Munich, Tschichold had begun work on the first.

This was called *Uhertype Standard Grotesk* and was closely modelled on Monotype's *Gill Sans*; indeed, many of the characters are identical. The reason for this likely to have been Uhertype's demand for popular typefaces that had already proven their commercial viability. This is reinforced by the fact that Tschichold was given so little time – initially just six months to complete six typefaces – suggesting that originality was never an intended outcome. Tschichold's Egyptian typeface was called *Ramses* and appeared in 1935. This time the typeface was remarkably close to Georg Trump's *City* (Trump was a colleague from Tschichold's teaching days at Meisterschule für Deutschlands Buchdruker). Shortly after, development of the Uhertype system began to falter, principally because of unsurmountable problems with the machine itself causing a major funding source to withdraw in 1938. The company closed in 1940.

Tschichold's first book after leaving Munich was published in 1935. *Typographische Gestaltung* (Typographic Design) is A5 format (21 x 14.8 cm), printed and published by Benno Schwabe. Tschichold later described *Typographische Gestaltung* as more prudent than *Die Neue Typographie*; it certainly provided a more pleasant reading experience. The text is set in Monotype *Bodoni* arranged within generous and variegated margins, with headings set in Trump's *City*. The paper is off-white, softer and warmer to the touch, the cover boards are encased in a blue cloth with a printed paper label on the spine. The dust jacket is printed in two colours on uncoated paper. It is an alluring document, almost intimate when compared to *Die Neue Typographie*. Danish, Swedish and Dutch editions quickly followed.

However, it was not until after the war that Tschichold declared his final disillusion with New Typography, set out in an article titled 'Glaube und Wirklicheir' (Faith and Reality). He explained:

> It seems to be no accident that this [New] typography was practised almost exclusively in Germany and hardly found acceptance in other countries. In particular, its intolerant attitude corresponds to the German inclination to the absolute, its military will to order and claim to sole domination correspond to those terrible components of the German character that unleashed the rule of Hitler and the Second World War.[12]

This uncompromising statement is a rejection of any autocratic ideology that aimed to prescribe intolerance in place of the rich variety of human practice. Before 1923, Tschichold had had a deep affinity with the craft and scholarship of calligraphy, typography and printing, so this was a reversion – the rediscovery of human endeavour and accomplishment. Following publication of *Typographische Gestaltung* in 1935, Tschichold travelled to Denmark to give lectures and to Britain, where the publisher Lund Humphries mounted an exhibition of his work in their London offices, organized by Eric (Peter). This would lead to Tschichold being commissioned to design Lund Humphries' stationery and then the 1938 volume of *Penrose Annual*, printed and published by them. Shortly after his exhibition, the journal *Typography*, edited by Robert Harling, printed the first serious article on Tschichold's work to be published in the UK. This was followed by an invitation to present a talk to the Double Crown Club. Established by Oliver Simon, Stanley Morison and Francis Meynell, the club was at the heart of British New Traditionalism but happily pursued an open-minded attitude towards divergent ideas regarding type and typography (the lively open discussion that followed Tschichold's talk included contributions from Maholy-Nagy – briefly living in London before moving on to New York – and Herbert Read).

It is easy to see that why the welcome received by Tschichold, especially from Eric Gregory, Ruari McLean and Oliver Simon, all admirers of German printing culture, would make his decision to take up the offer from Penguin Books to work in England much easier so soon after the war. Tschichold's prodigious work at Penguin, from 1947 to 1949, established what was, effectively, the final legacy of British New Traditionalist typography.

Penguin Books were printed in vast numbers (most titles were expected to achieve at least 500,000 sales) and occupied the presses of numerous printing companies around Britain. Tschichold's reform of Penguin's books began by establishing the role of the typographic designer as an independent practitioner, outside the printing industry and yet in control of every aspect of the final printed outcome. His *Composition Rules*, set out on four A5 pages, was a guide for printers – comprising elemental but essential instructions on issues such as spacing for words and punctuation marks, the setting of footnotes and page numbers, and other finer details of composition. It was through these basic rules, along with the collaboration of vigilant copy-editors, that Tschichold gained control of typographic standards across all Penguin publications. He was, of course, merely demanding standards to which any self-respecting printing office would aspire. That compositional instructions were deemed necessary, and enforced in such a public manner, was deeply resented across the print industry, but printers wanting to retain lucrative work

from Penguin had no alternative but to comply and abide by Tschichold's rules.

Tschichold's finest typeface, *Sabon*, was also his last, designed between 1964 and 1967. The German Master Printers' Association had decided they wanted a typeface that would look identical whether produced from hand-composed foundry type, Monotype matrices or line cast by a Linotype. The Association stipulated that the appearance of the typeface, its weight and x-height, should be based on the popular Monotype *Garamond* of 1922, but 5 per cent narrower to add efficiency to its merits. Tschichold appears to have relished working to a constricted brief and within the confines and complexity of its technical demands.

The type specimen sheet that Tschichold used as his original source, for both the roman and italic, had been printed by Konrad Berner who, in 1580, had taken over a successful printing and type founding business in Frankfurt from Jacob Sabon. Berner, unusually, included the punchcutter's name of each typeface on each specimen sheet, and Claude Garamond appears several times. Tschichold's drawings for the roman were based on a Garamond; the italic was based on type cut by another Frenchman, Robert Granjon.

Because Linotype technology required that the italic be the same width as the roman, Tschichold's italic had to be considerably wider than Granjon's. Another consideration for Tschichold – one necessary for all twentieth-century revivals of fifteenth- and sixteenth-century types – is that Garamond cut his type to be printed onto a rough-textured, dampened, hand-made paper (and of uneven thickness), meaning that the sixteenth-century printer had to apply considerable pressure to ensure a fulsome contact between type and paper. In the 1960s, power-driven, precision-built presses and the use of smooth, even, dry, machine-made paper meant that the contact between type and paper required little more than a 'kiss' to transfer a clean and bright image of the type to the paper surface. So, to achieve the same printed outcome that Garamond aimed for, Tschichold drew his characters comparatively heavy.

Tschichold's completed drawings were handed to the technical experts employed at Frankfurt by all three joint manufacturers. Two weights were ordered. The semi-bold required sufficient contrast to allow it to be used in conjunction with the *Sabon Regular* as a distinctive, bolder type, but, at the same time, not so heavy as to exclude its independent use for work such as bibles

and prayer-books where the type is generally small and the paper thin.

The apparent effortless success of *Sabon* is deceptive. It was cut by Monotype's Frankfurt works where the Stempel foundry, which manufactured matrices for Linotype, was also based. Considering the enormous technical demands, the design-to-manufacturing process went remarkably smoothly – but harmony was precisely what Tschichold sought. *Sabon* is a typeface tempered by a strong and principled sense of restraint and propriety. The text of *Penrose Annual*, vol. 61 (1968), was set in *Sabon* and included a glowing appraisal by Monotype's John Dreyfus.

Opposite and above: Jan Tschichold, *Sabon*, cover and spread from the type specimen published by Stempel. *Sabon* was released jointly by Monotype, Linotype and Stempel in 1967.

äbcdefg

£$1234

Berthold Wolpe GERMANY/GREAT BRITAIN 1905–1989

Berthold Wolpe grew up as part of a Jewish family in Offenbach am Main, where his father practised as a dentist. When he was seventeen, he met Rudolf Koch, one of the most respected type designers, calligraphers and lettering teachers in Germany, who was working for the Klingspor foundry in Offenbach. On finishing secondary school education, Wolpe was apprenticed as a bronze caster at a bell foundry and one of his first experiences as a typographer was drawing and engraving the lettering that became an integral part of the bells.

Wolpe also attended lettering classes at Offenbach's Technische Lehranstalten (Technical Institute) where Rudolf Koch had established a workshop three years previously and whose students designed metalwork and tapestries as well as lettering. In 1929 Wolpe became a teaching assistant to Koch, and by this time was also teaching calligraphy at the Kunstschule (Art school) in Frankfurt. His talent and dedication clearly impressed – he was invited to become a member of the Offenbacher Werkstatt, a small, informal group or inner circle, consisting of Koch and about six of Koch's pupils. They met and worked in the attic rooms of the school building where they carried out lettering projects under Koch's guidance.

Wolpe was involved with the 1927 *Offenbacher Haggadah*, a book commissioned by Siegfried Guggenheim that contained songs, prayers, explanations and instructions for a Seder evening.[1] While the book itself (a limited edition of 300) is set in Koch's *Jessen* typeface, Wolpe created the Hebrew lettering. He was involved in a number of Koch's projects, including some editions of the ABC-Büchlein (alphabet books) in 1934. He designed his first typeface in 1932, called *Hyperion*,[2] a distinctive italic for which the punches were cut by Paul Koch (Rudolf Koch's son) in one size only. The Bauer type foundry then produced a full range of sizes which were used in two books designed by Wolpe: *Handwerkerzeichen* (Craftsman's Marks) in 1936, and *Schmuckstücke und Marken* (Jewellery and Brands) in 1938. But the type was not made commercially available until after the war.

Opposite: Berthold Wolpe, a drawing of the *Albertus* lowercase characters. *Albertus* was initially released as a set of titling capitals in 1932. Lowercase and other characters were added by 1940.

Below: Berthold Wolpe, *Hyperion*, 1932.

ABCDEFGHIJKLMNOPQRSTUVWXYZ
abcdefghijklmnopqrstuvwxyz 123456

Wolpe's first visit to England was in 1932, when he met Stanley Morison at Monotype. Morison was a great admirer of Koch and they often met when he visited Germany,[3] and so it is likely Wolpe had been introduced to Morison previously. Morison was impressed by lettering Wolpe had made in bronze and invited him to design a typeface for the Monotype Corporation based on the bronze letters. The result would be *Albertus*. It was destined to be a huge success, but the circumstances for Wolpe during the period of its design were enormously strained. After 1933 and the rise to power of the Nazi Party, the situation for Wolpe in Germany rapidly deteriorated. Koch had lobbied on Wolpe's behalf, but died suddenly in 1934 aged fifty-seven. In 1935 Wolpe lost not only his teaching positions, but was also forbidden to pursue any work as a designer. Thanks to his contacts in England, principally Francis Meynell – politically connected, typographer, publisher, and admirer of Koch – Wolpe was able to emigrate there, taking his mother and sister with him.

On his arrival Wolpe met Morison to discuss the progress of *Albertus* and, probably on Morison's recommendation, he began working at the Fanfare Press in Bedford Square. Charles Hobson, a colleague of Morison, had recently sold the Press, but the new owners, London Press Exchange Ltd, had kept Ernest Ingham in charge of printing. Fanfare would achieve an excellent reputation for fine printing, sufficient for Francis Meynell to commission it to print eleven editions of his renowned Nonesuch Press books. Wolpe was in stimulating company, and would stay there for the next four years.

Later the same year, *Albertus* (named after Albertus Magnus, the thirteenth-century German philosopher and theologian) was released by Monotype. *Albertus Titling* appeared first in the *Monotype Recorder* of summer 1935. A roman upper- and lowercase set followed in 1938; bold and light versions arrived shortly afterwards in 1940. A highly distinctive typeface, the

Right: Berthold Wolpe, *Tempest Titling*, from a specimen sheet published by the Fanfair Press, *c.*1936.

228 Type Designers of the Twentieth Century

crisp and substantial letterforms were based on characters cut by Wolpe into metal with a chisel, not drawn onto paper with a pen. This, as Wolpe himself explained, 'gives [Albertus] a sharpness without spikiness, and as the outlines of the letters are cut from the outside (and not from the inside outwards) this makes for a bold simplicity and reduces the serifs to a bare minimum'.[4]

The London Press Exchange Ltd was an advertising agency, and sometimes influenced Wolpe's activities. *Cyclone*, designed by W. Ingram, was a typeface adopted for the branding of BOAC (British Overseas Airways Corporation, the state-owned British airline established in 1939), though not exclusively; *Cyclone* was cut by Monotype and used by Wolpe and others at the Fanfare Press on numerous jobbing projects.[5] Wolpe was also tasked with designing typefaces for the exclusive use of the Press. *Tempest Titling* (1936) was the result of lettering drawn for a book jacket design for a Louis Golding novel, *The Pursuer*. This was one of many covers Wolpe designed for the publisher Victor Gollancz while at Fanfare. Intended purely for display work, *Tempest Titling* was bought and cut in two sizes by Monotype at 48 and 60 point.

During this highly productive period at Fanfare, Wolpe also designed two typefaces commissioned by Monotype: *Sachsenwald* in 1937, a bold calligraphic blackletter, but with romanized capitals with the British reader in mind (though also sold in Germany until 1941), and *Pegasus*, also in 1937. *Pegasus* was commissioned by Monotype to be the text counterpart to Albertus but did not fare well. It was cut in only one size by Monotype and then overlooked. However, when the Victoria and Albert Museum mounted an exhibition[6] to celebrate Wolpe's seventy-fifth birthday in 1980, *Pegasus*

Top: Berthold Wolpe, pen and ink drawings for *Pegasus*, 1937.

Above: Berthold Wolpe, *Sachsenwald*, 1937.

was adapted for composition on the Linotype VIP filmsetter, a process aided by Matthew Carter. Wolpe designed new italic and bold versions. Four years later, Linotype released *Pegasus* for digitial setting.

As the inevitability of war became ever more real it was proving impossible for Wolpe to organize the correct paperwork to stay in Britain; when war broke out in 1939 he was 'relocated' to Australia. Once again, someone – this time Morison – was able to extricate Wolpe and got him back to England in 1941. Later the same year he met Margaret Smith, a painter and sculptor in wood and stone, and they were married. Once married to a British citizen Wolpe was finally granted permission to permanently stay in Britain, and in the same year he began working for the publisher Faber & Faber in London.

At that time, Richard de la Mare (son of the poet Walter de la Mare) was in charge of book design at Faber & Faber and much else – he was director for twenty years and chairman for ten, having been at the firm since it was founded in 1925. He had already assembled a formidable team of freelance book jacket artists including Barnett Freedman, Rex Whistler, Edward Bawden, McKnight Kauffer, Paul Nash, Eric Fraser and Reynolds Stone. He had long admired the work of Wolpe, and was pleased to lure him away from Fanfare.

The 1930s had been a distinguished decade for Faber & Faber, a period in which the format and house style had been securely established. Wolpe must have found the atmosphere within the design department particularly congenial, especially after the trials of the previous eighteen months. The war years demanded an economy of means that worked in Wolpe's favour. It enabled him to demonstrate how calligraphy and typography alone, often using just one or two colours on a plain ground, could replace the more elaborate art and process work that the company had experimented with during the previous decade. The war also influenced the appetites of readers and the topics of books published. Political and military topics were, of course, popular, but also books on what today would be called 'self-sufficiency' were much in demand: farming, gardening, bee-keeping, pig-curing and many more. Some of Wolpe's most resourceful and effective design work appeared on these utilitarian wartime books. 'Legibility and clarity; the dust jacket is a poster for the book' was his clarion call.[7]

Wolpe shared his studio at Faber & Faber with David Bland, who was head of the department, which also included six production/

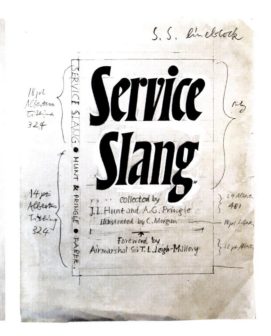

Above left: Berthold Wolpe, *Albertus*, single specimen sheet published by Monotype. c.1940.

Above right: Berthold Wolpe, original artwork for Faber & Faber's book cover for *Service Slang*, 1943.

design assistants. Although Wolpe did not design every cover, he always snatched the authors and books he wanted – well in excess of 1,500 between 1941 and 1975. Authors were understandably delighted not just to have their titles published by Faber & Faber, but adorned with a Wolpe jacket. Many of the great writers, and particularly those published in the 1950s and 1960s – Auden, Eliot, Larkin, Hughs, Golding, Plath and Beckett among others – came to be defined (and reputations enhanced) by Wolpe's authoritive, calligraphic lettering and by the emphatic presence of *Albertus*, often referred to as 'Faber lettering'.[8] In Wolpe's hands, *Albertus* was capable of infinite flexibility and expressiveness.

Despite his prodigious output for Faber & Faber, Wolpe continued to teach and he attached great importance to this work. He taught at the Camberwell College of Art (1948–53) and at the Royal College of Art within the school of graphic design (1956–75), and also ran a lettering course at the City and Guilds School of Art (from 1975 onwards). He also undertook a number of distinctive projects such as a new masthead for *The Times* (1966), as well as the popular British icons of the 1950s, the *Eagle* comic and its sister paper *Girl*, both published by the Hulton Press. He also created two new typefaces: floriated capitals called *Decorata* for the Westerham Press in 1955, and an italic to complement Edward Johnston's *Underground Alphabet* typeface for London Transport called *LTB Italic* in 1973, but not implemented.

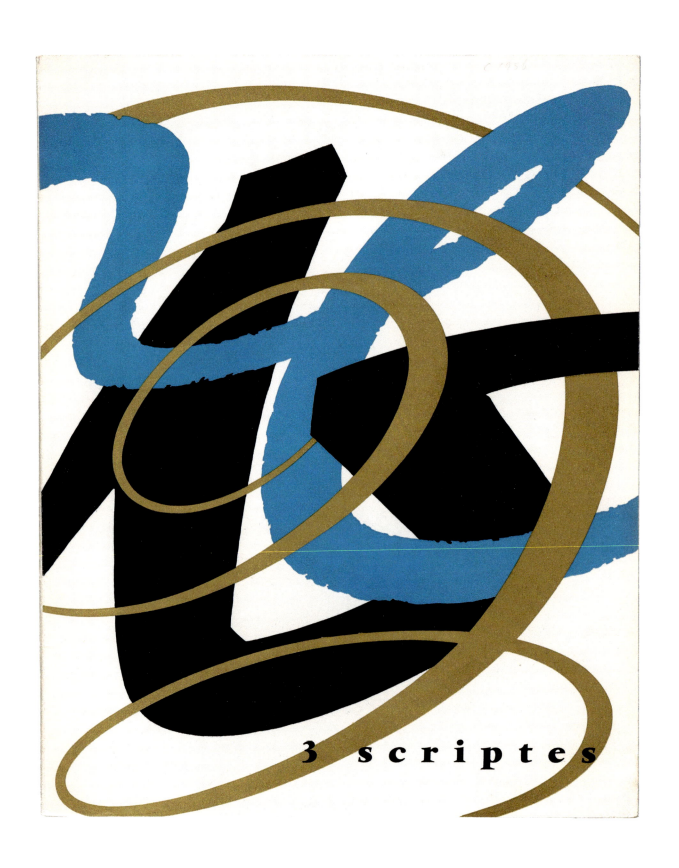

Roger Excoffon FRANCE 1910–1938

Roger Excoffon was born in Marseille. His father owned a flour mill, and also served as a judge in Marseille's court of trade. When his elder brother decided to become a lawyer, Roger followed suit. He studied law at the University of Aix-en-Provence; when he gained his degree he moved to Paris to study law and philosophy at the Sorbonne University. However, in Paris Roger discovered contemporary art, and in particular the dynamism distilled in the paintings of Georges Mathieu and Hans Hartung. A dramatic change of direction then took place.

Excoffon spent the next ten years, from 1930, painting and drawing, but he never exhibited or sold anything. With a war imminent, Excoffon was depressed, realizing how little he had achieved – especially since 1936, having a young family to consider. 'At thirty years old I was a failure, a damp squib; I had done nothing. I passed my time observing, drawing, painting. I possessed some means, though very modest, which allowed us to live in Paris meagrely; middle-class but simultaneously as young foes of convention'.[1] The outbreak of the Second World War forced Excoffon to re-evaluate his life.

His experience as Gunner Excoffon in the artillery was brief and uneventful. Armistice between France and Germany took place on 22 June 1940 and Excoffon briefly returned to Marseille, where he heard that Robert Alexandre's advertising agency in Paris required a commercial artist. He applied and got the job. For him the next five years of French occupation were spent in the company of illustrators, typographers and writers, while learning about print and the printing.

Of the French type foundries still in business following the war, the three most significant were Deberny & Peignot, Fonderie Typographique Française (FTF), both in Paris, and Fonderie Olive. Although not as large as its Parisian rivals, Fonderie Olive, a family run business based in Marseille, was directed by the young and ambitious Marcel Olive who had taken over from his father shortly before war broke out. In 1945 it was finally possible for Olive to consider how the company might expand and compete with its rivals. Olive's wife was Roger Excoffon's sister, and over lunch one day Olive asked his brother-in-law if he would take over as art director of Fonderie Olive's agency in Paris. Excoffon later explained, 'I had never held a paid position in my

Opposite: Roger Excoffon, cover of a type specimen booklet for Fonderie Olive, featuring three of Excoffon's script typefaces: *Choc* (black), *Mistral* (blue) and *Diane* (yellow ochre), 1956.

life [a typical exaggeration]. I was 35 years old and responsible for a family with two children. My answer was "yes".'² Excoffon's only practical experience of type design was two weeks during the war spent drawing an inline version of *Banville* for Olive at the foundry in Marseilles. He did a good job, although he did not enjoy the experience. However, the opportunity to work in Paris was a huge bonus. For Olive it must have been a gamble, but it turned out to be the beginning of a productive, lucrative and remarkably creative partnership.

Ensconced in Olive's Paris agency, Excoffon was responsible for the design of all advertising and general promotion of the foundry's typefaces through specimen sheets, leaflets, trade magazines and exhibition stands, as well as general ephemera such as stationary, business cards and labels. In addition, Excoffon found himself supervising the design of typefaces, and as the only draughtsman in the Olive agency studio he quickly realized he needed assistants in-house to help render the precise forms required. Most important of these was José Mendoza y Almeida, who had worked as a graphic designer for Clichés Union, a photo-engraving company, and who then spent a year working for Maximilien Vox before joining the Fonderie Olive's Paris agency. Excoffon learned quickly from the expertise he gathered around him, and when Marcel Olive suggested that a typeface that had been developed a few years earlier should be revisited, refined and made ready for production, Excoffon decided to undertake the task himself.

The original version, registered by Olive in 1942 and probably cast and marketed immediately after Liberation in May 1945, was called *Cabourg*.³ It had many similarities to Cassandre's *Peignot* (released in 1937). In Excoffon's version, now named *Chambord*, the contrast in line thickness is less pronounced, the overall weight a little bolder. He also altered the form of some of the capitals – adjustments which then required the whole character set to be redrawn. *Chambord* is superior to both *Cabourg* and *Peignot* although, in the circumstances, Excoffon should not be given sole credit for the design of *Chambord*.

As if to demonstrate *Chambord*'s superior readability over its rivals, one of the first advertisements on its release took the unusual form of a long text (coincidentally, Charles Peignot had done the same when promoting Cassandre's *Peignot*), whose content amounted to a company manifesto describing a respect for tradition but expressed in a distinctly cool yet elegant

Above: Roger Excoffon and François Ganeau, *Chambord Medium, Semi-bold, Bold* and *Condensed*. Fonderie Olive, 1946–47.

Chambord – described as being the very hallmark of French typographic modernity. An advertising campaign was devoted to *Chambord* throughout 1948, and it became the foundry's first significant national success.

Chambord's triumph was marred by accusations that Excoffon had seen proofs of a typeface in development at Deberny & Peignot named *Touraine* and that *Chambord* was a blatant copy. In fact, *Touraine* was basically Cassandre's *Peignot* but with new alternative and more traditional cuts (entrusted to Guillermo, father of José Mendoza) of eight lowercase characters ('a', 'e', 'g', 'h', 'm', 'n', 'r' and 'u'). Begun around 1942, for reasons unknown *Touraine* was not released until late in 1948 – and, importantly, after the release of Excoffon's *Chambord*. It has been suggested that Peignot moved to sue Olive, although no official documents appear to exist.[4] It is also not known if Excoffon had a copy of *Touraine* but in a later conversation with Peignot he implied, perhaps mischievously, that he had. This conversation was relayed to John Dreyfus who later wrote:

> Charles Peignot once told me with a chuckle that when he suggested to Excoffon that the similarity between *Chambord* and *Touraine* was a little too close for comfort, Excoffon tried to set Peignot's mind at rest by assuring him that he had kept Cassandre's design in front of him all the time he was working on *Chambord* – 'just to make sure that he didn't copy a single letter'.[5]

Peignot and Excoffon apparently remained good friends regardless of the fierce commercial and creative rivalry between their respective foundries. However, the difficulty of establishing the legitimacy of authorship and ownership of a typeface's design had never been better illustrated. Later, during the 1950s when Peignot was involved in the development of phototypesetting,[6] he and others (including Excoffon) founded the Association Typographique Internationale (ATypI) with the purpose of fighting against illegal copying of type designs. Peignot explained, 'I created ATypI as a place where artists and industries could regroup to fight against the copy. If artists are not protected like authors and creators are in other domains, they will renounce typographic creation'. It is interesting to note the names described as being the ten European typographers best qualified to assist in settling the framework and policy of the Association: Stanley Morison, Konrad Bauer, G.W. Ovink, Walter Tracy, Jan van Krimpen, Hans Mardersteig, Jan Tschichold, Max

Above: Roger Excoffon, *Banco*, 1951.

Caflisch, Roger Excoffon and Hermann Zapf. Peignot's cause met with minimal success.[7]

Fonderie Olive, helped greatly by the success of Excoffon's *Chambord* and a reinvigorated advertising industry in the postwar years, provided the incentive for Marcel Olive to concentrate on developing new display types – typefaces that did not have to be cut in ten or fifteen sizes, all in roman, italic, and three or four weights. Display faces could, instead, be highly effective in just three or four sizes, making its manufacture cheaper and sales highly profitable.

Excoffon's second type for Olive was more original than *Chambord*. Named *Banco* – an allusion to a term used by gamblers playing baccarat – it is all but impossible to classify. *Banco* is a sans serif, yet also cursive type, but without direct reference to any historic scripts. As such, its extraordinary appearance in 1951 came to represent, for good or bad, the decade in which it was designed. It was either 'expressing France's regained freedom and light-heartedness'[8] or, alternatively, the renunciation of everything for which France had once been admired – elegance, sophistication and flagrant intellect. Chosen by jobbing printers, signwriters and neon sign manufacturers alike, it was applied to every kind of business in which speed, expediency and cheapness was the primary concern. It is not surprising, then, that *Banco* came to represent what many considered to be a shabby decline in French graphic culture and inner-city landscape during the 1950s. Oxcoffon explained in *Le Courrier*, July 1951, the reason for its popularity, especially where competition between small businesses was acute: 'The violence of *Banco* was prefigured in the cacophony of advertising campaigns. This forceful typeface

Below: Roger Excoffon, *Mistral*, 1953.

was designed not to talk but to shout'. Such a statement might have been good for business, but it only reinforced the belief that *Banco*, so redolent of the period, epitomized what many saw as a postwar moral decline in French culture.

This conclusion was given added credence by the fact that *Banco* was produced by Fonderie Olive with the sole intention of stealing a march on its chief rival, Deberny & Peignot. It had begun when Excoffon saw an article in a trade journal concerning the work of type designer Marcel Jacno. Alongside the text was a photograph of Jacno working on a new typeface, called *Jacno*, for Deberny & Peignot. What the country's premier foundry was planning would naturally be of interest to any other foundry, but especially to Excoffon who knew that Olive sought nothing

Above: Roger Excoffon, *Choc*, Fonderie Olive, 1955. Some accented 'a's were subtly redrawn, giving emphasis to *Choc's* calligraphic spirit.

better than to publicly outmanoeuvre his rival. As Excoffon later explained:

> The next thing I did – to be perfectly honest – was to indulge in some industrial espionage. I took my magnifying glass and examined the photo as closely as I could, focusing on the typeface that Jacno was drawing. I looked at what could be seen of it, though quite faint, and managed to get an idea of the style of the letters. I immediately talked this over with Marcel Olive. Then I rapidly made some sketches for a few letters ... not identical, but of the same family, and notified Marcel Olive. He said 'Banco', but on condition that the type be ready within two months. The rest is a success story.[9]

As they had done with *Chambord*, Fonderie Olive launched *Banco* before Deberny & Peignot's *Jacno* and, as intended, stole a march on their rival. Perhaps due to a lack of time, *Banco* was cast as a titling typeface only.

Despite the questionable moral issues (although, as evidenced throughout this book, there was a cavalier attitude towards intellectual copyright throughout the type founding industry), *Banco* is not only a more innovative typeface to *Jacno* it is also significantly different, and despite Excoffon's candid statement about the origins of *Banco*, accusations of plagiarism were never made. However, to no one's surprise, *Banco* itself was copied by various foundries including a close version called *Ritmo*, designed by Aldo Novarese for the reputable Nebiolo foundry in Turin.

Above right: Roger Excoffon, cover of a Fonderie Olive type specimen using half-tone screens within which a number of Olive's display faces are shown, *c*.1955.

Banco was the first of what would become a series of display typefaces by Excoffon that were characterized by their energy, boldness and gestural lines, and which doubtless owed their origins to the paintings of Georges Mathieu and Hans Hartung so admired by Excoffon as a student. *Mistral* and *Choc* were based on Oxcoffon's own handwriting, with *Mistral* (1953) being reminiscent of a soft-grade pencil on textured paper in which the lowercase letters are ingeniously designed to connect and flow into each other; it was a considerable technical achievement. *Choc* (1955) is heavier; it was the result of various efforts to design a bold weight for *Mistral*. It is heavier towards the top (as is the case with *Banco*), more compact, and distinctly brush-like in appearance.

Excoffon was fascinated by half-tone screens, and had on several occasions used them to good effect on Fonderie Olive promotional literature since the early 1950s. Perhaps inspired by the early monochromatic Op Art paintings of Paris-based artist Victor Vasarely, begun in 1956, Excoffon began experimenting with an enlarged print of a half-tone screen by rolling it up and looking through the tube and imagining letterforms that replicated the effect. That Marcel Olive encouraged Excoffon in this speculative venture demonstrates their mutual trust and shared sense of creative spirit – all the more remarkable considering the inevitable problems that lay ahead in attempting to reproduce such complex letterforms in metal.

According to José Mendoza y Almeida, who led the project:

> Excoffon made sketches of the outlines of each character and in the studio shading was added by airbrush. The airbrush shading was converted to a dot-screen [which then had to be hand-rendered]. It was quite a challenge to transfer the drawings with a pantograph and to scale these complex drawings in different type sizes to the matrices.[10]

Below: Roger Excoffon, *Calypso*, 1958.

The typeface was called *Calypso*, incorporating capitals and essential punctuation only. It was cast in four sizes: 20, 24, 30 and 36 point.

It was not until 1962 that Excoffon revealed the project that had preoccupied him, on and off, for seven years. Initially called *Catsilou*, his *Antique Olive* is a sans serif – 'antique' being a common name for 'sans serif' in France – with unusual horizontal expansiveness and unusual inverted stress (by now a hallmark of Excoffon), and horizontal strokes wider than vertical strokes throughout. It also has an exceptionally large x-height, leaving minimal space for ascenders and descenders. These characteristics were the result of Excoffon reading Émile Javal's findings concerning legibility, recounted in *Physiologie de la lecture et de l'écriture* (Physiology of Reading and Writing);[11] his findings had influenced a number of twentieth-century type designers, notably T.L. De Vinne and Morris Fuller Benton. Javal concluded that the reader's eye moves along the top of the x-height in a series of movements, rather than a smooth glide along the centre of each word as previously supposed. Javal's other key finding was that clarity of form within the x-height was crucial, and that reading was made easier if individual letterforms flowed from one to another (without touching) to form distinctive word-shapes. Hence, Excoffon's emphasis being placed on the top of the x-height rather than the base, his extremely large and open x-height and, wherever possible, strokes – for example of the 'c' and 's' terminating vertically. *Antique Olive* was first released in a wide, ultrabold weight called *Antique Olive Nord* in 1958. The complete family, including four weights and various widths, was released four years later in 1962.

Antique Olive was the last typeface in France to be created on a commercial scale for casting as metal foundry type for use in hand-setting. This was also, in part, the reason for its lacklustre sales. Another was that Fonderie Olive's customers, most of whom were smaller to middle-sized printing concerns, catered

Below: Roger Excoffon, *Antique Olive Nord*, Fonderie Olive *c.*1961.

ABCDEFGHIJKLMNOPQ RSTUVWXYZ abcdefgh ijklmnop qrstuvxyz

to the needs of advertising rather than for books or magazines, and so had little use for what was essentially a textual typeface. It is often said that *Antique Olive* was designed to compete with *Univers* and *Neue Haas Grotesk* (*Helvetica* from 1963), and although it is likely this was an initial incentive, the final result is both imaginative and distinctive – the polar opposite characteristics of *Univers* and *Helvetica*.

Although famous – infamous in some quarters – for his typefaces, Excoffon also became renowned for his graphic design work, which grew substantially after 1956 when he formed his own design and advertising studio: Urbi & Orbi (U&O). His best-known work was for Air France in 1958, which included *Antique Olive Nord* for the new logo. Its design became a milestone in French graphic design, beginning on Friday 23 May 1958, around noon, while Excoffon was working on initial ideas for the logo. He asked José Mendoza to compose the words 'Air France' with the new *Antique Olive Nord* characters for an appointment with his customer in the afternoon. Mendoza started work; forty-five minutes later it was finished. Excoffon took the artwork and presented it to the Air France managers who immediately accepted it. The logo remained unchanged for more than fifty years.[12]

Excoffon continued to act as art director for Fonderie Olive, although it often meant that he was 'missing' from one or other studio. The issue was resolved in 1959 when the design studio at Fonderie Olive was closed and moved to U&O. Excoffon left U&O in 1971 to create Excoffon Conseil. Marcel Olive and Excoffon remained on excellent working terms. When Olive retired, he sold Fonderie Olive to the Haas foundry.

Left: Roger Excoffon, poster for Air France with the (dark blue) Air France logo using *Antique Olive Nord*, composed by José Mendoza in 1958. The bold, gestural brush-strokes that form the airplane are reminiscent of Ecoffon's typefaces, particularly *Choc* and *Banco* which, in turn, evoke the dynamism of the paintings of Georges Mathieu and Hans Hartung, which Excoffon admired when a student.

PART THREE
Phototypesetting

Introduction

After a decade of development and trials, the first commercially viable machines designed to set type photographically were introduced in the US in 1953, bringing more than 500 years of printing with metal type to an end. The next three decades of continued intense development in photocomposition[1] was a desperately difficult period for all traditional type foundries, whose glorious reputations very suddenly appeared to be irrelevant.

The key advantage offered by phototypesetting over the hot metal type casting system was simply the elimination of metal type, which in turn was only possible because of the growing popularity of offset lithographic printing. Phototypesetting technology also had the distinct practical advantages of being compact, clean and relatively quiet and odourless, meaning that typesetting could now be done in the designer's own studio or, indeed, in any office environment.[2]

In reality, phototypesetting machines proved too complex to use and maintain, and too expensive with new, much-improved models arriving too quickly for design studios to buy. Instead, phototypesetting technology was limited to larger-scale publisher/printers, while a brave new breed of specialist independent typesetting companies (or 'type houses') were established to serve what was by now a capricious but insatiable graphic design community. In this way, phototypesetting took typography away from both the composing machine operators and far smaller number of hand-compositors.

Lithography, as with xerography, serigraphy and gravure printing, relied on photographic processes and yet, until the arrival of phototypesetting, they all still required letterpress printing, be it from hot or cold metal type systems, to provide high quality printed 'reproduction proofs' printed on smooth baryta paper. These proofs were cut and then pasted into position on art board to be photographed again and transferred to lithographic plates.

As well as being fast, lithographic printing also enabled multiple (usually four) colours to be printed simultaneously and was therefore capable of perfectly accurate registration and pristinely reproduced fine halftone photographs. Letterpress was superior for the printing of textual material, but could not

Previous page: A phototypesetting studio at Oxford University Press, c.1970s. Early phototypesetting machines were boxes with a keyboard and a short, single-line display that showed glowing generic letters which 'marched' from right to left across the screen as the typesetter typed on the keys. The choice of typeface, its size, leading, and column width were programmed into the machine but were at no point visible to the typesetter.

The display was also not long enough to show a complete line (often only fifteen to twenty characters were visible) and so the typesetter was effectively setting the text blind. When the end of a line was reached the machine would set – expose – the line of type onto a roll of photo-sensitive paper inside the machine. The typed line was not stored in memory and so correcting an error – of which there were many – would require the whole line to be retyped.

compete with lithography for full-colour work on either quality or efficiency. The combination of photography and lithography had already pushed metal type to the margins, and so the development of photographic typesetting technology was not entirely unexpected. Nevertheless, its effect was still calamitous for many traditional type foundries.

The Uhertype company, based in Munich, was established by Edmund Uher in 1925 and made considerable progress in the development of photocomposition – so much so that, after a second and far superior prototype was built in 1932, the company hired Jan Tschichold to design a number of typefaces that took acount of the machine's specific technical requirements. The creative potential of the technology was enthusiastically reported by R.B. Fishenden, then editor of the *Penrose Annual*:

> In display composition any part of the work can be set at unusual angles, letters or lines can be overlaid with line or suitable tints, backgrounds introduced, or line designs with ease and with greater speed than would be possible with similar complicated work set in [metal] type. In fact, many of the effects produced would be quite impracticable if an attempt were made to set them typographically.[3]

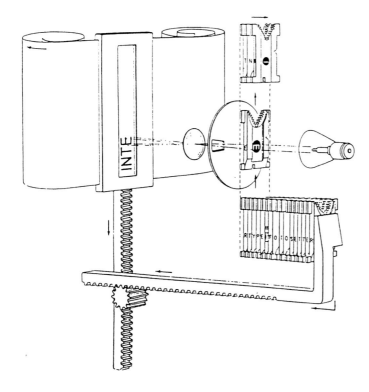

Left: The operating system of the Intertype Fotosetter. Released in 1946, it was one of the first-generation mass-market phototypesetting machines and preceded the Lumitype Photon by three years. It was based on hot metal typesetting technology, with the metal casting machinery replaced with photographic film. The light source remains stationary while precise mechanisms move the paper up and down and right to left. The size of the letter was set by adjusting the distance between the matrices and the paper.

However, by 1937 its engineers were losing momentum as technical issues with the machine caused delays and spiralling costs; in 1940, with the uncertainties created by a world war, the company was closed down.

The first commercially viable phototypesetting (or photocomposition) machine was invented in 1946 by René Higonnet and Louis Moyroud.[4] Both were electrical engineers (with no previous knowledge of type manufacture or design) at a subsidiary of International Telephone & Telegraph in Lyon, France. They called it the Lumitype. Finding no one in France willing to invest in the development of their invention, Higgonet and Moyroud turned to the American corporation Lithomat, which decided to back them; Higonnet and Moyroud moved to the US to continue their research and development. A prototype of their first commercial machine, called the Lumitype Photon, was presented in New York in 1949.

Development of the Lumitype Photon progressed slowly, and it was not until 1953 that the first book to be typeset entirely by the Lumitype Photon was published. This was *The Wonderful World of Insects*, published in New York by Rinehart & Company.[5] The extended colophon records:

> In 1949, the Graphic Arts Research Foundation, Inc. of Cambridge, Massachusetts was formed to provide high-level research in the printing industry. It had as its objective the creation of new, better and less costly printing methods. In the Higgonet-Moyroud, or Photon photographic type composing machine, the Foundation has perfected an entirely new, faster and far more versatile means of composition which does not employ metal type.

The following year, a Lumitype Photon typesetting machine was used for newspaper work, and the Lumitype Photon 200 was commercially released in North America in 1956. Despite being

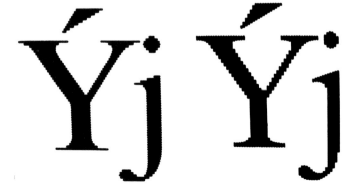

Right: Characters scanned horizonally and vertically at 28 tracks per centimetre. Horizonal tracking was found to be far less disruptive to the letterforms than vertical.

expensive it was a huge success, and Photon Inc. grew to become a major company with sales and service offices around the world.

The Photon phototypesetter utilized binary calculation and stroboscopic light technology. At the core of the machine was a glass 'matrix' disc on which a typeface, or indeed several typefaces, was printed in negative form. The disc span at high speed through which a beam of light would flash to expose the required individual letterforms onto a moving roll of photographic paper. An adjustable lens enabled the projected images of letters to be set at the required size (variably between 6 and 16 point). The matrix disc could hold 1,440 characters – for comparison, the 1950s Monotype matrix could hold approximately 225 characters, and Linotype's approximately 180 characters. Charles Peignot, who had been involved to a limited degree with the development of the Uhertype, now took the opportunity to partner his Paris-based type foundry Deberny & Peignot with Photon Inc., and guided Adrian Frutiger to design *Univers* for the Lumitype Photon. This was the first commercially successful typeface designed for phototypesetting technology.

Monotype and Linotype, aware of the inevitable devastating consequences of phototypesetting, had wisely been developing their own machines. Monotype, who had begun research work as early as 1944, produced the Monophoto in 1954. Linotype produced the Linofilm in 1958. But despite their impressive type libraries and considerable brand loyalty from the printing industry,[6] they discovered that changing tastes were undermining their grip of the market. Companies calling themselves type foundries – but with no experience in the design or development of type, typesetting or, indeed, anything type-related – were also entering the fray. This was only viable because the copying (pirating) of typefaces was all but impossible to prove and was rife. For independent typesetting companies, knowing what, exactly, a customer was asking for could be problematic. Clark E. Coffee, founder of Graphion, a phototypesetting company in San Francisco explains:

> There was a wonderful period in the late 1970s when most of the important typefaces were owned by, or under exclusive license to Intertype, Ludlow, Mergenthaler [Linotype] and Monotype, so the growing new companies simply copied these fonts and renamed them. Phototypesetters like ourselves had to keep conversion lists so we'd know that when a customer asked for '*Toms Roman*', he'd been dealing with a Compugraphic system. The same type would

be called '*London*' on a GSI or Singer machine, or '*Times Roman*' on a Mergenthaler. The fonts were about as similar as anyone could make them, but the tail on a letter Q might be longer or shorter to justify this outright theft by claiming that theirs was a unique face.[7]

There were technical issues that also had to be resolved. It had been realized early in development that the transfer of an image from a glass matrix onto photographic paper via a flash of light meant that the corners of letterforms appeared softened or rounded. To counteract this distortion, the form of each letter had to be adjusted. Adrian Frutiger, then a young designer almost fresh out of college, was employed by Peignot to redraw numerous classic typefaces to alleviate the distortion caused by the Lumitype Photon system. It was a miserable experience, as he explained:

> ... to think of the sort of aberrations I had to produce in order to see a good result on Lumitype! V and W needed huge crotches in order to stay open. I nearly had to introduce serifs in order to prevent rounded-off corners – instead of a sans serif the drafts were a bunch of misshapen sausages! [8]

With the introduction of phototypesetting, type designers did not take the opportunity to rectify stylistic foibles excused by the physical rectangular boundaries of mechanical typesetting technology of metal type. For example, when copies of 'classics' such as *Garamond*, *Caslon* and *Baskerville* were redrawn, the model used was generally a twentieth-century version – complete with stunted descenders – rather than returning to their original forms. The new flexibility, however, did give rise to new and sometimes elaborate script faces which could benefit from the lack of lateral constraints to allow elaborate overlaps. Another, and unfortunately, more memorable effect of the lateral versatility was the deplorable but briefly popular instruction 'set close, but not touching'.

Below: A 'marching display' incorporated in the GB Keyspeed 75 keyboard, so-called because the characters 'march' right-to-left as the typesetter keys in the text. Only cap characters were available for display on this machine so 'real' capitals were indicated by a dot above the character. The display facilities on other machines varied.

Type Type

For investors in phototypesetting technology, the fact that such a system was capable of producing all sizes of type from a single font was a huge financial benefit compared to the time-consuming practice of optical compensation conscientiously applied to each individual size of a metal typeface. To abandon the principal entirely would risk the technology losing all integrity, yet the allure of larger profit margins proved irresistible and so a compromise solution was devised. This took various forms, but typically the type designer would be required to produce three sets of drawings with appropriate adjustments to represent three size-categories of type: small (6 and 7 point), medium (8 to 12 point) and large (13 to 24 point). These 'masters' were designed to enable something close to uniformity of weight and balance across every required size of the typeface. This meant that a buyer had to purchase three masters, but it was not uncommon for just the medium master film to be bought and then used arbitrarily to set type beyond the range of sizes for it was designed. The results were predictably awful and yet they were seen often enough for phototypesetting to gain a reputation for producing dreadful results – despite the cause being the misuse of the system rather than the system itself. Not surprisingly, new hot metal typefaces continued to be cut and enthusiastically promoted, often at the same time as their release in film – Jan Tschichold's *Sabon*, released in 1967, was a particularly successful example. *Barbou* was the last Monotype hot metal typeface and was released in 1968. The final Monotype caster was built in 1987.

For the operator, early phototypesetting machines had a screen large enough to display just one or two lines of text – depicted as ocr-like characters, not the actual typeface. Plain horizontal and vertical lines or 'rules' were the only available design aids. The operator worked from marked-up copy provided by the designer. Output was limited to the width of the roll of photographic paper

Above: Two diagrams demonstrating the restriction of metal type (left) versus the freedom of phototypesetting technology – a major selling point for phototypesetting technology.

held within the machine. Once delivered to the designer, the photographic print-outs (called 'printed proofs', or 'galley proofs'– terminology from letterpress printing was commonly retained) were cut and pasted into position onto art board. The smell of the waxing machine, used as an adhesive to provide a thin coat of warm molten wax to the back of each piece of text, pervaded studios throughout the phototypesetting period.

A significant improvement in phototypsetting technology came with the introduction of the German engineer and inventor Rudolf Hell's typesetting machine, the Digiset 50T1, in 1965. It was a technological hybrid: analogue at one end with letters still being exposed photographically, and digital at the other end with the film or glass 'matrix' having been replaced by a numerical description that enabled letters to be created within a grid of squares (called a 'bitmap'). This phototypesetting process was known as 'digital photocomposition',[9] and marked an initial stage in what would, some twenty years later, become the digital revolution.

As with Lumitype Photon, Hell established his own type design program. Designing type for the Digiset required that drawings of each letter be transferred to a 100 by 200-unit grid by hand. Early digital typefaces were *Marconi* and *Edison*, designed by Hermann Zapf, and later *Demos* and *Praxis* by Gerard Unger. Unger chose to use a grid of white squares and fill each required square, black on white. Zapf did the opposite; he used a grid of black squares and painted out the unwanted squares with white paint – reminiscent of the punchcutter cutting away unwanted metal to leave only a pristine letterform. Nevertheless, it was a procedure Zapf described as being 'no joy for a type designer'.[10]

Beginning in 1972, the German inventor and entrepreneur Peter Karow developed a type design system called Ikarus at his URW Software and Type company in Hamburg. The origins of Ikarus can be traced back to the company Aristo and their 'Co-ordinatograph with numerical continuous path control' – or 'flatbed plotter' – designed in 1959 for use in the shipbuilding industry to plot complex shapes via a series of x-and-y coordinates on a prepared grid. Entrepreneur Walter Brendel realized that the concept of a flatbed plotter could be adopted to plot and cut master patterns for quick and precise reproductions of letterforms in phototype technology and consulted Karow at URW. Karow developed a working process described as 'hand-digitization', using a digitizing tablet and a sensor to trace marks on hand-drawn letterforms and convert them into digital vector outlines. The outline of a curve was plotted using Bézier curves. The primary advantage of outline fonts was that, unlike a bitmap font, letters are described as lines and smooth curves instead of individual pixels, and can also be scaled up or down with no loss of fidelity. (A bitmap font required a separate font to be drawn for each size, and since smaller sizes have fewer pixels with which to describe them, huge variance in appearance between a 6-point and 36-point character of the same typeface was inevitable). The Ikarus digital system was launched at the 1975 ATypI conference in Warsaw and enabled subtlety, sophistication, and something approaching the human hand to return to the process of creating letterforms.

By the early 1980s several other type design systems had been developed, notably Donald Knuth's Metafont, the Xerox Alto Font Design System, and the Camex Letter Input Processor – all developing the concept of digitizing an outline. Around the same time, John Warnock and Charles Geschke developed the page description language called PostScript, that could also be used to describe vector-based fonts. It received widespread recognition in 1985 when it was successfully implemented in the Apple LaserWriter. This, combined with the Apple Macintosh desktop computer incorporating Adobe's PageMaker, would herald the start of a new era – and the rapid end of photocomposition.

Below left: The rendering of letters with a fixed screen of dots means that detail is lost as a character is reduced in size.

Below: A Bézier curve always has at least two anchor points (AP), and one or two control points (CP). The control points are moved to create the required shape of curve between the anchor points.

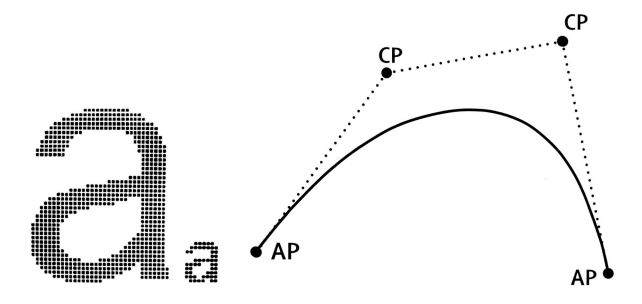

Max Miedinger SWITZERLAND 1910–1980

Max Miedinger was born in Zurich. He was apprenticed at the age of sixteen to Jacques Bollmann, a printer in Zurich, where he worked as a compositor in the book printing department. On completion of his apprenticeship he worked for various companies while attending evening classes at the School of Arts and Crafts in Zurich. In 1936, aged twenty-six, Max went to work as a typographer in the advertising department of Globus, a popular chain of department stores. He remained at Globus for ten years. Shortly after the Second World War he got a job with the Haas Type Company (Haas'sche Schriftgiesserei), where he was a typography consultant and type sales representative until 1956, when he decided to work freelance as a graphic designer. It was at this point that Max was commissioned to design a sans serif typeface.

This commission was at the instigation of Eduard Hoffmann, then co-manager of the Haas Type Company with his uncle Max Krayer. Hoffmann was born in 1892 in Zurich. As a student, he studied technology and engineering in Zurich, Berlin and Munich. In 1917, aged twenty-five, he was made an assistant under the direction of his uncle at the Haas type foundry. In 1937, Hoffmann became co-manager of the company and, after his uncle's death in 1944, became sole manager.

In the mid-1950s Hoffmann realized the company needed a sans serif typeface to serve the new Swiss International Style being pioneered with great success by Ernst Keller, Max Bill, Josef Müller-Brockmann and Armin Hofmann. Before the Second World War geometric or 'constructed' sans serifs, such as *Erbar* and *Futura*, had dominated, but in the aftermath of the war a less mechanical, more neutral sans style had gained popularity. For many designers *Akzidenz Grotesk*,[1] designed by Günter Gerhard Lange and released in 1896 by the Berthold type foundry in Berlin served this purpose and had become the preferred sans serif. The sales of Haas's own more neutral-styled sans serif types – *Französische Grotesk* from 1900, and its revised version *Normal Grotesk*,[2] 1943 – were both falling. Hoffmann needed a contemporary version of *Akzidenz Grotesk*, and he also knew his company was in a race with the Bauer type foundry in Frankfurt and Deberny & Peignot in Paris.

In 1956, when Miedinger left Haas to work as a freelance designer, Hoffmann promised that 'If I have an idea for a new

Opposite: Max Miedinger and Eduard Hoffmann, *Helvetica Bold Italic.* Cover by Hans Neuburg and Nelly Rubin, 1960.

Above: *Französische Grotesk,* Haas type foundry, c.1900.

**Festakt im Kunsthaus
ZEITUNGS-INSERATE**

**Hôpital de Payerne
CHANSON BELGE**

**Posthaus Lenk
JUGENDHEIM**

Regina Bar

Neukirch

Sichem

Above: *Normal Grotesk*, reworked from their own *Französische Grotesk* and released by Haas, c.1943.

typeface I'm sure you will be able to design it'.[3] It is likely that he already had in mind the sans serif he needed, because he offered a project to Miedinger soon afterwards. Hoffmann and Miedinger had contrasting personalities. Hoffmann was shy but had a steely determination and a clear vision of what was needed; Miedinger was more affable and he could draw and therefore make Edouard Hoffmann's ideas a reality whilst contributing ideas in the process. It was agreed that the project would be a collaboration and the typeface would be called *Neue Haas Grotesk*. Although it was, from the outset, to be a contemporary version of *Akzidenz Grotesk*, Hoffmann insisted they must also take account of Haas's own landmark early sans serif, *Normal Grotesk*.

At the Bauer type foundry in Frankfurt, Walter Baum, head of the design studio since 1949 and his senior, Konrad F. Bauer (not related), were working on *Folio*. Both were experienced type designers and jointly responsible for several successful typefaces for the Bauer type foundry, the most prominent being *Fortune*, the first Clarendon typeface with a matching italic. *Folio* was modelled more closely on *Akzidenz Grotesk* than either Hoffmann and Miedinger's *Neue Haas Grotesk* or Frutiger's *Univers*.

At Deberny & Peignot in Paris, Frutiger was also looking at *Akzidenz Grotesk* while designing *Univers*, but he was making changes by taking out features he considered expendable and adding a subtle sophistication, seen most clearly in finely graded, subtly squared arcs. *Univers* was conceived as a large cohesive family structure from the outset, as was *Folio*, although Frutiger was by far the more ambitious.

Hoffmann and Miedinger's *Neue Haas Grotesk* remained close to *Akzidenz Grotesk*, but became cleaner and more refined. It is rounder than *Univers*, though its curves remain modelled. Like *Univers* it has a large x-height but all strokes terminate horizontally or vertically to give it a more robust, severe and confident appearance. More importantly, *Neue Haas Grotesk* had clarity, objectivity and consistency; it seemed to have no obvious historic references, despite its starting point being *Akzidenz Grotesk*, and in so doing avoided appearing mechanical without reverting to overt humanistic characteristics. Together, Hoffmann and Miedinger gave *Neue Haas Grotesk* the expressionless stare that postwar typographers sought. It was released in 1957.

With the help of handsome brochures and interest generated at the Graphic 57 trade fair in Lausanne, *Neue Haas Grotesk* proved to be a success – but its sales were held back because the Haas type foundry was still cutting type by hand and only producing foundry type for hand-composition. Haas was owned by the Stempel type foundry in Frankfurt, who in 1961 decided to adapt *Neue Haas Grotesk* for Linotype production in Germany (Stempel was in turn owned by Linotype GmbH, known informally as 'German Linotype'). Modifications such as narrowing the bold typeface and adjusting the italic were made to enable it to fit Linotype matrices, and in 1963 *Neue Haas Grotesk* was ready for re-release. Unable to market a new Stempel typeface with a name that included 'Haas' they looked for an alternative that would embody the spirit of the typeface and decided on 'Helvetia' (the Latin name for Switzerland). Hoffmann suggested an alternative – *Helvetica*, meaning 'Swiss' – a subtle but important difference and a name that aligned *Helvetica* even closer to the new Swiss International Style of typography. This was agreed.[4]

Miedinger is almost unanimously credited with the design of *Helvetica*, primarily because he was the person holding the pencil. But if his working relationship with Hoffmann is compared to that of Victor Lardent and Stanley Morison when designing *Times New Roman*, the credit for *Helvetica* could have been reversed. The difference, of course, is that while the 'almost pathologically shy'[5] Hoffmann was willing to deflect all credit for the design of *Helvetica* towards Miedinger, Morison was quite the opposite – gregarious, outspoken and utterly self-confident – and although he never sought to diminish Lardent's role in wielding the pencil, Morison still took all the credit for the design of *Times New Roman*. It helped, of course, that Lardent, like Hoffman, was modest to a fault and never showed any interest in claiming credit.

During the next thirty years the *Helvetica* family was enlarged, adding new weights and widths. It was adapted for photocomposition and then for the first generation of digital typesetters. To return a semblance of order to what had become a rather chaotic collection, *Helvetica* was overhauled, rationalized and extended in 1983 – from ultra-light to black, and from condensed to extended – by the Stempel design studio under the guidance of René Kerfante and Wolfgang Schimpf, working in consultation with Erik Spiekermann. Called *Helvetica Neue*, and now with an extended family of fifty-one variants, every character was redrawn for use on Linotype's Linotronic range of typesetting machines. To add unity to this increased and diverse range, a numbering system was introduced, not dissimilar to that created for *Univers* in 1957.[6]

In 1984 *Helvetica*, together with *Times* and *Courier*, made up the core font set[7] for Adobe's PostScript.

ABCDEFGH
IJKLMNOPQ
RSTUVWXYZ
&.,:;!?[]*
abcdefghijklm
nopqrstuvwxyz
12345678

Above: Max Miedinger and Eduard Hoffmann, *Neue Haas Grotesk*, 1957.

Eurostile

sintesi espressiva del nostro tempo

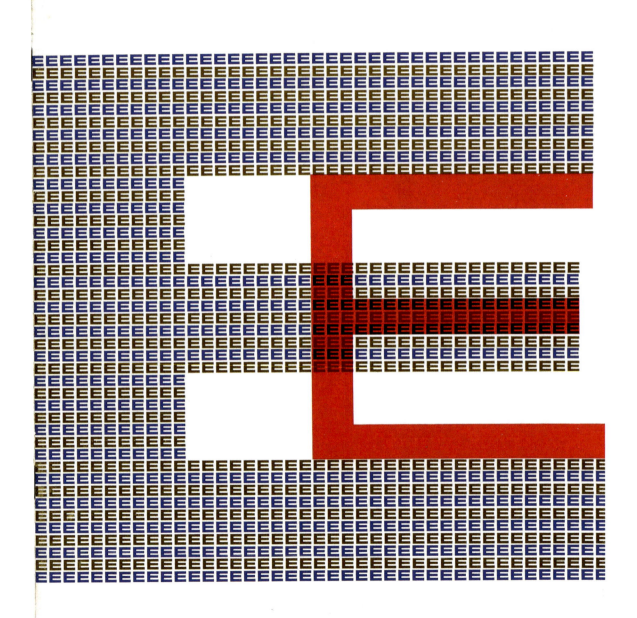

Aldo Novarese ITALY 1920–1995

Aldo Noverese was born in the small village of Pontestura in north-west Italy. The family then moved to Turin, where his father worked as a customs agent. In 1930 Aldo began his studies at the Scuola Artieri Stampatori, a printing school where he experimented with woodcut, etching and lithography. He then specialized in typography at the Scuola Tipografica e di Arti Affini Giuseppe Vigliardi-Paravia, a specialist school where he studied under the direction of type designer Alessandro Butti, who was also a designer at the Nebiolo type foundry in Turin. By the late 1920s, around the time that Renner's *Futura* was released, the Nebiolo foundry had responded with a geometric sans serif designed by Butti called *Semplicità*, which proved very popular in Italy and helped encourage the company to set up an in-house design studio. Opened in 1933, it was called Studio Artistico; Giulio Da Milano, who had been involved in the design of *Semplicità*, was appointed its first art director. His tenure was successful (*Titano*, *Neon*, *Razionale* and *Veltro* were all designed during his reign) but brief – in 1936 Alessandro Butti took his place. Butti recruited Novarese, then just sixteen years of age, to begin work as a designer.

   Nebiolo was established in 1852 and thrived in the first half of the twentieth century, not only as a type foundry but also as a major manufacturer of printing presses, allied tools and equipment. Before the establishment of Studio Artistico, Nebiolo's catalogue consisted mainly of display typefaces cast from matrices that were acquired (or copied) from German and French foundries. For example, the heavy slab serif *Egiziano Nero*, which first appeared in a Nebiolo type specimen leaflet in 1920 with the name *Tondo Nero Normale*, was probably electrotyped from Stevens Shanks *Antique No. 6*,[1] (which in turn was originally an 'Egyptian' shown by Vincent Figgins in London in 1815.[2]) Such practices were rife across the industry; however, once Studio Artistico was established the output from Nebiolo became more distinctive and standards radically improved.

Opposite: Alessandro Butti and Aldo Novarese, *Eurostile Bold Extended*, which was released as *Micrograma* in 1952 as a titling typeface designed by Butti. The lowercase was added and minor adjustments made to the capitals by Novarese and then re-released as *Eurostile* in 1962.

Below: Alessandro Butti, *Semplicità*, 1930.

Marchese di Saluzzo

Alessandro Butti was a reticent but determined character. Meticulous to a fault, he was reluctant to pass anything that he was not absolutely sure was right – not just technically, but also morally. An example of this was *Augustea*. This typeface was issued in 1949 as a titling typeface, but the project had been initiated much earlier. In 1938 Butti went to Rome, accompanied by the young Novarese, and together they photographed the Trajan column and hundreds of other Imperial roman inscriptions – all of which, of course, were capitals. When he returned to Turin Butti studied the photographs, then compared the variant examples and made numerous drawings and eventually, about eleven years later, allowed *Augustea* titling to be released. Before its release, and during the next two years, Butti worked on a lowercase *Augustea* to accompany the caps. The general opinion within Nebiolo was that the lowercase was ready to be put into production, but Butti refused to allow its release, not because he was dissatisfied with his drawings but for fear that adding a lowercase would offend the 'majesty of Roman lapidary'.[3] It was not until 1964, six years after Butti's death, that *Augustea* was 'reprised' as *Nova Augustea*, this time with lowercase letterforms. Novarese certainly made amendments to the lowercase that Butti had designed, but Butti's major contribution was conspicuously ignored when *Nova Augustea* was released and full credit given to Novarese.[4]

Novarese worked closely with Butti on many more typefaces, but their most successful were probably *Microgramma* in 1952 and *Recta* in 1958. Butti had designed *Recta* before 1952 (the year he was made redundant). *Recta* is a neutral sans serif pre-dating Frutiger's *Univers* and Hoffmann and Miedinger's *Neue Haas Grotesk*, both of which were released in 1957. In fact, it was not until the Nebiolo management saw the arrival and success of these typefaces that they quickly put *Recta* into production and released it in 1958. Novarese then expanded *Recta* into a large family of various widths and weights in the years that followed. *Microgramma*, a distinctive quadratic, caps-only sans serif, was also designed by Butti shortly before his dismissal. Fifteen years later Novarese designed a set of lowercase characters to accompany the caps and added a condensed version, and re-released as *Eurostile*. Its square-like forms with their distinctive rounded corners make this one of the most easily recognised and evocative typefaces of the twentieth century, encouraged by its resemblance to the pervasive form of the mid-century television screen from the 1950s and 1960s.

Hébridas
ESCUDO

Above: Aldo Novarese, *Ritmo*, modelled on Roger Excoffon's *Banco*, 1955.

ABCDEFGHIJKL MNOPQRSTUV WXYZ abcdegh ijklmnopqrstvwx 1234567890

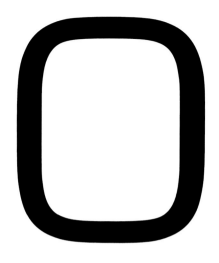

Above: Alphonso Butti and Aldo Novarese, *Eurostile Regular*, 1962.

In the postwar years and early 1950s the Nebiolo company was experiencing severe financial difficulties and many employees were made redundant, including, as mentioned earlier, Butti, who left in October 1952 then aged just fifty-eight. Novarese, recognized as a prolific designer as well as a dashing new figurehead for Nebiolo, took his place as art director of Studio Artistico and quickly revived its status and helped stabilize the company. Its success during the latter 1950s and early 1960s was heralded as signifying a newly reinvigorated and optimistic Italy after the country's severe deprivations during and immediately after the Second World War.[5]

The output of Nebiolo's studio (which never exceeded five designers)[6] had always been primarily display type, servicing the hundreds of small to medium Italian printing shops specialising in jobbing rather than book work. When the economic situation in Europe finally improved in the 1950s it was quickly followed by a rise in demand for display types, especially those that reflected a lighter, more carefree attitude. This was demonstrated by Roger Excoffon's *Chambord*, *Mistral* and *Banco* – the last of which was closely copied by Novarese's studio and called *Ritmo*. Two others, *Cigno*, and *Slogan* (both free-flowing scripts), also owed much to Excoffon.

Probably Novarese's first original, and arguably most successful, display typeface was *Stop*, designed in 1971. Its heavy forms are vaguely stencil-like, simplified to the point that many of the characters are recognizable only when used in combination with others. It was described at the time as 'futuristic', being vaguely reminiscent of those fonts designed specifically for

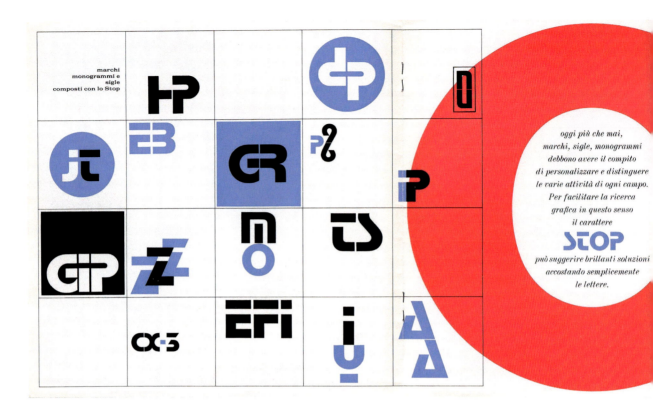

Above: Aldo Novarese, *Stop*. Centre spread from a typically elaborate type specimen published by Nebiolo, 1971.

machine recognition. Alongside this and other distinctive display typefaces he also designed a classic *Garamond* in 1956 called *Garaldus*, loosely based on the proportions of the typeface cut for Aldus Manutius by Francesco Griffo.

Before the mid-1960s, and despite state assistance, Nebiolo found itself once more in serious financial trouble. The company had long been dependent almost entirely on the sales of foundry type for hand-setting, and consequently made no investment whatsoever in phototypesetting technology. Exports were poor, and even the extended *Recta* family, which the company had hoped would rival *Univers* and *Neue Haas Grotesk*, had proved less successful than expected. The naivety of the Nebiolo management is demonstrated by the predictable failure of *Garaldus*. It was released at a time when virtually all publishing houses set their books on Monotype or Linotype composing machines (some had already switched to photocomposition), and so a text typeface produced for hand-setting was doomed to commercial failure. Although a few Nebiolo typefaces from the early 1970s onwards had also been released as Linotype matrices, no investment in equipment or strategic alliances were ever made

ABCDEFGHIJKLMNOPQQuRS
abcdefghijklmnopqrsſtuvwxyz

to embrace new technology – a hesitancy that would prove to be the downfall of the foundry. In 1976, following another financial setback, the company was bought by the Italian automotive company, Fiat. Two years later, the type foundry and cast-iron foundry branches were closed.[7]

Novarese had already left the company in 1975 to work as a freelance designer. His reputation was such that he continued to work independently without any reduction in output. He had also taught throughout his career at his old school, Vigliani-Paravia, and in 1964 had written *Alfa-Beta*, a book about type and typography (re-released in 2020). Novarese continued to draw a variety of typefaces for a disparate range of new technologies developed during the next twenty years, including phototypesetting, dry-transfer (or 'rub-down') letters, and later for digital systems such as Berthold, Visual Graphics Corporation (VGC), Haas/Stempel, Agfa Compugraphic, International Typeface Corporation (ITC) and others. However, none matched the success of *Stop* or the results of his early collaborative work with Butti.

Of his later typefaces, *Novarese*, released in 1978, remained well known, due in part to its name, but also because, having been commissioned by the Haas type foundry, it was then licensed to ITC in 1984. It is small serifed with a low contrast between its thick and thin strokes and a large x-height. The italic is unusual in that it is a combination of cursive lowercase and upright capitals, echoing early Venetian use of italics.

Later typeface designs include *ITC Symbol* (1984, a condensed text face similar to *ITC Novarese* but with even smaller serifs, and *ITC Mixage* (1985), a sans serif that matches both families harmoniously. *Arbiter* (1989) for Berthold is an unusual blend of squarish forms, small straight serifs, and long sharp terminals, as well as rather whimsical ball terminals; a formulated culmination of over fifty years of typeface design.

ABCDEFGHIJKLMN
OPQRSTUVWXYZÀ
ÅÉÎabcdefghijklmn
opqrstuvwxyzàåéî&
1234567890($£.,!?)

ABCDEFGHIJKLMN
OPQRSTUVWXYZÀÅ
abcdefghijklmnopqr
stuvwxyzàåéîõøü&1
234567890($£.,!?)

Top: Aldo Novarese, *Garaldus*, 1956.

Above top: Aldo Novarese, *Arbiter*, 1989. *Arbiter* attempts to bring arbitary styles harmoniously together.

Above bottom: Aldo Novarese, *ITC Novarese*, 1978.

Zur Typographie des Buches

Eine neue

Antiqua-Schrift

von der D. Stempel AG

in ihrer Anwendung

im Werksatz

Hermann Zapf GERMANY 1918 – 2015

Hermann Zapf was born in Nuremberg during a particularly grim period for Germany. Defeat in the First World War was followed by severe food shortages, which reached a peak in 1920.[1]. He left school in 1933 with the ambition of pursuing a career in electrical engineering. However, when the Nazi Party came to power Zapf's father, who was a trade union official at a large car factory, was sacked from his job and briefly imprisoned for his assumed communist sympathies. This also meant that Zapf was not allowed to attend the Ohm Polytechnic Institute in Nuremberg as planned. As a result, he was forced to find an apprenticeship.

Zapf was good at drawing, and his teachers, who were aware of the family's political problems, had suggested he become a lithographer. Despite his folder of artwork having met with approval, the inscrutable authority of the Nazi regime meant that, on asking about his political views, employers dared not accept him. The last printing company in the telephone directory – Karl Ulrich & Co. – to his surprise and good fortune did not ask him any political questions. They agreed that his work was excellent but, unfortunately, they did not do lithographic work. They offered him, instead, an apprenticeship as a photo-retoucher, and said that if he agreed he could begin work the following week. Zapf accepted. He rushed home to consult a dictionary in order to discover what he had agreed to and, in February 1934, began his four-year apprenticeship.

In 1935 a memorial exhibition was held in Nuremberg of work by Rudolf Koch, who had died the previous year. Zapf was captivated and bought a copy of Koch's book, *Das Schreiben als Kunstfertigkeit* (The Art of Writing) which led him to Edward Johnston's *Writing & Illuminating & Lettering*, and he began teaching himself calligraphy. His new skill was recognized at Karl Ulrich & Co. and he began to specialize in the retouching of lettering.

In February 1938, on the final day of his apprenticeship, Zapf handed in his notice. A few days later he went to the Werkstatt Haus zum Fürsteneck[2] in Frankfurt, a workshop run by Paul Koch,[3] son of Rudolf Koch, together with master printer Fritz Arnold. Paul Koch was a highly skilled punchcutter who cut types designed by his father and others, including Victor Hammer, for

Opposite: Hermann Zapf, *Palatino* on the cover of a type specimen published by the Stempel foundry, 1949.

whom he worked in Florence, and Berthold Wolpe. Zapf spent much of that year at Koch's workshop learning punchcutting and fine printing on a hand press. It was here that Zapf's career in typography truly began. Gustav Mori, a director at the Stempel type foundry, heard of Zapf's work and in 1939 recruited him for the company. It was here that Zapf first met the superlative punchcutter August Rosenberger.

Later that same year, Zapf began work on his first typeface for Stempel, a blackletter he called *Gilgengart* (in honour of a sixteenth-century book of religious texts). Zapf learned quickly as the work progressed. He also came to understand the whimsical nature and influence of political dogma. Blackletter had been heralded as a model of German cultural and social heritage by the Nazi Party, but then quite suddenly its use was outlawed and branded a 'Jewish concoction' when they discovered that blackletter was apparently indecipherable to readers outside Germany (not helpful to a government intent on global rule). Nevertheless, *Gilgengart* was hand-cut by Rosenberger and eventually released in 1941. A second version, with narrower and slightly more restrained capitals, was designed shortly after but released much later.

Zapf spent much of the Second World War working in a cartographic unit, drawing detailed maps of the Spanish rail network. As the war came to a close he was captured by the French, but after just a few weeks was released and allowed to make his way back to his parent's hometown of Nuremberg. As part of a programme organized by the German Federation of Trade Unions, Zapf was appointed as a part-time teacher and gave his first calligraphy lesson in 1946. The following year Zapf went to Frankfurt, where the Stempel type foundry offered him a position as artistic director of the in-house printshop. He was not yet thirty years of age and they did not ask for qualifications or references. All he had were three sketch books of drawings and writing done during the war, plus an exceptional set of twenty-five calligraphic alphabets he had completed in 1941. These had been left with August Rosenberger when Zapf was called up for military service, and which in the intervening years Rosenberger brilliantly hand-engraved into plates of lead. This was achieved in between, and sometimes during, the devastating bombing raids over Frankfurt.

An early task that Zapf was elated to undertake at Stempel was the design and production of a book in which Rosenberger's

Above: *Gilgengart I* was designed 1938–39 and released in 1941. *Gilgengart II*, a revised version of *Gilgengart I*, was released c.1951–52.

La fontana di Valle Giulia all'Alba
La fontana di Valle Giulia all'Alba

twenty-five engraved lead plates could be printed. *Feder und Stichel* (Pen and Graver) was printed on Stempel's own press in 1949 and published as a limited edition of just eighty copies on Japan paper and a further 500 on Fabriano. The publishing of *Feder und Stichel* had a second and for Stempel, at least, a more pressing purpose – to introduce a new typeface, *Palatino*, also designed by their young new art director, Hermann Zapf. The impact of this slim book was exceptional. There had certainly been a resurgence of interest in calligraphy after the war, but it was the fact that these twenty-five pages had been lettered by a self-taught twenty-three-year-old Zapf and engraved by Rosenberger in defiance of the bombs that rained on Frankfurt which caught the imagination. Such was the demand that a further 2,000 were printed in 1952, this time with an introduction in English.[4]

In the aftermath of the war, Frankfurt became the centre of West Germany's book trade. Its type foundries needed new roman types, and on his arrival at Stempel Zapf had immediately begun work on a roman type called *Novalis* that was initially drawn with a broad nibbed pen. Despite it being cut in medium and bold weights and corresponding italics, Stempel decided, finally, not to go any further with production. It was following this disappointment that Zapf began work on *Palatino* in 1948, this time closely aligned with fifteenth-century Venetian types. The first trial cuts were made in 1949, and the foundry version was released in 1951. A Linotype version was released the same year. The open counters that make *Palatino* such a legible letter were designed to overcome the poor quality of paper, a major problem for German printers at that time. The weight of the type was also designed to be slightly heavier in order to adapt to the lithographic and gravure printing processes of the period.

Zapf's intention had been that *Palatino* should be used for display rather than book work, which is why he maintained the distinctive calligraphic characteristics in some of the letters.[5] However, this did not discourage some book typographers, especially in the US, who pressed Stempel to provide alternative characters to replace the 'problem' calligraphic characters (the 't' with its unusual 'ascender', for example).[6] Zapf eventually designed a lighter weight *Palatino*, and, in the process, reduced its

ABCDE
GHIJK
LMNO
PQRST
UVWX
YZ 123
456789

Top: Hermann Zapf, *Palatino*, c.1949–50 (top line) and *Aldus*, 1952–53.

Above: Hermann Zapf, *Sistina*, a titling typeface, 1950 (see also p. 268).

calligraphic characteristics to provide a more 'bookish' typeface. He planned to call it *Palatino Book* but the sales department at Stempel decided that it should be marketed as a separate typeface and named it *Aldus* – despite Zapf's protest that it had nothing in common with the types of Aldus Manutius. *Aldus* was released in 1952–3. (The name *Palatino* was also decided by Stempel, after Giovanbattista Palatino, a sixteenth-century calligrapher. Zapf had proposed it be named *Medici*.)

Incidentally, in 1956 when Stempel was preparing to print a grand *Palatino* type specimen, Zapf asked Rosenberger, who had cut the *Palatino* punches, to make an engraving from a sketch Zapf had made of Rosenberger's work bench showing his files, gravers and all other paraphernalia essential in the cutting of punches. Stempel refused to allow its use. Their reason, according to Zapf, was that the management considered such a display would be contrary to the image they proffered of Stempel as a modern, efficient, forward-looking company whose products were the outcome of 'scientific' methods, rather than the reality which was a craft that dated back 500 years. Stempel's attitude was by no means uncommon – and that Zapf argued for the recognition of Rosenberger's role is to his credit.

With the design of *Palatino* complete and successfully in production, Zapf went to Italy in the autumn of 1950 where he visited Rome, Florence and Pisa to study at first-hand roman inscriptional letters. When he returned, he designed *Sistina*, a robust though elegant titling typeface, based on the sketches made in Italy.

This period, between 1948 and 1954, was a hugely productive period for Zapf, whose contribution to Stempel was instrumental in helping the company get back on its feet. Much of his work was for extensions to fonts or for missing sizes of fonts already in the extensive Stempel type library. But he also designed *Saphir* (decorative capitals, 1952), *Virtuosa* (a script, 1952–3), *Janson* for Linotype (1952), several Greek alphabets and, most significantly, a newspaper typeface, *Melior*.

During his visit to New York in 1951, where an exhibition of his work had been mounted, Zapf visited Linotype's Brooklyn headquarters to study the effects of various newspaper printing processes, chiefly rotary letterpress and web-fed lithography, and to consider the technical modifications required of type to alleviate adverse effects. *Melior* was the result of these deliberations; it appeared in 1952. It is distinctive and

Top: Hermann Zapf, *Saphir*, Linotype, 1952.

Above: Hermann Zapf, *Virtuosa II*, Linotype, 1953. This was designed to provide a simpler alternative set of characters to the popular *Virtuosa I* released the previous year.

sophisticated but also sturdy; the latter quality is particularly noticeable in the strong squared serifs (beneficial when used for rotary letterpress printing). *Melior's* letter-shapes are based on a squared-off circle (or 'super-ellipsoid'). It has been sited that this distinctive characteristic was inspired by the writings of Piet Hein, a Danish polymath who held that the super-ellipsoid provided an aesthetic unity superior to that of Euclidean geometry and whose theory was, for a brief period, very popular across a range of creative disciplines during the 1950s. (It possibly influenced Butti in his design of *Microgramma*.) The clarity and efficiency of *Melior* made it attractive to newspaper and magazine editors and designers, and remained a popular choice for much of the twentieth century.

In the midst of this burst of activity Zapf also designed what is his most original and most easily recognized typeface: *Optima*. Work began around 1955, and it was released in 1958. Although classified as a sans serif, *Optima* has a subtle swelling at its terminals that suggest bud-like serifs. Zapf called it 'a seriless roman' and initially called it *Neu-Antiqua* (New Roman), but this was later changed by Stempel. The classical geometric proportions of *Optima* are based on sketches made in Italy from inscribed letterforms he discovered on an ancient Roman gravestone in Florence. The original intention was that it should be a display face, but when Zapf showed proofs to Monroe Wheeler, head of exhibitions and publications at The Museum of Modern Art in New York in 1954, Wheeler explained that there was a need for an elegant sans serif typeface that could be used for extended texts in art books, magazines and similar publications. With this encouragement Zapf decided to make it a text type. Sebastian Carter has suggested it takes 'the comfortable round proportions of a transitional face such as *Baskerville's* [while] shedding the serifs with no distortion of its essential nature and no sense of anything missing.'[7] Despite its humanist lines, the italic follows the convention of a sans serif typeface and is a sloped roman.

At the end of 1956, and still only aged thirty-eight, Zapf resigned from his position at Stempel; administrative work was becoming an increasing burden and threatening to stifle any possibility of creative work, although he left on excellent terms. As a freelance designer his time was occupied working on books, teaching and lecturing, all of which offered the opportunity for travel. He had recently completed and published

Janson

ABCDEFGHIJKL
MNOPQRSTUV
WXYZabcdefgh
ijklmnopqrstuv
wxyz1234567
890 ?!*&

MELIOR
Standard Technik

Above top: Hermann Zapf, *Janson*, Linotype, 1952.

Above middle: Hermann Zapf, *Optima*, 1958.

Above bottom: Hermann Zapf, *Melior*, 1952.

the landscape format *Manuale typographicum* (1954), printed from hand-set metal type, and a second volume of *Manuale typographicum* (1968) which was hand-set but with additional setting achieved by mechanical composition. A third *Manuale*, this time *Manuale phototypographicum*, was planned to be set using photocomposition but was, unfortunately, abandoned for financial reasons. Zapf was a constant enthusiastic advocate for new technology, and it is tempting to imagine a fourth *Manuale* dedicated to digital typographic technology (Rudolf Hell had invented the Digiset photocomposition machine in 1964 and Zapf was fascinated by its possibilities). Two other books of note are *Typographische Variationen* (1963) and the privately issued *Orbis Typographicus* (1980).

Teaching continued throughout his life. From 1972 to 1981 he lectured in typography at the Technical Institute in Darmstadt, Germany, but his advocacy of computer-aided type composition was disparaged and so, as Zapf explained, 'I had no choice but to go to the United States. The Americans were more open to such new and unconventional things and they still have something of their old pioneering spirit'.[8]

Zapf was appointed by the Rochester Institute of Technology (rit) to take over when Alexander Lawson retired in 1976. The intention was to establish a professorship for typographic computer programs, the first of its kind in the world. Zapf agreed

Below: Hermann Zapf, *Manuale Typographicum*, with a display of *Sistina*, 1954.

and taught there from 1977 to 1987, flying regularly between the US and Germany. At Rochester he was able to develop his ideas on digital typography with help from connections made in companies such as IBM and Xerox, as well as discussions with the computer programming specialists within RIT. In 1991 Zapf used this experience when he began work on a typesetting program called the Hz-program, developed in conjunction with URW Software & Type GmbH in Hamburg. This was later acquired by Adobe Systems who incorporated it in InDesign.

In distinct contrast, an earlier teaching appointment, again in America, would lead to a private commission resulting in a very different outcome. In 1960 Zapf had been invited to become a visiting professor of design at the Carnegie Institute of Technology in Pittsburgh. The following year, he was commissioned to design a typeface for the exclusive use of the world-renowned Hunt Botanical Library situated on the Institute's campus (founded by Rachel McMasters Miller Hunt). The early 1960s were effectively the last years of the metal type era and the manufacture of such a typeface, especially for private use, was expensive. However, the Hunt Botanical Library's publications were all still printed by letterpress from metal type. Hunt had been an apprentice at Cobden Sanderson's Doves Bindery in London, and she was encouraged in this venture by Jack Stauffacher, typography professor at Carnegie who was a long-time admirer of Zapf's work. The punchcutting and casting of what was eventually called *Hunt Roman* was undertaken by Arthur Ritzel at the Stempel type foundry. Zapf explained that he wanted to 'create a transitional type that would not take over the historic peculiarities of *Baskerville*'.[9] Because *Hunt Roman* was intended for hand-setting only, Zapf was not limited by the various unit systems essential to mechanical composing machines, nor by the common stipulation that it must be economical in the amount of space it took up on the page. The result is a truly beautiful face featuring a large x-height, generous width and regal counters. It was cut in four sizes with the 18-point pilot size completed in May 1962. No italic was designed.

The exclusivity of *Hunt Roman* makes its beauty all the more alluring. Other digital typefaces Zapf later designed – such as *Marconi* and *Comenius*, both 1976 – bear resemblances. However, the nature of the letterpress printing process for which *Hunt Roman* was designed ensures that it will always appear crisper than any of its descendants.

«We like an honest books and dear boo cheapness that doe manship or a big e think should disqu ferior work with a

Marconi
Marconi
Marconi
Marconi

Top: Hermann Zapf, *Hunt Roman* (much enlarged), designed to be hand-cut and cast in metal type by the Stempel type foundry, released in 1962.

Above: Hermann Zapf, *Marconi*, designed for the Digiset digital typesetting system, released in 1976.

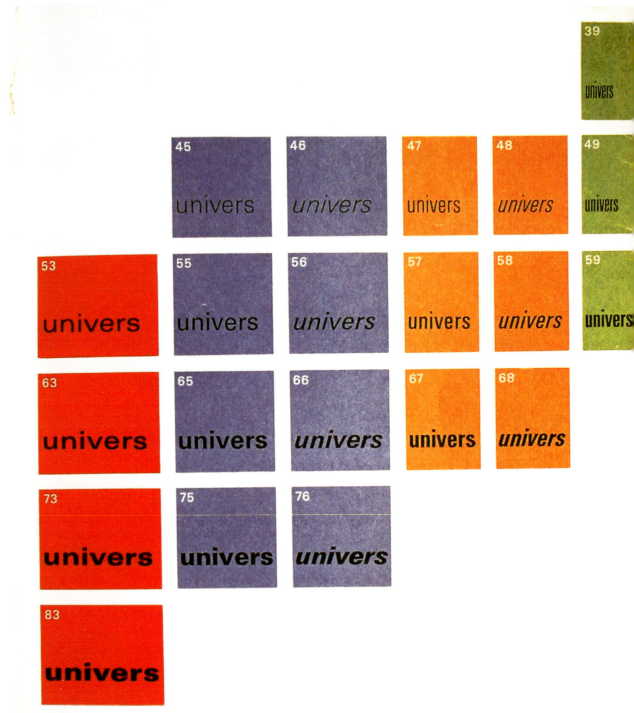

21 variations sur un thème unique

Adrian Frutiger SWITZERLAND 1928 – 2015

Adrian Frutiger was born and educated in Switzerland. His father was a weaver, and as a child Frutiger helped him. This work augmented the importance of technique grounded in craftsmanship and an appreciation of essential materials. In 1944, at the age of sixteen, Frutiger began a four-year apprenticeship as a compositor to the printer Otto Schlaeffli at Interlaken, while attending classes in woodcut and drawing at the Gewerbeschule (Trade School) in Bern.

In 1949 Frutiger transferred to the Kunstgewerbeschule (School of Applied Arts) Zürich, where for the next two years he studied graphic techniques in conjunction with lettering, including monumental inscriptions from Roman forum rubbings. It was while he was a student there that he produced a remarkably accomplished synopsis of the development of the western alphabet, with specimen scripts cut in the side grain of planks of wood. His precocity was further demonstrated by a sans serif typeface he also began work on and which would later resurface as *Univers*.

On leaving college Frutiger got a job working as a graphic designer at Alfred Willi Mann and Walter Käch in Zurich, but his career began in earnest when he joined the renowned Paris-based Deberny & Peignot type foundry in 1952. Its director, Charles Peignot, was concerned about the future of foundry type manufacture. Mechanical metal composition – principally, the Monotype or Linotype systems – was mainly used for setting quantities of textual type, so Peignot had concentrated his company's typeface development on display types for hand-composition for jobbing work undertaken by printers and specified by designers of advertising and other printed matter. But by the 1950s Peignot was anticipating other challenges, in particular photocomposition and dry-transfer (or 'rub-down') adhesive lettering, and he was determined that Deberny & Peignot remain at the forefront of such developments.

In 1952, Peignot took the opportunity to partner with the American-based company Photon Inc. This company had patented the 1944 invention of two French engineers, Louis Moyroud and René Higonnet, who created the first photographic type composition system,[1] called the Lumitype in France. The transfer of letters printed on a glass disk via a beam of light onto

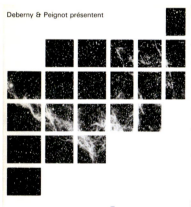

Opposite: Adrian Frutiger, *Univers*, 1957. Here the original Deberny & Peignot type specimen cover shows the classic grid of the twenty-one variants, each with its own index number.

Above: Adrian Frutiger, *Univers*, 1960. By now the iconic diagramatic grid was so well known that Deberny & Peignot were confident enough to playfully remove all the information pertaining to the Univers family and replace them with an image of the universe.

light-sensitive paper caused certain distortions to the letters – most notably the softening of outer corners and the filling-in of inner-corners. Realising that he needed a range of amended typefaces that took account of and, in effect, 'corrected' these distortions, he was looking for a young designer with a sound knowledge of typographic form but who was also open-minded and enthusiastic about new technologies. With foresight or good fortune, he discovered the young Adrian Frutiger and invited him to Paris.

One of Frutiger's earliest tasks at Deberny & Peignot (prior to working on typefaces for the Lumitype) was to design a script capable of competing with Excoffon's recently released *Mistral* by Fonderie Olive. Up until this point it had always been Marcel Olive who was trying to keep up or second-guess his major rival Charles Peignot. Now, for the first time, Olive had released an original and highly popular typeface and so it was Peignot who felt he had to respond. The task was given to Frutiger whose answer was *Ondine*, released in 1954.

It is a script face but with none of the panache or technical acumen of *Mistral*. *Ondine* is reminiscent of uncial and Carolingian minuscule writing, with gently swelling main strokes, sharp terminals, open counters and the illusion of a slight back-slant. Frutiger explained that he:

> ... wrote the letters with a broad pen on tracing paper and put them in an enlarger (the capital letters had to be 20 cm tall). I produced precise drawings from these, used white transfer paper to copy the type to black card and then cut the letters out with scissors. That way I could spread them out in front of me.[2]

It is probable that the vague sense of Arabian exoticism was unintended; 'ondine' is a French term for water nymphs. This and the two preceding typefaces he designed, *Président* and *Phoebus* (both 1953), came to be regarded by Frutiger as 'practice work'.[3]

For the Lumitype system Frutiger found himself having to redraw the classic repertoire: *Garamond, Baskerville, Bodoni* among others for its matrix disks. It was a depressing experience. He later wrote: 'the fonts [I redrew] don't have any historical worth'.[4] But when Peignot decided he needed a sans serif to add to the growing Lumitype range of typefaces Frutiger saw an opportunity, and persuaded him to allow the development of a design he had begun as a twenty-one-year-old student in Zurich (rather than adapt *Europe*, as was Peignot's suggestion; Deberny &

Above: Adrian Frutiger, *Ondine*, 1954.

Peignot had acquired the rights to distribute Paul Renner's *Futura* in France under the name *Europe*). Trials were made and approved, production went ahead, and *Univers* was released in 1957.

In the same year, *Folio*, designed by Walter Baum and Konrad Bauer for the Bauer foundry in Germany, and *Neue Haas Grotesk*, designed by Max Miedinger and Eduard Hoffmann for the Haas foundry in Switzerland, also appeared. *Univers*, along with its two rivals, represented an attempt to provide a 'neutralized' sans serif whose style was 'no style'. This new typography emanating from Switzerland (described as The Swiss Style or International Style) was cultivated by a second generation of Bauhaus-influenced designers such as Max Bill, designer, artist, and teacher, and Ernst Keller, influential Principal and teacher at the Kunstgewerbeschule in Zurich – where the young Frutiger, eight years previously, had sketched his first ideas for *Univers*.

Initially, the most distinctive feature of *Univers* was that it comprised a family of twenty-one variants. This was planned at the outset; the typeface was designed within a programme that was demonstrated by a grid-like presentation with each variant bearing an index number. While this gave an air of cool, systematic objectivity, the sophistication of *Univers* depended on traditional drawing skills and assured modulation – it was an innovative typeface based in Swiss craft and tradition.

Although *Univers* was originally conceived to take advantage of the cost- and space-saving potential of phototypesetting (Deberny & Peignot advertised each of their Lumitype glass master discs as replacing three tons of brass matrices), the company also arranged licensing deals with type foundries, the most notable being the Monotype Corporation. Arguably the required amendments made for Monotype composing machines – leading to some characters being fractionally wider – improved Frutiger's typeface. *Univers* was certainly a major success for Monotype with several weights being among their bestselling typefaces (second only to Morison's *Times New Roman*), despite being released in 1963–64 – by which time many type historians assume the era of metal type was finished.

The success of *Univers* was due to skilful unobtrusive detailing. Frutiger eliminated virtually everything but the essential form of each letter. Yet it is the most visually sensitive as well as the most rational of the postwar sans serifs, a point cleverly emphasized by the iconic representation of its numeric system identifying its different styles.[5] It was also the most original. Miedinger and

Above: Adrian Frutiger, *Univers*, roman and slanted, 1960.

Hoffmann had, in the main, taken *Akzidenz Grotesk*, still popular among Swiss typographers, and 'polished it up';[6] *Folio* is modelled even closer on *Akzidenz Grotesk*, and despite its elegant promotion by the Bauer foundry was the least commercially successful of the three sans serifs released in 1957 – all of which emphasises what a remarkable feat Frutiger had achieved with *Univers*. It corresponded to the ideal of 'total design', epitomized by Dutch designers Wim Crouwel and Benno Wissing who named their all-encompassing design studio Total Design in 1963, and where *Univers* was virtually adopted as the national typeface of the Netherlands. In the US and Germany, graphic designers preferred *Helvetica*. Frutiger later caustically – but with justification – characterized the difference as '*Helvetica* is the jeans, and *Univers* the dinner jacket'.[7]

Although designed and manufactured in the heart of Paris, the origins of *Univers* are firmly set in Switzerland. There, Emil Ruder, influential writer, teacher, graphic designer and a leading disseminator of International Style ideology, also actively supported *Univers*, first in the journal *Neue Grafik* and then in a special issue of *Typographische Monatsblätter* (with German, French and limited English texts), in which the Monotype cutting of *Univers* made its first appearance.[8] The international platform provided by *Typographische Monatsblätter* was hugely influential in establishing *Univers* as a truly 'universal' typeface, eminently suited to the intentions of the International Style. It did, of course, also attract some, though limited, criticism. Karl Gerstner, a prominent graphic designer and writer who would later help guide Swiss typography out of the ultra-cool impasse it had created – complained that *Univers* (and *Helvetica*) was too smooth, too regular in tone. Regardless of whatever aesthetic or ideological assets to which it aspired, *Univers* was certainly not a 'functional' typeface: 'what has ocular clarity may appear monotonous when read'.[9]

Surprisingly, Frutiger agreed. Talking in 1977 about the recent implementation of the typeface he designed for the signage of the new Paris airport, Charles de Gaulle, Frutiger's explanation of why he resisted the pressure to adopt *Univers*, is reminiscent of Gerstner's remarks: '*Univers* would not suit either the general aesthetic and architectural concept or the principles of optimum legibility … The characters of *Univers* are a little too "smooth" for sufficiently rapid and accurate reading on indicator panels.' The new typeface he designed was originally called *Roissy*, the

ABCDEFGHIJKLMNOP
QRSTUVWXYZ   .,:;?!-–"
abcdefghijklmnopqrstu
vwxyzß & 1234567890

name of the new airport when first commissioned in 1968 (and completed in 1972), but renamed *Frutiger* by Linotype in 1974. It proved groundbreaking – a highly efficient sans serif but with personality and bonhomie.

Frutiger's distinctive character and improved readability comes largely from the design of its terminals, formed so that each character works collectively (rather than independently, as in *Univers* and its ideological rival *Helvetica*) to form a connection with its neighbours. For example, with *Frutiger*, the curves and terminations of the 'c' and the 's' encourage the eye to move smoothly across to the next character. In contrast, the curves and terminations of the same characters in *Univers* turn downward to deny connectivity. It is the ability of each character to make a connection with its neighbour that helps to make *Frutiger* feel warmer and inviting.

The period in which type was considered better if it was anonymous was relatively brief. Frutiger was happy to return to a warmer, more sociable and readable type, and was never particularly complimentary about *Univers*, saying that once completed it held 'little interest' for him. He wrote in the Linotype specimen booklet for *Frutiger* that it was time for the mechanistic nature of *Futura* and *Kabel*, and the anonymity sought by *Helvetica* and *Univers*, to make room 'for a type design which has the freehand rhythm of writing as opposed to "constructivism" ... to allow the appearance of clearly identifiable characters within the harmonious word-image'.[10]

Frutiger designed many typeface families over approximately sixty years, but *Frutiger* remained his greatest achievement. In hindsight *Frutiger* might appear to be a relatively mild rebuff to the doctrine of the International Style; but coming from the designer of *Univers* – for many the apogee in that movement's reductive doctrine – *Frutiger*, a distinct and amenable typeface, was a sign to young Swiss typographers that the Swiss straightjacket had, at last, fallen away.

Above left: Adrian Frutiger, *Frutiger*, Linotype, 1974.

Wim Crouwel THE NETHERLANDS 1928 – 2019

Crouwel was born in Groningen, a northern Dutch province, and spent his early teenage years there during German occupation. His father, Jacobus, was a printer. After the war Crouwel studied art, but he was equally fascinated by the modernist design he saw featured in magazines at the town library and remodelled his bedroom accordingly. In his early twenties he built a houseboat; this huge technical challenge was undertaken in an efficient and logical manner by ensuring the proportions of the boat were based on the standard measurements of the sheets of wood required, including its open-plan interior and furniture.

Crouwel studied at the Academie Minerva (Art School) in Groningen, where he saw a poster designed by A.M. Cassandre for the Étoile du Nord express train and began to consider the possibility that design might be a career. He moved to Amsterdam in 1951, primarily to study graphic design by attending evening classes at the Instituut voor Kunstnijverheidsonderwijs (Institute for Applied Arts) later renamed the Gerrit Rietveld Academy. During the daytime Crouwel worked for an exhibition design company while occasionally also working for Dick Elffers, a highly respected graphic designer whose clients included the Rijksmuseum, Amsterdam.

During this period, he discovered Swiss Typography and was astonished by the daring and simple clarity of their typography:

> I met Müller-Brockmann on one of my trips to Switzerland. He later introduced me to his friends: Armin Hofmann, he was a teacher; Emil Ruder, Chief of the Basel School of Arts; Richard Lohse and Max Bill. In 1957, I became a member of the AGI (Alliance Graphique Internationale), I got to know Müller-Brockmann really well and we became good friends. I was absolutely highly influenced by his posters.[1]

Crouwel's preference for lowercase letters came from his interest in Bauhaus theory concerning elemental functions of typographic form. His interest was drawn to the theory that simplicity was essential to clarity, but as with everything else that Crouwel did, aesthetics also played a critical role – believing that the shape of the letters themselves had a deep impact on the way the information they carried was perceived.

Opposite: Wim Crouwel, detail of a page from *Kwadraatbladen*, a 20-page magazine dedicated to his *New Alphabet*, 1967.

An example of this was Crouwel's redesign, with Jolijn van de Wouw, of the Dutch telephone directory in 1977. In the pre-digital era, every owner of a telephone had a telephone directory; an essential document, it had a weighty physical presence in every home, office, shop, school and telephone kiosk, ensuring that from an early age everyone learned how to use it and became familiar with its distinctive page layout. Telephone directories were printed in their millions and updated annually and, over time, each country developed its own, subtlety different way of organizing precisely the same information. These small differences came to represent something akin to a national identity. Hence, when Crouwel and Van de Wouw offered a radical change, it became not just a national but an international story.

Crouwel and Van de Wouw were able to demonstrate that their solution would not only make the directory easier to use, but also significantly reduce the amount of paper required by using lowercase only, reducing the size of type (*Univers*), and by the editing and reorganization of the information. The justification for such radical change was a saving in cost to the environment as well as to their client's annual print bills. This attention to aesthetic, cultural and environmental impact caused the Netherlands to be perceived outside its borders as a liberal, forward-looking country where radical solutions were welcome.

However, within the Netherlands there were complaints, primarily about the small size of type, but also from some who protested that they 'didn't want to be known as a number' (telephone numbers were placed first followed by names). Some aspects of the directory were amended in a redesign forced upon Crouwel and his design studio a few years later – including an increase in type-size, causing the reduction of four columns per page to three. A special set of numerals, slightly wider to incorporate larger counters to aid recognition, was designed by Gerard Unger and Chris Vermaas. Remarkably, the most radical aspect of the original design – the all-lowercase typography – was maintained.

Below: Wim Crouwel and Jolijn van de Wouw, the Dutch telephone directory, using *Univers*, 1977.

33 01 61	**kwekerij de witte lelie,** kanaalwg 18/b	33 03 55	**motorhome,** kerkstr 22, bromf hdl	33 02 39	**osterwei, b. van,** fuutstr 37
33 01 16	**laan, t,** berkenstede 57			33 02 46	**otten, i,** keizersgrt 819/a
33 01 19	**laan, a,** beukenwg 29	33 05 62	**mottighuizen, l,** middenwg 44	33 04 17	**ottenoord, l,** radboud 41
33 02 73	**laan, pieter,** j jongkindstr 91	33 05 73	**muis, r w d m,** beukenwg 19	33 06 10	**otter, p,** javastr 12
33 07 48	**laan, w,** zwaluwstr 18	33 01 43	**muistemakers, h j,** kalfjesln 88	33 05 63	**outeren, r s,** berkenstede 16
33 01 67	**laar-nyhoff, mw b s,** kalkoenstr 5	33 06 66	**mulder, k,** wormerstr 16	33 06 62	**paarlbank, n,** kerkstr 18/1
33 02 84	**lakeman, g,** wielingenstr 181, drogist	33 02 33	**mulderije, c. vd,** kerkstr 111/1	33 03 43	**padjesmand, j. van,** kanaalw
		33 04 54	**muziekhandel libretto,** n beetsstr 44	33 04 57	**panacras, ds w,** javastr 29
				33 04 20	**panbaker, dr th tj,** kalfjesln 3

Crouwel's work for the Dutch PTT (postal services) was done under the auspices of Total Design. This multi-disciplinary design consultancy was founded in 1963 by Wim Crouwel and Benno Wissing, and based in Amsterdam. Wissing, five years older than Crouwel, had worked as a graphic designer since 1949 for, among others, the Boymans Van Beuningen Museum in Rotterdam. His posters were chiefly typographic and, like Crouwel, his approach to organizing information was systematic; the grid being a dominant feature in his work. In 1962 Wissing teamed up with Kho Liang Ie for his largest assignment to date – the internal signage system for the new Schipol Airport. The result, utilizing *Akzidenz Grotesk* with no capitals except for gate numbers ('B3' etc.), was a resounding success. It was during the Schipol Airport project that Wissing joined Crouwel and Frisco Kramer, an industrial designer, to create Total Design (often reduced to TD). They were joined soon after by graphic designer Ben Bos.

The prime objective in setting up TD was to stop major Dutch companies looking abroad when offering large-scale complex design commissions. By this criterion, TD was a huge success, serving prestigious clients such as De Bijenkorf, the Dutch Post Office, Peter Stuyvesant, Amsterdam Stedelijk Museum, the Schiphol Airport, the Dutch Pavilion for the 1970 Osaka World Fair among many others.[2] TD was also the precursor of similar multidisciplinary design consultancies – Wolff Olins (1965) and Pentagram (1972), both London based, being early prime examples. Success attracted more clients and inevitably the number of employees increased. By the end of the 1960s there were over forty, making TD (and the Netherlands in general) an attractive place to gain valuable experience for a new generation of graphic designers from around the world. From its beginning it was Crouwel who came to personify the agency, often acting as its spokesperson and, in effect, a distinctive walking advertisement; he was very tall and very slim, and had his suits tailor-made as soon as he could afford it.

Although the design of the PTT telephone directory caused international reverberations, the work that first brought Crouwel to international attention began as a low-key personal exercise. He was interested in the way letter-forms reflected the limited technical capacities of the machines – typically, that letters on low-resolution video screens appeared rough and irregular due to the technology's inability to display curves. It was during a visit

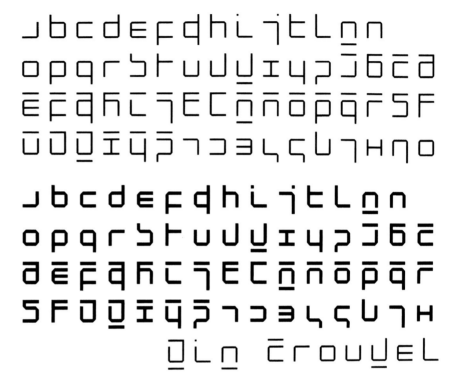

Above right: Wim Crouwel, *New Alphabet*, two (of three) weights, 1967.

to a major print and paper exhibition in Düsseldorf that Crouwel saw the Hell company's Digiset digital typesetter and was appalled by the print-outs he saw. Not only were the conventional typefaces employed horribly distorted, but their form changed radically at every change of size; the grid of dots remained the same, and so as a letter got smaller there were fewer dots available with which to describe it (see p. 251).

Crouwel came away intrigued by the idea of creating a typeface specifically for the crude grid of dot-matrix print technology that would enable each character to maintain its formal appearance, regardless of the size it was printed. The result, made public in 1967, was *New Alphabet*. Its first appearance was in *Kwadraatbladen* (Square Format) no. 23, a journal edited by Pieter Brattinga and published by the printing company Steendrukkerij de jong in Hilversum for distribution primarily to designers. Serendipitous or calculated, the timing of its public debut was perfect. Computer technology was a hugely topical subject of discussion; exhibitions showing its social implications and its creative potential were taking place everywhere.[3] Nevertheless, Crouwel could not have foreseen the remarkable response his *New Alphabet* would receive. It was reported in the national and regional newspapers, he was invited to give lectures both at home and abroad, and numerous articles were published in the specialist design press. It was a radical-looking type with no illusions whatsoever about its artificial appearance – 'new forms for new technologies' became the mantra. It proved popular enough to be manufactured in 'rub-down' form by Letter Press, a Dutch subsidiary of Mecanorma, Letraset's chief rival.

New Alphabet was a single lowercase typeface with letterforms made up of rectangular segments drawn on a grid of (mostly) five by nine units with 45° bevelled corners. Every character was the same width. About half the characters were easily recognizable, but many others – for example, 'a', 'g', 'j', 'k', 'm', 's', 'v', 'w', 'x' and 'z' – if viewed singularly, were not. But Crouwel was not concerned by criticism regarding legibility because, as he repeated many times, the typeface had been an experiment and was never intended to be used. Without doubt, what helped to give *New Alphabet* such resonance was the design of its presentation. The long-established square format of *Kwadraatbladen* was the perfect vehicle for a typeface whose key form was also a square. Despite its experimental status, *New Alphabet* has an elegant and seemingly effortless authority which it has retained despite the transformations that digital technology has wrought in the meantime.

Below: Wim Crouwel, *Vierkant*. The original uppercase character set created for the 1972 *Drupa catalogue*. This version was recreated by Crouwel and David Quay (The Foundry) c.2012.

One of Crouwel's first clients whilst still working as a freelance had been the Van Abbemuseum in Eindhoven, for which he designed catalogues, invitations and posters until 1964. When Edy de Wilde, director of the museum, became director of the Stedelijk Museum in Amsterdam he took Crouwel with him. Succeeding the renowned designer Willem Sandberg, Crowel had sole responsibility for the Stedelijk's identity until the end of De Wilde's directorship in 1985. He designed almost all its posters and catalogues by developing a modular grid system that provided visual consistency to the museum's graphic identity.

Crouwel wanted to test how far the explorative intent of the typographer could progress while maintaining the primary function of typography. With the cultural authority of the Stedelijk he was able to push the semantic extremities of typography – modifying, sometimes drastically, the appearance of type, adjusting letterspacing and word spacing to intensify or qualify meaning. While the grid underpinned all the posters, Crouwel's inventive prowess was the other, equally important, presence. Whimsical choice of colour (puce green for a Fernand Leger poster), humour (a blown-up balloon-shape alphabet for Claus Oldenburg), as well as the uneasy juxtapositions of image and word and the closeness of words to the edges of the poster, make it clear that Crouwel never stopped testing the formal limits expected of type and typography.

The use of humour helped keep Crowel's typography relevant long after Modernism. There are several photographs of Crouwel not only dressed like a Starfleet commander, but also striking a feigned thespian pose: hands on hips, feet apart and with his head turned looking, one imagines, 'to where no man has gone before'. Such self-deprecating humour often accompanied Crouwel's work and helped raise it above mere function. Gerard Unger, who worked with Crouwel at Total Design for a brief period shortly after leaving college, described Crouwel's work as owing its visual power rather less to functionalist formula and more to artistic talent. In fact, Crouwel described himself as a 'functionalist troubled by aesthetics'.[4]

Long before Crouwel had effectively retired, a counter-culture that spurned the plodding orthodoxy of monolithic corporate identities – what had effectively been the mainstay of Total Design – had arisen. 'Form follows function' had been replaced by 'form follows fun'. A dramatic cultural shift had taken place and Crouwel discovered that his *New Alphabet*, once the ultimate of cool modernist statements, had been transformed into a jovial and irreverent post-modernist statement appearing, for example, on the record cover of Joy Division's *Substance*, designed by Brett Wickens.

Crouwel did not succumb to Postmodernism but, importantly, he did not decry it either. As the culture of graphic design moved away from Modernism, Crouwel's status oddly grew as exhibitions of his work were mounted and his earlier typefaces – *New Alphabet, Gridnik* (initially designed for Olivetti and then used on PTT stamps), *Catalogue* (the Oldenburg alphabet), *Stedelijk* (used on the Vormgevers poster) and others – were digitally redrawn by David Quay and Freda Sack at The Foundry in London and issued as part of their Architype series.[4] The success of this partnership, established in 1996, encouraged Crouwel to design two new faces with Quay – *Ingenieur* and *Vierkant* – both of which were based on lettering drawn for exhibition catalogues and posters in the 1960s and 1970s.

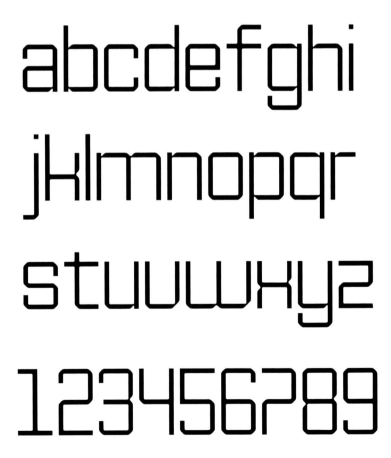

Left: Wim Crouwel, *Ingenieur*, designed for the Ewald Mataré exhibition poster, 1964. Recreated by Crouwel and David Quay (The Foundry) in 2012.

nimodeh
frtuscjbal
pqkgvwy

Bram de Does   THE NETHERLANDS 1934 – 2015

Bram de Does was born into a typographical family. His grandfather had started a small jobbing print business in Amsterdam called Systema; the business was then passed to De Does's father, Abraham. During the Second World War the business was forced to close; Abraham could not get a work permit from the Germans, and his Linotype machinery and equipment were confiscated to be melted down to make armaments. Abraham survived by passing his customers on to other firms in return for a percentage; he then rebuilt Systema after the war.

Bram de Does excelled in mathematics and was passionately interested in music, taking violin lessons from the age of eleven. He seriously considered applying to study at the music conservatory but was unhappy with the syllabus. Impetuously, he decided to change course and become a maker rather than a player of musical instruments, before realizing that in the austere post-war period such work was impossible to find. Finally, and perhaps inevitably, he began helping in his father's printshop.

Most of the typefaces at Systema were bought from Lettergieterei Amsterdam, but for one of his customers Abraham had bought some *Romanée*, Jan van Krimpen's handsome design for the Enschedé foundry, and the young De Does was smitten. He began to interest himself seriously in type – based as he was in Amsterdam, De Does was able to use the library of the Dutch equivalent of the Federation of Master Printers and examine their rich collection of books on typography. He was even allowed to take home on loan a copy of Enschedé's 1768 *Proef van Letteren*, the primary document in the cataloguing of the famous firm's rich historical type holdings. At the age of eighteen, having spent less than one year in his father's printshop, De Does designed Systema's type specimen book.

De Does enrolled in the three-year print management course at the Amsterdamse Grafische School (Amsterdam Printing Trade School) which included enough 'hands-on' work with type and press to satisfy his practical preoccupation.

> We were subtly invited to work in a 'modern' or 'fresh' manner and by all means avoid symmetry. I soon rebelled against such a foolish principle imposed on us and started setting symmetrical texts with nicely spaced small capitals. I needed to be so obstinate to gain a sense of self-esteem in that small community.[1]

Opposite: Bram de Does, working drawings for *Lexicon 1,* December 1989.

His teacher, M.H. Groenendaal, was broad-minded enough to support him and encourage his printing experiments. As well as *Romanée*, De Does also discovered *Bembo* (a Monotype revival) and later described these two faces, when letterpress-printed on an off-white, lightly textured paper, as 'love at first sight which has never left me'.[2]

On leaving college De Does had a brief spell in the sales office of an Amsterdam printer before being offered a design job in 1958 at the distinguished Joh. Enschedé & Zonen in Haarlem, where the infamous Jan van Krimpen ruled with renowned zeal. Such was the reputation of Van Krimpen's temper that De Does entered the building with trepidation. But within two months, and before he had even met him, Van Krimpen suddenly died.

Nevertheless, De Does confessed that he did not fit in comfortably at Enschedé, a traditional firm where employees at management level – which included senior designers – were expected at the very

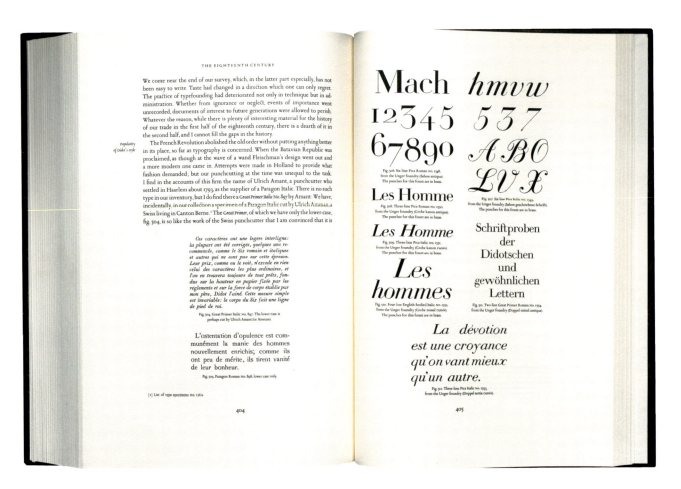

Below: Bram de Does, *Romanée*, as used in Harry Carter's 1978 English translation of *Typefoundries in the Netherlands,* originally written in 1908 by Charles Enschedé.

least to wear a jacket and tie. Sem Hartz, who took over as art director from Van Krimpen, always dressed immaculately as, of course, had Van Krimpen. In contrast, De Does preferred a loose-fitting jumper. This might have been the reason that some within the upper-echelons at Enschedé concluded that De Does 'lacked managerial drive'.[3]

He left in 1962 to work for the Querido publishing house, but resigned after four months and went through a difficult period of reassessment. Before a year had passed, however, Sem Hartz, who knew De Does well enough to know that his preference for casual clothes was not a reflection of his approach to work, had persuaded him to return to Enschedé. Indeed, De Does was a perfectionist, so much so that he was nicknamed 'puntje in, puntje uit' among the compositors at Enschedé because of his frequent instructions to insert or remove a point space.

On his return De Does's task was the design of annual reports, commemorative volumes and type specimens, as well as overseeing the work of other designers. He also became closely involved with the company's move into photocomposition. Enschedé had invested in the Mark 3 Monophoto in 1967, but like many designers De Does was dissatisfied with the appearance of early Monophoto faces, especially the deplorable Monophoto version of *Bembo*. For many years all of Enschedé's more prestigious work continued to be letterpress printed.

In 1968 De Does was promoted to chief typographic designer, but still managed to avoid administrative responsibility. Beginning around 1970 he attempted, with his wife and family, to establish a parallel career in bio-dynamic market gardening while continuing to work two or three days a week for Enschedé. The plan lasted three years. A more significant, and a far longer-lasting, endeavour was his private press, Spectatorpens, set up around 1961. The printing was done in his father's printshop in the evenings using *Romanée*.

The 1970s were a volatile time at Enschedé. The technology concerned with the making of type was changing. Phototypesetting, though still considered by many to be crude and inept, was under rapid development as type foundries, including Monotype, Berthold and Linotype, as well as many new companies with no typographic pedigree, fiercely competed to dominate. It was certain that this new technology, or something similar, was going to replace metal type; a rudimentary digital technology was already in use and its development causing much speculation. Perhaps it was the inevitability of the seismic change fast approaching that caused the management at Enschedé to take a renewed interest in the company's incomparable history that resulted in De Does being given a project that would take up much of the next decade.

The task was to design and oversee the printing and binding of Harry Carter's English translation of *Typefoundries in the Netherlands*, a text originally written in 1908 by Charles Enschedé. The book is a history of Dutch type until 1900, utilizing the outstanding collection of original types, punches, strikes and matrices preserved within the Enschedé Museum. All of the text samples were set in original or recast hand-set types, with the body text set in *Romanée*. This was to be De Does's crowning accomplishment at Enschedé. The prestige of the project meant that he was able to insist that a single pressman be responsible for printing the whole book, with a 'reserve' in case of illness, plus two hand-compositors and a further four employees – all of whom worked solely on the task for a year. The finished book, the last to be printed entirely by letterpress at Enschedé, was published in 1978.

The transition from metal type to phototypesetting was a gradual process at Enschedé, taken over ten years. The first generation Monophoto typesetters had lacked particular characters in certain fonts and this caused De Does to attempt, with the help of Henk Drost, Enschedé's last punchcutter, to design the missing characters. 1978 was also the year that Enschedé finally decided to replace its Monophoto typesetters with second-generation phototypesetting machines from the Swiss company Bobst Graphic (which would become Autologic in 1981 when ownership moved to the US). When Bobst Graphic asked if they could add *Romanée* to the Bobst type library, the management at Enschedé asked De Does for his opinion and he advised against it. His main objection concerned the issue of optical sizing, explaining that each of the designated sizes of Van Krimpen's *Romanée* had been cut with the necessary adjustments to the distribution of weight to ensure optimum readability at each size. De Does was all too aware that a highly refined serifed typeface like *Romanée* would be particularly susceptible to the anomalies created by current phototypesetting technology. He

Below: Bram de Does, *Trinité 1, 2,* and *3*, showing the regular weight with their three different ascender and descender lengths.

abbbcdddefffggghhhiiijjj

suggested that a new typeface, one designed specifically for the new technology, would be a better option. To his surprise the Enschedé management agreed and invited De Does to design it.

The result was *Trinité*, released in 1982. The process began by studying *Romanée* and, to a lesser degree, *Bembo* and Eric Gill's *Joanna*, but also looking closely at small Bible types in order to study spacing and proportions. De Does did this by photographing characters and enlarging them, and then refining his drawing skills by working over these and experimenting with their structure and form. The name *Trinité* derives from the fact that the final font family has three variants, each with a different length of ascender and descender while retaining the same width.

Left: Cover of Autologic's house journal showing Bram de Does' *Trinité 1, 2,* and *3*, published by Autologic in association with Joh. Enschedé, 1982.

The result is arresting, and yet its distinctive appearance does not interfere with legibility or rhythmic flow. Indeed, 'rhythmic flow' is probably its most distinctive feature. In an interview with Jan Middendorp,[4] De Does explained, 'Early Renaissance [printed] pages present a stronger, more regular overall image. I discovered two factors which contribute to that impression: the fact that characters are subtly slanted [to the right] and that the serifs are slightly longer towards the right'. The slant that De Does gave *Trinité* is, indeed, subtle: 1° for characters with a top serif – 'b', 'h', 'i', 'k', 'l', 'm', 'n'; slightly more for 'a', 'd', 't', and slightly less for 'j', 'p', 'r'. But this, combined with the asymmetric foot-serifs, the fact that every line is curved, and that capitals are considerably shorter than ascenders, helps to provide the forward momentum – the 'forward swing',[5] that De Does sought.

Trinité was released as a typeface for the Autologic company under license from Enschedé. It was successful for a period, but wider acceptance was hampered by the rapid rate of development in digital technology. When Enschedé replaced its Autologic phototypesetters with the Linotronic digital system, they kept one Autologic phototypesetter purely for setting *Trinité*. With the technology for which it was designed having been superseded, *Trinité* was in danger of extinction. Peter Matthias Noordzij, type designer and admirer of *Trinité*, explained to De Does that he should digitize the font using Ikarus, but De Does was not enthusiastic about learning another technology and offered Noordzij the job of doing it for him. Noordzij agreed, and then approached Enschedé to ask what their future plans were for *Trinité*. Their answer, effectively, was nothing.

This was a time of radical change at Enschedé. The company had outgrown its city centre location and was about to move its printing activities to purpose-designed buildings on the outskirts of Haarlem. The old type-founding machines were no longer needed, and the production of metal type discontinued. Noordzij argued that a digital version of *Trinité* would announce the beginning of a new era for the company – as the publisher of digital fonts. Cautious at first, the management then agreed to a variation of the plan. Noordzij was to establish a small-scale digital 'foundry' with himself as its principal, so that the venerable Joh. Enschedé & Zonen, established in 1743, could continue as The Enschedé Font Foundry (TEFF). The long-term plan was that the extensive collection of typefaces held by the Enschedé library could be digitized.[6] The first of these was *Trinité*, re-released in 1992. Following its successful new identity as a PostScript font, *Trinité* quickly became a standard typeface in Dutch book design.

During the digitization process of *Trinité* De Does had taken the opportunity to make minor modifications, and although he now considered certain aspects of the face to be impaired – for example, the angle of the italic not providing enough contrast with the roman, or the contrast in stroke thickness not being quite sufficient – he had no appetite to undertake the design of another typeface. However, in 1989 Bernard C. van Bercum, the designer of the twelfth edition of *Vale Dale's Dictionary* of the Dutch Language – a venerable three-volume monument – was interested to see what a digital version of *Trinité* at 7 point would look like. He approached De Does who initially offered to modify some of the characters, such as the counters of the 'a' and 'e', to improve legibility at the smaller size, but then realized that this was a rare opportunity to design a typeface for a specific purpose as well as revisit the minor faults in *Trinité*. He offered to design a test page free of charge.

De Does and Noordzij were already working together on the digital version of *Trinité*, and now the teamwork extended to the new provisional typeface and the *Vale Dale Dictionary* test page. The starting point was the preliminary research De Does had done previously for *Trinité* and especially the small types he had studied such as the 4.5 point *Bible* font from Monotype. The editorial board of the *Vale Dale Dictionary* compared the De Does face with several alternatives and decided to offer him the commission. The new face, appropriately called *Lexicon*, was first seen in 1992 when the new edition of the *Vale Dale Dictionary* was published.

Lexicon has two versions: the original dictionary version with its very short ascenders and descenders, and a second version (which took a further three years to complete and was released as part of the TEFF library in 1997) with ascenders and descenders of a more conventional length. It is a more rugged, more multi-purpose typeface than *Trinité*, capable of functioning not only at small sizes but also at low resolution or when printed onto a coarser paper, a fact confirmed when it was chosen for both text and headlines by the prestigious evening newspaper *NRC Handelsblad*, replacing Stanley Morison's *Times New Roman*.

Above: Bram de Does, in collaboration with Peter Matthias Noordzij, *Lexicon 1*, shown here at 12 and 7 point, 1992. *Lexicon 2* has taller, more standard size ascenders.

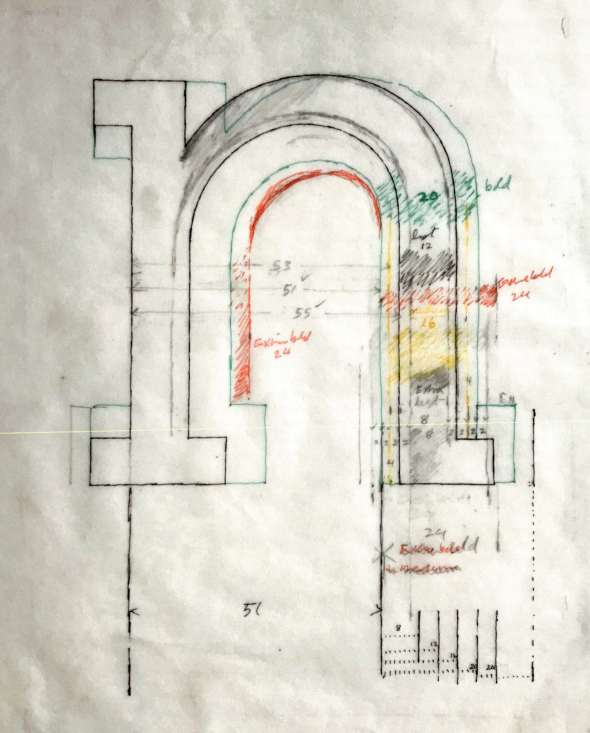

Margaret Calvert GREAT BRITAIN 1936 –

Margaret Calvert was born in South Africa and spent her early years there. In 1949, aged thirteen, together with her mother, sister and accompanied by a small stray dog, she sailed from South Africa to England, docking at Southampton in January 1950 where they were met by a bevy of English relatives.[1]

In London she attended St Paul's Girls' School. Then, aged seventeen, Calvert became a student at Chelsea College of Art where she embarked on a four-year course in illustration (two-year Intermediate followed by a two-year National Diploma). Calvert impressed her tutors, but she never felt that illustration was the right subject for her. Looking back on that time she realized that what she aspired to be was a designer, but the field of graphic design was virtually unknown in UK education at that time.[2] As an illustration student she was advised to steer well clear of typography.

In her final year, a new tutor, Richard 'Jock' Kinneir (1917–1994) arrived in the studio and made an impression on Calvert: '[T]here was something about his attitude which I liked'.[3] It was certainly enough to make her begin attending more regularly. Kinneir was, in fact, in the process of setting up his own design practice.[4] He had been a student at Chelsea School of Art himself, attending from 1935 to 1939, and after the war had been employed as an exhibition designer by the Central Office of Information, the UK government's own marketing and communications agency. In 1950 he moved to the Design Research Unit (Milner Gray, one of its founders, also taught at Chelsea). DRU – it was rarely called by its full name – was the first British design consultancy combining expertise in architecture, graphics and industrial design; it was a genuine precursor to the multidisciplinary design consultancies such as Total Design in Amsterdam and Pentagram in London. DRU played a major role in the Festival of Britain exposition in 1953.

In 1956 Kinneir left DRU to start his own design practice, and shortly after its launch was commissioned to design the signage at Gatwick Airport. He obtained the job almost by chance. As Calvert explained:

> His neighbour, David Alford, worked at the architectural practice Yorke, Rosenberg & Mardall, who were designing Gatwick – a hugely

Opposite: Margaret Calvert, working drawing for *Calvert*, c.1979–80.

prestigious project. They happened to be standing together in a bus queue waiting to catch a Green Line bus to Hyde Park Corner when during their conversation Alford said, 'We've got this job, and we need someone to do signs, are you interested?' Kinneir said 'Of course', although he knew very little, if anything, about signing large buildings.

Calvert had completed her final exams when Kinneir said, 'I've got this job and I need an assistant'. 'What does it involve?' Calvert asked. 'Well, it's Design', he replied, '–nothing like what you have been doing here'.[5] It was 1957, and Calvert had just turned twenty-one.

Designing the signage for Gatwick proved to be a huge learning curve for Kinneir as well as Calvert, and involved a great deal of research into typefaces, their varying functions and, especially, the nature of legibility. The need for a logical, systematized arrangement of all information across the whole signage system, including sizes and placement of the signs themselves, quickly became apparent to Calvert. The Gatwick management had requested a colour-coded system, but after rigorous testing Kinneir and Calvert found that white letters on green[6] proved most effective, and so this was maintained throughout.

The Gatwick project was well received and, as a result, Colin Anderson, chairman of the P&O Line shipping company, commissioned Kinneir to design a baggage labelling system (Anderson claimed many of the P&O porters were illiterate) The task was passed to Calvert. When Anderson was appointed chairman of a new government committee created to oversee the design of the signage for the new British motorway network, Kinneir was duly commissioned to do the work.

The system of traffic signs used in Britain after the Second World War had evolved through many years of amendments and modifications, going back to the beginning of the century. The Ministry of Transport was forced into action because Britain's first motorway, the Preston Bypass (later to become part of the M6 motorway) was due to open in 1959, and it was clear that current sign regulations were inadequate for motorway traffic.

The Preston Bypass became the test bed for draft designs proposed by Kinneir and Calvert. Following German and American models, both of which had substantial motorway networks, the committee had already decided that uppercase and lowercase type should be used rather than capitals, as had been used on Britain's roads since 1933. Both the American *FHWA Series* (or '*Highway Gothic*' as it was unofficially called, initially

Above: Comparison between Margaret Calvert and Jock Kinneir's *Transport* and David Kindersley's *MOT Serif*, using capitals only with the information ranged left. Despite the additional cost, the committee chose the Kinneir-Calvert solution.

designed by Theodore Forbes)[7] and the German *DIN* alphabet system[8] had their advocates on the committee. It had also already been decided that white lowercase lettering on a blue background should be used, as it was in Germany.

After the first meeting, Kinneir received a letter from Anderson:

> I am anxious you shouldn't embark upon inventing an alphabet of a character quite 'new'. We have, as a committee, got into the habit of accepting the general weight and appearance of the German alphabet as being the sort of thing we need! I think therefore something on those lines is what the Committee believes it wants …[9]

The request was ignored. It was felt that the *DIN* alphabet suffered from rather narrow and rectangular letterforms. Nor was Calvert impressed by the fact it had effectively been designed by engineers. She later wrote that they felt '…the German sans serif … although demonstrably effective, would not sit well in the English landscape. So we started from scratch, with a specification for the ideal letterform, having looked at other possibilities (including adapting the typeface *Akzidenz Grotesk* – a major influence regarding proportion and overall appearance)'.[10]

Akzidenz Grotesk and similar sans serif typefaces had been revived by type foundries in mainland Europe during the 1950s, and the Berthold type foundry had recently reissued the family in 1955. This was then followed by a several new typefaces aiming to achieve the same level of anonymity. While the clarity of the results was generally admired, Kinneir and Calvert also decided that a sense of 'Britishness' should be infused into their alphabet. For this they looked to Edward Johnston and Eric Gill.

There are details – such as the curve on the end of the lowercase 'l' that mirrors the distinctive tails they devised for the 'a' and 't', and the high vertex of the 'M' – that are reminiscent of Edward Johnston's *Underground Alphabet*. Elsewhere, Calvert explained:

> The obliquely cut curved strokes of the letters a, c, e, f, g, j, s, t and y, were specifically designed to help retain the word shape of place names when slightly letterspaced; a necessary compromise to offset the effect of 'halation', when viewed at the appropriate 'decision-making' distance, in full glare of headlights.[11]

These features were also intended to provide a more open and inviting sensibility to British motorway signage than that seen

in European signage systems. The final version was named *Transport*.

The Preston Bypass was officially opened in 1959. The new signs immediately came under attack from several quarters, most notable being those associated with prewar typographic revivalism, including Stanley Morison who helped Reynolds Stone draft a letter of protest.[12] But it was David Kindersley who took the lead. Kindersley was an eminent stone engraver, lettering and type designer, consultant to Letraset International (for whom he devised a character-spacing guide) and had been an apprentice to Eric Gill when Gill's studio was at Piggots in 1935. Kindersley was appalled by the new signs, and *The Times* received and published a letter from Kindersley in which he made a series of criticisms,[13] the fundamental issues being the use of upper- and lowercase and the choice of a sans serif typeface.

Kindersley argued that while upper- and lowercase offered a more distinctive word-shape this was only helpful when the word-shape was already familiar – with place names, this would be unlikely. Secondly, he argued that serifs would help reinforce the characters at those points most vulnerable to a loss of definition in poor weather conditions or the glare of headlights. Kindersley argued that his suggestions would result in smaller sized signs, thus saving money and being less of a blot on the landscape. When the ministry replied stating, probably erroneously, that the signs were still at an experimental

Above: Maquette of a motorway sign demonstrating Calvert and Kinneir's proposed combination of lettering and diagramatic information.

stage, Kindersley, without invitation, proposed his own set of letterforms – serifed and capitals only.

Using *MOT Serif* (perhaps with minor modifications), a typeface that Kindersley had designed for the Ministry of Transport for local street signs some eight year previously, he had dummy signs constructed so that direct comparisons could be made with the Kinneir-Calvert signs. The design of his proposed alphabet was dictated by the need to ensure that each letter was distinct from all others. In so doing, he designed a set of letters that had very little in common with the conventions of visual unity governing how letters relate and interact with each. This gave his signs a distinct homespun quality, nothing at all like the clean-cut, modern appearance that the committee sought for its new, state-of-the-art motorway system.

Nevertheless, in true democratic fashion, tests were initiated by the Road Research Laboratory in 1959 to settle the issue. Rather comically in retrospect, a small group of volunteer airmen from Benson Airfield in Oxfordshire found themselves seated on a tiered platform, in the middle of the airfield, while a car drove towards them at thirty miles per hour. Signs were mounted on its roof composed of place names, with each sign using different letters: Kindersley's *MOT Serif*, the Kinneir-Calvert *Transport*,[14] and, for good measure, the Johnston-based London Transport standard. (In 1933 Johnston's *Underground Alphabet* had been adopted as part of the London Transport brand.)[15] Kindersley's serifed letters proved to be fractionally (3%) more legible than *Transport* – a negligible amount given the primitive conditions governing the test, and certainly insufficient to persuade the committee to re-think their choice of Kinneir and Calvert's *Transport*. Perhaps unknown to Kindersley, international politics had also been a significant and constant factor throughout in the committee's deliberations. Britain was negotiating to enter the European Common Market, and Anderson had been told that it would be helpful if the new traffic signage system was seen to be closer to European norms. Hence the apparently unreserved support of the committee from the outset towards sans serif, upper- and lowercase letters, and the use of a blue background. *Transport* was duly accepted.

Kinneir's studio had set the benchmark and was immediately asked to undertake the second, and far more complicated, task of designing a traffic signage system to be introduced across the entire UK. European standards and the Vienna Convention became obligatory, and so symbols and images (modified and redrawn versions taken from the 1949 Geneva Protocol) had to replace 'instructional' words. This meant, for example, that the urgency to STOP should no longer be lost during the effort to translate and comprehend the instruction: 'halt at major road ahead'. It was at this point that Calvert became a partner and the studio renamed Kinneir Calvert Associates.

On 1 January 1965, their new national road signage system became law. Calvert later commented, 'We always thought the Swiss and Germans were better – there was an inferiority complex in this country. [But] when we'd done our road signs I thought – they're not aggressive, there's something rounded about the characters, and the colours and the coolness and the straightforwardness of them.'[16] Indeed, from 1965, Britain had a road signage system widely considered to be the best in the world.

Throughout the rest of the 1960s Kinneir Calvert Associates were fully occupied and the studio grew. David Tuhill was brought in to manage the peripheral, though essential, printed material emanating from major signage systems that also acted as corporate identities, and in 1970 the company became Kinneir Calvert Tuhill Associates. Two of the most significant British transport institutions – the British Airports Authority and British Railways – commissioned Kinneir Calvert Tuhill to undertake a complete overhaul of signage. Important as the BAA task was, it was the design of *Rail Alphabet*, a crucial part in British Rail's new nationwide identity programme coordinated by DRU, that made the greatest impact on public sensibilities.

British Railways (as it was publicly known until 1966) had been nationalized in 1948 but still operated in regional sectors, each holding on to their own identity. By the early 1960s it was decided that a new, all-encompassing corporate identity was needed to pull these sectors together and eliminate the existing assortment of styles and motifs that so graphically demonstrated the current confused nature of the business. British Railway's most frequently used typeface was *Gill Sans*, often seen on aluminium station signs printed in all-capitals, generously spaced and reversed out of a darker colour – an elegant design inherited from the London and North Eastern Railway. Nonetheless, used in this way it was considered rather 'austere and bossy' and 'increasingly out of place in the more informal 1960s'.[17]

Despite its elemental nature, Kinneir recognized that, like other aspects of typography, a sign system must reflect something of its time and place to be fully effective. He later wrote that it would not suffice that a sign 'explains what needs to be understood clearly. How it was said, tone and inclination sensed from the colours, surface, materials, size, age and placement also had to be right'. Hence the demise of the elegant *Gill Sans* signs. 'It has to be acknowledged that the functions of public inscriptions reside more in their content than their form', continued Kinneir, 'on a utilitarian level one letter style could serve all purposes adequately, if bleakly. Yet this apparently functional view of lettering ignores the important role of style in giving information, as well as the part lettering plays in the environment.'[18]

Rail Alphabet, apart from also being a sans serif, was very different in appearance to *Transport*. Kinneir and Calvert realized that a passenger standing on a station platform will generally have time to read and take in the immediate environment, so speed of interpretation was not the chief concern. The result of Kinneir and Calvert's deliberations was a slightly heavier, more compact and more closely spaced set of letterforms, applied almost exclusively as black text on a white background. It has many similarities to *Helvetica* and, like *Helvetica*, it also has close ties to *Akzidenz Grotesk*. *Rail Alphabet* was also used by Kinneir and Calvert

Below: Margaret Calvert and Jock Kinneir's *Rail Alphabet*, in a page from the British Rail corporate design manual, 1965.

for the signage of Glasgow Airport (white on dark blue, to tie in with the colour of the Scottish flag) as well as other transport hubs, notably DSB, the Danish Railway Corporation.

In the UK, *Rail Alphabet* began to disappear in the 1990s when British Rail was privatized and split back into a number of smaller companies. (DSB used it until 1997.) However, the national UK network of stations became the responsibility of Railtrack, a separate company set up to manage the infrastructure of the railway system. They commissioned The Foundry, run by David Quay and Freda Sack, to design a new custom typeface which was called *Brunel*.

The typeface, which was eventually called *Calvert*, was originally designed in the 1970s for the visual identity of the new French town of St Quentin-en-Yvelines. The typeface is essentially 'Rail Alphabet with slabs',[19] and was rejected for being 'too English' – but it was resurrected several years later for Newcastle's Tyne and Wear Metro system, which opened in 1980. Calvert's suggestion that the slab serif form reflected Newcastle's distinctive architecture sounds perfunctory, but she was doubtless keen to break away from the universal use of sans serif letterforms in transport networks. This was one of Calvert's last jobs in

Below: Inspecting the signage for Newcastle's Tyne and Wear Metro system, 1980. The typeface was later named Calvert by Monotype when they issued it later the same year.

ABCDEFGHIJKLMNOPQ
RSTUVWXYZ abcdefghijklm
nopqrstuvwxyz 1234567890

**ABCDEFGHIJKLMNOPQ
RSTUVWXYZ abdefghijklm
nopqrstuvwxyz 1234567890**

partnership with Kinneir, who retired in 1979. Monotype issued it as a typeface in three weights later the same year, and it was their decision to name it *Calvert*.

In 1987 Calvert was appointed head of the graphic design department at the Royal College of Art by Derek Birdsall. Kinneir had previously held the same post from 1964 to 1969 – demonstrating the high level of responsibility that had been placed on Calvert within the company by the 1960s. She had had close ties with the RCA since 1966, when she was invited by Misha Black, then head of industrial design, to teach his students. She later joined the graphic design department on a one-day-a-week contract, at the request of Richard Guyatt. Calvert held the position as head of graphic design at the RCA until 1989, when her title changed to acting course director (after Birdsall walked out having had a row with the Rector, Jocelyn Stevens, over the nature of the course).[20]

Calvert taught at the RCA in various capacities while at the same time continuing with her own consultancy work. For example, in 2008 she worked with Henrik Kubel, Danish born co-partner of the A2-TYPE foundry in London, on a digital conversion of *Rail Alphabet*. Kubel had been a student at the RCA and was taught by Calvert. The digitally translated *Rail Alphabet* became a multipurpose typeface in six weights, renamed *New Rail Alphabet*. (Some letters were redesigned and hand-drawn by Calvert.)

Above: Margaret Calvert, *Calvert Light* and *Calvert Bold*, released by Monotype, 1980.

PART FOUR
Digitization

Introduction

Individually constructed computers began to appear in mainframe form during the 1950s, usually housed in purpose-built, air-conditioned rooms within government departments and universities. Initially users generally had little or no direct contact with the machine, but were required to prepare tasks for the computer elsewhere on other equipment, for example, in the form of punch cards, which were delivered. The results – and cards – might be ready for collection the following day. The complexity and fragility of mainframe computers was infamous and a cause of frustration as much as wonderment.

By the mid-1960s phototypesetting was incorporating computer technology, but it was not until the 1970s that computers became relatively small and cheap enough to influence what was fast becoming a highly competitive marketplace. In 1972 there were more than 100 different phototypesetting machines available to choose from; most were a hybrid of complex and delicate electromechanical processes linked to digital technology. The analogue aspect meant that these machines remained large and resolutely immobile. Nevertheless, when problems arose they were generally due to hardware (mechanical) problems – strobe timing errors causing base line errors, or erratic spacing between the characters. Such failures were common, yet fixing them was complex, expensive and inevitably required the services of a specialist-trained engineer.

When Steve Jobs introduced the Macintosh computer on stage in 1984, he unzipped the carrying case, lifted out the computer by its handle, plugged it in and turned it on. The purpose of these simple actions was to demonstrate how familiar and 'everyday' it was. Apple's new computer was mobile and accessible; making it work was as easy as turning on a television, and its design was inclusive. Jobs demonstrated applications such as MacWrite and MacPaint, but what impressed the audience above all was the clarity of the screen, user-friendly graphic interface and mouse.[1] The Macintosh was remarkably intuitive to use: instead of keying in codes, all the user had to do was 'point, click, cut and paste'.[2] It cost $2,495.

During the previous three decades, phototypesetting had swept away virtually all remaining hand-composing departments within the printing industry, while compositors who had

Previous page: Lundgren+Lindqvist, a design studio in Gothenburg, Sweden, 2010. Unlike the bulky computers that had cluttered design studios in the year 2000, modern versions were now so inconspicuous as to be just part of the furniture. What is more, without the paraphernalia of pencils, pens, precision drawing instruments, inks, brushes, paint, paper, glue – to say nothing of drawing tables with parallel motion, studio cameras and light boxes – the emphasis now rested on the cognitive rather than physical activities that once took up so much studio space and the designer's time.

However, disappearing along with these tools are the highly skilled specialist craft disciplines that barely a decade earlier were still nurtured and prized because they were essential to the successful function of a design studio. These time-consuming activities slowed down the design process as other hands and eyes became involved and inevitably influenced the way a design solution finally appeared. Despite the designer receiving all the credit the design process was rarely a solo effort – a fact particularly pertinent to type design.

In contrast, the creative independence afforded the designer by the computer has enormous advantages, economic as well as creative. However, the dangers of gleaning all information, insight and influences from a screen will prove highly reductive. An incentive to step away is a necessity. Note the mix of graphic design, typography and art books among the catalogues, paper samples and colour swatches. The poster is by Wim Crouwel.

performed hot-metal typesetting on, for example, Monotype or Linotype machines, had retired – often prompted by union-negotiated 'buy-out' incentives. A few transferred their knowledge of typography and keyboarding skills to phototypesetting machines, but with the much-hyped arrival of the Macintosh desktop computer – especially combined with a Laserwriter equipped with PostScript software in 1985 – the phototypesetting era came to an abrupt end, and there were few who regretted it. The digital age had arrived.

In fact, 'PostScript age' is more appropriate. PostScript, designed by Chuck Geschke and John Warnock at Adobe,[3] was the computer language that enabled both text and images to be passed within and between processing units and printers, allowing typesetting to be done on the designer's own desk. Adobe licensed PostScript to manufacturers of laser printers, most notably Apple. The designer was no longer dependent on the services of any outside agency.

Until this point it is likely that neither Adobe nor Apple had given much thought to type, typography or typographers (reminiscent of Monotype and Linotype's initial attitude almost 100 years earlier). PostScript laser printers were fitted with an odd assortment of fonts – chosen, no doubt, to fulfil the perceived needs of an office worker with responsibility for producing correspondence, memos, newsletters, reports and

Below: The IBM System/370–165 mainframe computer, newly installed at the Bosch headquarters, Stuttgart, 1971.

agendas. However, if a laser printer could output *Times*, *Helvetica*, *Courier* and *Symbol*,[4] clearly other more interesting typefaces could be uploaded, given the software. No longer tied to a composing machine, typefaces could now be bought (on a 3.5-inch floppy disc), and used on any computer. Proprietary type systems that tied typefaces to a manufacturer's machine had ended.

A program to enable the design of whole pages on-screen was the final component. Desktop publishing was launched by Aldus Corporation with PageMaker in July 1985 in conjunction with Apple, making it possible to create typography on screen and view the results on paper without leaving the studio. Almost as soon as desktop computers became available, so too did the software that enabled the design of typefaces; it was no longer confined to a tiny number of trained designers with privileged access to expensive hardware. Almost overnight, any individual equipped with a computer and a copy of Fontographer software (released in 1986) could establish his or her own 'typefoundry'.

From the outset, Steve Jobs at Apple directed public perception of the Macintosh computer as being a liberating tool, a force to promote rather than repress individuality. It should be remembered that the arrival of the computer was considered by many in the design community to be a genuine threat to creative freedom. But, as Emily King explained, 'Apple computers became associated with counter-cultural forces, but they were acceptably rebellious, not dangerously revolutionary'.[5] Jobs must surely have been grateful to magazines such as *Emigre* with Zuzana Licko and Rudy VanderLans (from 1984), and *Fuse* with Neville Brody and Jon Wozencroft (from 1991), who applied the newfound freedom they discovered in digital technology to typeface design. Licko and Brody's typefaces reaped outrage from the status quo; a reaction they will have found reassuring.

Designers of digital letterforms could now work alone, developing ideas all the way from an elemental idea to their final and complete form. In this sense, the conditions of a digital type designer were not dissimilar to those of the hand punchcutter – before technical limitations were imposed by the mechanization of type composition or, indeed, the opinion of a type designer.

Larger digital type design enterprises were also established from the start. Adobe in California was a glamorous frontrunner, creating its own digital font studio in 1983 led by Sumner Stone called Adobe Originals. Its success was due primarily to the excellent work of the company's leading in-house type designers:

Above: The Macintosh, also known as the Mac 128k because it came with 128kb of Random Access Memory (RAM). The CRT monochrome monitor measured 9 inches (23 cm).

Carol Twombly and Robert Slimbach. Stone chose to develop two of the most coveted 'classic' typefaces – *Caslon* (designed by Twombly) and *Garamond* (designed by Slimbach) – using impeccable historic sources and assimilating craft methods, something Adobe were at pains to illustrate and explain in a series of printed promotional booklets.

But while Adobe was attracting the limelight, Bitstream, founded two years earlier in Cambridge Massachusetts, can claim to have been the first digital type company. Two of the founding partners, Matthew Carter and Mike Parker, were both originally from England and happily drew on their knowledge and admiration of European typography. Bitstream became a forerunner in establishing the independent marketing of type, but its strategy of speedily offering digital versions of popular pre-existing typefaces in vast numbers received vigorous criticism.

Meanwhile, some long-established companies who had played a major role in the design and making of type and/or typesetting machinery in the first half of the twentieth century have survived by reorganizing or merging with other media-based companies. Monotype became Monotype Imaging Inc. in 2004, having previously been Agfa Monotype when it acquired the International Typeface Corporation (ITC) in 2000. As Monotype Imaging Inc. it acquired Linotype Hell in 2007, Bitstream Inc. in 2012, FontShop in 2014 and URW in 2020. As the various compound names suggest, all these influential companies had been through transformative times, focused on survival rather than pursuing future-focused ventures. Nevertheless, their best work remains the benchmark for designers of digital type today.

Independent digital outfits, which began to appear in the 1990s, continued to proliferate. After the euphoria at gaining the tools to make and distribute type, the initial positivity of many type designers dissipated when they realized how difficult it was to earn sufficient revenue from the sale of type alone. The arrival of FontShop in 1989 – effectively a publishing house for digital typefaces – was hugely important. Digital type foundries have adopted differing strategies to lure type users into purchasing typefaces; from 'exclusivity' to cheap and cheerful 'mega-bundles'. Meanwhile, serious-minded independent type designers have found a workable strategy somewhere between these extremes, producing quality fonts, manageable license agreements and reasonable pricing.

abcdefghijklmnopqrstuvwxyz ABCDEFGHIJKLMNOPQRSTUVWXYZ 1234567890
abcdefghijklmnopqrstuvwxyz ABCDEFGHIJKLMNOPQRSTUVWXYZ 1234567890

Matthew Carter GREAT BRITAIN/USA 1937–

Matthew Carter was born in London. His father, Harry Carter, was a highly respected typographer and authority on the history of type-founding and punchcutting techniques who, among many accomplishments, worked closely with Francis Meynell as co-designer and print-overseer of Meynell's Nonesuch Press books. After the Second World War he became Head Printer at His Majesty's Stationery Office (HMSO), which was effectively the Government's printing office and at that time one of the largest publishing establishments in the world. Harry Carter also translated and edited the English edition of Charles Enschedé's *Typefoundries of the Netherlands* (later designed by Bram de Does). Perhaps without even realizing it, Matthew Carter absorbed the craft of printing and a fascination for the design of printed material from the books, visitors and conversation that filled the house.

Carter was schooled at Charterhouse, a private boarding school, from the age of seven until eighteen. He was offered a place at Oxford, the plan being that he would study English with the vague notion that he might end up in a bookish activity of some sort. The opportunity arose to take a year out between school and university and so, in September 1955, he travelled to the Netherlands to spend twelve months on an internship programme at the Enschedé printing house in Haarlem, where he learned how to cut punches by hand. (Van Krimpen, the senior designer at Enschedé, was a long-time friend of Carter's father). The idea of the Enschedé internship programme was to provide a broad introduction to the world of design and printing. The first department Carter arrived at was the type foundry and he quickly became fascinated in all its aspects, but especially in punchcutting, and spent the entire year devoted to this. By the time he left Enschedé he had the equivalent of a journeyman's knowledge of punchcutting and matrix making.

By this time the idea of going to university no longer held any interest whatsoever. Carter expected his father – who at this time was the archivist for Oxford University Press (OUP), appointed at Stanley Morison's suggestion – to contest the decision, but was surprised to discover that he was, in fact, sympathetic. He even found him work at the OUP, where the young Carter was given the task of designing and assembling a small museum within

Opposite: Matthew Carter, *Charter*, designed for Bitstream specifically to function on low-resolution output devices such as fax machines and 300 dpi laser printers, 1987.

the company buildings in which historical material could be displayed.

As a distinguished typophile, his father was able to introduce Carter to people who could help him, but the problem was that what he had enjoyed learning so much at Enschedé had quickly become an all-but-obsolete craft. He did receive a number of small engraving and punchcutting jobs, but more significant was a period spent in Verona working at the Officina Bodoni with Giovanni Mardersteig, and then at Monotype where he worked on several typefaces including the cutting of a semi-bold weight for *Dante*,[1] a typeface designed by Mardersteig.[2]

In 1960, when he was twenty-three, a friend of the family gave Carter the means to spend three months in New York. It proved to be something of an epiphany. Everything he knew about typography had come from his father's connections – New York offered an entirely new perspective, and for Carter a new purpose for type. He was especially impressed by the work of Lou Dorfsman, Herb Lubalin and Push Pin Studios (primarily Seymour Chwast and Milton Glaser), whose use of type – witty, expressive, almost illustrative – was a revelation. He also discovered the work of the previous generation of American type designers, including Dwiggins, of whom little was known in Europe at that time, along with Goudy and Cooper. Their personalities shone through their work, which was rather shocking to a young potential type designer from Britain where personality was suppressed, its presence considered uncouth. Carter spent his evenings in New York's jazz clubs.[3]

On his return to London he continued his freelance work until 1963 when he got his first salaried job, which was at Crosfield Electronics. The main business of the company was electronic equipment for the printing industry, but they had recently established a side-line selling and, a little later, manufacturing, the Franco-American designed phototypesetting system, more commonly known in Europe as Lumitype and Photon in America.[4] When a customer bought a Lumitype phototypesetting machine they could specify the typefaces they wanted, and these would be supplied on glass disks. Crosfield did not have the expertise to design the fonts and so this was to be Carter's job. Fortuitously, this required that he spend time in Paris where another branch of the Lumitype-Photon concern nestled within the distinguished old type foundry of Charles Peignot's Deberny & Peignot.

*AaBbCcDdEeFfGgHhIi
JjKkLlMmNnOoPpQqRr
SsTtUuVvWwXx YyZz
1234567890 /(&)/ éüîåçœ*

At that time the Swiss type designer Adrian Frutiger was also working in the Deberny & Peignot studio. Frutiger, always measured and quietly spoken, had considerable experience designing or adapting typefaces for phototypesetting, and was extremely helpful to Carter on practical issues. Roger Excoffon, more exuberant and outward-looking – and also running his own very successful advertising agency Urbi & Orbi (U&O) – was also influential, giving Carter the confidence to begin designing his own typefaces. Until this point Carter had only known how to make type, now he was learning how to design it.

During his time in New York, Carter had visited the Linotype company in Brooklyn and met British type-designer Mike Parker, who was then assistant to Jackson Burke, head of typography. In 1965, when Burke had to retire due to ill-health, Parker became director of typographic development and offered his own previous position to Carter, who readily accepted.

When Carter moved to New York, Linotype had a successful photocomposing system called Linofilm. Virtually all the tedious work of converting their metal types to photocomposition had been done, so there was now time for Parker and Carter to begin exploring the new opportunities that photocomposition technology offered and which had been impossible with metal type. The most obvious, they concluded, was in the design of script faces. The physical, rectilinear boundaries that dominated metal type design no longer existed, meaning that the space

Above: Matthew Carter, *Snell Roundhand*, 1966.

Below: Matthew Carter, *Galliard*, 1978, released by Linotype and reissued by the International Type Corporation in 1982.

ABCDEFGHIJKLNOPQRS
TUVWXYZ abcdefghijklm
nopqrstuvwxyz 1234 4567890

between phototypeset letters was infinitely flexible.

Carter created three scripts: *Cascade*, which has similarities to the rough-edged, nonchalant calligraphic typefaces of Roger Excoffon, and *Snell Roundhand*, both from 1965–66, followed by *Shelley* in 1972. *Snell Roundhand* is a connected cursive script based on the work of the seventeenth-century Puritan writing master Charles Snell; the typeface had been ignored during the transition to mechanized typesetting due to the impracticality of the large overhangs of its capitals. *Snell Roundhand* was celebrated as a demonstration of the 'technical liberation from the constraints of metal typecasting rather than the pursuit of a particular aesthetic'.[5] *Auriga*, a mécane (slab serif) typeface designed around 1965, before Carter's move to New York, was released by Linotype in 1970.

Carter returned to London in 1971 while continuing to work for Linotype. Parker had felt for some time that a distinguished, old-style typeface, designed specifically for photosetting, was missing. This was discussed and Carter's solution, released in 1978, was *Galliard*. It was based on the types of the French punchcutter Robert Granjon (1513–1589), which had been the starting point for a previous important twentieth-century typeface, Monotype's *Plantin* in 1913. Carter had come into contact with Granjon's type during the 1950s when an intern at Enschedé. His father was doing research work at the Plantin-Moretus Museum in Antwerp, and Carter had helped in identifying and indexing Granjon's punches, matrices and type.

Galliard (meaning 'a lively dance') is an exuberant interpretation, drawn freely rather than working on transparent paper over photographic enlargements. It was rapturously received on its release. Aaron Burns, president and one of the founders of International Typeface Corporation (and a close friend of Parker), bought a licence in 1981 to manufacture *Galliard*,

Above and right: Matthew Carter, *Bell Centennial*, 1978.

using copies of Carter's drawings. *ITC Galliard* was announced in the December 1981 issue of *U&lc* (Upper & lowercase) magazine. The additional exposure offered by ITC helped *Galliard* become a popular modern classic.

Much later, when Adobe bought a licence for *Galliard*, according to Carter they did a particularly poor job in converting it to digital technology. It was one of the first typefaces they bought; at that time they assumed their market was essentially the standard commercial office rather than the designer's studio and, as a consequence, the integrity of their early typefaces was of little concern. But once the combination of PostScript and the Macintosh had been so successfully been established Adobe realized that standards had to improve if their typefaces were to gain credence within the graphic design community. As a result Adobe hired Sumner Stone and the Adobe Originals studio was established.

When Carter co-founded Bitstream Inc., a digital type foundry, in 1981, he was able to produce his own digital version of *Galliard* that was an accurate copy of the original Linotype and ITC version – and included all the additional characters that had not been possible to include previously.[6] In 1992, Carter and Cherie Cone (one of the founding partners of Bitstream) established a new, smaller company called Carter Cone Type Inc., and *Galliard CC* was tweaked again and newly released.

Back in 1978, the same year that *Galliard* was first designed, Carter designed what might be considered its antithesis: *Bell Centennial*, a typeface commissioned by the American Telephone and Telegraph Company (AT&T Corporation from 1982) for use in their telephone directories.

The first time AT&T took an interest in the typography used in their telephone directories was 1937, after seeing the achievements of Chauncey H. Griffith, head of typographic development at Linotype, in improving the legibility of newspapers. Griffith was asked to design a typeface specifically for Linotype composition of all at&t telephone directories. The result was *Bell Gothic*, which became the standard for directory composition for the next forty years. Griffith, renowned for his collaboration with numerous type designers without claiming any credit, this time made *Bell Gothic* his own. It was not until the early 1970s and the introduction of new technologies that AT&T became concerned about the efficacy of *Bell Gothic*.

Typographic composition of their directory was being done using cathode ray tube (CRT) typesetting, and printed on high-

MANTINIA · MCMXCIII
CAPS AᴬBᴮCᶜDᴰEᴱFᶠGᴳHᴴ
AND IⁱJᴶKᴷLᴸMᴹNᴺOᴼPQQ
SUPERIOR RᴿSˢTᵀUᵁVⱽ
CAPs WᵂXˣYʸ&&ZᶻÆŒŒ
FIGURES 1234567890
SMALᴸ·CAPˢ ACEHIORSTUWYZ
LIGATURES H̱V̇CTH̄UPLA
TTŒTUTWTYMEMPMDMB̄E
ALERNATIVES T&YR̄QQ
TALᴸ·CAPITALˢ ITLY

speed offset lithography presses. These new production methods adversely affected Griffith's *Bell Gothic*. Letterforms (especially lighter weight faces) began to evaporate; their strokes became thinner or disappeared completely at the intersections of straight and curved strokes. Printers tried to compensate for this erosion by over-inking the printing plates, but while this helped to thicken the strokes, it created numerous other problems – counters filled in and the strokes of different characters ran into each other, making 'c' and 'l' become 'd', 'r' and 'n' became 'm', '3' resembled '8', '5' resembled '6' and so on. It was apparent that a new typeface had to be designed that would also compensate for the inherent characteristics of the photocomposition.

Once more they approached Linotype. This time it was Mike Parker who met AT&T's representatives and who then passed the project to Carter. The result was called *Bell Centennial*. Carter developed four styles: *Name and Number, Address, Sub Caption* and *Bold Listing*. The differentiation of visual hierarchy between weights was crucial. He made the *Name and Number* face heavier and wider, increasing its prominence over other information. Also, the width of the least important and therefore less prominent *Address* face was decreased; this reduction would more than make up for the added width of the *Name and Number* face. This allowed more information to fit in a small space, saving paper, print time and transport and, consequently, creating a huge reduction in costs.[7] Carter designed each character to optimally function at a specific size (6 point) and resolution. This involved creating each character, pixel by pixel, on gridded paper.

The unique aspect of *Bell Centennial*'s forms, and only apparent when enlarged, is the distortions incorporated to solve a technical problem during production. Since the phonebook was printed at high speeds and on low-quality paper, the ink had a tendency to spread, especially so with inside corners which became rounded. Because even the slightest amount of ink spread greatly affects the shape and, therefore, the legibility of 6-point characters, Carter included 'ink traps' – notches cut into corners and joins – to compensate. When *Bell Centennial* became available as a retail type family in digital form, designers discovered these distinctive characteristics and used them at large size for display work. Alex Kaczun is attributed to wrapping the shapes with bezier curves to create a vector-based font.

By the end of the 1970s, there appeared a new wave of digital imaging companies such as Scitex and Camex; these smaller, fast

Above: Matthew Carter, *Mantinia*, 1993.

growing companies introduced powerful, if expensive, digital systems that enabled whole pages of magazines and newspapers to be set intact. Carter and Parker realized that Linotype was in danger of becoming a technical backwater. Along with Cherie Cone, the Letter Drawing studio manager, and Rob Friedman from finance – both also unhappy with the direction Linotype was heading – they decided to join together and form Bitstream Inc. They also enticed the other nine best type designers from Linotype to join them.

Bitstream Inc. was set up in 1981 in Marlborough, Massachusetts, and was the first company dedicated to the design and marketing of digital typefaces independent of the manufacture of typesetting systems.[8] Bitstream made a hugely successful start (Scitex was an early client), which in turn attracted a host of new investors. But after two or three successful years it became clear that the stellar growth predicted by its financial backers was not going to materialize, and pressure to diversify into hardware changed the direction and culture of the company. As a result, Carter found himself with ever-decreasing opportunity to design,[9] and in 1991 he left Bitstream. The following year he and Cherie Cone set up Carter & Cone. Reenergized, he designed *Mantinia, Walker, Sophia, Elephant, Big Caslon, Alisal* and *Miller* all in quick succession.

Nothing demonstrates the flexibility of digital technology, or Carter's new-found sense of freedom and purpose, more than *Walker*, a typeface designed for the Walker Art Center in Minneapolis. At its core it is a plain sans serif capital alphabet but with a set of five different 'snap-on' serifs which can be used as connectors as well as terminals.

The multiplicity of options *Walker* offers the designer was described at the time as being a groundbreaking post-modernist statement. Carter avoids such 'absolutist' labels, advocating tolerance of the experimental nature of young type designers, and has consistently supported the radical democratization of type made possible by the personal computer. He is not, however, an uncritical pluralist. Concerning the unprecedented rise of type design activity during the late 1980s he said, in characteristic understatement, 'The results are not always wonderful'.[10]

Above top: Matthew Carter, *Sophia*, 1993.

Above: Matthew Carter, *Walker*, 1995.

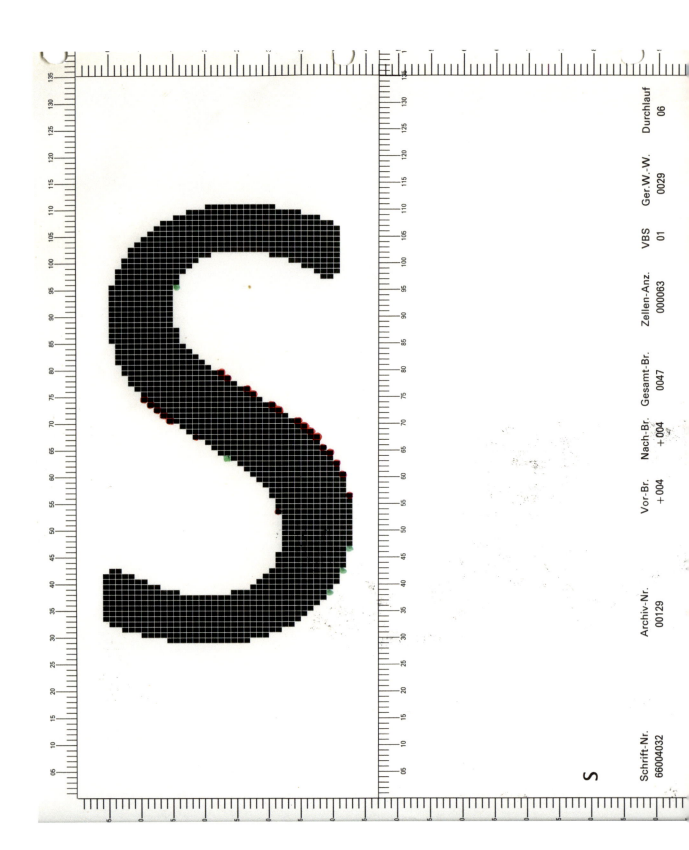

Gerard Unger THE NETHERLANDS 1942 – 2018

Unger was born in Arnhem. His father, Adam, was head of the publicity department of the textile manufacturer Rayon. His grandfather had been a compositor in the printing trade, and Unger's father took great interest in the design and printing of books (part of his job was to edit and oversee the production of the company journal, *Rayon Revue*, designed by Otto Treumann). He often brought home exhibition catalogues and rare books, mostly French – he was an enthusiastic Francophile – and amassed an impressive collection.

Disastrously, the house and much of its contents, including the library, was damaged during the Battle of Arnhem in September 1944. The whole population of Arnhem was forcibly evacuated and the city looted. When the family eventually returned to their house, five-year-old Unger was able to pick up the damaged books, including some printed by Christophe Plantin as well as notable twentieth-century material, and 'improve' them with his pencils.[1]

After compulsory military service, Unger studied at the Gerrit Rietveld Academy (then the Institute for Applied Arts) in Amsterdam from 1963 to 1967. He had already begun to draw type, having been inspired by seeing an exhibition of work by Jan van Krimpen for the Dutch PTT. Unger suffered from a mild form of dyslexia (a condition surprisingly common among type designers), and found he enjoyed drawing and studying the characteristics that help distinguish each individual letter on paper. In this way his career began in the typical way – by imitating the work of a master. At that time the graphic design course at the Rietveld Academy was concerned with the solving of general commercial communication problems; type design was not on the curriculum. Unger was fascinated by the fiercely contrasting views of his tutors, and tried to take what he thought the best from deeply held opinions. Pragmatism would be a notable characteristic throughout his career.

Unger began his career as an assistant to Wim Crouwel, spending six months at Total Design. It was an illuminating experience:

> Wim is an absolutely charismatic leader. He's charming and outspoken, and when he explained design you thought 'this is it, this is the solution, here's the way to do it'. I had a very tough time

Opposite: Gerard Unger, a bromide proof of *Praxis Bold* with corrections following advice from Max Catflisch, 1978. The red marks indicate pixels to be deleted, the green marks indicate where pixels are to be added.

freeing myself from that influence, convincing myself that I had different ideas.²

A few months after Wim Crouwel's *New Alphabet* appeared in 1967, Unger published a counterproposal in the same *Kwadraatblad* magazine series,³ in which he argued that it was perfectly possible to adapt type design to new technology without having to resort to such a radical redesign of so many of the characters. In fact, Unger had been invited by Crouwel to write this counterproposal, a gesture that Unger has since described as being remarkably generous: 'he wanted to give me a chance to make my voice heard'.⁴ It is equally likely that Crouwel sought to add fuel to the debate. Unger's article was presented written by hand in Dutch with an English translation typewritten on the back. Unger considered handwriting (not calligraphy) to be the basis of type design.⁵

On leaving college Unger went to work in an advertising agency, a counterintuitive decision but typical of Unger's questioning of a standard trope: '"Graphic design good. Advertising bad" – I thought that was all nonsense'.⁶ Unger was then offered two more interesting jobs in quick succession: a part-time evening teaching post at the Rietveld Academy, and a commission to design a typeface for Enschedé's Pantotype machine. The venerable Enschedé en Zonen in Haarlem was seeking to diversify as metal type became gradually obsolete – the Pantotype machine was an engraving system used for making signs and nameplates for hospitals, municipal buildings, corporate headquarters etc. This occupied Unger for two days a week, and provided invaluable experience working with Henk Drost, Enschedé's last punchcutter. Sem Hartz had already designed an alphabet for the system, which was called *Panture*. This was an elegant face comprised solely of roman capitals, but their complex, refined form meant that the engraving process took a long time. Unger designed *Markeur*, a sans serif face that could be cut far more efficiently. The cutting procedure involved a rotating blade, and so Unger incorporated rounded corners and slightly widened the terminals to compensate.

Right: Gerard Unger, *Markeur*, 1972.

Above: Gerard Unger, *M.O.L.*, 1974. Photograph taken in 2018, at the last station to take down the signs.

Unger's next typeface – called *M.O.L.* (Metro-Ondergrondse Letter) – also had rounded corners, but for a different reason. In 1973 Unger formed Sign Design in partnership with Paul Mijksenaar, and in collaboration with Total Design they put in a bid to design the signage for the Pompidou Centre in Paris. The bid was not successful, but Unger and Mijksenaar were invited to join a working group led by Pieter Brattinga (publisher of Crouwel's *New Alphabet* in *Kwadraatbladen*, and Unger's response) for designing a signage system for the Amsterdam Metro. This would require both illuminated and printed signs. The illuminated signs were lit from within, which had the effect of softening the corners of the letters.

To maintain visual parity between both sets of signs, Unger designed a sans serif alphabet with rounded corners so that the printed letters (white on blue) appeared the same as the illuminated letters. The project was officially completed in 1977. Unger was gaining a reputation as a type designer undaunted by new technology – in fact, one who appeared to revel in overcoming what many would consider the crippling restrictions it imposed. In 1975 Unger set himself up as an independent type designer but was then promptly approached by Rudolf Hell, creator of the first digital typesetter, the Digiset 50T1. It was the beginning of a fruitful working relationship that would last almost fifteen years.

By the mid 1970s phototypesetting was giving way to digital technology. Although the Digiset 50T1 is generally considered to be the first digital typesetter, there remained elements of phototypesetting technology within its process. Letters were still exposed photographically at the end of the composing process, but the revolving disc holding a font in negative form (as in phototypesetting) had been replaced in the Digiset by a numerical description; the letters were now 'memorized' and stored within the machine as a matrix of square dots (pixels). It was this information that could then be beamed by spots of light through a cathode ray tube (CRT) in the composing process – described at the time as 'digital photocomposition'.[7]

Hell had licensed several popular typefaces including *Futura*, *Times* and *Univers* for adaptation to the Digiset, and contracted Hermann Zapf to design Digiset's first original typeface, *Marconi*, released in 1975. Designing type for the Digiset required master drawings to be made on a CRT grid with 120 horizontal positions and 100 vertical positions per em (12 points). Three type-size

Hollandse Med.
Sheldon

ABCDEFGHIJKLMN
OPQRSTUVWXYZ
abcdefghijklmnop
qrstuvwxyz 12345

ABCDEFGHIJKLMN
OPQRSTUVWXYZ
abcdefghijklmnop
qrstuvwxyz 12345

Above top: Sjoerd Hendrik De Roos, *Hollandse Mediaeval*, 1912.

Middle: Jan van Krimpen, *Sheldon*, much enlarged (original is 7 point), 1947.

Above: Gerard Unger, *Demos*, 1975 and Gerard Unger, *Praxis*, 1977.

ABCDabcdefgh ijklmnopqrstu

ranges (up to 9 point, 8–18 point, 16 point and above) were required,[8] with each glyph being drawn by hand, pixel by pixel. Unger eventually persuaded Hell to let him design his own typeface for the Digiset.

Demos was 'the result of technical as well as aesthetic considerations'.[9] As with the solution for the *M.O.L.* signage, Unger designed the form of *Demos* to the cognate characteristics of the technology by rounding the corners on *Demos*'s serifs, effectively preempting – and embracing – the limitations inherent in the technology. (This is similar to the thinking that had led Crouwel to design *New Alphabet*.) Unger had already been working for a year on *Demos* before he was given the formal go-ahead in March 1975. It was released later the same year, shortly after Zapf's *Marconi*.

The open and robust form of *Demos* is, in part, influenced by De Roos's *Hollandse Mediaeval*, a typeface he had been familiar with since childhood. The short tail on the 'g' and 'e' and short foot on the 'k', for example, as well as its open counters, are all reminiscent of *Hollandse Mediaeval*. But *Demos* also has a tall x-height, strong (though blunt) serifs and the tensive curves characteristic of Jan van Krimpen's *Sheldon*. Designed for 7 point only, *Sheldon* was commissioned by the Oxford University Press to use in the printing of bibles, which it was assumed would be read in poor light. However, *Demos* (meaning 'populace') was designed to have a far wider range of applications, meaning it also had to be spatially economic. This was achieved by giving *Demos* a strong horizontal emphasis that, Unger argued, eliminated the need for the additional leading normally required by a typeface with such a large x-height. It was completed in the early 1980s.

The italic *Demos* was sloped electronically with no input from Unger. The results were less than ideal, and caused Unger to consider the possibility of a sans serif version of *Demos* as an alternative to the sloped italic (Van Krimpen had envisaged the same with *Romulus*). The idea quickly gathered momentum, and in 1977 *Praxis*, a sans serif counterpart to *Demos*, appeared. When it was suggested at Hell that an italic version be made by electronically slanting *Praxis* Unger offered *Flora*, a genuine italic – albeit with a minimal slant – derived from experiments he had made in the early 1970s using felt-tip pens. Its subsequent protracted development, caused largely by ongoing technological changes, meant that *Flora*, named after Unger's newborn daughter, was not released until 1984.

Above: Gerard Unger, *Flora*, 1984.

Hollander

Although *Demos, Praxis* and *Flora* were not originally conceived as a serial (serif, sans serif and italic) family, they are, undoubtedly, closely related. Unger himself referred to these three faces as a 'family' but chose to give them separate names: 'It is one of the typographer's pleasures to find interesting combinations of disparate faces. I don't want to prescribe anything to the user and therefore have consciously unlinked the members of the family.'[10]

In 1977, the year *Praxis* appeared, Unger was invited by Edy de Wilde, director of the Stedelijk Museum, Amsterdam, to have an 'Atelier' exhibition – a series of small but prestigious exhibitions mounted within the Stedelijk to promote upcoming artists and designers. De Wilde's invitation is evidence that Unger's work with the Digiset system was attracting attention, but not all of it was positive. John Dreyfus, in 'New Types for New Technology' – an article for *The Times Literary Supplement* – suggested that the character of Unger's type was 'too insistent', meaning its distinctive form might be a distraction for the reader (not an uncommon criticism for a genuinely new typeface). But Hermann Zapf was more penetrant, arguing that Unger's approach toward technology was too conciliatory: 'that way the technology would never improve'.[11]

Flora was possibly the first typeface to be designed with outlines using the Ikarus system. Ikarus was developed by Peter Karow (technical director and co-founder of URW Software & Type GmbH in Hamburg) in 1974 and adopted at Hell during 1976. In the early 1980s Hell's Digiset, with its CRT grid-restrictive technology, was replaced with the Laser Digiset whose laser beam technology provided far higher resolution while the Ikarus software programme enabled the outlines of the letters to be defined in curves. Ikarus restored something reminiscent of drawing to the design process – albeit on screen.

The refinement enabled by the new technology was eagerly utilized by Unger for his next typeface, as he was keen to return to the sophistication and subtlety of a drawn line. This was also the first time Unger felt it appropriate to look further back, in fact to seventeenth- and eighteenth-century publishers in Utrecht, for inspiration. Laser technology also encouraged Unger to return to the design of sharp corners. The outcome was *Hollander*, a typeface that Unger would equate with the Dutch landscape. Flat wide-open spaces are created by a distinctive horizontal top curves (reminiscent of William A. Dwiggins's *Electra*) that are

Above: Gerard Unger, *Hollander*, 1983.

ABCDEFG
HIJKLMN
OPQRSTU
VWXYZ a
bcdefghij
klmnopqr
stuvwxyz
12345678

Above: Gerard Unger, *Swift*, 1987.

stretched to provide a series of broad and sweeping arches when set. Combined with prominent left-leaning serifs on top of the ascenders, these give *Hollander* a firm, yet panoramic, wind-swept, and heroic appearance.

During work on *Hollander* Unger also made sketches for a semibold version which, instead, evolved into what would be his most popular and bestselling typeface, *Swift*, released in 1987. At the beginning of the 1980s there was only a small number of types suitable for newsprint, with most newspapers still using either Monotype's *Times New Roman* (Stanley Morison, 1932) or Linotype's *Excelsior* (Chauncey H. Griffith, 1931 – one of the Legibility Group of typefaces begun in 1928). From the outset, *Swift* was specifically designed as a newspaper typeface and so the subtle flexure of *Hollander's* serifs was replaced with something simpler and distinctly more angular in character. Importantly, it was capable of withstanding the demanding conditions of fast web-fed presses and coarse paper, remaining eminently readable at a smaller text size and yet also offering an attractive headline. Despite the rationality Unger brought to bear, *Swift* retained the taut elegance of *Hollander* while gaining a more confident and robust character. This new, sharp clarity became a hallmark of Unger's later work. A matching sans serif type, *Argo*, was designed in 1989.

Argo – basically Swift with its serifs removed – was the first typeface Unger designed and digitized for himself. It had begun while *Swift* was still in the early stages of development, but it was not until 1987 that Unger was contracted to design four variants of the typeface. Further progress was halted when Hell hit a financial crisis. The digital transformation of the 1980s had caused huge ructions within the printing business and all its related industries. The reputations of type foundries, built upon decades, sometimes centuries, of craftsmanship, innovation and expertise very suddenly evaporated. Former rivals sought support from each other and merges became commonplace. In 1989 Hell's design studio was closed when the company merged with Linotype (they would later be subsumed within Heidelberg).[12] Unger was given *Argo* as part of the leaving deal, which he licensed in 1990 to Frank Blokland's newly formed Dutch Type Library (DTL). While technological change very rapidly altered the way type was created, a more significant change for Unger was that digital design tools such as Fontographer were by now widely available. Throughout the 1970s and early '80s he had been one of a very small number of type designers:

Gulliver

There was Matthew Carter, Adrian Frutiger, Hermann Zapf; they were older than I was. I did not have many contemporaries. And suddenly in the mid 1980s, early 90s, there was a wave of young designers from the Hague, Arnhem, and then Britain, Germany… and the picture changed completely. Since type design [went] digital, the number of type designers has multiplied unbelievably.[13]

Unger, who continued to teach throughout his career, welcomed the democratizing effect of digital tools but, like Blokland, was well aware of the lack of professionalism among some of the new 'foundries'. In fact, Blokland set up a research, design and production studio called Type Unlimited International (TUL), with his former trainee Gerard Daniels, to ensure that all typefaces published by the Dutch Type Library were of a professional standard.

Following Linotype's merger with Hell in 1990, Unger was told that Linotype would no longer develop or promote his typefaces.[14] As a result, Unger's next newspaper typeface, *Gulliver*, completed in 1993, was issued by Unger himself and produced at TUL. *Gulliver* grew out of Unger's continuing experiments with legibility and space-saving. Its counters were made as large as possible, with the effect that *Gulliver* at 8.5 point provides the same visual impression as *Times New Roman* at 10 point. With its slightly condensed form and short serifs (in contrast to *Swift*), *Gulliver* can be set tighter to save space on the page without appearing cramped.

Gulliver was the first typeface for which Unger worked almost exclusively on screen. Using a combination of type design software and QuarkXpress (which allowed the user to expand or contract the character-width), he made the fullest possible use of increasingly sophisticated digital technology.

The marketing of *Gulliver* was rather unique. Potential customers were told that *Gulliver* would be available only to organizations and companies whose design and printing 'will do justice to *Gulliver's* space-saving capabilities' – principally newpaper and high-volume magazine publishers. In return, vetted customers were promised a degree of geographic exclusivity and that there would be no more than 100 licensee members worldwide. This exclusivity was given additional credence by giving licensees membership of the Gulliver Club. Initially this strategy appeared to work as the number of members had reached forty-five by 2010, but then quickly dwindled. *Gulliver* was later withdrawn from the market.[15]

Above: Gerard Unger, *Gulliver Regular*, 1993.

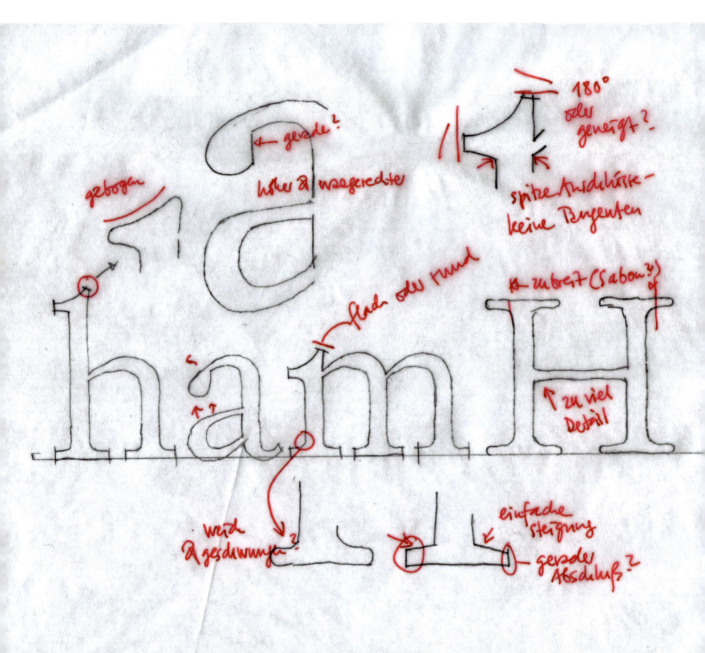

Erik Spiekermann GERMANY 1947 –

The eldest of four children, Erik Spiekermann was born in Stadthagen, a small town near Hanover in Lower Saxony. His father trained as a mechanic and was a lorry driver. The Spiekermanns lived modestly, and with his father working away from the home for long periods Erik often found himself acting as a substitute head of the family.

    He was a precocious child – always busy learning, and involving himself in drawing, painting and music projects. At the age of seven he discovered a commercial printing company nearby, and became a regular presence there after school. He was allowed to stand next to the printer and watch how a pristine sheet of white paper was placed on the proofing press, to see it rolled over the locked-up type, and then watch as the paper was lifted off the press and held up to check the inked letterforms. The family moved to Bonn in 1957; their house was, fortuitously, close to the university press. Once more, Spiekermann was able to talk his way in. His fascination was noticed, and at the age of twelve an old platen press and a small amount of type was given to him as a gift. At high school Erik not only wrote for the school magazine but also designed, typeset and was able to 'supervise' it being printed.

    Just after his seventeenth birthday, and while still attending high school, Spiekermann moved to Berlin. He explains:

> Berlin had no draft at the time, and my dad, having spent the war in a U-Boat – which apparently with a survival rate of 10% wasn't much fun – didn't want his sons to ever wear a uniform and follow stupid orders. So he sent me to Berlin where I lived on my own, making a living chalking on the sidewalks and busking.[1]

Spiekermann was eventually able to use one of his father's connections to get a job at the Buck printing press in Munich, and then in 1966 at the Mercator printing press, owned by the *Tagesspiegel* newspaper. He worked at both presses for two or three afternoons a week while also studying as a student; he read art history and English studies at Berlin's Free University. Music was also an important part of his early life. He co-founded a music club and regularly performed with a guitar, wearing an English-inspired three-piece suit. It was through a music friend that Spiekermann got a summer job at the Troubadour café in

Opposite: Erik Spiekermann, early sketch for a serifed version of a proprietary typeface for Deutsche Bahn, named *DB Type*, c.2002. *DB Type* eventually comprised a family of six: *DB Head*, *DB Sans*, *DB Sans Condensed*, *DB Sans Compressed*, *DB Serif* and *DB News*.

London; his ability to speak fluent English would prove to be a huge advantage in his career.

While Spiekermann was at university, he started collecting type and old printing presses. The 1960s was a period when printing technology was rapidly changing – photocomposition was replacing 'redundant' letterpress equipment, which could be obtained gratis. Spiekermann rented a factory floor and began designing and printing small jobs; these were mostly posters, record covers and fliers for fellow musicians, usually for fun rather than money. In 1973 he passed on his printing and distribution enterprise to his brother, and for the first time worked as an employee – as director of pre-press at a printing company called Format. It was short-lived. Later the same year the house that he and his English wife and son were renting was sold, and they decided to move to London.

The next seven years spent in England left an indelible mark, the most obvious being a growing Anglophilia with an affectionate grasp of British popular culture – acquired from the students Spiekermann taught at the London College of Printing as well as, no doubt, British television and the 'popular' press. He was also working as a typographer for a typesetting company

Right: An advanced sketch by Gerry Barney for the new postal services typeface, *PT55*, with correction notes by Erik Speikermann, c.1982. Rejected by the Deutsche Bundespost, it would reemerge as *FF Meta* in 1985.

ABCDEFGHIJKLMNOP
QRSTUVWXYZabcdef
ghijklmnopqrstuvwx
yz 1234567890(&.,£)

called Filmcomposition, who set type onto film using Berthold phototypesetting machines and, through Spiekermann's contacts with the renowned Berlin-based Berthold company, was able to obtain all the latest typefaces. From 1978 he also worked as a freelance designer at the Wolff Olins design consultancy, where he found himself acting as an advisor on work for major German clients such as Volkswagen, Audi, Faber-Castell and the Bank für Gemeinwirtschaft.

Spiekermann wondered why these weighty German institutions were coming to an English design consultancy – or more to the point, why was there was not a German design consultancy on a par with Wolff Olins or, indeed, Henrion Design Associates, Pentagram, Fitch & Co, or Minale Tattersfield? At this time, nine of the ten largest design consultancies in the world were based in London. He concluded that it was, rightly or wrongly, the size and the international reach of these consultancies that attracted major corporations. International companies were more comfortable talking business with a consultancy whose own scale and breadth could demonstrate its understanding of what it meant to run a multinational operation. In 1979 Spiekermann set up MetaDesign in Berlin together with three partners; his ambition was to establish a German design consultancy to match those in London.

MetaDesign's early years were volative. By 1983 the partners wanted to go in different directions, and the company was bought by the London-based Sedley Place Design who wanted an office in Berlin. However, prior to the takeover, MetaDesign had been in talks with the Deutsche Bundespost to redesign their entire corporate identity; when Sedley Place Design took over, Spiekermann was retained to act as a consultant on the project. The Deutsche Bundespost had previously used *Helvetica* on everything, which Spiekermann explained was not only

Above left: Erik Spiekermann, *FF Meta Medium,* 1991.

already used by dozens of other major German companies but also happened to be 'boring and bland'. Spiekermann presented designs for an original typeface which he called at that time *PT55* (PT for 'Post Type' and 55 indicating the weight – borrowed from Frutiger's *Univers* system which he had digitized in 1985 at Stempel AG on their Ikarus system). The brief Spiekermann set himself was that *PT55* should function regardless of printing methods, including low-resolution desktop printers, on all papers, and at very small sizes. For Spiekermann it also had to be the antithesis of *Helvetica*.

The result was a logical but also a distinctive and characterful typeface that exuded a positive attitude. *PT55* has generous counters despite being narrower than *Helvetica*, and a subtle, balanced stroke contrast. It shares the refined humanistic contours of sans serif types such as Hans Eduard Meier's *Syntax* (1968). *PT55*, however, was rejected on the grounds that its distinctive appearance would 'cause unrest'.[2] Deutsche Bundespost, despite having funded the project, decided to continue using *Helvetica*. Describing his frustration, Spiekermann

Below: Erik Spiekermann, *ITC Officina*, c.1989. A busy, elaborate, and compelling two-colour, four-page type specimen.

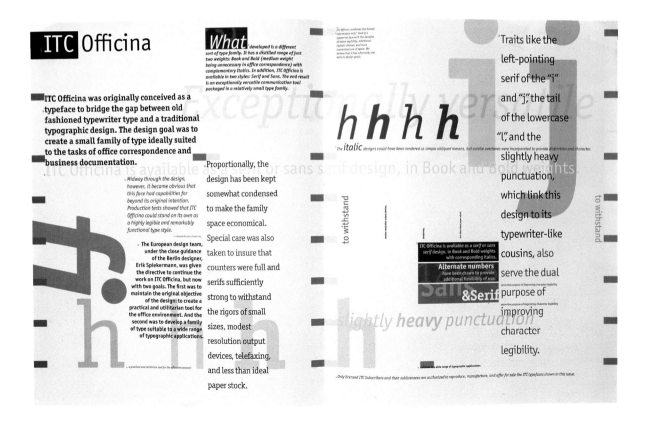

said: 'It's pretty disheartening. 550,000 people work for the Deutsche Bundespost, yet nobody dares go out on a limb. That's why ideas are discussed until they're no longer recognizable, or they are simply shoved in a drawer so that nobody has to deal with anything that might actually change things.'[3] Spiekermann emphasized at the time and since that *PT55* was not a solo effort; some initial work was done by Michael Bitter from Bielefeid University of Applied Sciences, which was refined into preliminary ideas by Gerry Barney and Mike Pratley at Sedley Place Design.

Following the sale of MetaDesign (the new owners changed the name to Sedley Place Design: Berlin), Spiekermann briefly worked with a group of colleagues in a large house at 58 Motzstaße, Berlin, while living on the top floor, before founding hksw GmbH (the initials of the four partners in alphabetic order). Spiekermann then founded MetaDesign GmbH (MetaDesign Company Ltd.) which in 1990 became MetaDesign Plus when additional partners joined. The company moved to Potsdamer Platz and then, along with FontShop, to Bergmannstraße.

Spiekermann had set up FontShop with his wife Joan and Neville Brody in 1989, describing it as a publishing house – not a type foundry – for digital typefaces. Since 1995 FontShop has also hosted the annual typography and design conference, TYPO Berlin, with offshoots in London and San Francisco. It has become the world's largest manufacturer/independent publishing house for typefaces, with over 100,000 fonts from 100 libraries. Not surprisingly, one of FontShop's earlier typefaces, is *FF Meta*, 1991 – Spiekermann's final version of *PT55*. ('FF' stands for FontFont, a digital type library established in 1990.) Ironically, *FF Meta* was so successful and became such a common sight that it was dubbed 'the *Helvetica* of the 1990s'. The *FF Meta* family has been expanded considerably over the years, comprising *FF Meta Plus* (1993), *FF Meta Correspondence* (1996), *FF Meta Condensed* (2001), *FF Meta Headline* (2005) and *FF Meta Serif* (2007).

Shortly after Letraset bought the International Typeface Corporation (ITC) in 1986, Spiekermann was invited to be on the advisory board – whose purpose was to identify gaps in the ITC library of typefaces and to commission new typefaces. In January 1988 Spiekermann presented a written outline concept for *ITC Officina*, which he described as 'a correspondence face', a typeface 'for business correspondence that reads better, takes up less space than *Courier* or *Pica*, but still doesn't look too much

Above: Erik Spiekermann, a comparison between *Meta* (top: *Meta Antiqua Book* and *Meta Book*) and *Unit* (*Unit Slab Regular* and *Unit Regular*).

like a proper "designed" typeface'; in other words, an unpretentious workhorse for everyday business use. Such a typeface, Spiekermann explained, should be 'neutral, and not make a comment about its content'.[4] It was released in 1989 as *ITC Officina Sans*. *ITC Officina Serif* followed, together with further weights, in 1995, using the occasion to expand the family to include small caps and old-style (non-lining) numerals. *Officina Display* was created by Ole Schäfer for the redesign of *The Economist* (London) in 2001 and adapted by Christian Schwartz for release by ITC. (Schwartz first met Spiekermann when an intern in 1998 and would become a stalwart collaborator.)

During the late 1980s and throughout the 1990s, MetaDesign enthusiastically incorporated digital technology; Spiekermann's engagement with new media has played a significant role in MetaDesign's success. This fusion of communication design with computer technology required substantial ongoing investment in hardware and software for design companies who, it should be remembered, had previously required no more than a drawing table and a process camera. By the end of the 1980s new companies were emerging that were founded by young 'digital native' designers, who were neither concerned nor intimidated by computers. Spiekermann, excited by what he had seen in Silicon Valley, set up Meta Design West in San Francisco in 1992 and his first client was Adobe.[5] In the following years the San Francisco office grew to 170 employees. Spiekermann left in 2001 over 'policy disagreements',[6] and set up the United Designers Network.

The typeface *Unit* was based on a first draft of a bold headline face, essentially a straightened and more businesslike version of *FF Meta* that Spiekermann had proposed for Deutsche Bahn in 2002 (who rejected it). *Unit* was then developed by Christian Schwartz as the 'house' typeface for United Designers Network. (Meanwhile Spiekermann, drawing on his experience with Deutsche Bundespost, continued working with Schwartz on a new corporate design for Deutsche Bahn.) Spiekermann described *FF Unit* as '*FF Meta* without the puppy fat'; it was released by FontShop in 2003.

The United Designers Network did not last long. The name was too long and too ambiguous, and by this time Spiekermann was aware that his name had become too valuable an asset to ignore. He changed the company name to SpiekermannPartners. The final move came in 2009, when SpiekermannPartners merged with the Amsterdam company Eden Design & Communication to become EdenSpiekermann. With offices in Amsterdam, Los Angeles, Berlin, Singapore and San Francisco it currently has over 100 employees.

Spiekermann has been involved in the design of many corporate typefaces, but the most significant has been for the DB Deutsche Bahn (named *DB Type*), begun in 2002 and finally completed in 2006 and which has become the typeface most closely associated with postwar Germany. The full bespoke family was designed with Christian Schwartz to provide visual consistency across a broad range of communication on screen and in print: *DB Sans*, *DB Serif*, *DB Head*, *DB Sans Condensed*, *DB Sans Compressed* and *DB News*.

Spiekermann was awarded the German Federal Design Prize in 2011 for the Deutsche Bahn project and his associated work on the passenger information system for BVG (Berlin Transport), for 'having made a significant contribution to the look of Germany'. Appropriately, long-time colleague Christian Schwartz was awarded the German Design Award and the Prix Charles Peignot in 2007.

Below: This award-winning bus timetable booklet from BVG (Berlin Transport) incorporates various members of Erik Spiekermann's *DB Type* family.

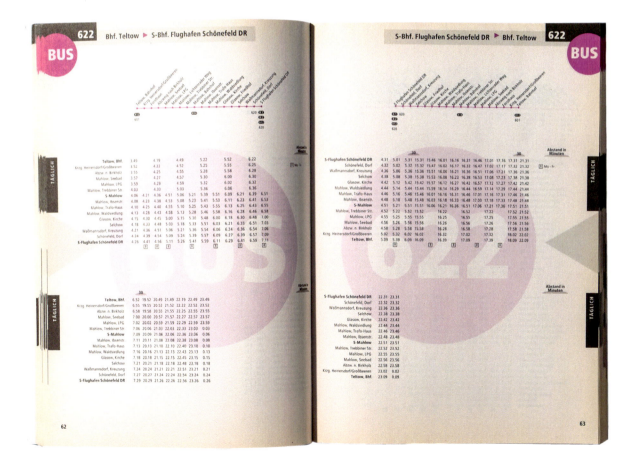

FEATURING RUUD STOP DNA STORE BY COH DAR\YDORP RELIVEN\KOORBNRAB\NIRGLAG MOT

Neville Brody GREAT BRITAIN 1957 –

Neville Brody was born in Southgate, a suburban area of North London. He attended Minchenden Grammar school and then, in 1975, gained a place on the foundation course at Hornsey College of Art, a place of political cause célèbre still reverberating from the student uprising of 1968.[1]

A year later he began studying for a Bachelor of Arts degree in graphic design at the London College of Printing (LCP), a dismal towerblock located south of the River Thames in Elephant & Castle. The LCP student body was eighty per cent local printers' apprentices,[2] attending college on 'day-release' and who considered art students studying graphic design – the remaining twenty per cent – to be interlopers; or 'flashy little stylists' as Beatrice Warde had called them.[3] The graphic design students were equally combative. Brody derided the printing students for carrying a rolled-up copy of *The Sun* newspaper (a 'red-top' harbinger of absurd headlines and topless 'page three' girls) in their back pocket as a badge of primal solidarity. For Brody, the attitude of the printing trade was encapsulated in a phrase he regularly heard when delivering artwork – after a sharp intake of breath and a shake of the head: 'You can't do that, mate!'[4]

In 1975 the Sex Pistols had their first headline performance. It was held at St Martin's College of Art and Design to the north of the Thames, just a short distance away from the LCP, and their contempt for establishment conventions was palpable. It was the beginning of a movement that would radically influence almost every aspect of creative endeavour during the next decade. Brody had become a student in order to learn the rules of typography, but 'the punk explosion blew all of that out the window'.[5]

An important part of Punk sensibility was that the status quo, and the rules by which its judgments were made, were no longer relevant. Indeed, an anti-design (or 'no design') affectation pervaded all aspects of popular culture, but especially so in fashion and print. Jamie Reid – encouraged by his art school friend Malcolm McLaren, manager of the Sex Pistols – was a leading proponent, and designed the Sex Pistol's seemingly impromptu record sleeve, *Never Mind the Bollocks, Here's the Sex Pistols* (1977), to be more an impromptu hazard warning than an invitation to buy.

Opposite: Neville Brody, *Antisans*. There were eighteen issues of *FUSE* between 1991 and 2001 and two more were added when a commemorative boxed set was published in 2012 by Taschen. This poster is for no. 20.

As a student, Brody designed posters for college music events, and contacts made in the process provided him with occasional record cover commissions. His main income on leaving college was working for Rocking Russian, an agency started by Alex McDowell, who was about the same age as Brody and who (with Sebastian Conran) had staged that first Sex Pistols headline concert at St Martin's. Rocking Russian was set up with money from his various music interests – he would later become a major art director in Hollywood.[6] Brody worked with McDowell for almost two years, a period of near abject poverty living in a squat in Covent Garden.

The large number of independent record labels, especially Fetish and Stiff Records, proved a vital resource for Brody – not just enabling him to earn a little money, but also by offering him the freedom to pursue his own ideas while learning about printing technology and having the thrill of seeing his work on display in record shops: 'The record shop was as valid a showcase as the framed environment of art galleries, I thought this area was the only one that would offer any chance of experimentation.'[7] At this point, Brody was focused on image-

Below: Neville Brody, *The Face* magazine, May 1984. Note the inclusion of politics (Livingstone) and feminism (Greer).

Below right: Neville Brody, *Insignia*, originally designed as a headline typeface for *Arena* magazine, which in turn was derived from Brody's *Arena* masthead, 1986.

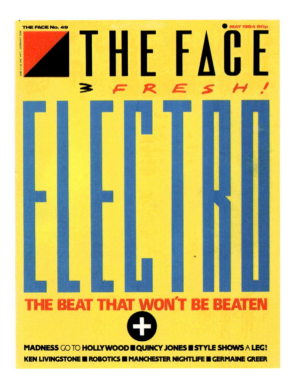

making, his practice closer to illustration than graphic design, while typography remained alien territory. Conventional typesetting for Brody was an excruciating procedure, requiring hand- or type-written copy to be 'marked up' to provide detailed instructions explaining what the designer required the phototypesetter to achieve. Frustration and a lack of time or budget caused Brody to use type as little as possible.

This changed when he met Nick Logan in 1979. Logan had been editor of the monthly magazine *New Musical Express*, a hugely successful magazine in its heyday during the 1970s. When he met Brody he was editor of *Smash Hits*, but he was eager to establish a popular magazine that was more ambitious in scope. In 1979 Logan presented his idea for a new magazine to his employers Emap Publishing. *The Face*, he explained would be a well-produced, well-designed and well-written monthly with music at its core but, crucially, with expanding coverage of the subjects that informed it; from fashion and film to nightclubbing and social issues'.[8] Emap turned it down and so, with a tiny budget of £7,000, Logan published *The Face* independently. The first issue appeared on 1 May 1980 and was an immediate success. It included a short feature written by Brody, who had met Logan in his basement office on Broadwick Street and showed him his portfolio of work. The following year Brody's name began to appear in *The Face* as a designer before becoming its art director. Brody explains: 'The first design I did for *The Face* was a feature on Kraftwerk, as a test of what I might bring. Nick Logan said afterwards that he could not have designed that himself, and consequently brought me in as designer'.[9]

Brody described *The Face* as:

> a living laboratory where I could experiment and have it published. Our golden rule was, 'question everything'. If a page element existed just as taste or style, it could be abandoned. Page numbers could be letters or shapes increasing in size. We could start the headline on the page before. We had disasters and near misses in every issue. We had two weeks to art direct everything, then a week to lay it out. It was pre-computer so everything was traced by hand ... It certainly wasn't a nine-to-five job. You had to be obsessed to make it work.

Although Brody knew little about the conventions of textual typography, he had closely studied the use of typography by the Dadaists, Futurists, and the work of Alexander Rodchenko (his college first year thesis compared the work and intent of Dadaism and Pop Art). Commissions to design record covers had allowed him to indulge in creating type that functioned primarily as image rather than information – emotive expression was infinitely more important than legibility. Once employed as the art director of a magazine, something Brody had never imagined himself doing, his instinct was to maintain the expressive potential of type by imbuing not only headlines but also textual matter with expressive intent, as an extension of the images with which text shares the page.

Headings were often designed and hand-drawn for specific articles and then recycled from time to time. One of the most successful of these was called *Typeface* 3 within the studio, but later named *Industria*: 'The geometric quality of the type was authoritarian, drawing a parallel between the social climate of the 1930s and 1980s.' Headlines were drawn with a Rotring pen and compass on blue graph paper, and then filled in with a felt-tip pen and ink. The artwork that Brody drew had to be completed so fast that last-minute errors were 'touched up' with Tippex and reduced to the required size using a photo-mechanical transfer (PMT) camera.

During his five years at *The Face* Brody slowly refined his use of typography; he maintained the interdependent nature of word and image, but added clarity and reduced the sense of anarchy. At this time Brody also worked on covers and a redesign for the *New Socialist* magazine and the style-conscious London listings magazine *City Limits*, all of which was boosting Brody's typographic confidence as his range of graphic experience grew.

When Brody left *The Face* in 1986 to art direct *Arena*, another Logan publication, he purposefully and controversially turned to *Helvetica*, an intentionally neutral typeface and the antithesis of

Above: Neville Brody, *Industria*, 1984. Fonts designed for *The Face* were initially assigned numbers (this was no. 2) but renamed following digitization for marketing purposes.

Top right: Neville Brody, *FF Blur Bold*, 1992.

his own, highly distinctive hand-drawn display types. His aim was to reduce the disharmony he had willingly employed for *The Face*. For Brody, the use of *Helvetica* – usually *Black* (*Helvetica's* heaviest weight) and often only in lowercase – represented the cool, neutral language of information graphics.[10] But more than that, *Helvetica* signified for Brody a 'bland, non-emotive place where the reader could take stock'.[11]

It was while designing *Arena* that, in September 1987, Brody first borrowed a Macintosh computer. Although sceptical, Brody had seen the quarterly magazine E*migre*, published by Rudy VanderLans and Zuzana Licko in California – E*migre* covers were commonly displayed amongst the music magazines in the Virgin Record Megastore on London's Oxford Street – and realized that the computer was going to revolutionize the way type was designed and used. That same year, QuarkXpress desktop publishing software was launched (quickly replacing PageMaker) to make typographic specifications a thing of the past. A whole page could now be seen and designed on screen in 'What You See Is What You Get' (WYSIWYG) mode, then transferred to an external disk and passed to a digital typesetting agency who could quickly deliver high-resolution print-outs.

Digital typesetting agencies functioned entirely independent of the printing industry and competition meant that an ever-growing range of fonts became available. Most importantly, the digital typesetters' role was not interpretive – they simply processed and printed material given to them by the designer. The print-outs were delivered and then cut and pasted into position on art-board. For Brody, as with many typographic designers, the allure of the computer was the independence and personal control it provided.

In addition, new programs such as Altsys' Fontographer and Letraset's FontStudio meant that anyone could now design type, although these early software programs were complex and rather inhospitable for all but the most determined. The single most important software for Brody was Aldus Freehand. This pre-dated Illustrator, and worked with Fontographer, which was the first ever PostScript drawing program for the computer: 'I was amazed by how you could design a typeface in Fontographer, pull it into Freehand, then set it, and even slant it backwards'.[12] There were also fax machines, photocopiers and the studio PMT camera, all of which, either individually or in combination, could provide startling and immediate results without leaving the studio. For

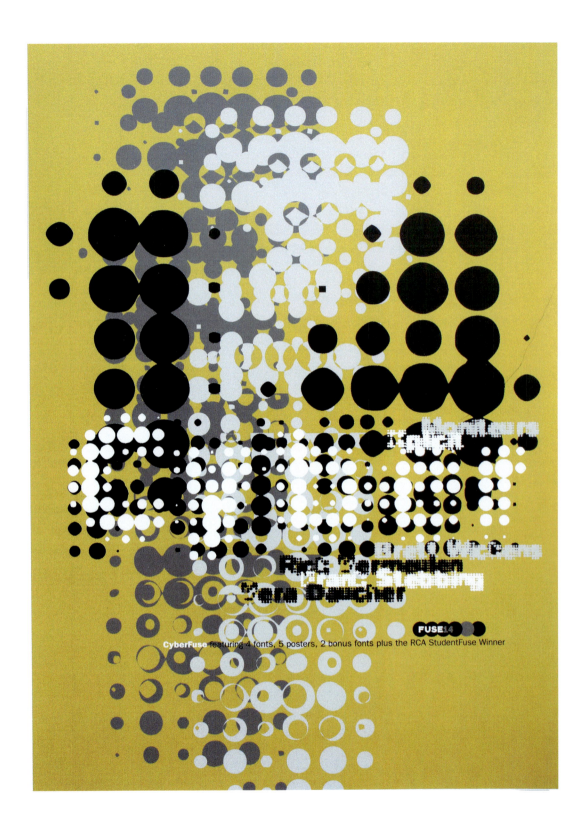

example, Brody experimented with the focus and exposure settings on his PMT camera to distort letterforms – although the final version of *Blur* (1991) was created entirely on the Mac. It was 'blurred' in PhotoShop, traced in Freehand then copied and pasted into Fontographer.[13]

This DIY ('Design It Yourself') methodology was seen as the ultimate antidote to the formality underlying Modernism, and resulted in Brody's work being celebrated as the embodiment of Postmodernism – although not by Brody. 'I hated post-modernism, with its façade and decorativeness; I saw myself as a modernist'.[14]

Ironically, despite it now being possible to obtain crystal-clean, high-resolution digital typesetting, there was a flood at this time of distressed, or 'dirty', DIY letterforms – initially appearing on club fliers, record covers and posters, but then transferring to mainstream advertising, upmarket magazines, television and film, a fascination epitomized by Kyle Cooper's title sequence to the film *Se7en* (1997). Meanwhile Brody had become notorious – a household name no less – and at the age of thirty-one, in the midst of a remarkable media brouhaha he was given a one-man exhibition in 1988 at the Victoria and Albert Museum, London, attracting 40,000 visitors. (The exhibition then toured around Europe before arriving in Toyko two years later.)

That same year, Brody met David Berlow and Erik Spiekermann at an ATypI conference in New York. By the time they met again at the next conference, in 1990, Berlow had co-founded Font Bureau in New York and Spiekermann had co-founded FontShop International in Berlin; both were publishing houses for digital fonts. Later the same year, Brody and Spiekermann founded FontFont – a digital type library. The development and marketing of FontFont became the main focus for FontShop.

Brody had already had three typefaces released by Linotype: *Industria*, *Arcadia* and *Insignia*, in 1986–7. Now he enlisted Berlow's Font Bureau to work[15] on another five typefaces, originally designed for *The Face* and *Arena*, for release through FontFont. (At this point FontShop did not have sufficient resource to

Opposite: Neville Brody, *CyberFuse*, in a poster blending the ideas incorporated in the typefaces designed for *FUSE magazine* no. 14, 1995.

Below: Neville Brody, *Pop*, 1992; *Tyson*, 1993; and *Harlem*, 1993. Brody's output of display faces at this time was prodigious and

undertake such work.) Tobias Frere-Jones, then a junior designer at Font Bureau, went to London to 'help make sense of [Brody's] wild geometric designs'[16] by preparing *FF World*, *FF Tokyo*, *FF Tyson* and *FF Dome* for release in 1993, as well as *FF Harlem*. In remarkably quick time, and due in large part to Brody and Spiekermann's shared renegade reputations (and diametrically contrasting characters), FontFont became the new foundry young designers sought to work with. Brody wanted FontFont to resemble a record store where new designs – potential 'hit singles' – could be seen and bought. As with the music industry's weekly top twenty hits, trends would cause typefaces to quickly fade and make way for the next new typeface; a perpetual cycle of typographic renewal.

To give emphasis to the radical nature of FontFont, Brody and Jon Wozencroft, encouraged by Spiekermann, set up a new magazine to be published and distributed by FontShop International.[17] Called *FUSE*, 'a fusion of the printed word with electronic language', its purpose was to highlight the creative potential of digital typography by providing a vehicle where designers could challenge, without inhibition, conventional thinking about the form and function of type and the visual languages and codes that are used. *FUSE* took the form of a brown card box with the title silkscreen-printed on the surface and its opening sealed with a wraparound printed label. Each issue had a theme. Its contents comprised: an editorial; a disc containing four typefaces, each produced by a different contributor; four A2, two-colour posters, each displaying a typeface, plus an 'introductory' poster. Production was overseen by Spiekermann.

FUSE was launched in the summer of 1991 to euphoric acclaim and squeals of protest in equal measure. Several of the early typefaces feigned commercial application, but by volume 10 such concerns were long forgotten. Brody later explained:

> We were thinking about how most communication had developed abstract forms that dispensed with standard information, like sculpture, painting and music. We called it 'Freeform Typography', and were interested in how the actual form of a letter has emotive, manipulative and expressive qualities. Freeform used written language as if it was visual sound.[18]

Meanwhile, Brody had left *Arena* the previous year and became art director of magazines *Per Lui* (Italy) and *Actuel* (France). In 1994 he established Research Studios in London, with offices in Berlin, Barcelona and Paris. This reflected the fact that most of

Above: Neville Brody and Luke Prowse, *Times Modern*, demonstrating the font's ability to convey different kinds of information.

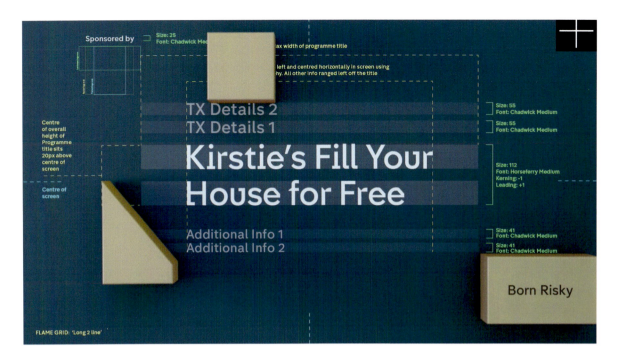

Channel 4

Brody's major assignments after his exhibition at the V&A were from outside Britain – for example, the design of stamps for PTT (the Dutch postal services), signage for the National Gallery of Germany in Bonn, and corporate work for ORF (the Austrian national television and radio broadcaster).[19] More recently, however, Brody was commissioned by *The Times* newspaper to direct the redesign of their *Times2* features section, in 2005, and then the following year to design a new bespoke type family: *Times Modern*.[20] It was designed to function at a smaller size than the previous typeface to allow more text to be squeezed onto the paper's new smaller pages. Other major projects included corporate typefaces for Samsung, Coca-Cola and Channel 4, and the design of the BBC website. In 2010 Brody also art-directed the magazine *Arena Homme+*.

Above: Neville Brody, corporate typeface and specification of the Channel 4 on-screen identity, 2015. Two bespoke typefaces are incorporated: *Horseferry* for headlines, and *Chadwick* (named after the streets that Channel 4 occupy).

CHARLEMAGNE

Carolingian capitals were originally used for titles, to contrast with and enliven text. The typeface that Carol Twombly of the Adobe type staff has designed, Charlemagne, can be effective in the same role in today's book typography. It is useful as well in other display uses, especially when the design calls for a more adventuresome or dynamic quality than conventional Roman capitals provide.

The Charlemagne typeface was inspired by capitals such as those found in the tenth-century Carolingian manuscript, *The Benedictional of St. Aethelwold*. Twombly began this design by sketching a handful of letters whose generous bowls, swelling stems, and accentuated serifs captured the exuberance of the manuscript's title lettering. Twombly scanned these drawings into Adobe's computer system, which enabled her to make the many adjustments necessary to fine type design directly on the computer screen. After completing the regular-weight design, Twombly carefully modified it on-screen to create the bold weight.

Charlemagne regular and bold were designed for use in posters, book titles, packaging, and other display applications; the letters look their best at 18 points and larger. For the best results, care should be taken to optically letterspace any job that is typeset in a titling (all-capital) typeface.

Top right: letterforms from "The Benedictional of St. Aethelwold," 960–980 A.D. (Episcopal liturgical blessings). Photo courtesy of the British Library, London.
Bottom right: Carol Twombly's pencil sketches for Charlemagne.
Letterforms are 96-point Charlemagne regular.

AGKMSZ

Carol Twombly USA 1959–

Carol Twombly was born in Concord, Massachusetts, the youngest of five children. She was initially interested in sculpture and went to Rhode Island School of Design. There she was taught by Charles Bigelow, began to explore the creative potential of graphic design and became intrigued by typography. Twombly later said, 'I discovered that communicating through graphics – by placing black shapes on a white page – offered a welcome balance between freedom and structure'.

   Charles Bigelow (1945–) had studied typography with Jack Stauffacher at the San Francisco Art Institute and with Hermann Zapf at the Rochester Institute of Technology. He taught type design, typography, and the history and theory of writing at the Rhode Island school. Gerard Unger was invited to teach digital typography there for a semester. Bigelow and his design partner, Kris Holmes, encouraged Twombly's interest in type design by inviting her to work as a designer in their studio during summer months. After graduation, Twombly spent an unrewarding year working in a Boston graphic design studio, but was then invited by Bigelow to join a small group of students in a newly formed digital typography program that he had established (supported by Donald Knuth, creator of the Metafont digital program in 1979) at Stanford University, California. The unique two-year program focused on computer science and typographic design.

   After successfully completing the program, Twombly worked at Bigelow and Holmes's studio for the next four years (when Bigelow and Holmes were fully occupied with *Lucida*, a typeface initially completed in 1984–5 but with an ever-extending family). It was during this period that Twombly entered her first type design in an international competition sponsored by Morisawa Ltd, the Japanese manufacturer of phototypesetting fonts and equipment. To her surprise, she won first prize in the Latin text

Opposite: Carol Twombly, *Charlemagne*, from a specimen published by Adobe Originals, *c.*1989.

Below: Carol Twombly, *Mirarae*, 1984.

ABCDEFGHIJKLMNOPQRSTVW
XYZ abcdefghijklmnopqrstvwx
yz 1234567890 (!&$£?)*

category; in 1984 Morisawa licensed and marketed her design under the name *Mirarae*. It has a large x-height and a calligraphic line accentuated by a slight inclination to the right. Soon afterwards, she was asked to add a bold version.

Around this time, Morisawa was in talks with Adobe regarding the development of Japanese PostScript fonts, and her success at Morisawa no doubt helped Twombly gain a part-time position at Adobe working under Sumner Stone. In 1988, she became one of Adobe's two full-time type designers (the other being Robert Slimbach, who had joined the previous year) on what would be called the Adobe Originals program.

The Adobe Originals program was led by Stone (1945–), who had arrived at Adobe in 1985. His initial primary interest had been calligraphy, which he had discovered under Lloyd Renolds, a charismatic teacher in the spirit of Edward Johnston, while at Reed College, Oregon (as had Kris Holmes). He then set up his own lettering studio in Sonoma, California, while studying mathematics at the Sonoma State University. It was here that he became interested in the design of letterforms on computer. This led in 1979 to Stone working for Autologic as director of typographic development until 1983 and then, after a brief period with Camex in Boston, he moved to Adobe. While director of

Below: Carol Twombly, *Trajan*, a caps only typeface, in an Adobe type specimen booklet published c.1989.

ABCDEFGHIJKLMNOPQRSTUV
WXYZ abcdefghijklmnopqrstuvwxyz
1234567890 1234567890 {(!?@£$&*)}
*ABCDEFGHIJKLMNOPQRSTUVW
XYZ abcdefghijklmnopqrstuvwxyz
1234567890 1234567890 {(!?@£$&*)}*

typography at Adobe, Stone designed the extensive *Stone* family in 1987.[1]

Twombly's first independent design projects for Adobe were two typefaces designed in quick succession, *Trajan* and *Charlemagne*, both based on historical models and completed by 1989. Twombly, who always started with hand-drawings, revealed a deep affiliation with the historical roots of these two titling typefaces. *Trajan* is a pure, crisp restrained version of the famous incised roman capitals at the base of the Trajan column. Several missing letters had to be designed, as well as lowercase, numerals, punctuation marks and symbols. *Charlemagne* was inspired by the capitals found in tenth-century Carolingian manuscripts. A bold version was added later. These two faces were quickly followed by a third: another caps-only sans serif typeface called *Lithos*, based on *c.*400 BC Greek inscriptional lettering but lightened by a cursive touch. All three were immediately very popular.

In 1990 Twombly completed her first major type family: *Adobe Caslon*. It is modelled on the enormously popular typeface designed by renowned sixteenth-century British type founder and printer, William Caslon. Twombly's *Adobe Caslon* is considered by many to be the best text typeface to emanate from the Adobe design studio, and remains popular as a text face today. She based her design on Caslon's specimen pages, printed around 1734 (see p. 18) but added many of the features now expected as standard in a high-quality digital text font, such as small caps, non-lining (old-style) numerals, swash letters, ligatures, alternate letters, fractions, subscripts and super-scripts, and even ornaments. Although italic non-lining numerals are included, there are no italic small caps.

She then collaborated with Slimbach on the large and versatile sans serif type family, *Myriad*, issued in 1991. *Myriad* is an open

Above left: Carol Twombly, *Adobe Caslon*, 1990.

ABCDEFGHIJKLNOPQRSTUVW XYZ abcdefghijklmnopqrstuv

and informal humanist sans serif and its italic form is a 'true italic' (not a slanted version more commonly designed to accompany a sans serif). Twombly described the design process as being one of swapping and reworking each other's drawings in an attempt to create a 'homogenous' design. However, in retrospect, she also admitted the experience had been 'too hard' to consider repeating. From the outset, the brief had been to design an independent, anonymous sans, but they found this all but impossible, perhaps because of their typographic roots in calligraphy. Neither was happy working on the project, and Twombly eventually withdraw to its periphery.[2] When eventually released in 1991, much was made of the similarity of *Myriad* to Adrian Frutiger's *Frutiger*, released in 1974. They are, indeed, similar. Frutiger took Adobe to task over it, and Slimbach and Twombly endured professional criticism and personal anguish.

This book contains many examples of blatant copying by foundries of rival's typefaces, undertaken apparently with no moral concern and with little or no criticism. However, Slimbach and Twombly did not set out to design *Myriad* to look like *Frutiger*. The fact that it eventually did, consciously or not, demonstrates just how difficult it is at the end of the twentieth century to design a truly original, 'anonymous' sans serif. It also highlights the brilliance of Martin Majoor's achievement in creating *Scala* two years earlier (see p. 348).

In 1993 Twombly, wishing to take a new direction, created *Viva*, a vivacious display face; the following year she went further in that direction with *Nueva*. Twombly released her last typeface in 1997 – a hybrid serif/slab serif typeface, called *Chaparral*. Despite its slab-like serifs, *Chaparral* retains its strength and charm by a combination of flowing curves and powerful angularity. Twombly took a lead from 'old-style' book types, keeping the contrast low and varying the stroke widths only when necessary. As a result, *Chaparral* not only works exceptionally well in the relative quiet of a running text, it also has sufficient character to be noticed when set as a headline.

Myriad
Myriad

Top: Carol Twombly and Robert Slimbach, *Myriad*, 1991.

Above: Comparison between Carol Twombly and Robert Slimbach's, *Myriad*, 1991 (top), and Adrian Frutiger's *Frutiger*, 1974.

ABCDEFGHIJKLMNOPQRST
abcdefghijklmnopqrstuvwxyz
12345678 *abcdefghijklmnopqr*

As well as many ongoing projects, including enlarging the Latin set for *Adobe Caslon*, Twombly also spent thousands of hours working on a new type format called Multiple Master. The aim in Multiple Master (MM) font technology was to allow the user of MM fonts to create the precise font required by adjusting its parameters. For example, *Myriad* in its MM version had two axes: 'weight' and 'width'. This font therefore included four separate 'master designs' of each character: light compressed, light extended, bold compressed and bold extended. Characters of any weight or width in between these endpoints could be produced by interpolating between the character outlines of these master designs. Italics, of course, required another four master designs.

MM Myriad was released in 1996. MM eventually gave the results intended and, indeed, found a limited market but insufficient to warrant further development, and it was eventually abandoned.[3] Possible explanations for its failure are that typographers found it inconvenient to work with type families that are not clearly defined (MM fonts did not have traditional style names, such as light, bold, condensed and extended, but instead a number quantifying the interpolation value for each axis). But most surprising (to Adobe at least) was that the concept of limitless variation simply did not have the appeal expected.

It was at this moment, in 1999, and having reached the age of forty, Twombly decided to retire to the foothills of the Sierra Nevada and devote her time to alternative, non-digital creative pursuits.

VIVABCDEFGHIJKLMNOPQ
abcdefghijklmno 1234567

**NUEVABCDEFIJKLNOPQRSTU
abcdefghijklmnopq 12345678**

Top: Carol Twombly, *Chaparral Regular*, 1997.

Left top: Carol Twombly, *Viva Regular*, 1993.

Left bottom: Carol Twombly, *Nueva Bold*, and *Nuava Regular Italic*, 1994.

Above: Adobe's Multiple Master technology enables the designer to adjust a given typeface to any width or weight.

Carol Twombly

FF Scala is named after the Teatro alla Scala (1776–78) in Milan. There were two reasons for this name: FF Scala was made especially for a concert hall, the Vredenburg in Utrecht, and the design has it roots in around the time Teatro alla Scala was built, the mid-eighteenth century. Furthermore the word 'scala' has the meaning 'a whole range', which FF Scala certainly is: from A to Z and from **serif** to **sans serif**, from light to **black** and from formal to DECORATED.

As first released (1991) FF Scala had only four styles: Regular, *Italic,* **Bold** and SMALL CAPS. Since then FF Scala has grown to 28 styles.

FF Scala & FF Scala Sans: two typefaces, one form principle

FF Scala and FF Scala Sans are two different typefaces sharing a common form principle. The character of a seriffed typeface mainly arises from the form principle and from elements such as serifs and contrast of the strokes. A sans serif design depends almost entirely on the form principle. FF Scala Sans was made simply by cutting the serifs off from the characters of Scala and by adjusting their contrast. So the skeletons of both FF Scala and FF Scala Sans are identical.

THE SKELETON OF BOTH FF SCALA AND FF SCALA SANS

Martin Majoor THE NETHERLANDS 1960 –

Martin Majoor was born in Baarn, in the Dutch province of Utrecht. An interest in letters was encouraged by his grandfather, who had a lingerie shop and bought lettering books to help him create his own shop displays. Having shown an interest, Majoor would be given used copies for Christmas. His father, meanwhile, was a keen chess player and Majoor remembers him bringing home from his chess club crude dot matrix print-out records of the chess moves. Though these were barely legible, Majoor could not resist trying to design letters of his own from the same matrix.[1]

Majoor enrolled at the Arnhem Art Academy in 1980, the same year as Fred Smeijer, and they became good friends. Unlike the Royal Academy in The Hague, the Arnhem Art Academy did not have a course concerned with the design of type or letterforms. Yet a number of its graduates have become some of the Netherland's best-known type designers; so much so that Arnhem is often referred to as the second 'alphabet city' (after The Hague). This reputation is due almost entirely to the work of Evert Bloemsma, Martin Majoor and Fred Smeijers, all of whom graduated in the early 1980s and, as type designers, were largely self-taught. Their interest in the history, disciplines and crafts associated with type design – calligraphy, letter carving and punchcutting – was considered largely irrelevant within a broadly based Bauhaus-style curriculum, that focused on modernist theory and practice. Thus the younger Majoor and Smeijers were encouraged to discover that Bloemsma's graduation exhibition included his own typeface: *Balance*.[2] They determined that they too would find a way of making the curriculum serve their own purpose rather than that laid out by their tutors.

For his student placement in 1984 Majoor worked at the URW type foundry in Hamburg, where he used their Ikarus system – the first digital type design system (invented at URW by Peter Karow) – to digitize his first typeface *Serré*. It was never released. This was Majoor's first encounter with computers. On graduation Majoor was immediately employed in the research and development department of Océ, a major manufacturer of laser printers (Smeijers would shortly join him). Majoor's job was to design digital typefaces for the Océ printer, but he quickly

Opposite: Martin Majoor, *FF Scala and FF Scala Sans*, a spread from the type specimen published by FontShop, c.1993.

realized that the primitive 300dpi technology, though standard at that time, was unable to cope – causing thin lines and finer serifs to break up or disappear. The budget for research and development was generous enough to allow Majoor to attend a specialist short course at Bitstream in Boston, US, on the production of digital typefaces for laser printers.

After two years at Océ, Majoor was required to undertake military service; as a conscientious objector, he was allowed to work in the social or cultural sectors for two years. To fulfil this obligation Majoor worked as an assistant graphic designer at the state-run Vredenburg Music Centre in Utrecht, where the design department was headed by Jan Willem den Hartog, who knew Majoor from the Art Academy in Arnhem. Den Hartog had been one of the first to introduce Apple Macintosh computers, but when he realized that none of the fonts available for Pagemaker at that time included small caps or non-lining (old style) numerals, he suggested that Majoor design a proprietary typeface for the Vredenburg Centre in 1988.

That typeface would become *Scala*, a type family designed to be sufficiently robust to withstand the detrimental effects of laser printers, photocopiers and fax machines. It was one of the first new typefaces to be designed for the Macintosh that included all ancillary characters required for book texts. The proprietary agreement was generous, in that *Scala* would remain exclusive to the Vredenburg Centre for one year only. The distribution and resultant international recognition of the face occurred suddenly and unexpectedly in 1990.

Erik Spiekermann was looking for fonts to distribute under his new FontFont label. He saw Majoor's typeface at Type 90 (the ATypI conference held in Oxford in 1990) and asked Majoor for the rights to license *Scala* in tandem with fonts from four other young Dutch designers: Max Kisman, Just van Rossum, Erik van Blokland and Peter Verheul.[3] *Scala* was the first text face to be distributed by FontFont. A huge boost for Majoor, and a bestseller for FontShop. However, what turned *Scala* into one of the most influential twentieth-century typefaces was the fact that Majoor added a companion, *Scala Sans*, which was released in 1993 also by FontFont.

Combining serif and sans serif versions within the same family was not an entirely new idea. Van Krimpen had made detailed drawings and had four weights of a sans to accompany his seriffed *Romulus* in the 1930s, but although trial cuts were made it went no further. The completion of the *Scala* family, therefore, caused quite a furore. *Scala Sans* is a true translation of *Scala's* formal proportions and so inherits its humanist proportions: 'two typefaces, one form'.[4] The *Scala Sans Italic* is a true calligraphic italic (other major sans serif faces at that time – *Univers, Frutiger, Helvetica* – had sloping romans). Robin Kinross described *Scala* as 'a text-face without exact historical precedents, but rooted in tradition'.[5] Certainly, the *Scala* family's indeterminate historical references enable it to allude to typographic tradition while remaining non-partisan; it was described by Emily King as 'a kind of soft-edged modernism'.[6] In 1997 Majoor augmented *Scala* with additional variations to the family: light, black and condensed, plus a set of four display versions called *Scala Jewels*.

Throughout the 1990s, *Scala* and *Scala Sans* were the only available typefaces by Majoor, who explained that he was only concerned with creating typefaces for specific typographic purposes and had no interest in the speculative design of type or of being a servant to the whims of font buyers. Indeed, Majoor waited nearly a decade before publishing another typeface, although in the intervening years he worked on several commissioned typefaces, most notably for the Dutch telephone company PTT (discussed later). The impetus for *Seria*, Majoor's second family of typefaces, was his dissatisfaction with the use of *Scala* for longer literary texts. *Scala* is a remarkably versatile typeface, but Majoor began to consider adding to the *Scala* family by providing a version with lengthened ascenders and

Below: The close structural relationship of the *Nexus* family of fonts demonstrated by Majoor, 2004.

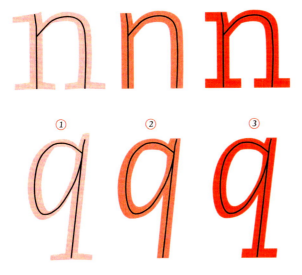

1 Nexus & Nexus italic
ABCDEFGHIJKLMNOPQRSTUVWXYZ
abcdefghijklmnopqrstuvwxyz 1234567890
ABCDEFGHIJKLMNOPQRSTUVWXYZ
abcdefghijklmnopqrstuvwxyz 1234567890

2 Nexus Sans & Nexus Sans italic
ABCDEFGHIJKLMNOPQRSTUVWXYZ
abcdefghijklmnopqrstuvwxyz 1234567890
ABCDEFGHIJKLMNOPQRSTUVWXYZ
abcdefghijklmnopqrstuvwxyz 1234567890

3 Nexus Mix & Nexus Mix italic
ABCDEFGHIJKLMNOPQRSTUVWXYZ
abcdefghijklmnopqrstuvwxyz 1234567890
ABCDEFGHIJKLMNOPQRSTUVWXYZ
abcdefghijklmnopqrstuvwxyz 1234567890

descenders. He decided, instead, to create a new face. He studied two twentieth-century fine book typefaces: Bruce Rogers's *Centaur* and Bram de Does's *Trinité no. 3*. Jan van Krimpen's types, most of which are of similar proportions, were also studied. Work began in 1996 and the result was *Seria*, released in 2000 in two forms: *Seria* and *Seria Sans*, each accompanied by almost vertical italics – not disimillar to Van Krimpen's italics for *Romanée*, 1949.

Nexus grew out of *Seria*, as Majoor explains:

> *Nexus* started as an alternative to *Seria*, a typeface I had designed some 5 years earlier. *Seria* has some strong features like extremely long ascenders and descenders, and an upright italic … I started working on an alternative version of *Seria*, with shorter ascenders and descenders. But soon this design developed into a new typeface, with numerous changes in proportions and details, and with a redrawn italic. The result [*Nexus*] was a workhorse typeface like *Scala*, but with all the features that *Seria* had for book work.[7]

When the *Nexus* family (*Nexus Serif*, *Nexus Sans*, *Nexus Mix* and *Nexus Typewriter*) was released in 2004, it was one of FontShop's first OpenType font families. The term 'Mix' is used by Majoor to describe the slab serif: a 'mixture between a sans and a serif'. The origin and purpose of an unannounced 'fourth' interloper, *Nexus Typewriter*, is ambiguous – even FontFont literature describes it as 'an enigma wrapped within a riddle'.[8]

In the early 1990s, Jan Kees Schelvis, a friend and fellow teacher at the Academy at Arnhem – and also the designer of the PTT Telecom phone book's covers and introductory pages – explained to Majoor that there were growing concerns within the company about the directory. Schelvis had already approached Ootje Oxenaar of the art and design department of PTT to let

Right: Martin Majoor, *Telefont List* and *Telefont Text* and variants, 1993.

him know that he would like to propose a redesign. When he spoke with Majoor about the project, they concluded that a new typeface would be essential. Schelvis suggested the idea of a new typeface to Oxenaar, who was enthusiastic but thought Gerard Unger should be the person to design it. Nevertheless, a meeting was set up and both Schelvis and Majoor went to present their ideas. The outcome was that they were asked to write a report and provide a visual proposal.

The significance of the meeting's outcome for Schelvis and Majoor cannot be overestimated. The Dutch telephone book had last been comprehensively redesigned in 1977 by Wim Crouwel and Jolijn van de Wouw. Theirs was a remarkable achievement; radical and uncompromising, its modernist credentials – most distinctive being the use of lowercase type throughout – created enormous international interest. In the years that followed, the original design had been eroded by concessions forced upon Crouwel, with the result that by the early 1990s, functionality had reached an all-time low. Following the privatization of PTT Telecom in 1989, the company conceded that the phone book needed a fundamental overhaul.

When Scheivis and Majoor returned to present their ideas to

Below: Martin Majoor, *Telefont List*, testing the effectiveness of 'spikes and inktraps', 1993.

Above: Martin Majoor, *Telefont*, as applied in the *Dutch Telephone Directory*, 1994.

Oxenaar at PTT Telecom, they explained that the new directory should include postcodes and that the use of capital letters should be reinstated at the start of proper names. They also proposed a return to telephone numbers before names (as initially and controversially instigated by Crouwel) and, critically for Majoor, a new typeface that he promised would save space, paper and money. Oxenaar was supportive and offered them three months to develop their ideas into a workable visual form.

The deadline was March 1993. Final approval was given at the end of 1993 following a conclusive presentation to PTT Telecom and TeleMedia – PTT's sole amendment being that names must appear before telephone numbers.

Before the decision had been made to design a new type, Majoor and Schelvis had studied as many telephone directories as they could find. The last landmark in telephone directory typeface, *Bell Centennial*, had been designed by Matthew Carter in 1978 – a low-resolution bitmap typeface for CRT typesetting machines. It incorporated 'spikes' and 'inktraps' necessary to negate the ordeal of the typesetting process and high-speed web-offset printing. After comprehensive tests, Majoor found that such compensations were no longer necessary.

Majoor designed two typefaces for the new directory: *Telefont List* and *Telefont Text* (the name was his father's idea). Majoor relied significantly on collaboration with Fred Smeijers, who by this time had completed the core family of his own impressive 'full-blooded sixteenth/twentieth-century Low-Countries typeface': *Quadraat*.[9] Schelvis, meanwhile, concentrated on the overall information and wayfinding design.

For the listing Majoor designed the robust and simplified 'industrial' *Telefont List*. Initial capital letters and minutely judged word-spaces were deployed. Turnover lines were indented, a procedure that aided function and offended modernist principles. Postcodes were set in a reduced size. *Telefont Text*, designed for the continuous text on introductory pages, has a more generous width, a little more distinction in height between upper- and lowercase. The set includes small caps and non-lining numerals.

The typography of the Majoor *Dutch Telephone Directory* was acclaimed for its visual assurance, gained in large part by maximizing the distinction in weight between names (in bold) and addresses. In spite of the paper-saving efficiency of the type design and diligent editing, the sense is that information has ample space in which to function. The care taken over every detail exemplified a new spirit in typography – intelligent, efficient, free of histrionics and yet fully aware of tradition, in effect it is Modern Traditionalism.[10]

In 2018 PTT Telecom announced that the last printed telephone directory had been published.

Zuzana Licko CZECHOSLOVAKIA/USA 1961 –

Zuzana Licko and her family emigrated to San Francisco, California, from Bratislava when Czechoslovakia was still under communist rule. Her father taught biomathematics at the University of California, and encouraged Licko's involvement with computers during the summer holidays when she helped him with data processing work. Her ambition was to become an architect, and she gained a place in the College of Environmental Design at the University of California, Berkeley. The university had recently closed its Visual Studies program, but many of the associated classes, such as photography, letterpress and typography continued and were offered to architecture students as a means to broadening their skills and cultural horizons. Once on campus, Licko realized she was more interested in these marginal classes than she was in architecture, and finally graduated with a degree in graphic communications instead.

Licko was still an undergraduate when, in late 1982, she met Rudy VanderLans and the following year they were married. VanderLans had studied at the Royal Academy of Arts in The Hague and graduated in 1979. He worked as an intern at Total Design in Amsterdam, and as a junior designer at Form Vijf and Tel Design in The Hague. In 1981, aged twenty-five and feeling disillusioned by graphic design, he decided to go back to university to do graduate studies – and since he also wanted to see more of the world, he chose to study photography at the University of California.

Both Licko and VanderLands were pursuing freelance design work after classes in search of a career direction. VanderLans was hired by the *San Francisco Chronicle* newspaper to work as a graphic designer and illustrator (he had gone to the interview under the impression that he was applying for a job at *Chronicle Books*). In 1984, the year Licko graduated, the Macintosh desktop computer was launched. In her final year, Licko attended a computer graphics class and was given access to a terminal on which she experimented, generating line drawings through coding. The process was counter intuitive and so slow, in fact, that projects were batch-processed overnight.

The launch of the Macintosh was accompanied by a new magazine, *MacWorld*, and the editor invited illustrators from the San Francisco Bay area, including Licko and VanderLans,

Opposite: Zuzana Licko, *Mrs Eaves*, in a type specimen published by *Emigre*, 1996.

to come and see the new machine. The first Macintosh was a primitive little box-like computer that could do very little except render coarse, low resolution images. Nevertheless Licko, having experienced the frustration of working with mainframe computers, immediately recognized its potential. The editor at *MacWorld* offered to lend them one for the weekend. They were smitten and bought one. Macintosh user-groups started up almost immediately, and Licko attended several sessions with the UC Berkeley group. It was here, by chance, that she discovered FontEditor software.

By this time, one issue of *Emigre* magazine had been published, established by VanderLans and two Dutch friends. Frustrated at not being able to get their photographs published or into galleries, they decided that a magazine might act as a vehicle for their work. The first issues included poetry, short stories and architectural projects as well as photography. A typewriter was used in place of typesetting to save on costs, but having seen the Macintosh computer Licko and VanderLans realized they could now render their own fonts.[1] Although expedient, the results were far from satisfactory. Early computers had very little memory, and so the 'type' that the designer saw on screen was no more than a very crude interpretation of the chosen typeface, meaning typographers were designing text virtually blind. Licko decided that an embryonic typeface was needed, so simple in its construction that its appearance on screen would be precisely the same as it would later appear in printed form – an outcome popularly described at the time as, 'What You See Is What You Get' or 'WYSIWYG'.

The Macintosh gave a new and unique focus to what Licko and VanderLans were doing, and it was a tool they enjoyed mastering. It enabled everything they had learned about design to be reassessed, and its restrictive means gave them every reason to break with convention. Licko explained:

> The Macintosh was unveiled at the time I graduated. It was a relatively crude tool back then, so established designers looked upon it as a cute novelty. But to me it seemed as wondrously uncharted as my fledgling design career. It was a fortunate coincidence; I'm sure that being free of preconceived notions regarding typeface design helped me in exploring this new medium to the fullest.[2]

Emperor
Oakland
Emigre
Universal

Above: Zuzana Licko, *Emperor, Oakland, Emigre,* and *Universal,* all c.1984.

A 'cute novelty' is a charitable description – in fact, many designers were horrified by the idea of peering at a small screen for hours trying to create something that would take a minute or two with a pencil and paper. To suggest that the computer was a creative tool seemed a ridiculous notion to many at that time.

When Licko first began designing bitmap fonts in 1984 there was no plan to start a type foundry; it was *Emigre* that encouraged this option. The third issue was the turning point for Licko's typeface experiments – and for the magazine – because this issue was typeset using her low-resolution typefaces: *Emperor*, *Oakland*, *Emigre* and *Universal*. Perhaps to Licko's surprise, the potential of these typefaces, whose appearance became closely associated with new digital technology, was immediately recognized as having a wider range of creative applications. Inquiries about their availability began to arrive.

For a brief period, this turned Licko into a typesetter. Because many of the designers who wanted to use Licko's typefaces did not yet have a Macintosh she was selling typesetting using her fonts, typing the required words in the required typeface as instructed and providing a print-out. Meanwhile, *Emigre* magazine provided Licko with a reason to continue developing other fonts as well as providing the means to promote them. In turn, Licko's type made a huge contribution to the magazine's unique character, as well as providing a cost-effective and efficient means of typesetting.

When designers began buying Macintoshes, they asked Licko to supply the fonts on a disc and this was the eureka moment – when Licko realized that she could make copies of her fonts and sell them without limit. Licko took charge of all the technical aspects of font manufacturing, administration and planning, as well as designing most of the fonts. Meanwhile, VanderLans concentrated on *Emigre*, conducting the interviews, doing much of the writing as well editing and design. (The other founders had left in 1987.)

Both VanderLans' *Emigre* and Licko's typefaces became the focus as well as the means of debate; what was said in the magazine was inseparable from how it looked. The confidently large (approximately A3) format was like no design publication seen before. Interviews with young designers barely out of college – such as David Carson, Edward Fella, Jeffery Keedy, US), Nick Bell, The Designers Republic, Vaughan Oliver (UK), – were fulsome, kept raw and incisive. VanderLans' pages were complex,

Above: Zuzana Licko, demonstrating how the high-resolution *Base 900* family has adopted key elements of the low-resolution *Base 9* (designed on a 9-pixel-high grid). A detail from the *Base 900* type specimen, 2010.

Zuzana Licko **359**

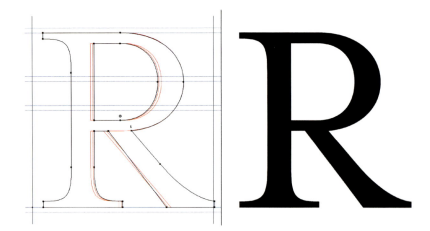

an underlying structure might be hinted at but then cut through by a text that, apparently, could not be constrained. Meanwhile, Licko's type defied everything typographers had been taught – the 'unreadable' was now being avidly read.

Understandably, the cool authority that had formed the basis of Modernism was threatened and the reaction from some of its practitioners was vitriolic, but *Emigre* readers were happy to see the establishment riled and faltering in the wake of what was, after all, a small independent magazine run by two young designers in Berkeley (a city that still feels like a village) and barely out of college. But possibly the most startling aspect behind all of this was the Macintosh – a tool previously described as a creative cul-de-sac.

Licko's early elemental bitmap fonts (*Emperor, Oakland, Emigre* and *Universal*) were later grouped together and named the *Lo Res* family. By the 1990s, Licko was exploring the opportunities offered by improving digital type technology while holding on to the distinctive appearance of the *Lo Res* family. The *Base 900* family is a high-resolution adaptation of *Base 9* which was designed on the same 9-pixel-high grid as *Lo-Res 9 Narrow*, and demonstrated Licko's continuing interest in technological constraint serving as a source of inspiration.

Her challenge when drawing *Base 900* was to find the right balance between 'normalizing' the design of *Base 9* while maintaining its original character. In achieving this, the most distinctive element carried over to *Base 900* from *Base 9* was the triangular spur detail. In *Base 9*, to suggest the 'negative' space created where the rounded stroke meets the upright, a pixel was removed to open up the area. This open square became the

Above right: Zuzana Licko, *Mrs Eaves* in development.

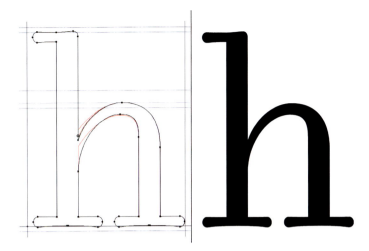

triangular wedge shape that became the prominent feature of *Base 900*.

By the mid 1990s, and in line with improving digital sophistication, Licko was exploring richer and infinitely more complex type forms. *Mrs Eaves* and *Filosofia* both appeared in 1996. It is no coincidence that the arrival of these two faces coincided with a radical overhaul of *Emigre* magazine's design. In 1995 VanderLans reduced the format to A4 – a more conventional magazine proportion – and adopted a relatively conventional textual appearance. These changes, in turn, marked a change in editorial stance. VanderLans explained: 'Instead of focusing on the designers' intentions and the designer's work, we decided to turn the tables and look at how this work is impacting our culture.' It was decided that longer, more in-depth texts required more conventional, less distracting letterforms with which to hold the reader's attention.[3]

For this Licko turned to *Bodoni*, originally cut by the Italian Giambattista Bodoni towards the end of the eighteenth century; it was a typeface she had long admired. Licko was aware that the bold vertical stance of Bodoni did not offer a particularly comfortable read. After closely studying a copy of Bodoni's *Manuale Tipografico* (1818) at the Bancroft Library in Berkeley, she designed *Filosofia*, effectively from memory, using Fontographer to draw directly on the computer. Far from being a revival of Bodoni, *Filosofia* should be viewed as a homage, or 'interpretation'.[4] On the *Emigre* website the term 'anthropological modernism' is used in conjunction with *Filosofia*, a description supported by the presence of organic fleurons also designed by Licko.

Above left: Zuzana Licko, *Filosofia* in development.

To provide a more amiable reading experience Licko reduced the amount of contrast between the thick and thin strokes (this also helps *Filosofia* withstand reduction to smaller sizes), and provided subtlety bulging serif endings. These mimic the unintentional effect often seen in printed samples of Bodoni's work caused by the pressure of ink against paper during printing. Other distinctive features are the ball terminals of the 's' and '3'. All of this gives Licko's *Filosofia* a softer, yet robust and infinitely more human quality if compared to the numerous twentieth-century *Bodoni* revivals.[5]

The regular version of the *Filosofia* family is designed to be used in text, while *Filosofia Grand* is designed for display applications and characterized as more refined and delicate. An additional variant included in the *Grand* package is *Unicase* – a version which uses a single height for characters that are otherwise separated into uppercase and lowercase, with additional stylistic variants to provide more flexibility for headline use.

Licko's *Mrs Eaves*, released in 1996, is based on *Baskerville*, a typeface cut for the English printer and publisher John Baskerville by John Handy in 1757. Licko named *Mrs Eaves* after Sarah Eaves, who was Baskerville's live-in housekeeper, eventually becoming his wife following the death of her previous husband. Like *Baskerville*, *Mrs Eaves* has a near vertical stress, departing from previous 'old style' models such as *Caslon* and *Garamond*, but not quite reaching the upright stance of Bodoni's 'modern style'. As with *Filosofia*, Licko reduced the contrast in stroke-width to provide a rounded, more luscious and generous appearance. This also countered the anaemic reproduction at smaller point sizes in digital revivals of *Baskerville*. To compensate and create a lighter-looking page, Licko lowered the x-height and widened the proportions to provide generous counters. She later developed two companion variants – *Mr Eaves Sans* and *Mr Eaves Modern* – both strikingly supple sans serifs. *Mr Eaves Sans* is the variation that relates more closely to the serif version, while *Mr Eaves Modern* provides simpler and more geometric-looking shapes.

Licko may be the less outspoken of the *Emigre* partnership, but it was her typefaces that carried *Emigre*'s message far beyond its pages and in so doing attracted the hostility of senior design modernists. Licko's apparently innocuous line – 'people read best what they read most' was met by a level of outrage that is hard to fathom today. The statement is a playful reiteration of Stanley

Morison's 'Familiarity is the first law of legibility',[6] but turned on its head by suggesting that typefaces as diverse as *Helvetica*, *Times New Roman* and her own *Emperor* are, in fact, not intrinsically legible at all but simply become legible through use.

Massimo Vignelli called Licko's work 'garbage'. Her response was a euphemistic shrug, to say how much she admired Vignelli's work and carry on. Their exchange of correspondence was published in *Emigre*, no. 69 and includes Vignelli's apology.[7]

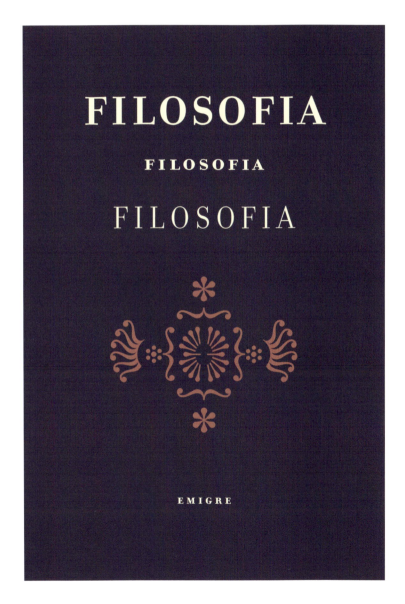

Left: Zuzana Licko, *Filosofia*, with decorative fleurons, from the cover of an *Emigre* type specimen, 1996.

REDISTURBED

Jeremy Tankard GREAT BRITAIN 1969 –

Jeremy Tankard was born in Crewe, Cheshire. The family moved to Sandbach where his father was publicity manager for the truck company ERF. They then moved to Lincolnshire in 1983 in time for Jeremy to start his O-level studies, after which he began his A-levels. But after the first year of the two-year course he 'jumped out and then jumped into the Foundation course at Lincoln College of Art in 1986' where he remembers 'excitedly reading about Muriel Cooper's progressive work at the MIT Media Lab' and 'using a light pen on a computer to do life drawings'.[1]

Tankard gained a place on the BA Graphic Design course at St Martins School of Art and Design in London.[2] His typography tutor in the first year was Nicholas Biddulph who, with Nicolette Gray, established the Central Lettering Record as a resource and reference archive representing the full range of lettering practice. Biddulph was renowned for 'arriving at his classes with a mass of material from the archive, dumping it on a desk and negotiating it visually in the most wide-ranging and cross-historical manner'.[3]

The college was unusual in that it was one of very few to retain a letterpress workshop – a work space Tankard explored and where he learned how to use a Berthold typesetter. At the same time, Central was also one the first art colleges[4] in the UK to introduce computer technology to graphic design students. This was initially set up as a specialist part-time course – 'Computers in Graphic Design', established by Gillian Crampton Smith. Tankard, who had grown up with Sinclair ZX81 and Spectrum 48k computers, was quick to take advantage of these facilities, especially once WYSIWYG (What You See Is What You Get) via the laser printer enabled a much-improved typographic output. Nevertheless, these machines were slow; so slow that Tankard realized it was far quicker to nip into the letterpress workshop and set text by hand, print, and then cut and paste in the studio. However, during Tankard's three years at St Martin's the computing facilities increased to provide college-wide access and by 1990, when Tankard applied to the Royal College of Art (RCA), he was a confident and enthusiastic user of digital technology.

In 1990 Margaret Calvert was head of the graphic design department at the RCA. Derek Birdsall, the previous incumbent, had little interest in computers and had brought in Alan Kitching (previously a partner with Birdsall at Omnific Design) to

Opposite: Jeremy Tankard, *Redisturbed*, 2010, a refined version of *Disturbance*, 1993. From the cover of a type specimen designed by Tankard.

365

aBCDefGHIJKLm
NOPQRStUVWXYZ

aBCDefGHIJKLm K
NOPQRStUVWXYZ R

establish a letterpress workshop at the College and act as a counter to the emerging wave of digital enthusiasm. The development of digital facilities at the RCA was due in large part to Richard Doust, a full-time Senior Tutor and who was Tankard's personal tutor. Doust had moved to the RCA from St Martin's, where he had taught on the 'Computers in Graphic Design' course. When he arrived in 1987, the RCA had just one Mac 128k – the original Apple Macintosh personal computer. Calvert, a passionate advocate of drawing, nevertheless decided to act against college policy and bought several more Macs and a laser printer, enabling Doust to begin setting up a small computer studio to ensure graphic design students had their own, unrestricted access to digital technology.

The allure of Kitching's letterpress studio (richly aided by print 'technician' Mike Perry) dominated the RCA student shows[5] during the early 1990s and Tankard, feeling frustrated by what he felt was an entrenched way of thinking by core lecturers, spent a great deal of his first year with Kitching and Perry gaining a tacit, in-depth knowledge of wood and metal type and printing. Letterpress, Tankard, realized, was the ultimate 'WYSIWYG' system; in fact, it was more so, because it was possible to print any typeface in any colour and on a paper of choice. Having barely survived his first year, Tankard, along with a small number of other students, began to use the new digital facilities and started designing their first typefaces. Using an early version of Fontworks, Tankard designed *FF Disturbance*, which attracted critical acclaim outside the confines of the RCA.

FF Disturbance, like Thompson's *Alphabet 26*, is a unicase typeface

Above right: Jeremy Tankard, *FF Disturbance* shown above a stage development of the revised version, *Redisturbed*, released in 2010. Tankard's intention was to take the idea of a unicase alphabet further and treat it as a conventional text type by adding all the characters, typographic elements and details expected today. Tankard reasoned that the unfamiliar unicase letterforms are less problematic today than they had been in the recent past.

– a combination of upper and lowercase letters. Since uppercase models are used for the characters 'B', 'D' and 'H', there are fewer ascenders overall, resulting in some unfamiliar word shapes. However, the three-quarter-height ascenders of 'K' and 'L', along with the use of an unusually large number of ligatures, add vertical elements usually provided by capital letters. Ligatures are commonly limited to a small number of character-combinations such as 'fi' and 'fl', but Tankard wanted to explore what new forms were possible by extending the number and variety of ligatures to assist in flow and rhythm; this is now a familiar feature in many of Tankard's typefaces. In the final version, ten ligatures were added to the standard ones. *FF Disturbance* was released in 1993 by FontShop International. Much later, from around 2000, Tankard began heavily revising and refining Disturbance to improve the quality of outline, increase weight and glyph range and make use of optical scaling. Renamed *Redisturbed*, it was finally released in 2010.

   Tankard had not set out to be a type designer, but during the second year of study his determined interest was, at least in part, an act of defiance fuelled by his graphic tutors' antagonism towards his interest in digital technology. (Doust and Kitching were exceptions.) 'I ignored my tutors because they discouraged me from exploring typography and for not allowing me to engage in free-thinking! I wanted to explore how language is enhanced, altered, interpreted, and formed by letters, and examine the extent to which forms can be disrupted.'[6] Tankard has always regarded technology, be it analogue or digital, as a challenge, never a constraint.

Below: Jeremy Tankard, *Bliss*, 1996.

ABCDEFGHIJKLMNOPQRSTUVWXYZÀÁÂÃÄĀĂ
ÅĄÆǼĆĈČÇĎĐÈÉÊĚËĒĖĘĜĞĠĢĤĦÌÍÎĨÏĪĬIJĴ
ĶĹĽĻŁĿŃŇÑŅÒÓÔÕÖŌŎŐØǾŒŔŘŖŚŜŠŞŢŤ
ŦÙÚÛŨÜŪŬŮŰŲẀẂŴẄỲÝŶŸŹŽŻŊÐÞ

abcdefghijklmnopqrstuvwxyzàáâãäāăåǻąæǽćĉ
čçďđèéêěëēėęĝğġģĥħìíîĩïīĭıijĵķĺľļłŀńňñņòóôõ
öōŏőøǿœŕřŗśŝšşßťţŧùúûũüūŭůűųẁẃŵẅỳýŷÿ
źžżŋðþ

Tankard's thesis – exploring the American designer Bradbury Thompson's ideas concerning unicase fonts and the merits or otherwise of Thompson's *Alphabet 26* [7] – was unorthodox in both content and appearance. Tankard set his thesis in the first version of *FF Disturbance*. 'My tutors said "You can't do this to the alphabet. It's ugly. There are reasons for things being the way they are. It's disturbing." Bingo, I had a name for the typeface!'[8]

On graduation Tankard began working at Addison Design, a major (if short-lived) design consultancy in Britton Street, Clerkenwell, just around the corner from Alan Kitching's own typography studio. Here Tankard met Kitching's assistant Kelvyn Smith and, once more, found solace in the letterpress workshop, a sanctuary from the discomfort and frustration of working in corporate design. For similar reasons, Tankard also began teaching one day a week[9] and, keen to visit the type museums of Europe, went 'Inter-railing at every opportunity'. In 1994 he moved to the more congenial Wolff Olins studios and remained there until 1998.

During his six years in corporate design, Tankard began work on several typefaces in his own time, including *Bliss* (which he had started while at the RCA) as well as *Blue Island*, *The Shire Types*, and *Alchemy*. He then decided to take a six-month sabbatical to travel around Australia, and on his return was determined to work as an independent type designer. He resigned from Wolff Olins and began working from his London flat before finding a studio space at the Canalot Studios, Kensal Road. Finally, in 2003 he and his wife moved to Cambridge and set up Jeremy Tankard Typography.

The possibilities of making one character flow naturally into the next were explored to the full in Tankard's *Blue Island*. This grew out of a development project at Wolff Olins, when Tankard found himself working for the luxury jewellery company Bulgari.

Above: Jeremy Tankard, initial sketch for Bulgari and the genesis for *Blue Island*, c.1994–98.

Right: Jeremy Tankard, *Blue Island* in development, 1997, and released by Adobe in 1999. The comments in pencil

368   Type Designers of the Twentieth Century

He had been asked to look at the possibility of adapting the typography of the company name for use in new markets. One of several concepts that Tankard designed was of letters linked or interlocked, to invoke the way the jewels of a necklace are connected. Then, as is often the case, the project dissipated. Nevertheless, Tankard continued to work on the 'interlocking letters' concept. He wanted to 'turn the forms inside out, so that many letters would appear to be made from the strokes of the letters that preceded or followed'.[10]

Tankard was interested in developing *Blue Island* as a Multiple Master typeface. MM had been developed by Robert Slimbach and others at Adobe, and Tankard had used it at Wolff Olins where he was regularly asked to 'make [letters] a bit heavier or a bit wider. In the end it just made sense to anticipate this and use mm's sliding bars to offer a quick solution'.[11] Tankard approached Adobe with *Blue Island* and received an encouraging reply from Carol Twombly, then manager of type. Tankard was offered a contract to complete the typeface and given some sketches from Slimbach to consider. However, it was Twombly who remained Tankard's main contact.

Signing a contract with Adobe was one of the factors that persuaded Tankard to resign from Wolff Olins, although the company left his place open should he want to return. Over the next twelve months reinforced FedEx envelopes containing print-outs and extensive comments winged back and forth across the Atlantic, with the result that *Blue Island* became increasingly harmonious, balanced and fluid in appearance. It was decided, however, that forcing every character pair to link would be counterproductive, as Tankard explained: 'It's similar to how we write informally, where we may naturally join some letters of a word and not others.' In the final design, the illusion of most letters being created from both preceding and following letters was achieved without recourse to additional or 'alternative' characters. This was at the insistence of Adobe. Tankard would have preferred to have at least a small number of alternative characters – for example, he wanted to include a reversed 'o' to enable additional linkage options.

The alphabetic forms were the first to be signed off, followed by the accents, and finally the spacing. Adobe then took the font in-house in November 1998 to complete the character set, fine-tune and fully test it. In February 1999 *Blue Island* was added to the Adobe Originals collection and it won a Type Directors

Club Type Design Competition 2000 Award. It had been three years in the making and Tankard admitted that 'working with Adobe had been an excellent education'. (The conversion of *Blue Island* to Multiple Master had been rejected almost at the outset, Twombly's explanation being that 'MM tech [is] only used for text faces, not display faces'.)[12]

The groundwork for the sans serif *Bliss* had begun when Tankard was still a student at the RCA. Its genesis was Edward Johnston's seminal book *Writing & Illuminating & Lettering*, first published in 1906. Tankard was intrigued by the expressive humanistic potential of letters, and especially in Johnston's *Underground* lettering system which, despite its elemental design, was imbued with the idea of 'Englishness'; a quality that was manifest in letters that are 'softer, more flowing and fulsome in their curves'.[13] Eric Gill offered Johnston advice on his design and Johnston's *Underground* lettering became the basis for his own *Gill Sans* – which, since 1945, has often been warmly referred to as the national typeface of Great Britain.[14]

Qualities that convey a humanistic disposition are particularly apparent in Tankard's earlier pencil drawings for *Bliss* in which,

Below: Jeremy Tankard, *The Shire Types*, 1998. Seen here in a spread from *TypeBookOne*, published by Jeremy Tankard Typography, 2004.

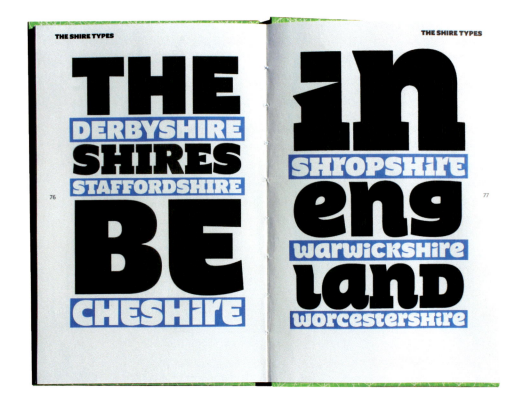

despite being sans serif, lines have a distinct brush-like quality. This aspect, although tightened as the typeface developed, is still perceptible in the stroke terminal detailing, while a relaxed natural flow was preserved overall to maintain a warm personality. *Bliss* was kept as uncomplicated as possible, as Emily King has explained: 'It is a face that seems straightforward because it is imbued with so much that we already know'.[15] *Bliss* was released in 1996.

The theme of 'Englishness' was explored again, but this time more overtly, in Tankard's hugely ambitious *Shire Types*. This time his inspiration was the heavyweight Clarendons, Egyptians and vernacular forms of English lettering developed from hand-drawn signage a hundred years before Johnston's *Underground Alphabet*.

Begun before he went to Australia in 1996, and immediately picked up again on his return, *The Shire Types* was a wide-ranging concept: a 'family of Shires' at the heart of Britain's Industrial Revolution to be represented by letterforms based on each Shire's vernacular type styles. Tankard eventually decided on a family of six distinct, though inextricably linked fonts, all sharing the same ultra-heavy weight. Derbyshire, Staffordshire and Shropshire represent the industrial North Midlands – including Birmingham and the so-called 'Black Country', justifying the dense weight of these typefaces. The forms became rounder for a more gentile Cheshire, and then softer and more rural for Warwickshire and Worcestershire.

As work progressed the scheme became less explicit and increasingly intuitive, as the all-too-close geographic proximity of the six shires eventually eliminated the possibility of relying entirely on distinctive local type styles. Instead, Tankard began exploring through type the landscape and histories of the different shires:

> Derbyshire and Staffordshire use only capital letters, and have industrial strength. Cheshire and Shropshire incorporate historical ideas of mixing capitals and lowercase letters to give a more uncial feel. Warwickshire and Worcestershire are more rural, these types echo the rolling hills through the use of softer, rounder detailing inherited from more script-like letters.[16]

The Shire Types was released in 1998 to huge acclaim. Despite its vernacular origins, its distinctive appearance attracted attention from further afield. Tankard was commissioned to add Cyrillic

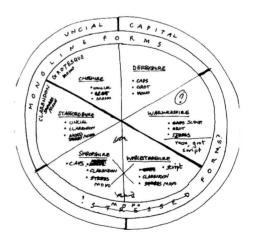

Above: Jeremy Tankard, the initial scheme for the *Shires Type*, c.1996.

Jeremy Tankard 371

and Greek versions, followed by an Arabic version which he designed in conjunction with Arabic calligrapher and type designer Mourad Boutros.

Alchemy was originally a commission from the agency Publicis for a whisky campaign. Tankard took inspiration from the manuscripts of the Middle Ages, and in particular the magnificent *Lindisfarne Gospels* (c.689 AD) with its rich diversity of Anglo-Saxon hand-drawn capitals. *Alchemy* is a set of capitals designed in a single weight, to which a variegated texture is added by the inclusion of many alternate characters, ligatures and sizes.

The genesis for *Enigma* was a number of sketches that Tankard made during a visit to the Plantin-Moretus Museum in Antwerp in 1996 (on route to the ATypI conference in The Hague), but it was not begun in earnest until May 1998. What had caught his eye was the *Groot Canon roman* (c.1570), designed by Hendrik van den Keere. This was a narrower roman with a large x-height – a major innovation at that time, where weight, form and proportion were designed for a readership also used to reading blackletter texts.[17] Another characteristic Tankard noted was its high arches with flatter top curves, something that Tankard had also seen in William A. Dwiggins's *Electra* typeface of 1935. While it is surmised that Van den Keere cut flatter top curves to reflect something of

Below: Jeremy Tankard, *Alchemy,* and a late *Alchemy* proof with amendments, 1998.

the angularity of blackletter, Dwiggins had employed similar forms to reflect what he described as modernity, the 'snap and speed' of the age: 'take your curves and stream-line 'em'.[18] The whiplash effect of the top curves provided visual stress to the horizontal. Something of the 'streamlined' curves by Dwiggins and Van den Keere remain in *Enigma* – notably in the 'n' and 'm' which, along with some distinctively crisp internal shapes in, for example, the 'a' and 'c', especially in the italic, help provide a sharper, cleaner impression.

When first published in 1999, *Enigma* comprised four versions (regular, regular italic, bold and bold italic), but was expanded in 2013 with the addition of light and heavy weights as well as new 'Display' and 'Fine cuts'. *Shaker* is a sans serif complement to *Enigma* and was released in 2000. Although available as a typeface in its own right, *Shaker* (which began by Tankard painting out *Enigma*'s serifs) retains sufficient visual reference to act as an extension of the *Enigma* family. However, Tankard had always intended that *Shaker* should offer a greater choice of widths and so it finally offered condensed, standard and wide, with each available in five weights.

The text of this book is set in *Enigma Text Regular* (10 point) and the captions are set in *Shaker Light* (9 point).

Below: Jeremy Tankard, *Enigma Regular*, 1999 and (bottom) *Shaker Regular*, 2000.

ABCDEFGHIJKLMNOPQRSTU
VWXYZ 1234567890!@£$%^(&)
abcdefghijklmnopqrstuvwxyz

ABCDEFGHIJKLMNOPQRSTU
VWXYZ 1234567890!@£$%^(&)
abcdefghijklmnopqrstuvwxyz

Tobias Frere-Jones USA 1970 –

Tobias Frere-Jones grew up in Brooklyn in a scholarly household. His brother Sasha would go on to be a music critic, his British-born mother was the daughter of the publisher Alexander Stuart Frere CBE, and his father, Robin Carpenter Jones, was a copywriter for advertising agencies who wrote opera librettos at the weekends.

 Literature was an important part of Frere-Jones's childhood, but he also became interested in the letters with which books and other objects functioned. During a visit to London to see his grandmother he realized that the street signs, food packaging and book covers looked different from those in America. On discovering that it was typography that gave these items their distinctive 'Britishness', he became fascinated with the form of letters. Designing type was a process somewhere between writing and drawing, and once he had discovered that this was a profession from which he could, potentially, earn a living, he was determined to know everything about it.

 Clear in his goals, in 1988 Frere-Jones enrolled at the Rhode Island School of Design to study graphic design. The course taught him how to use type – but at no point how to design type – and so he applied for an internship with David Berlow at the Font Bureau digital type foundry in Boston, and was accepted. One of his earliest typefaces, *Dolores*, was designed in 1988 for his brother's rock band. During a course trip to Europe, Frere-Jones met Erik Spiekermann at the Font Shop International offices and showed him *Dolores*. Spiekermann recognized the potential of the nineteen-year-old and offered him a contract; *Dolores* was released the following year.

 While an intern at the Font Bureau, Frere-Jones found himself developing full character sets of several display faces designed by the British designer Neville Brody: *FF Typeface Four, FF Gothic, FF Tokyo, FF Tyson, FF Harlem* and *FF Dome*. Frere-Jones explains: 'Spiekermann had plenty of people on hand [at FontFont] but Brody just wanted to work with Berlow and his team, which just happened to include me.'[1] Berlow then sent Frere-Jones to Brody's studio in London to work as a graphic designer and gain a broader work experience. As such, type design was not intended to be part of his work there. However, at this time Brody was editor (with Jon Wozencroft) and designer of the digital/print hybrid

Cast iron & brickwork of American cityscapes

Opposite: Tobias Frere-Jones, a developmental sketch of an ampersand for *Armada* begun in 1987 when aged seventeen.

Above: *Armada Regular* (with ampersand).

magazine *FUSE*, and he invited Frere-Jones to contribute. The result was a typeface he called *Reactor* and Brody included it in *FUSE* no. 7, 1993. Other experimental typefaces by Frere-Jones for *FUSE* quickly followed: *Fibonacci* in 1994, and *Microphone* in 1995. At the time Frere-Jones explained: 'The contortions of the 1990s will fall out of favour, but not before showing what these [digital] tools can do'.

While splitting his time in his final year between college and his internship at the Font Bureau, Frere-Jones worked on other fonts of his own, including *Garage Gothic* and *Nobel*. On graduating from Rhode Island School of Design in 1992, he was offered a position by the Font Bureau 'at the very bottom of the ladder'[2] and moved to Boston. He was promoted to Senior Designer around 1996.

When Frere-Jones first arrived at the Font Bureau offices as an intern the company had only recently been established by its co-founders David Berlow and Roger Black, but it quickly gained a reputation for its clinquant list of clients, including *The New York Times Magazine, Playboy, Newsweek, Esquire, Rolling Stone* and *The Wall Street Journal*. As well as Berlow and Black, Frere-Jones met with Matthew Carter was a frequent collaborator with the company.

During his seven years at the Font Bureau, Frere-Jones's most significant typeface was *Interstate*, designed between 1993 and 1999. *Interstate* is based on several components of the *Federal Highway series* (B, C, E, and E modified), commonly called *Highway Gothic*. The FHWA Series is a signage alphabet that was designed by a team led by Dr Theodore W. Forbes in 1949 with drawings probably done by signwriters J.E.Penton and E.E.Radek.[3] While its optimal purpose was signage, *Interstate* has refinements that have tempted some to consider it suitable for setting text. Indeed, Font Bureau recommended it for 'Newspaper, Magazine, Book, Web and Corporate use.'[4] While still in Boston Frere-Jones worked

Below: Tobias Frere-Jones, *Interstate*, designed while at the Font Bureau, Boston, between 1993 and 1999. It is currently available in eight weights with each weight available in two widths.

ABCDEFGHIJKLMNOPQRSTUVWXYZ abcd efghijklmnopqrstuvwxyz 1234567890 **ABC DEFGHIJKLMNOPQRSTUVWXYZ abcde fghijklmnopqrstuvwxyz 1234567890&)**

on another, but very different signage typeface, this time for the Whitney Museum, New York. The brief (from Michael Rock in 1995–6) was to 'create a sans serif that isn't too far away from *News Gothic* and *Gill Sans*'.[5] Frere-Jones returned to the cut angles incorporated in *Interstate* to give *Whitney Sans* a distinctive character. However, in 1998, with the typeface and several weights finished the management of the museum changed and the *Whitney* identity was discarded. A more restrained version of *Whitney Sans* (i.e. without the 9° angles) was adopted by the United Nations Fund for Population Assistance.

In 1999 Frere-Jones left Font Bureau to return to New York, where he began working at the Hoefler type foundry (renamed Hoefler & Frere-Jones in 2005), prominently placed in the Cable Building at Broadway and Houston. Jonathan Hoefler and Frere-Jones had known each other for many years, shared a passion for typographic history and had competed for clients.[6]

The Hoefler type foundry gained two important and very different early commissions soon after Frere-Jones's arrival: one from *The Wall Street Journal*, and the other from *GQ* magazine. *The Wall Street Journal* realized that readers of its regular stock listings had often passed retirement age and frequently struggled to read the type set in 6 point or less. The journal needed a typeface that was not only easier to read at small sizes, but was also economical on space and took account of the variable quality of image when printed on newsprint paper. The typeface being used at that time was *Helvetica Condensed*. The problems faced by Frere-Jones were essentially the same as those faced by Matthew Carter when he designed *Bell Centennial* for AT&T between 1975 and 1978, but while Carter had to design each character pixel by pixel Frere-Jones had a choice of vector drawing progams with which to create a solution. The outcome in 2000 was *Retina*.

The concept for *Retina* concerned emphasizing the unique features within each letter. This called for simplification in some cases and greater complexity in others to provide information 'that can be quickly interpreted as successful indicators of individual letters', Frere-Jones explained.[7] As with Carter's *Bell Centennial*, notches, or ink traps, are cut into each character to compensate for ink spread so that the act of printing effectively 'completes' the characters. (Martin Majoor concluded that such compensations were no longer necessary when designing *Telefont* in 1994 (see p. 353).

Many newspapers now use *Retina* not only for stock listings

Top: Tobias Frere-Jones, *Retina Microplus*, 1999, and *Retina Standard*, 2016. The latter was part of the extended family designed for a broad range of print and digital applications.

Above: Tobias Frere-Jones, *Whitney Sans*, c.1998. The 9° angle was calculated to provide a recognizable character for use in signage and on posters but which effectively disappears when used at text sizes. Ironically, the year new management cancelled *Whitney Sans* it earned Frere-Jones his first design award.

but also for sports scores, classified ads, movie and tv listings, and other high-density information. *Retina MicroPlus* is the name given to the smallest sizes. For headlines and larger sizes of text, *Retina Standard* was developed with more conventional proportions and details, while preserving the essential form of *Retina MicroPlus*.

The technical success of *Retina* was widely reported, and the 'distortions' incorporated by Frere-Jones in order for it to work made *Retina* instantly recognizable when reproduced at larger sizes. Type, typography and printing became, briefly, a widely reported topic, and Frere-Jones and Jonathan Hoefler, in a frenzied case of media hyperbole, were described as 'The Beatles of the typography world'.[8]

The *Gotham* family of typefaces began with a commission by the editors of *GQ* magazine who wanted a geometric sans serif that was 'masculine, new, and fresh'. The relative freedom of the assignment enabled Frere-Jones and Hoefler to explore their long-time common interest in New York postwar building signage, especially the kind that had been physically made – cut into stone or cast in metal. They used the seemingly plain, geometric lettering from New York's Port Authority Bus Terminal as the project's touchstone, a typeface free of historic (and generally non-American) affectation.

Both Frere-Jones and Hoefler had grown up in the city and both had noticed the formidable lettering over the entrance to the Port Authority Bus Terminal on 42nd Street and 8th Avenue. It is a strikingly plain geometric letter, but it is not a letter that a type designer would draw – instead, it is the kind of letter an

Below: Tobias Frere-Jones, *Gotham Bold*, 2000.

Bottom: The New York Port Authority Bus Terminal sign. The terminal building was opened in 1950.

ABCDEFGHIJKLMNOPQRSTUVWXYZ
abcdefghijklmnopqrstuvwxyz1234567

engineer would 'make'. The solemn weighty appearance of these letters, today a faded gold, is the result of a logical process that had little to do with aesthetics, 'engineered rather than designed', but conceived to have the hefty swagger and pride that is seen so often in the signage of New York's older (and fast disappearing) commercial districts. Frere-Jones searched for other signs from the era that might add to the typeface that was forming in his mind. Thousands of photographs were taken from across the city – liquor store signs were particularly pertinent – and he began to realize that as New York's mid-century buildings were torn down, the vernacular letters on their facades, expressing so much about what America was, or aspired to be, was also disappearing. With *Gotham*, Frere-Jones wanted to mark a distinctly American time and place.

When drawing *Gotham*, Frere-Jones used the mathematical reasoning that came with the tools of a mid-century draftsman, allowing the letters to avoid any sense of character-wide grid. This process gave the design of *Gotham* a quality quite different from the geometric sans serifs, while its vintage New York sources distinguish it as a notably American typeface. In 2002, the *GQ* exclusive licence expired and the typeface was released for public use. The family has since expanded to sixty-six styles and four widths, each in eight weights all with accompanying italics. It has been used in newspapers, corporate logos and film posters, and packaging on brands such as Coca-Cola, Netflix, Crest and countless others. Most significantly, and no doubt chosen for the distinctive, traditional American values that underpin it, *Gotham* was used in the 2008 US presidential elections and then Barack Obama's successful run in 2009.

When Frere-Jones set up his own company, Frere-Jones Type, in New York, he also released *Mallory*. Leaving Hoefler & Frere-Jones had been fraught, both emotionally and professionally, and he later admitted that '*Mallory*'s original purpose was to keep me together in a difficult time'. *Mallory* is a sans serif with carefully modulated curves that recall not only Eric Gill – and by default Edward Johnston – but also other British stalwarts such as Reynolds Stone, David Kindersley and Michael Harvey. As Frere-Jones explained, 'There is a leap of faith ... in releasing a typeface. One can only hope that the research and effort will find a receptive audience both in users and readers. But I've come to believe that typefaces carry stories best when they have stories of their own.'[9]

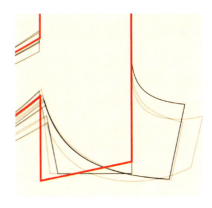

Top: Tobias Frere-Jones, *Mallory Book,* 2014. This is just one of the 115 weights and five widths available.

Above: Tobias Frere-Jones, *Mallory,* revealing all developmental versions of lowercase 'a' from first draft to final release.

Chronology of Twentieth-century Typographic Development

1885 The Linotype typesetting and casting machine first used by the *New York Tribune*.

1887 The Monotype typesetting and casting machine in production.

1888 Emery Walker delivered his lantern lecture on type and printing.

1891 *Golden* designed and Kelmscott Press founded by William Morris.

Electricity used to power newspaper presses by the *Birmingham Gazette*, Britain.

1892 Karl Klingspor takes over the Rudhard Foundry at Offenbach.

1893 The Merrymount Press established by Daniel B. Updike in Boston, Massachusetts.

The Doves Bindery established at Hammersmith, London, by T. J. Cobden-Sanderson.

1894 The Ashdene Press, established by C. H. St John Hornby.

St Bride Printing School established in London.

1895 Journal, *Pan*, launched in Germany.

First issue of the *Penrose Annual*. Printed by Lund Humphries from 1897 and published by Lund Humphries from 1906.

1896 The Vale Press, established by Charles Ricketts in England.

1897 The Monotype typesetting and casting machine launched.

1898 *Akzidenz-Grotesk*, designed by the Berthold type foundry, Berlin.

1899 Launch of journal *Die Insel*, rival publication to *Pan* in Germany.

1900 ***Doves Type*, designed by Emery Walker and T. J. Cobden-Sanderson.**

The Doves Press founded by T. J. Cobden-Sanderson and Emery Walker, Hammersmith, London.

1902 ***Franklin Gothic*, designed by Morris Fuller Benton.**

The first issue of *The Monotype Recorder*, England.

1907 The Janus Press, founded by Carl Ernst Poeschel and Walter Tiemann, Leipzig, Germany.

1908 ATF established its typographic library, in Jersey City, presided over by Henry Lewis Bullen.

1910 ***Deutsche Schrift*, designed by Rudolf Koch**

1911 ***Kennerley*, designed by Frederic W. Goudy**.
Goudy also opens his Village Press Foundery.

Curwen Sanserif Titling, designed by Harold Curwen (released 1928).

The Ludlow Typograph type casting machine launched.

1912 *Imprint*, designed by John H. Mason (in collaboration with the Monotype drawing office).

Hollandse Mediaeval, designed by Sjoerd Hendrik de Roos.

1914	*Centaur*, designed by Bruce Rogers.
	The American Institute of Graphic Arts (AIGA) established.
	Harold Curwen takes over control of the Curwen Press, London.
	Frederic W. Goudy appointed as typographic advisor to the American Monotype Company.
1915	The Zilverdistel Press founded by F. van Rayen, in The Hague.
1916	*Underground Alphabet*, designed by Edward Johnston.
1917	The Pelican Press founded. Directed by Francis Meynell, assisted by Stanley Morison.
	The Intertype composing machine launched in New York.
1919	The Bauhaus established by Walter Gropius in Weimar, Germany.
1922	*Cooper Black*, designed by Oswald Cooper.
	Erbar Grotesk designed by Jakob Erbar.
	The Golden Cockerel Press established by Harold Taylor. Robert Gibbings takes over 1924.
	Printing Types written, designed and printed by Daniel B. Updike at his Merrymount Press.
	The Officina Bodoni founded by Hans (Giovanni) Mardersteig, Switzerland.
1923	Stanley Morison appointed as typographic advisor to the Monotype Corporation, London.
	First issue of *The Fleuron* published, edited by Oliver Simon, assisted by Stanley Morison.
1925	*Universal*, designed by Herbert Bayer (not put into production).
1927	*Futura*, designed by Paul Renner.
	Record Gothic, designed by Robert Hunter Middleton.
1928	*Gill Sans*, designed by Eric Gill.
	Romanée, designed by Jan van Krimpen.
	Book, *Die Neue Typographie*, written & designed by Jan Tschichold.
	International Society of Typographic Designers founded. (Initially called the British Typographer's Guild.)
1929	*Bifur*, designed by A. M. Cassandre.
	City, designed by Georg Trump.
	Metro, designed by William A. Dwiggins.
1932	*Abertus*, designed by Berthold Wolpe.
	Times New Roman, designed by Stanley Morison & Victor Lardent.
1935	Bruce Rogers's *Lectern Bible* completed for Oxford University Press.

	Journal, *Signature*, launched, edited and designed by Oliver Simon.
	Penguin Books founded by Allen Lane, London.
1938	Bauhaus exhibition at the Museum of Modern Art, New York.
1940	Journal, *Print,* founded by William Edwin Rudge, US.
1946	Lumitype photocomposing machine invented.
	The Type Directors Club (TDC) founded in New York.
1947	Jan Tschichild appointed as head of typography at Penguin Books.
1949	**Palatino, designed by Hermann Zapf.**
	Journal, *Typographica*, edited and designed by Herbert Spencer.
1950	Lumitype Photon typesetting machine used for newspaper work.
1951	**Banco, designed by Roger Excoffon.**
1952	**Dante, designed by Hans (Giovanni) Mardersteig.**
	Adrian Frutiger appointed designer for Fonderie Deberny & Peignot.
	Aldo Novarese appointed head of design at the Nebiolo foundry.
1953	First book to be phototypeset is published in the US.
1954	Monophoto typesetting machine produced by Monotype.
1955	Publication of Beatrice Warde's *The Crystal Goblet: Sixteen Essays on Typography.*
1956	Lumitype Photon typesetting machine made launched.
1957	**Neue Haas Grotesk, designed by Eduard Hoffman and Max Miedinger.**
	Univers, designed by Adrian Frutiger.
	Folio, designed by Konrad Friedrich Bauer and Walter Baum.
	Association Typographique Internationale (ATypI) founded.
1958	Journal, *Motif*, launched, edited and designed by Ruari McLean.
	Journal, *Neue Graphik*, launched and edited by Josef Muller-Brockmann and others, Switzerland.
1959	Letraset type lettering system. Dry-transfer sheets launched 1961.
1961	Digiset phototypesetting machine launched by Rudolf Hess.
1962	**Eurostile, designed by Alessandro Butti and Aldo Novarese.**
	Transport, designed by Jock Kinneir and Margaret Calvert.
1965	*The Journal of Typographic Research* launched in America.
1966	**New Alphabet, designed by Wim Crouwel.**
1967	**Sabon, designed by Jan Tschichold.**
	International Typeface Corporation (ITC) founded.
1970	Publication of *Letter and Image,* written and designed by Robert Massin.
1973	Launch of journal *U&lc,* designed and edited by Herb Lubalin.

	Ikarus vector system developed by Peter Karow in Hamburg..
1975	***Demos*, designed by Gerard Unger.**
1977	Apple Computer, Inc. established and the Apple 2 'personal computer' launched.
1978	***Galliard*, designed by Matthew Carter.**
1980	Magazine, *The Face*, launched. Neville Brody appointed as designer then art director the following year.
1981	Bitstream founded by Matthew Carter and Mike Parker.
1982	PostScript, enabling type and image to be combined on screen, launched by Adobe Systems.
1984	***Emperor*, designed by Zuzana Licko.**
	Journal, *Emigre*, launched by Rudy VanderLans and Zuzana Licko.
	Apple Macintosh computer launched.
1985	Emigre Fonts established by Zuzana Licko and Rudy VanderLans.
1986	Fontographer, developed by von Ehr, released.
	QuarkXpress launched by Quark, Inc.
	Publication of *Twentieth Century Type Designers*, written and designed by Sebastian Carter.
1987	***Swift*, designed by Gerard Unger.**
1988	Exhibition of Neville Brody's work at the V&A, London.
	Carol Twombly appointed as type designer at Adobe Systems.
1989	***Trajan*, designed by Carol Twombly.**
	Adobe Originals (type design) program established under Sumner Stone.
	Adobe Systems develops PhotoShop.
1990	FontShop International founded by Erik and Joan Spiekermann.
1991	***Meta*, designed by Erik Spiekermann.**
	***Scala*, designed by Martin Majoor.**
	Magazine *FUSE* launched, designed by Neville Brody and edited by Jon Wozencroft.
	Multiple Master technology launched by Adobe Systems.
1992	Publication of *Modern Typography*, written and designed by Robin Kinross.
1996	***Blur*, designed by Neville Brody.**
1999	***Enigma*, designed by Jeremy Tankard.**
	***Gotham*, designed by Tobias Frere-Jones.**
	Adobe launches InDesign to challenge QuarkXpress.

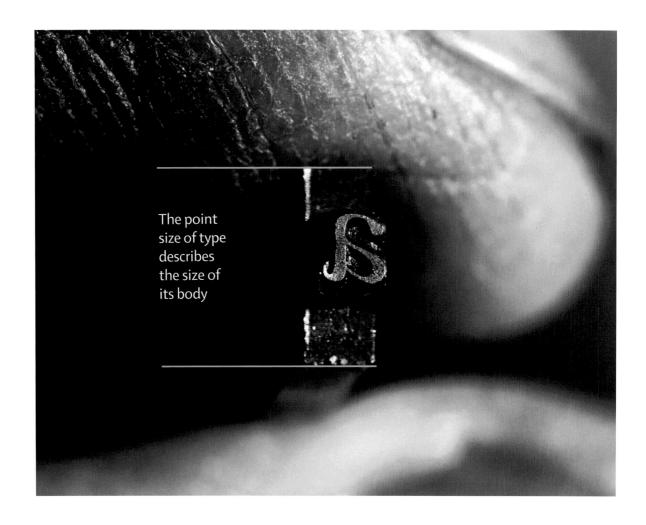

This 10-point glyph/sort/character/letter
(all terms used to describe this object)
was created on a Monotype caster.

Letterform Terminology

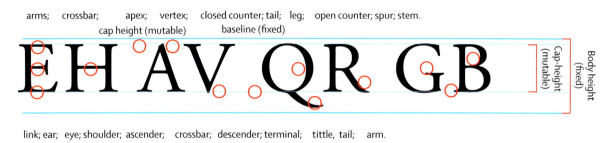

arms; crossbar; apex; vertex; closed counter; tail; leg; open counter; spur; stem.
cap height (mutable) baseline (fixed)

EH AV QR GB

link; ear; eye; shoulder; ascender; crossbar; descender; terminal; tittle, tail; arm.

gea b t qy ij k .:;

common ligatures (availability varies)

common diacritics:
acute; umlaut/diaeresis; circumflex; cedilla; angstrom; tilde

ff fi ffi ffl é ü î ç å ñ

Adobe *Garamond* roman   Adobe *Garamond* italic   *Arial* roman   *Arial* sloped roman

gaeu *gaeu* gaeu *gaeu*

The terminology used to describe the various parts of a letter are not universal. However, terms used by the author or quoted by others in this book are included here and on the following pages.

Glossary

Bézier curve
Bézier curves are used to model smooth curves on-screen. They are used in typeface design because the paths they create can be scaled infinitely.

Bitmapped
A typeface generated from a set pattern of dots (each dot representing a pixel).

Blackletter
Blackletter is characterized by tight spacing and condensed lettering. Evenly spaced, heavy verticals dominate the letterform to give the page a dark texture. The first books printed in Europe by Gutenberg used a style of blackletter called *Textura*, used at that time for handwritten liturgical books.

Book sizes
Terms such as *folio*, *quarto* and *octavo* were used by bibliographers to describe the size of a book. When presses were of a regular size it was usual to describe the size of a book based on the number of leaves (or sheets) in each gathering: eight leaves (sixteen pages) per gathering forming an *octavo*, four leaves (eight pages) formed a *quarto*, two leaves (four pages) formed a *folio*. *Octavo*, therefore, was the smallest size book and *folio* the largest. These terms, which remained popular for much of the twentieth century have, for the most part, become meaningless today because of the increased variety of sizes of printing presses and differing binding methods.

Colour
Term used to describe the tone of a page of text.

Contrast
'Contrast' refers to the different widths of line used in a given typeface. For example, *Bodoni* has a high contrast – very thick and very thin lines – *Futura* has a low contrast. 'Monoline' is used to describe a typeface whose lines are all the same width.

Counter
The enclosed or partially enclosed space within a letter, for example, the 'O' and 'C'.

CRT (Cathode Ray Tube)
An electronic means of transmitting letter images formed of lines or dots on to output film or paper.

Diacritics
Ancillary mark or sign added to a letter. Accents are one type of diacritics. In the Latin alphabet their function is to change the sound value of the letters to which they are added; in other alphabetical systems such as Arabic or Hebrew they may indicate sounds (vowels and tones) which are not conveyed by the basic alphabet.

Digitizing
The process of converting a character into coded data for storage in a computer's memory.

Display (or Headline) **typeface**
A category of typefaces designed to attract attention, as opposed to text typefaces. Display typefaces are usually intended for larger settings.

Double-storey
A double-storey 'a' or 'g' has two counters, as opposed to their single-storey variants which only have one.

Electrotype
First used in the 1830s, electrotyping is a process by which a physical copy of a page of metal type can be made. As with a stereotype, a mould is required that is formed from, for example, a page of type. Electrotyping involves a wet chemical process and the moulding material, made from wax or natural latex. The mould's surface is coated with a thin layer of fine graphite powder or paint, to make it conduct electricity. A wire is attached to the conducting surface, and the mould is suspended in an electrolyte solution. Electrotyping was also used to make copies of individual pieces of metal type. This enabled unscrupulous type foundries to pirate other foundries' type – having made minor adjustments to one or two characters, they could then market a font as their own design.

Fit
The type designer's spacing of characters – for example, close fitting type is described as having a 'tight fit'.

Founts, fonts and typefaces
A typeface is usually made up of many founts. A 'fount' historically refers to a complete case of metal type comprising all available characters (see glyphs or sorts) that make up one size and style of a typeface. A popular typeface such as *Helvetica* could occupy dozens of cases. For example, there would be a case each of 6 point, 8 point, 10 point, 11 point, 12 point, 14 point, 18 point, 24 point, 30 point, 36 point and 48 point *Helvetica Light*, and then a case each for the same sizes in medium and Bold, and perhaps a few sizes in ultra bold. Italic founts were then required in all the same sizes and weights with, again, each 'fount' of type requiring its own case. Then there were the various widths to consider. The storage of metal type took up an enormous amount of space.

Confusion concerning the meaning of 'fount' occurred at the same time that its spelling changed to 'font'. This coincided with developments in digital technology, and in particular OpenType. OpenType, the veritable standard for digital typefaces, provides 'space' for 65,000 glyphs. In other words, OpenType has enabled a case of type (or fount) to grow a thousand-fold and contain every size and style.

Today when buying a typeface from a digital type 'foundry' ('publisher' would be more appropriate), we don't buy a certain quantity of type, nor an individual size of type, although we do still usually need to specify the various weights and/or widths required. Nevertheless, having bought and stored them on the computer these fonts are all held in one place – effectively a single 'type case'. It is not surprising then that in recent years the term 'fount'– now 'font'– has tended to be used instead of 'typeface'.

Occasionally an italic or a different weight of a given typeface was released with its own name, as if it were a separate entity. For example, Eric Gill's *Perpetua*, whose italic was named *Felicity*, and Roger Excoffon's *Antique Olive*, which has an ultra-bold version called *Nord*. Such anomalies are generally due to impenetrable company politics and marketing strategies.

The conventional descriptions of fonts are by weight, width and style – listed here separately.

Glyphs and sorts
Each font is made up of many characters, known as *glyphs* or *sorts*. This describes any letter, numeral, punctuation mark or symbol within a given font.

Gravure
A method of intaglio printing, in which the image is engraved into a metal plate. The plate is then coated in ink and the surface wiped clean with a blade leaving the ink in the engraved areas. The paper is brought into contact with the plate under pressure enabling the ink to transfer to the paper.

Kerning
The built-in spacing of a typeface is intended to produce an even texture in any letter combination. Certain combinations, like 'LT', 'VA' or 'To' tend to look gappy and loose with the default built-in spacing. (A problem far more prevalent when setting metal type – less so with digital type.) Kerning is an additional adjustment to those problem pairs that corrects the excess or inadequate space. A more generously spaced font will need comparatively fewer kerning pairs. A page of text that has been properly kerned will appear as an even colour (tone/texture).

Latin alphabet
The Latin alphabet, so-called because it is the alphabet used to write Latin, is the standard method of writing in most Western and Central European languages, some Eastern European languages, and many other languages across the world. The Latin alphabet is also referred to as the roman alphabet. Many writing systems are not alphabetical but syllabic, like Chinese Hanji, Japanese Kana or Korean Hangul systems.

Leading
Lead strips inserted between lines of text to increase the vertical space between lines of metal type. In digital technology, adding 'interline spacing' is still described as leading, though the measurement is from baseline to baseline.

Letterpress
A method of relief printing, usually from metal or wood type. In practice, letterpress also includes printing from wood engravings, photo-etched zinc or brass plates ('cuts') or linoleum blocks – all of which can be placed alongside metal type and printed simultaneously. Letterpress printing was the usual form of printing text from the fifteenth century onwards, and remained in wide use for books and other uses into the second half of the twentieth century.

Ligature
Special characters that are two or three letters combined into one. In cases where two adjacent characters would normally bump into each other, a ligature allows the letters to stand together more gracefully. Common ligatures include 'fi', 'fl', 'ff' and 'ffl'.

Lining numerals
Numerals that sit on the baseline and uniform height.

Lithography (and offset lithography)
A method of planographic printing in which the inked image is transferred from a plate to paper. The lithographic process is based on the repulsion of oil and water; the image on the dampened plate is oil-based and attracts the ink, whilst the plate itself repels the ink. With offset lithography the inked image is transferred ('offset') from a plate to a rubber blanket and then to the printing surface.

Lowercase
The small letters in a typeface. The name refers to the days of composing metal type by hand when the case of small letters was placed below the upper case holding capital letters.

Matrix
1. A bar of brass or copper with the image of a single character incized using a punch, to create what is effectively a mould from which a metal character can be cast for use in letterpress printing.
2. Photographic negative, usually on a strip of film or a glass disc, on which hundreds of characters are printed. Used in phototypesetting.
3. Code page used in digital type design and manufacture.

Measurement
The point system of type measurement was introduced more than 200 years ago, and has been used universally for the last 100 years for describing the size of type. The main unit of measurement is the pica, or em. In modern British-American typographical measurement the pica equals 12 points (.166044 inches, 4.2175mm), and 1 point equals .013837 inches (.3515mm). A pica, therefore, is approximately one sixth of an inch; a point is approximately one 72nd of an inch. With digital typefaces the point has been rounded up to exactly one 72nd of an inch.

The point system is problematic for two main reasons. Firstly, it has no coherent relationship to either the inch or the millimetre. Secondly, and more problematically, it is impossible to measure the (point) size of a typeface simply by looking at it on a printed page. This is because the size given to a typeface represents its body size (see p. 384). This is slightly larger, and variably so, than the printed letter. Every 10-point typeface has the same size body. However, the varying amount of space given to the x-height (which is the dominant visual feature of any typeface) will make, for example 10-point *Helvetica* appear far larger than 10-point *Perpetua*.

Basing the size of a typeface on its body made complete sense when type was metal. The body of the type was what was held in the compositor's fingers and, therefore, the obvious way to establish its size. When phototypesetting became available it had to function alongside letterpress, and so the method of describing type sizes remained the same.

However, the arrival of desktop digital technology in 1984 had long been predicted, and in the preceding decades there were several determined attempts to reform type measurement. None were acceptable. There is no part of a typeface – although the x-height and capital height were both serious contenders – that can be relied upon to identify the size of type on a printed page. For example, if the x-height is the measure, how do you determine the type size of a line of capital letters? Or how do you determine the size of a line of lowercase letters if the cap-height is used? Then historical and cultural issues came into play, to say nothing of the concern that a new system would impose aesthetic limitations on the type designer. Eventually all attempts ran out of steam.

Mechanical composition
Any form of mechanized typesetting involving a keyboard and caster. Monotype and Linotype were the two major systems.

Non-lining numerals (or Oldstyle numerals)
Numerals that have different heights, some aligning to the baseline, some below. Oldstyle numerals harmonize well with lowercase letters, and so are generally preferable to lining numerals within text.

Oblique (or Slanted or Sloped)
Oblique typefaces are sloped or slanted versions of the roman characters, that are then optically adjusted.

OCR (Optical Character Recognition)
In conjunction with early phototypesetting machines, OCR is the electronic conversion of keyboarded text into machine-encoded text for display on a screen.

Pantograph
A device of jointed metal rods used to reproduce a drawing at a different scale and in minute detail.

Pixel
The smallest single component of any digital image – including letterforms. The more pixels available to represent an image, the closer a curve can resemble that of the original drawing.

Postscript
The computer language that enabled both text and images to be passed within and between processing units and printers, and placed typesetting on the designer's desk.

Punch
A short steel bar, onto the end of which a character is engraved (or 'cut') by hand. When finished the steel bar is hardened and can then be stamped into a (softer) bar of brass or copper to form a matrix – effectively a mould – from which type is cast.

Roman
Used to describe the upright characters of a typeface to distinguish them from italic characters. Also used as an alternative term for the Latin alphabet.

Sans serif
Sans serif (also called 'grotesk' or 'grot') is a typeface without serifs. In America, sans serif type is often described as 'gothic', as in *Franklin Gothic*.

Signature (or section, gathering)
A sheet or group of sheets folded to form the pages of part of a book.

Small caps
An additional alphabet of capitals but about the same height, weight and width as lowercase letters.

Swash
An elegant extension on a letter form – a modification of an existing part, or an added-on part.

Titling
A capitals-only typeface, usually including numerals and a limited range of punctuation.

Tittle
The dot over the 'i' and 'j'.

Typeface family
Typefaces that are designed as a closely related group – usually including sans and serif, and sometimes a slab serif version. An early successful type family is Martin Majoor's *Scala*, which includes (a serifed) *Scala* and a *Scala Sans*, both in a variety of weights and two widths.

Weights (of type)
The full range generally comprises: hairline, thin, extra light, light, book (which might be lighter or heavier than regular, depending on the whim of its designer), regular, medium, semi-bold, bold, extra bold, ultra bold, heavy, black, ultra black.

Widths (of type)
The full range generally comprises: ultra condensed, condensed, semi-condensed, narrow, normal, extended, extra extended, expanded.

Notes

Introduction

1. According to some authorities, the French king, Charles VII, sent Jenson at the end of 1458 to Mainz, Germany, to gain information about the new invention of printing. It has also been suggested that while in Mainz he may have worked with Peter Schöffer (who took over Guttenberg's printshop). See Martin Lowry, *Nicholas Jenson and the Rise of Venetian Publishing in Renaissance Europe,* Blackwell, Oxford, 1991, pp. 49–51.
2. Andrea Torresani printed and published the first edition of Manutius's Latin grammar book the *Institutiones grammaticae* (published 9 March 1493). The establishment of Aldus's connection with an experienced printer like Torresani was probably the conclusive step that led Manutius to begin his own press.
3. It is known that Jenson sold copies of his roman types. Some forty printshops were using Jenson's types before 1500, so it is likely that even if Manutius did not have the means to cast Jenson's types within his own Aldine printshop he could probably have bought freshly cast Jenson types from elsewhere. Riccardo Olocco, 'Nicolas Jenson and the Success of his Roman Type', 2017: https://medium.com/http-c-a-s-t-com/nicolas-jenson-and-the-success-of-his-roman-type-9f0afeba4103 (accessed 13 December 2023).
4. See James Clough, 'Who was Francesco Griffo?' 2016: www.griffoggl.com/en/chi-era-francesco-griffo (accessed 13 December 2023).
5. See Juliet Spohn Twomey, 'Whence Jenson: A Search for the Origins of Roman Type', *Fine Print*, no. 15, 1989, p. 134.
6. Riccardo Olocco, 'Nicolas Jenson and the Success of his Roman Type', 2017: https://medium.com/http-c-a-s-t-com/nicolas-jenson-and-the-success-of-his-roman-type-9f0afeba4103 (accessed 13 December 2023).
7. The Joh. Enschedé en Zonen type foundry have matrices dating from 1492 and in good condition. See Harry Carter, *A View of Early Typography,* Hyphen Press, London, 2002, p. 21.
8. Robert Granjon's *Civilité*, used between 1557 and 1566, was an attempt to design a typeface that replicated a formal, business handwriting of the time. It met limited demand.
9. Riccardo Olocco, 'The Influence of Jenson on the Design of Romans', 2018: https://medium.com/http-c-a-s-t-com/nicolas-jenson-and-the-success-of-his-roman-type-9f0afeba4103 (accessed 13 December 2023).
10. Hendrik D.L. Vervliet, *The Palaeotypography of the French Renaissance,* Brill, Leiden and Boston, 2008, p. 105.
11. May Morris, in her introduction to vol. 15 of *The Collected Works of William Morris,* Longmans, Green & Company, London, 1912, p. xv.
12. William Morris, *The Ideal Book; Essays and Lectures on the Arts of the Book,* University of California Press, Berkeley, CA, 1982, p. 69.
13. David McKitterick (ed.), *Stanley Morison & D.B. Updike, Selected Correspondence,* The Moretus Press, New York, NY, 1979, p. 65.
14. From Morison's essay 'Towards an Ideal Type' in *The Fleuron,* no. 2, 1924.
15. D.B. Updike, *Printing Types, Their History, Form and Use*, vol. 1, Oxford University Press, Oxford, 1922, p. 76.
16. For the nature of jobbing work and the development of the 'jobbing printer', see David Jury, *Graphic Design Before Graphic Designers: The Printer as Designer and Craftsman, 1700 to 1914,* Thames & Hudson, London and New York, 2012.
17. Thorne did not publish a catalogue between 1803 and 1820, and so it is impossible to say exactly when his *Egyptian* was produced.
18. Confusingly, sans serif letterforms were also initially called *Egyptian* and *Antique*, as well as *Gothic* and *Grotesque* – often reduced to *Grot*.
19. Fred Smeijers, 'Typography verses Commercial Lettering', *TypoGraphic,* no. 54, 1999.
20. See James Mosley, 'The Nymph and the Grot', *Typographica,* no. 12, 1965.
21. Geoffrey Dowding, *An Introduction to the History of Printing Types,* The British Library and Oak Knoll Press, London and Delaware, DE, 1998, p. 260.
22. Before 1600 it was more likely that a printer would take a set of their own matrices to a type founder from which to make the printer's type. After 1600 it was usual for the type founder to have a collection of their own matrices and who, typically, would publish a specimen sheet showing all the types they could cast from their matrices. See Harry Carter, *A View of Early Typography up to About 1600,* Hyphen Press, London, 2002, pp. 94–95 (first published in 1969 by Oxford University Press).
23. The unit proposed by Pierre-Simon Fournier was one seventy-second of the contemporary French inch, although this was never legally defined. See Andrew Boag, 'Typographic Measurement: A Chronology,' *Typography Papers,* no. 1, University of Reading, Department of Typography and Graphic Communication, 1996, p. 105.
24. Paul Nathan, *Printing Business,* Lotus Press, New York, NY, 1900, p. 36.
25. The type foundry Deberny & Peignot published *Les Divertissements Typographiques,* a quarterly designed by Maximilien Vox and first published in the autumn of 1928. It took the form of a folder holding a chosen number of

loose samples of graphic work using Deberny & Peignot founts.

William Morris and Nineteenth-century Perceptions of Technology

1. Peter Broks, *Understanding Popular Science*, Open University Press, 2006, p. 39, quoting a correspondent in *Cassell's Saturday Journal*, 1898.
2. John Hodgson, 'John Rylands Research Institute and Library', *Parenthesis*, no. 42, Fine Press Book Association, 2022.
3. Alum-rosin size was introduced in the mid-nineteenth century, alongside wood pulp. It was made from a mixture of alum (in this case aluminium sulphate) and rosin, the resinous material left over when turpentine is distilled. This type of alum is not chemically stable but it was cheap, could be added while the paper was being made rather than at a separate stage, and produced an excellent surface for printing at speed. Unfortunately, in moist conditions it generates sulfuric acid which attacks the paper, turning it yellow and making it brittle.
4. Alexis Weedon, *Victorian Publishing*, Taylor & Francis, Abingdon, 2016, p. 158.
5. The catalogue underwent several reincarnations; the number of exhibits quoted is taken from the final version. The catalogue did not include photographs. Also available was a 32-page booklet written by William Blades entitled *A Guide to the Objects of Chief Interest in the Loan Collection of the Caxton Celebration, Queen's Gate, South Kensington*, 1877.
6. These were *The Golden Legend*, *The Recuyell of the Historyes of Troy* (both 1892), *The History of Reynard the Foxe*, *The Order of Chivalry* and *The History of Godefroy of Boloyne and the Conquest of Iherusalem* (all 1893).
7. Chiswick Press was founded by Charles Whittingham I (1767–1840) and the name was first used in 1811. The founder's nephew Charles Whittingham II (1795–1876) took over the management in 1840. The press continued to operate until 1962.
8. The first issue of *The Century Guild Hobby Horse* appeared in April 1884. There were no further issues until 1886, when Mackmurdo started the magazine again with volume number 1. In 1893 it was renamed *The Hobby Horse*, but this only lasted for a further three issues. It closed in 1894.
9. Fiona MacCarthy, *William Morris: A Life for Our Time*, Alfred A. Knopf, New York, NY, 1995, p. 615.
10. Morris also had photographs (taken by Walker) of Leonardo Bruni Artino's *Historia*, printed by Jacobus Rubeus in 1476 using Jenson's type. See James Mosely's lecture 'Emery Walker's Photographs for the Types of William Morris' at the symposium *Gotico-Antiqua, Proto-Roman, Hybrid*: www.gotico-antiqua.anrt-nancy.fr (accessed 13 December 2023).
11. S.C. Cockerel, *A Note by William Morris on His Aims in Founding the Kelmscott Press*, Kelmscott Press, London, 1898.
12. William Harcourt Hooper was the Kelmscott Press's prime wood-engraver, who was responsible for translating most of Morris's decorative work as well as Edward Burn-Jones's illustrations into woodblocks. He also worked for several other private presses including C.R. Ashbee's Essex House Press, and taught Charles Ricketts and Charles Shannon how to cut on wood for their Vale Press books.

PART ONE: COLD METAL TYPE
Introduction
1. Giambattista Bodoni, *Manuale Tipografico del cavaliere Gambattista Bodoni* (3 vols), trans. Angelo Ciavarella, Ricci Editore, Palermo, 1965, p. 107.
2. Harry Carter, 'Letter Design and Typecutting', *Journal of the Royal Society of Arts*, October 1954, p. 885.
3. Paul Koch, 'The Making of Printing Types', *The Dolphin*, no. 1, 1933, p. 25.
4. For example, in Philadelphia in 1875, the type foundry MacKellar, Smiths & Jordan occupied five city blocks and employed approximately 300 people. Hermann Ihlenburg, a punchcutter at the company, is believed to have designed and cut more than eighty typefaces, without receiving any public credit from his employers.
5. F.C. Avis, *Edward Philip Prince: Type Punchcutter*, Glenview Press, London, 1967, p. 16.

Frederic Goudy
1. Kevin R. Donley, 'Arts and Crafts Movement: Frederic Goudy': www.multimediaman.blog/tag/arts-and-crafts-movement (accessed 13 December 2023).
2. 'Printing' was one of a collection of essays that formed the book *Arts and Crafts: Essays by Members of the Arts and Crafts Exhibition Society* (1893). In 1932 Goudy designed and cut another type which he called *Village No. 2*, and a year or two later cut an accompanying italic. Monotype bought the reproduction rights to *Village No. 2* and produced them for machine composition in two sizes.
3. Robert Wiebking (1870–1927) was born in Schwelm, Germany. His family emigrated to Chicago when he was aged eleven. By 1893 he had his own engraving business and was cutting matrices for various type foundries. In 1900 he formed the Advance Type Foundry with H.H. Hardinge, and together they designed various pieces of machinery including precision tools for matrix fitting and an automatic casting and finishing machine for type. The improvements enabled

Wiebking to cut the matrices for the 14-point size of Frederick Goudy's *Kennerley*, then cast and finish 400 lbs of the type in a little over forty hours. He also taught Goudy how to cut matrices.
4. Following the 1911 issue of the first *Typographica*, five more were issued at varying intervals. The second issue was published in June 1912, and included samples of *Goudy Oldstyle* (later to be renamed *Goudy Lanston*) as well as additional sizes of *Kimberley*. *Typographica* no. 3 was published in 1916, with a supplement the same year; no. 4 was published in 1926, no. 5 in 1927 and no. 6 in 1934.
5. Andrew R. Boone, 'Type by Goudy', *Popular Science*, 1942, p. 114.
6. For example, both were regular members of a small group who called themselves the Stowaways, 'a club with no purpose [other than to meet] for dinner and good fellowship' on a weekly basis. It ran from 1907 to 1937. Other members included Joseph Bowles, William Ketteridge, Carl Purlington Rollins, William Edwin Rudge, Rudolph Ruzicka and Frederic Warde. See Simon Loxley, 'Manhattan Mariners', *Parenthesis*, no. 22, Fine Press Book Association, 2012.
7. Kurt Beske, 'Craftsman in a Machine Age', *US Library of Congress Quarterly Journal*, 1977, p. 97. Goudy counted roman and italic as two designs. See also Frederic W. Goudy, *A Half Century of Type Design and Typography 1895–1945*, The Typophiles, New York, NY, 1946.

Bruce Rogers
1. Bruce Rogers, *The Centaur Types*, Purdue University Press, West Lafayette, IN, 1949, p. x (Introduction).
2. Ibid, p. 6.
3. Ibid, p. 6.
4. Bruce Rogers and James Hendrickson, *Paragraphs on Printing*, William E. Rudge's Sons, Mount Vernon, NY, 1943, p. 27.
5. This was Frederic Warde's description of the agreement ('capitals only') in his article written for *The Fleuron*, no. 4, ed. Oliver Simon, 1925. For further elaboration, see Jerry Kelly and Misha Beletsky, *The Noblest Roman: A History of the Centaur Types of Bruce Rogers*, David R. Godine, Boston, MA, 2016, pp. 52–53 and 56.
6. Robert Wiebking's Advance Type Foundry was purchased by the Western Type Foundry in 1914. When the Western Type Foundry collapsed in 1919, all its holdings were transferred to Barnhart Brothers & Spindle. BB&S asked Rogers if he was willing to allow *Centaur* to be made commercially available – Rogers declined. (ATF also made an offer which was declined.) The matrices were sent to The Metropolitan Museum where they were placed in storage.
7. 'Bruce Rogers Creates Monotype Centaur': https://www.historyofinformation.com/detail.php?id=3199 (accessed 13 December 2023).
8. Jerry Kelly, *100 Books Famous in Typography*, Grolier Club, New York, NY, 2021, p. 142.
9. For a full description of this episode, see Simon Loxley, *Emery Walker: Arts, Crafts, and a World in Motion*, Oak Knoll Press, Delaware, DE, 2019, p. 158.
10. Reported to Scott-Martin Kosofsky by David J. Way in personal correspondence. Quoted by Jerry Kelly and Misha Beletsky, *The Noblest Roman: A History of the Centaur Types of Bruce Rogers*, David R. Godine, Boston, MA, 2016, p. 72.
11. This was Warde's description of his position, rather than his formal position at the Mount Vernon Press. He did, however, work alongside Rogers and no doubt learned an enormous amount from the experience.
12. Bruce Rogers and James Hendrickson, *Paragraphs on Printing*, William E. Rudge's Sons, Mount Vernon, NY, 1943, pp. 50 and 58.
13. Printed as one volume in a limited edition of 1,000, and as two volumes in an edition limited to 200, folio size (465 x 325mm).

Frederic Warde
1. Simon Loxley, *Printer's Devil: The Life and Work of Frederic Warde*, White Label, Woodbridge, 2010, p. 27.
2. Ibid, p. 32.
3. Robert Seymour Bridges (1844–1930) was poet laureate from 1913 to 1930. Educated at Eton College and Corpus Christi College, Oxford, he went on to study medicine in London. Ill health forced Bridges to retire in 1882, and from that point on he devoted himself to writing and literary research.
4. Mary Monica Waterhouse Bridges's publication *A New Handwriting for Teachers* advocated the improvement of children's handwriting in schools by revisiting sixteenth- and seventeenth-century Italian letterforms. Her book was used in grades 1-9 for many years.
5. Simon Loxley, *Printer's Devil: The Life and Work of Frederic Warde*, White Label, Woodbridge, 2010, pp. 56–57.
6. Ibid. From a letter written by Warde to T.M. Cleland.
7. The Fanfare Press was set up by Charles William Hobson. Its progenitor was Hobson's Cloister Press in Manchester. Hobson had employed Walter Lewis as printer and Stanley Morison as typographic designer. However, the need to be closer to his larger accounts, plus financial difficulties, led Hobson to move his advertising agency to London. At this point, or just before, Lewis moved to become university

printer at Cambridge, and Morison became typographic advisor to the Monotype Corporation.

8. David Mckitterick, 'The Fanfare Press', *Matrix*, 18, 1998, p. 24. Under Ernst Ingham's leadership the Fanfare Press would be become one of the best fine press printers in Britain. Ingham retired as a director in October 1959. The Press closed in December 1966.

9. In fact, Rogers had trialled *Arrighi* with *Centaur* in an edition of the poet John Drinkwater's *Persephone*, published by William Edwin Rudge, Mount Vernon, NY, in 1926.

Emery Walker

1. John Dreyfuss, 'A Reconstruction of the Lecture given by Emery Walker on 15 November 1888', *Matrix*, no. 11, 1991.
2. May Morris, in her introduction to vol. 15 of *The Collected Works of William Morris*, Longmans, Green & Company, London, 1912, p. xv.
3. A set of these enlargements is now at the St Bride Print Library, bound in a volume (classmark 5826) with a bookplate of Talbot Baines Reed, director of the type foundry where Morris's first type was cast.
4. C.H. St John Hornby was a partner in W.H. Smith & Sons, but he set up his own press initially to print books for family and friends. The Ashendene Press continued until 1935, with a break during the First World War.
5. Roderick Cave, *The Private Press* (second edition), R.R. Bowker, Chatham, NJ, 1983, pp. 323 and 327–8.
6. Ibid. p. 328.
7. A second typeface was designed for Ashendene by Emery Walker in 1925 and called *Ptolemy* (from Ptolemy's *Cosmographia* of 1482, printed by Holle in Ulm, Germany). By this time, Edward Prince had died and an alternative punchcutter could not be found in England so Walker resorted to mechanical punchcutting.
8. Marianne Tidcombe, *The Doves Press*, The British Library and Oak Knoll Press, London and Delaware, DE, 2002, p. 14.
9. From Walker's 'Statement of Claim', part of court proceedings in the Emery Walker vs. Annie Cobden-Sanderson court case, 1923. This forms part of the appendices of Marianne Tidcombe, *The Doves Press*, The British Library and Oak Knoll Press, London and Delaware, DE, 2002, p. 229. Walker's comment concerning the 'over-inked' printing of Jenson's *Historia naturalis* is born out by Bruce Rogers's preference for Jenson's earlier printing of *De praeparatione evangelica* to be used as the model for his *Centaur* type.
10. Ruari MacLean, quoted by Roderick Cave, *The Private Press*, R.R. Bowker, Chatham, NJ, 1983, p. 122.
11. Francis Meynell, quoted by Roderick Cave, *The Private Press*, R.R. Bowker, Chatham, NJ, 1983, p. 123.
12. This episode has become legend. For the grisly detail, see Simon Loxley, *Emery Walker: Arts, Crafts, and a World in Motion*, Oak Knoll Press, Delaware, DE, 2019, and Marianne Tidcombe, *The Doves Press*, The British Library and Oak Knoll Press, London and Delaware, DE, 2002.
13. John Dreyfus, *The Book as a Work of Art: The Cranach Press 1913 to 1931*, Triton Verlag, Vienna, 2005, p. 238.
14. Frederick Compton Avis, *Edward Philip Prince: Type Cutter*, Glenview Press, London, 1967, p. 53.
15. The solicitors acting on behalf of Mrs Cobden-Sanderson (14 November 1922) asked for information from Walker's solicitor regarding 'lettering similar to that of the Doves Press which she understands is now being used in Germany'. Simon Loxley, *Emery Walker: Arts, Crafts, and a World in Motion*, Oak Knoll Press, Delaware, DE, 2019, p. 158.
16. John Dreyfus, *The Book as a Work of Art: The Cranach Press 1913 to 1931*, Triton Verlag, Vienna, 2005, p. 240.
17. Stanley Morison, *A Tally of Types*, Cambridge University Press, Cambridge, 1973, pp. 41–60.
18. Quoted by John Dreyfus, *Into Print*, British Library, London, 1994 (first published 1950), p. 92.
19. Frederick Compton Avis, *Edward Philip Prince: Type Cutter*, Glenview Press, London, 1967, p. 33.

Edward Johnston

1. Peter Holiday, *Edward Johnston: Master Calligrapher*, The British Library and Oak Knoll Press, Delaware, DE, 2007, p. 5.
2. Lethaby had been an art inspector for the London County Council when he successfully applied for the job as co-director of the Central School of Arts and Crafts in 1896 (his application was supported by William Morris who was on the board of governors). In 1902 he was promoted to sole principal and remained until 1911. Meanwhile, in 1901, he had joined the recently formed School of Design and Ornamentation at the Royal College of Art as a professor, where he remained until 1918.
3. Peter Holiday, *Edward Johnston: Master Calligrapher*, The British Library and Oak Knoll Press, London and Delaware, DE, 2007, p. 94.
4. Ibid. p. 85.
5. Marianne Tidcombe, *The Doves Press*, The British Library and Oak Knoll Press, London and Delaware, DE, 2002, p. 39.
6. Garard Meynell was cousin to Francis Meynell, book designer and publisher of the Nonesuch Press, and nephew to the publisher Wilfrid Meynell.
7. Denis Megaw, 'Twentieth Century Sanserif Types', *Typography*, no. 7, p. 32. Harold Curwen had designed a sans serif typeface before Johnston (between 1911 and 1913), albeit

capitals only. A lowercase would be added around 1924 and the fount made available for the Curwen Press to use in 1928.
8. Nicholas Pevsner, 'Patient Progress One: The Life and Work of Frank Pick', *The Architectural Review*, 1962, p. cxxxii.
9. John Dreyfus suggests that it was 'their mutual friend, Gerard T. Meynell [who] brought them together … to collaborate in designing a new typeface for London Underground' – from the introduction (p. 13) to a facsimile of *The Four Gospels*, published by Book Club of California, 1990. Gill withdrew from the project due to the pressure of sculptural commissions but, nevertheless, Johnston paid him ten per cent of the fee for his advice. Peter Holiday, *Edward Johnston: Master Calligrapher*, The British Library and Oak Knoll Press, London and Delaware, DE, 2007, p. 156.
10. Justin Howes, *Johnston's Underground Type*, Capital Transport, London, 2000, p. 28.
11. Edward Johnston, 'The Leicester Lectures', in *Lessons in Formal Writing*, edited by Heather Child and Justin Howes, Lund Humphries, London, 1986, pp. 92–3.
12. Walter Tracy, *Letters of Credit*, Gordon Fraser, Cambridge, 1986, p. 90. There was clearly a demand for Johnston's *Underground Alphabet* to be available in smaller sizes but, other than Johnston's own reluctance to allow this, there appears to be no reason for the cutting of *Granby* by Stephenson Blake as an alternative. See also Mike Ashworth: www.flickr.com/photos/36844288@N00/3732343807 (accessed 13 December 2023).
13. Ibid. p. 90. Charles Pickering had been a student under J.H. Mason at the Central School of Arts and Crafts.

PART TWO: HOT METAL TYPE
Introduction
1. *The Monotype Recorder*, 1902, p. 1. This was the house journal of the Monotype Corporation, and was sent free of charge to all Monotype users.
2. Christopher Burke, 'Monotype Typography', *The Monotype Recorder*, new series, no. 10, 1997, p. 5. The second Monotype typeface to be offered was *Old Style*, based on another Miller & Richard typeface that was cut by Alexander Phemister. It owed its origins to the types cut by William Caslon, based on Dutch designs, and which in turn derived from the earliest romans cut by Nicolas Jenson and Francesco Griffo in Venice.
3. The number of patterns designed and cut to create the required full range of sizes might be reduced to save costs. The results meant that smaller types might look over heavy, and larger types too light and weak.
4. Beatrice Ward, 'Cutting Types for Machines: A Layman's Account', *The Dolphin*, no. 2, 1935, p. 64. Frederic Goudy was one of very few designers who cut his own types using a pantograph machine.
5. D.B. Updike, *Printing Types: Their History, Form and Use*, vol. 1, 1922, p. 73.
6. Frederic W. Goudy, *Goudy's Type Designs* (originally published 1946), ed. by Paul A. Bennett, Myriade Press, New Rochelle, NY, 1978, p. 18.
7. Patrick Duffy, *The Skilled Compositor, 1850–1914: An Aristocrat Among Working Men*, Routledge, London, 2000, p. 68.
8. Richard Southall, *Printer's Type in the Twentieth Century. Manufacturing and Design Methods*, The British Library and Oak Knoll Press, London and Delaware, DE, 2005, p. 35.

Morris Fuller Benton
1. The typesetting machine with automatic justification – so-called 'self-spacing type' – involved reducing the number of character widths in a fount of type. See Henry Lewis Bullen, 'Discursions of a Retired Printer, no. vii', *The Inland Printer* 38, January 1907, p. 517. A full description with sample settings can be seen in the *American Type Founders Specimen Book of Type Styles*, available here: www.archive.org/details/americanspecimen00amerrich/page/n11/mode/2up (accessed 13 December 2023).
2. Electro-deposition made it possible for a foundry to duplicate the typefaces of its competitors simply by purchasing complete founts of type and electroplating copper onto them to make matrices.
3. By July 1893, ATF had consolidated from twenty-three down to fourteen foundries. These were: MacKellar, Smiths & Jordan, Philadelphia; Dickinson Type Foundry, Boston; Boston Type Foundry, Boston; Conner Type Foundry, New York; John Ryan & Co., Baltimore; Collins & McLeester, Philadelphia; Allison & Smith, Cincinnati; Cincinnati Type Foundry, Cincinnati; Central Type Foundry, St. Louis; St. Louis Type Foundry, St. Louis; Benton, Waldo & Co., Milwaukee; Cleveland Type Foundry, Cleveland; Marder, Luse & Co., Chicago; Palmer & Rey, San Francisco. See 'American Type Founders, Early History Through 1906': https://www.circuitousroot.com/artifice/letters/press/noncomptype/typography/atf/history-early/index.html (accessed 13 December 2023).
4. David Pankow, 'The Rise and Fall of ATF', *Printing History* 43/44, vol. 22, nos 1 and 2, 2002, p. 7.
5. Henry Lewis Bullen, 'Robert Wickham Nelson: An Intimate

History', *Inland Printer*, September 1926, p. 906.
6. Patrica A. Cost, *The Bentons: How a Father and Son Changed the Printing Industry*, Cary Graphics Arts Press, New York, 2011. p. 90.
7. Theodore Low De Vinne, 'The Century's Printer on *The Century's Type*', *The Century Magazine*, no. 5, March 1896, p. 795.
8. Quoted by Fred C. Williams, 'Theodore Low De Vinne's Type of the Century', *Type & Press*, no. 49, summer 1986, p. 1.
9. Ibid.
10. Shortly after the first two *Century* typefaces had been produced, it was decided to abandon the use of punches at ATF and instead to engrave matrices directly by machine.
11. Alexander S. Lawson, 'Anatomy of a Type: Century, Part 3', *Printing Impressions* 24, no. 8, January 1982, p. 62.
12. James Moran, *Stanley Morison: His Typographic Achievement*, Lund Humphries, London, 1971, p. 26.
13. Louis Émile Javal (1839–1907) was a French ophthalmologist, born in Paris. Javal's research influenced a number of twentieth-century type designers. His findings are described in a little more detail in the chapter on Roger Excoffen of this book.
14. Published under the title of 'The Relative Legibility of Different Faces of Printing Types', *American Journal of Psychology*, January 1912. Roethlein made comparisons of twenty-six contemporary typefaces, and reached the conclusion that *Century Expanded* and *Century Oldstyle*, along with *News Gothic*, *Bulfinch*, *Clearface* and *Cheltenham Wide*, were the best. However, her conclusions are considered somewhat suspect, since she concludes that *Cheltenham Oldstyle* and ATF's *Caslon No. 540* performed worst in the legibility tests.
15. Alexander S. Lawson, 'After 70 Years Century Typefaces Hold Their Own', The Alexander S Lawson (digital) Archive. Originally written 1 January 1965: www.alexanderslawsonarchive.com/bibliography/articles/composing-room (accessed 13 December 2023).
16. Phinney's *Taylor Gothic* was based on *Quentell*, a typeface designed by William Quentell for the Central Type Foundry in St Louis before it was taken over by ATF.
17. The designer of *Globe Gothic Bold* is unclear. Both Frederic Goudy and Morris Fuller Benton have claimed to have designed it. *Globe Gothic Bold* did not sell well and was not included in ATF's 1923 *Specimen Book*.
18. Mac MacGrew, *American Metal Typefaces of the Twentieth Century*, Oak Knoll Press, Delaware, DE, 1993, p. 143.

Rudolf Koch
1. William Morris, *A Note by William Morris on His Aims in Founding the Kelmscott Press*, 1895. Edition edited by William Peterson, Grolier Club, New York, NY, 1996.
2. At this point the company name was still the Rudhard foundry. The company had been bought by a wealthy manufacturer and his two sons, Karl and the younger Wilhelm, in 1892. The brothers took over its management in 1904 and named it Klingspor shortly after Koch joined in 1906. Wilhelm died in 1924.
3. In his *Deutsche Grammatik*, Jakob Grimm used capitals just for sentence openings and for proper names. The first edition of 1819 was set in blackletter with all the nouns capitalized, but the next edition of 1822 and all subsequent editions used roman type. See Robin Kinross, *Unjustified Texts*, Hyphen Press, London, 2002, pp. 133–6. Grimm also argued for the use of roman type in his famous revival of German fairy tales, but was wisely persuaded to have the work printed using a blackletter typeface.
4. Quoted by Robin Kinross, *Modern Typography*, Hyphen Press, London, 1992, p. 75.
5. Quoted by Sebastian Carter, *Twentieth Century Type Designers*, Lund Humphries, London, 2002, p. 59.
6. Quote attributed by Julius Rodenberg, a reputable writer and included in an article he had published shortly after Koch's death.
7. Walter Tracy, *Letters of Credit*, Gordon Fraser, Cambridge, 1986, p. 170.

Paul Renner
1. Paul Renner, 'Aforismen' (Aphorisms)', *Der Künstler in der mechanisierten Welt*, 1977, p. 165. Quoted by Christopher Burke, *Paul Renner: The Art of Typography*, Hyphen Press, London, 1998, p. 17.
2. Fritz Stern, *The Politics of Cultural Despair*, George Allen & Unwin, London, 1972, p. 8.
3. Paul Renner, 'Die Schrift unserer Zeit' ('The Script of Our Time'), *Die Form*, Jhg 2, Helf 3, 1927, pp 109–10. Quoted by Christopher Burke, *Paul Renner: The Art of Typography*, Hyphen Press, London, 1998, p. 16.
4. Paul Renner, 'Erinnerungen aus meiner Georg Müller-Zeit' (Recollections from my Georg Müller Period), *Imprimatur: ein Jahrbuch für Bücherfreunde* (Imprimatur: a yearbook for book lovers) unpaginated supplement, Jhg 9, 1939–40. See Christopher Burke, *Paul Renner: The Art of Typography*, Hyphen Press, London, 1998, p. 28.
5. 'Zur Kultur des Buches: 1' (On the Culture of Books: 1) *Allgemeine Buchhändlerzeitung*, 12 May 1910, p. 242.
6. The other co-directors were Emil Preetorius and Hans Cornelius, philosopher and art historian.

7. 'Wilfully bizarre' was Konrad F. Bauer's description of Renner's early unconventional characters. From a review by Brauer of recently released sans serif typefaces in *Imprimatur*, jhg 2, 1931.
8. Paul Renner, in a letter to Bauer type foundry, 14 March 1940. Quoted by Christopher Burke, *Paul Renner: The Art of Typography*, Hyphen Press, London, 1998, p. 96.
9. Paul Renner, *Schrift und Rechtschreibung* (Writing and Spelling), Pandora, Ulm, Germany, 1946, pp. 31–37.
10. Jost took part in a group visit organized by the Bund Deutscher Gebrauchsgraphiker (Union of German Commercial Designers), and a report on their findings was published in the journal *Gebrauchsgraphik*. Although the posters displayed on the Underground were praised, no specific mention of Johnston's *Underground Alphabet* was made.
11. Paul Renner, in a letter to Bauer type foundry, 14 March 1940. Quoted by Christopher Burke, *Paul Renner: The Art of Typography*, Hyphen Press, London, 1998, p. 96.
12. Paul Renner, 'Die Zukunft unserer Druckschrift' (The Future of our Printing Type) *Typographische Mitteilungen*, Jhg 22, Heft 5, 1925, p. 86.

Oswald Cooper

1. Quoted by Steven Heller, 'Telling and Selling: Oz Cooper', *Eye*, no. 7, 1992.
2. Oswald Bruce Cooper, *The Book of Oz*, Society of Typographic Arts, Chicago, IL, 1949.
3. Barnhart Bros. & Spindler was acquired by ATF in 1911. However, the agreement allowed BB&S to continue manufacturing and selling type independently until 1933.
4. The question has been raised as to whether *Cooper Fullface* and *Cooper Modern* are, in fact one and the same face. This is due to there being two different serial numbers for matrices in ATF's vaults.
5. The Continental Type Founders Association was founded by Melbert Brinckerhoff Cary Jr. in 1925 to distribute foundry type imported from European foundries across America. The influence of more modern European type design was thus felt in the US for the first time, and American foundries responded by imitating many of the more popular faces.
6. For example, Mac McGrew, *American Metal Typefaces of the Twentieth Century* (second edition), Oak Knoll Press, Delaware, DE, 1993, p. 105.

William A. Dwiggins

1. Paul Shaw, 'The Definitive Dwiggins', 2020, no. 131 – Reed and Dwiggins, Publishers. See: www.paulshawletterdesign.com/2020/11/the-definitive-dwiggins-no-131-reed-and-dwiggins-publishers (accessed 13 December 2023).
2. Updike was greatly interested in the history of printing types and in 1922 published *Printing Types: Their History, Forms and Use*. An extensively revised second edition was published in 1937.
3. Martin Hunter, *The Merrymount Press: An Exhibition on the Occasion of the 100th Anniversary of the Founding of the Press*, Harvard University Press, Cambridge, MA, 2005.
4. Paul Shaw, 'D.B. Updike and W.A. Dwiggins', *Parenthesis*, Fine Press Book Association, no. 26, autumn 2014.
5. Paul Hollister, 'Note, to be filled in a corner-stone', *WAD: The Work of WA Dwiggins Shown by the American Institute of Graphic Arts at the Gallery of the Architectural League* (catalogue) 1937, p. 8.
6. Paul Shaw, 'The Definitive Dwiggins no. 300 – W.A. Dwiggins meets Alfred A. Knopf', 2020. See: www.paulshawletterdesign.com/2020/07/the-definitive-dwiggins-no-300-w-a-dwiggins-meets-alfred-a-knopf (accessed 13 December 2023).
7. In 1919, Dwiggins and his cousin Siegfried created a fake series of interviews with publishing directors and book salesmen, to create an exposé of the shoddy quality of most trade books. They printed their 'findings' as a 24-page booklet, titled *Extracts from An Investigation into the Physical Properties of Books as They Are at Present Published*, and sold it for 50 cents. Knopf knew Melcher who, as editor, listed Dwiggins's booklet in *Publishers' Weekly*.
8. Quoted by Walter Tracy, *Letters of Credit*, Gordon Fraser, Cambridge, 1986, p. 177.
9. Sebastian Carter, *Twentieth Century Type Design*, Lund Humphries, London, 2002, p. 69.
10. James Mosley, Typefoundry blog, *Scotch Roman*, 2007: www.typefoundry.blogspot.com/2007/02/scotch-roman.html (accessed 13 December 2023).
11. William A. Dwiggins, letter to C.H. Griffiths dated 5 August 1932. The Chauncey Hawley Griffith Papers, University of Kentucky Libraries.

Eric Gill

1. Eric Gill, *Autobiography*, Jonathan Cape, London, 1940, p. 77.
2. Ibid, pp. 118–19.
3. Robert Harling, *The Letterforms and Type Designs of Eric Gill*, Eva Svensson, Kent, 1976, p. 17.
4. Eric Gill, *Autobiography*, Jonathan Cape, London, 1940, p. 115. For a brief period after sharing rooms with Johnston and before his move to Hammersmith, Gill lived in a block of worker's flats in Battersea Bridge Buildings – a (short-lived) gesture towards his political and social beliefs. Robert Harling,

The Letterforms and Type Designs of Eric Gill, Eva Svensson, Kent, 1976, p. 18.
5. Joseph Cribb was Gill's first assistant. This was arranged by Emery Walker. Cribb's father was a cartographer employed in Walker's company. Laurence, Joseph's younger brother, would also become an assistant to Gill.
6. Gill stayed in Ditchling until 1924, when he and his growing family, seeking a rural idyll and more privacy, moved to Capel-y-ffin ('Chapel at the border') in Wales. Although it could be reached in three hours from London, Capel-y-ffin was isolated and often wet, which made moving the heavy stones required for Gill's work particularly difficult. The stay was short-lived – after four years the family moved to the more practical surroundings of Pigotts Farm, a complex of buildings high on the hills above High Wycombe, Buckinghamshire, and conveniently close to Waltham St Lawrence and the Golden Cockerel Press.
7. Eric Gill, *Autobiography*, Jonathan Cape, London, 1940, p. 116.
8. Ibid, pp. 177–79.
9. Hilary Pepler, *The Hand Press, Ditchling*, Ditchling Press, Sussex, 1952, p. 1.
10. The Cuala Press was an Irish private press set up in 1908 by Elizabeth Yeats with financial support from her brother, and played an important role in the Celtic Revival of the early twentieth century. It was Emery Walker who advised Yeats to train as a printer at the Women's Printing Society, London. Originally named the Dun Emer Press, from 1908 until the late 1940s it functioned as Cuala Press.
11. Robert Gibbings, 'The Golden Cockerel Press', published in *The Woodcut*, 1927.
12. A 14-point roman was also made, presumably using the patterns made by Collinge that served to make the 18 point.
13. James Mosley, 'Eric Gill & The Golden Cockerel Type', *Matrix* 2, 1982, pp. 17–23.
14. Ibid, pp. 17–23.
15. Letter from Gill to Desmond Chute. Quoted by Robert Harling, *The Letterforms and Type Designs of Eric Gill*, Eva Svensson, Kent, 1976, p. 36.
16. Douglas Cleverdon went on to be a publisher of distinction, including a collection of engravings by Gill, and later the *Book of Alphabets for Douglas Cleverdon* (also by Gill). In 1927 he commissioned David Jones to make a set of copper engravings for *The Rime of the Ancient Mariner*, printed by the Fanfare Press, London, and published 1929. In 1939 he joined the BBC Radio's Third Programme as a producer – work included his adaptation of David Jones's major poem *In Parenthesis* in 1948, and the superlative premier of Dylan Thomas's *Under Milk Wood* in 1954.
17. Although *Futura* was released in 1927, Renner made a number of well-publicized illustrated lectures concerning his new typeface prior to its release, and so both its appearance and immanent release by the Bauer Foundry had been known well in advance.
18. Eric Gill, *Essay on Typography*, Sheed & Ward, London, 1931, p. 51.
19. Sebastian Carter, *Twentieth Century Type Designers*, Lund Humphries, London, 2002, p. 80.
20. From a letter by Gill to the *Monotype Recorder*, 1933. Quoted by Robert Harling, *The Letterforms and Type Designs of Eric Gill*, Eva Svensson, Kent, 1976, p. 54.
21. Martin Majoor, 'My Type Design Philosophy', 2023, see www.martinmajoor.com/6_my_philosophy.html (accessed 13 December 2023).
22. Robert Harling, *The Letterforms and Type Designs of Eric Gill*, Eva Svensson, Kent, 1976, p. 57.

Harold Curwen
1. Thomas Balson, unpublished typescript, private collection, 1950. Quoted by Brian Webb and Peyton Skipwith, *Harold Curwen and Oliver Simon*, Antique Collectors' Club, Woodbridge, 2008, p. 9.
2. Edward Johnston, 'The Leicester Lectures', in Heather Child and Justin Howes (eds), *Lessons in Formal Writing*, Lund Humphries, London, 1986, pp. 92–3.
3. 'Revival of Printing' was the title of a chapter in Holbrook Jackson's influential book, *The Eighteen Nineties*, Grant Richards, London, 1913.
4. 'Curwen drew a new sans serif type: his designs for it were finished in 1911, five years before Johnston completed his sans serif design for London Transport.' John Dreyfuss, *Matrix*, no. 5, 1985. Harold Curwen wrote that 'In 1912 I drew myself an address in block letters for private letter paper.' *Signature* 7, 1938.
5. Edward Johnston, 'The Leicester Lectures', in Heather Child and Justin Howes (eds), *Lessons in Formal Writing*, Lund Humphries, London, 1986, pp. 92–3.
6. Denis Megaw, 'Twentieth Century Sanserif Types', *Typography*, no. 7, 1938, p. 32.
7. Nicholas Pevsner, 'Patient Progress One: The Life and Work of Frank Pick', *The Architectural Review*, number cxxxii, 1942.
8. Brian Webb and Peyton Skipwith, *Harold Curwen and Oliver Simon: Curwen Press - Design*, ACC Art Books, Woodbridge, 2008.
9. Noel Carrington, 'Harold Curwen, Master Printer and Craftsman', *Matrix* no. 5, 1985, p. 35. Various proofs are illustrated in Brian Webb and Peyton Skipwith, *Harold Curwen and Oliver Simon: Curwen Press – Design*, ACC Art Books, Woodbridge, 2008, p. 30.
10. The first four issues of *The Fleuron*

were edited by Oliver Simon and printed by Curwen. The final three issues were edited by Stanley Morison who took the printing to Cambridge University Press.

Stanley Morison
1. Nicolas Barker, *Stanley Morison*, MacMillan, London, 1972, p. 32.
2. The article was credited as 'from our German Correspondent'. Kessler's production, *Die Odyssee*, with lettering by Eric Gill and published by Insel, was singled out for special mention.
3. Nicolas Barker, *Stanley Morison*, MacMillan, London, 1972, pp. 56–57.
4. Francis Meynell, *My Lives*, The Bodley Head, London, 1971, p. 135.
5. See Charles Lubelski, *Pride, Passion and Printing: The Life and Times of Percy Lund Humphries*, Croft Publications, Bradford, 2018; and Caroline Archer, *The Kynoch Press*, The British Library and Oak Knoll Press, London and Delaware, DE, 2000.
6. Lanston Monotype was the company name until 1931, when 'Lanston' was dropped.
7. French historian Jean Paillard raised doubts about the *Imprimerie Nationale* type being the work of Garamond. Paillard died in the First World War soon after publishing his conclusions in 1914. ATF's historian, Henry Lewis Bullen, had his own doubts if the '*Garamond*' his company was reviving was really Garamond's work, and discussed his concerns with ATF junior librarian Beatrice Warde. In a paper published in *The Fleuron*, no. 5, 1926, Warde revealed that the Imprimerie Nationale type had, in fact, been created by Jean Jannon, French printer, punchcutter and type founder, something she had discovered by examining printing credited to him in London and Paris and through reading the work of Paillard. (Warde's article was published under her pseudonym, 'Paul Beaujon'.)
8. Nicolas Barker, *Stanley Morison*, MacMillan, London, 1972, p. 121.
9. James Moran, 'Stanley Morison 1889–1967', *Monotype Recorder*, vol. xliii, no. 3, 1968, p. 11. William I. Burch took over as managing director from Harold M. Duncan who had held the position since 1900. In 1922 Duncan was ill (and would die two years later) and Burch was acting as his right-hand man.
10. There has been some debate regarding the exact date of Morison's appointment with Monotype, with Morison suggesting it might have been earlier. See Robin Kinross, *Modern Typography*, Hyphen Press, London, 1992, p. 57.
11. George William Jones was printer, designer and proprietor of the press at 'The Sign of The Dolphin'. In 1921 he was appointed by the British branch of the Mergenthaler Linotype Company to develop typefaces that would enhance their reputation. His projects included *Granjon* and *Estienne*, two families based on the typefaces of the French renaissance, and a revival of *Baskerville*, among many others. His partnership with Linotype draughtsman Harry Smith, who drew the production drawings for the typefaces at Linotype, was a key factor in Jones's success.
12. Mike Parker, introduction to Stanley Morison, *A Tally of Types*, reissued paperback edition, 2011, p. xvi.
13. Stanley Morison, *A Tally of Types*, Cambridge University Press, Cambridge, 1973, pp. 99–100.
14. Nicolas Barker, *Stanley Morison*, MacMillan, London, 1972, p. 211.
15. Ibid, p. 343.
16. Stanley Morison, *Printing the Times Since 1785*, Printing House Square, London, 1953.
17. Walter Tracy, *Letters of Credit*, Gordon Fraser, Cambridge, 1986, p. 196.
18. Only three *Times New Roman* lowercase letters vary in proportion to Monotype's *Plantin*: 'a', 'k' and 'o' are one unit wider. Seven of the capitals vary (four are wider and three narrower); all vertical measurements are virtually identical.
19. Robert Granjon (1513–1589) was the designer and punchcutter of the typeface on which Monotype's *Plantin* was based. The typeface is named after the printer and publisher Christophe Plantin (1520–1589).
20. Sebastian Carter, *History of the Monotype Corporation* (co-authors Judy Slin, Sebastian Carter and Richard Southall; edited by Andrew Boag and Christopher Burke), Printing Historical Society, London, 2014, p. 262.
21. Stanley Morison, *A Tally of Types*, Cambridge University Press, Cambridge, 1973, pp. 22–4.
22. Walter Tracy, *Letters of Credit*, Gordon Fraser, Cambridge, 1986, p. 206.

Jan van Krimpen
1. The editors were F. Ernest Jackson, Edward Johnston, J.H. Mason and Gerard Meynell of the Westminster Press, London, which was also the printer of the journal. The typeface *Imprint* was cut by Monotype specially for the journal, but was immediately made available to the print trade.
2. Gerard Forde, *Design in the Public Service: The Dutch PTT, 1920–1990* (exhibition catalogue), Design Museum, London, 1990, p. 9.
3. Sem Hartz, in Ruari McLean, *Typographers on Type*, Lund Humphries, London, 1995, pp. 118–19.
4. Quoted by Jan Middendorp, *Dutch Type*, 010 Publishers, Rotterdam, 2004, p. 38.
5. Ibid. p. 54.
6. John Dreyfuss, *Into Print*, British Library, London, 1994, p. 216.
7. Quoted by John Dreyfuss in the

introduction to *A Letter to Philip Hofer on Certain Problems Connected with the Mechanical Cutting of Punches*, David R. Godine, Boston, MA, 1972.
8. An anonymous reviewer of Van Krimpen's *Lutetia Italic* in *The Fleuron*, no. 6, 1928, noted that it was 'so good in itself that it cannot combine, with the proper self-effacement, with its roman'.
9. Walter Tracy, *Letters of Credit*, Gordon Fraser, Cambridge, 1986, p. 113.
10. Van Krimpen's *Memorandum* was published in *Matrix* 11 (1991) under the auspices of Sebastian Carter. Van Krimpen had given Will Carter (Sebastian's father) a type-written copy of the *Memorandum*. Quoted by Sebastian Carter, 'Stanley Morison and Jan van Krimpen: A Survey of Their Correspondence, Part 4', *Matrix* 11, 1991, p. 132.
11. Sem Hartz, in Ruari McLean, *Typographers on Type*, Lund Humphries, London, 1995, p. 120.

Hans (Giovanni) Mardersteig

1. Wolff also published several landmark illustrated books by artists including Oskar Kokoschka (1917), Ernst Ludwig Kirchner (1924) and Paul Klee (Voltaire's *Kandide*, 1920), as well as important artist's print portfolios. The company was liquidated in 1930 due to growing economic and political difficulties. After living in France and Italy between 1931 and 1941, Wolff emigrated to New York where he played an important role as a publisher of European literature in the US.
2. Warde, in a letter to T.M. Cleland, quoted by Simon Loxley, *Printer's Devil: The Life and Work of Frederic Warde*, White Label edition, Woodbridge, 2009, pp. 54–55.
3. This was the first of three versions of *Arrighi* designed by Frederic Warde. See the chapter on Frederic Warde.
4. Giovanni Mardersteig, *The Officina Bodoni: An Account of the Work of the Hand press 1923–77*, Officina Bodoni, 1980.
5. Hans Schmoller, *Two Titans: Mardersteig and Tschichold*, The Typophiles, New York, NY, 1990, p. 68.
6. Ibid, p. 71.

Robert Hunter Middleton

1. Bruce Rogers considered *Ludlow Eusebius* to be 'a more faithful reproduction of Jenson's letter than *Centaur* or *Cloister*'. See Rogers, *The Centaur Types*, Purdue University Press, West Lafayette, IN, p. 8.
2. See how the Ludlow machine works here: www.youtube.com/watch?v=25trV8M__k8&ab_channel=DonBlackLetterpress (accessed 13 December 2023).
3. *Procopius* may have been abandoned because of a heated dispute between McMurtrie and Clarence Hornung (1899-1997), who McMurtrie had employed to draw it.
4. Paul F. Gehl, *Chicago Modernism & the Ludlow Typograph: Douglas McMurtrie and Robert Hunter Middleton at Work*, Opifex, New South Wales, Australia, 2020, p. 10.
5. Although McMurtrie was associated with the company as director of advertising until his death (by heart attack) in 1944, he only worked full time for Ludlow for four years, from 1927 to 1931. Thereafter, he pursued other projects, mainly involving research, writing and publishing.
6. McMurtrie provided sketches only. While it is not known who worked on their development, it was probably Middleton who did the final drawings. Middleton never recorded an opinion of *Ultra-Modern*. Paul F. Gehl, *Chicago Modernism & the Ludlow Typograph: Douglas McMurtrie and Robert Hunter Middleton at Work*, Opifex, New South Wales, Australia, 2020, p. 21.
7. See the Chicago Design Archive: www.chicagodesignarchive.org/collection/27-chicago-designers-exhibit-2016 (accessed 13 December 2023).

Georg Trump

1. An italic for *Schneidler Mediäval*, named *Amalthea*, was released in 1956.
2. In the 1930 catalogue of an exhibition of work by members of the ring in Basle, Kurt Schwitters wrote that the ring consisted of '[Willi] Baumeister, [Max] Burchartz, [Walter] Dexel, [César] Domela [-Nieuwenhuis], [Hans] Leistikow, [Robert] Michel, [Paul] Schuitema, [Kurt] Schwitters, [Georg] Trump, [Jan] Tschichold, [Friedrich] Vordemberge-Gildewart, [Piet] Zwart', and that guest exhibitors included 'Cyliax, Kassák, Molzahn, and Teige'. An announcement for the Magdeburg exhibition of July 1929 has particularly impressive guest exhibitors: 'Otto Baumberger (Zurich), Herbert Bayer (Berlin-Charlottenburg), A.M. Cassandre (Paris), Walter Cyliax (Zurich), Theo van Doesburg (Paris), John Heartfield (Berlin), Lajos Kassák (Budapest), Moholy-Nagy (Berlin), Johannes Molzahn (Breslau), Oscar Nerlinger (Berlin-Charlottenburg), Karel Teige (Prague).' The final Ring exhibition was held at the Stedelijk Museum, Amsterdam, June–July 1931.
3. Christopher Burke, *Paul Renner: The Art of Typography*, Hyphen Press, London, 1998, p. 143.
4. Sebastian Carter, *Twentieth Century Type Designers*, Lund Humphries, London, 2002, p. 113.
5. Norbert Krausz, *Trump Mediaeval: The Story of its Creation and a Re-evaluation of its Historical Relevance* (dissertation, Reading University), 2015: www.typeculture.com/academic-resource/articles-essays/trump-

mediaeval-the-story-of-its-creation (accessed 13 December 2023).
6. Ibid. Georg Trump letter to Siefried Görwitz, 22 November 1951.
7. Ibid. p. 38.
8. Sebastian Carter, *Twentieth Century Type Designers*, Lund Humphries, London, 2002, p. 115.

A.M. Cassandre
1. The use of a pseudonym to protect future artistic aspirations was by no means uncommon. 'The Brothers Beggarstaff', used by British artists William Nicholson and James Pryde between 1894 and 1899, was one of the most famous.
2. Henri Mouron, *A.M. Cassandre*, chapter 1: www.cassandre-france.com (accessed 13 December 2023).
3. Maximilien Vox edited, designed and wrote most of the famous Deberny & Peignot journal *Divertissements typographiques*, and advised Peignot to buy the French rights to Paul Renner's *Futura*.
4. Michel Wlassikoff, *The Story of Graphic Design in France*, Gingko Press, Richmond, CA, 2005, p. 84.
5. *Arts et Métiers Graphiques Paris*, 15 January 1929. The journal was launched in 1927, and became a world forum for trends in the graphic arts.
6. Cassandre knew Alexey Brodovitch from his highly productive years spent working in Paris (1920–30). Brodovitch moved to New York in 1930, and from 1934 was creative director of *Harper's Bazaar* magazine.
7. Half-uncial emerged from the *New Roman Cursive*. One of the most important characteristics of half-uncial is that it is now effectively minuscule (lowercase) – for example, the letter 'D' now has an ascender and the letter 'P' now has a descender. While roman cursive characters were of a uniform height, half-uncial were not.
8. Georges Dangon, *Le Courrier Graphique*, November 1937.
9. André Lejard, 'Á propos d'une conception nouvelle de la publicité murale. Lucien Mazenod', *Arts et métiers graphiques*, January 1938.

Jan Tschichold
1. Jan Tschichold, *Leben und Werk des Typographen Jan Tschichold (Schriften 2:422)*, p. 16. Quoted by Robin Kinross in his introduction to the English translation of *The New Typography*, University of California Press, Berkeley, CA, 1998.
2. Alfred H. Barr, Jr., *Bauhaus 1925–1928*, Preface to the Catalogue of the exhibition, Museum of Modern Art (MoMA) New York, 1938, p. 7.
3. Jan Tschichold, *Die Neue Typographie*, Bildungsverband der deutschen Buchdrucker, Berlin, p. 7.
4. Robin Kinross, introduction to the English translation of *The New Typography*, University of California Press, Berkeley, CA, 1998, p. xvii.
5. Petra Eisele, Annette Ludwig, Isabel Naegele (eds), *Futura: The Typeface*, Lawrence King, London, 2017, p. 207.
6. The idea of a simplified, single alphabet (replacing the combination of caps and lowercase) in which 'our letters lose nothing but rather become more legible, easier to learn, essentially more scientific' was discussed by the engineer Dr Walter Porstmann in his book *Sprache und Schrift*, ('Language and Writing'), 1920. Moholy-Nagy quoted Porstmann's proposals in his writings on typography during 1925. Capital letters were abolished at the Bauhaus in the same year.
7. Bayer's *Universal*, plus Josef Albers, Van der Leck and Van Doesburg's experimental typefaces, have been digitized by David Quay and Freda Sack of The Foundry, London. However, the original founts were modified to improve functionality. See 'From Bauhaus to font house', *Eye*, no. 11, 1993.
8. Christopher Burke, *Active Literature: Jan Tschichold and New Typography*, Hyphen Press, London, 2007, p. 162.
9. In a letter to Joseph Albers (dated 8 December 1931). Christopher Burke, *Active Literature: Jan Tschichold and New Typography*, Hyphen Press, London, 2007, p. 166.
10. Ibid. p. 175.
10. On 11 March a squad of Röhm's Sturmabteilung (SA Storm Troopers) of the Nazi Party arrested Tschichold on the initiative of a zealous member, one of his neighbours. Only his wife Edith was at home so the SA took her hostage and let it be known they would release her only if Tschichold gave himself up. Tschichold was not in Munich at the time of the raid, but presented himself as soon as he could.
11. A second edition of *Die Neue Typographie*; updated and in a larger (A4) format, had been planned for 1932, but was abandoned by the publisher due to fear of political reprisal.
12. Quoted by Ruari McLean, *Jan Tschichold: Typographer*, pp. 131–9, David R. Godine, Boston, MA, 1975. The original article, 'Glaube und Wirklicheir', was published in *Schweizer Graphische Mitteilungen*, no. 6, 1946, p. 234.

Berthold Wolpe
1. A Seder evening is the most commonly celebrated Jewish ritual and includes the telling of religious stories, eating special foods and singing. The first edition of the *Haggadah* was published in 1927 and printed by Heinrich Cramer. Koch's *Jessen* was produced by the Klingspor type foundry.
2. *Hyperion* was originally named *Mattias Claudius*, but was later changed to avoid confusion with Koch's typeface *Claudius*.
3. Nicholas Barker, *Stanley Morison*,

4. Sebastian Carter, *Twentieth Century Type Designers,* Lund Humphries, London, 2002, pp 128–9.
5. It was named *Fanfare Bold Condensed Italic No. 2* by Monotype.
6. The Berthold Wolpe exhibition was presented first at the Gutenberg Museum in Mainz before it travelled to the Victoria and Albert Museum, London.
7. Deborah Hopson-Wolpe, Wolpe's daughter, quoted in a review from *Design Week* of the exhibition, *Berthold Wolpe: The Total Man*, held at The Lettering Arts Centre, Snape Maltings, Suffolk, 23 March – 24 June 2018: www.designweek.co.uk/issues/19-25-march-2018/berthold wolpe (accessed 13 December 2023).
8. Joseph Connolly, *Faber and Faber: Eighty Years of Book Cover Design*, Faber & Faber, London, 2009, p. xviii.

Roger Excoffon
1. François Richaudeau, *L'apprenti/The Novice*, 1910–1943, p. 16: https://excerpts.numilog.com/books/9782911220395.pdf (accessed 13 December 2023).
2. Sandra Chamaret, Julien Gineste, Sébastien Morlighem, *Roger Excoffon at al Fonderie Olive*, Bibliothéque Typographique, Amiens, 2010, p. 37.
3. Ibid. p. 81. Due to the occupation of France, precise dates of manufacture and distribution are not known. Nor is it clear why Marcel Olive decided to replace *Cabourg* with Excoffon's *Chambord*.
4. Ibid. p. 89. TheSpeedandGraceof Roger Excoffon.pdf (accessed 13 December 2023).
5. John Dreyfus, 'The Speed and Grace of Roger Excoffon', *International Typeface Corporation*: http://luc.devroye.org/JohnDreyfus
6. The Lumitype-Photon, 1954.
7. ATypI drafted a type protection treaty for presentation at an international World Intellectual Property Organization (WIPO) conference in Vienna in 1973. The delegates from the eleven countries who were present signed the agreement, but so far, the document has only been ratified by Germany and the UK.
8. Sandra Chamaret, Julien Gineste, Sébastien Morlighem, *Roger Excoffon at al Fonderie Olive*, Bibliothéque Typographique, Amiens, 2010, p. 127.
9. Ibid., p. 135.
10. As relayed by Joep Pohlen in 2023: http://luc.devroye.org/fonts-57974.html (accessed 13 December 2023).
11. Despite the title of Javal's book it is in fact concerned almost exclusively with the legibility of printed and written matter, and the physiological processes are investigated only in so far as they throw light upon this aspect of the subject, giving indications for increased facility and rapidity in reading.
12. *Roger Excoffon, a Master of French Graphic Design*, 3 May 2013: www.grapheine.com/en/history-of-graphic-design/roger-excoffon (accessed 13 December 2023).

PART THREE: PHOTOTYPESETTING
Introduction
1. Phototypesetting is sometimes erroneously referred to as 'cold type' to distinguish it from the 'hot type' letterpress composition machines it replaced. It should not, of course, be confused with foundry type used for hand-setting which, with the advent of composition machines was, and is still, often referred to as 'cold type'.
2. S.H. Steinberg, *Five Hundred Years of Printing* (new edition, revised by John Trevitt), The British Library, London, 1996, p. 220.
3. F.B. Fishenden, 'Uhertype at Waterlows', 1934. Unpublished typescript, held by St Bride Printing Library, London.
4. Phototypesetting machines had been patented before 1900 (for example, by Eugen Porzsolt in 1894 and the cinematographic pioneer William Friese-Green in 1898), although none came into general use until after the Second World War.
5. In addition to the regular trade edition, the publishers issued 1,000 numbered copies printed on high quality paper in two colours. These copies were issued in the traditional style of deluxe books in France, unsewn, in signatures in a printed wrapper and boxed.
6. Andrew Boag, 'Monotype and Phototypesetting', *Journal of the Printing History Society*, 2000, p. 57.
7. See: www.haagens.com/oldtype.tpl.html (accessed 13 December 2023).
8. Heidrun Osterer and Philipp Stamm, *Adrian Frutiger Typefaces: The Complete Works*, Birkhäuser, Basel, 2014, p. 80.
9. Ferdinand P. Ulrich, 'A brief overview of developments in digital type design': https://medium.com/@fpeulrich/a-brief-overview-of-developments-in-digital-type-design-561d9e63a122 (accessed 13 December 2023).
10. Ibid.

Max Miedinger
1. Akzidenz translates as 'commercial' or, in a printing context, 'jobbing'. The term 'jobbing' was used in the print industry for work other than book work. *Akzidenz Grotesk* was sold in America under the name *Standard*.
2. Haas's *Normal Akzidenz* was also known as *Accidenz-Grotesk* and *Akzidenz-Grotesk*, but despite having the same name the Haas version was quite consciously different from the original 1896 Berthold version – being more condensed and more square in appearance. *Französische Grotesk* was based on

Schelter & Giesecke's *Breite halbfette Grotesk* from 1890.
3. This was how Hoffmann's son described his father's promise to Miedinger in 1956. From the film *Helvetica*, directed by Gary Hustwit, 2007.
4. *Helvetica* was not available in Britain or the US until early 1965.
5. Ibid. Mike Parker's description of Hoffmann.
6. Johannes Erler, *Hello I Am Erik: Erik Speikermann: Typographer, Designer, Entrepeneur*, Gestalten, Berlin, 2014, p. 80.
7. Core fonts, though introduced by Adobe in 1984 as part of the PostScript page description language, did not see widespread use until March 1985 when the first laser printer to use the PostScript language, the Apple Laser Writer, was introduced.

Aldo Novarese
1. See: www.fontsinuse.com/typefaces/12073/egiziano (accessed 13 December 2023).
2. Vincent Figgins' great grandson, Richard Herbert Stevens, arranged the merger with P.M. Shanks in 1933 to form Stevens, Shanks.
3. Alessandro Colizzi, *Aldo Novarese and Alessandro Butti, a Story to be Rewritten*. Lecture given at ATypI conference, 24 September 2018: www.youtube.com/watch?v=TdSOmu3OvkM&ab_channel=ATypI (accessed 13 December 2023).
4. Ibid.
5. Novarese was imprisoned in 1939 for participating in protests against the Second World War. Following the 1943 armistice, with Italy divided between the German occupation and the American-led liberation, Novarese joined the partisan resistance. See: https://typenetwork.com/articles/aldo-as-ferrari-is-to-cars-novarese-is-to-type (accessed 13 December 2023).
6. Paul Shaw, *Archivio Nebiolo – A short Conversation with Alessandro Colizzi*: www.paulshawletterdesign.com.
7. Ibid.

Hermann Zapf
1. Hermann Zapf, *The Life Story of Hermann Zapf*: https://www.calligraphy.com.ua/wp-content/uploads/2010/05/ZapfBiography.pdf (accessed 13 December 2023).
2. The Haus zum Fürsteneck stood on the Weckmarkt corner of the Fahrgasse; it was destroyed during the 1944 air raids on Frankfurt.
3. Paul Koch died fighting on the Russian front in 1943.
4. The 1949 edition quickly sold out. In 1951, the Cooper Union in New York mounted an exhibition featuring Zapf's work alongside that of Fritz Kredel, wood engraver and book illustrator. Zapf was invited to the US and gave several lectures. The exhibition was organized by the American calligrapher Paul Standard, who then arranged for an English version of *Feder und Stichel* to be published. This second edition, *Pen and Graver*, printed by Stempel in 1952, was an edition of 2,000.
5. Alexander S. Lawson, *Anatomy of a Typeface*, Hamish Hamilton, London, 1990, p. 123.
6. The American type designer William A. Dwiggins was particularly vocal on this matter. See Alexander S. Lawson, *Anatomy of a Typeface*, Hamish Hamilton, London, 1990, p. 125.
7. Sebastian Carter, *Twentieth Century Type Designers*, Lund Humphries, London, 2002, p. 152.
8. *The Life Story of Hermann Zapf*: https://www.calligraphy.com.ua/wp-content/uploads/2010/05/ZapfBiography.pdf.
9. Jack Stauffacher & Hermann Zapf, *The Birth of a Typeface* (introduction), Pittsburgh Bibliophiles, Pittsburgh, 1965.

Adrian Frutiger
1. Adrian Frutiger, *Adrian Frutiger: Typefaces*, Birkhäuser, Basel, 2014, p. 50.
2. Hiedrun Osterer and Philipp Stamm, *Adrian Frutiger Typefaces: The Complete Works*, Birkhäuser, Basel, 2014, p. 50.
3. Sebastian Carter, *Twentieth-Century Type Designers*, Lund Humphries, London, 2002, p. 165.
4. Heidrun Osterer and Philipp Stamm, *Adrian Frutiger Typefaces: The Complete Works*, Birkhäuser, Basel, 2014, p. 80.
5. Monotype ignored Frutiger's numeric system, so what he called *Univers 83* appeared in Monotype literature as *Monotype Univers Ultra Bold Extended, Series 697*. When *Helvetica* was overhauled, extended and renamed *Neue Helvetica* in 1983, Frutiger's unique classification system was adopted.
6. Sebastian Carter, *Twentieth-Century Type Designers*, Lund Humphries, London, 1987, p. 165.
7. Martin Majoor, 'Inclined to be Dull', *Eye*, Spring, 2007.
8. Emile Ruder, 'Univers', *Neue Grafik*, no. 2, 1959, and 'Die Univers in der Typographie', *Typographische Monatsblätter*, vol. 80, no. 1, 1961.
9. Karl Gerstner, *Programme Entwerfen (Designing Programmes)*, Arthur Niggli, Teufen, 1964, p. 32.
10. The *Frutiger* type specimen, published by Linotype c.1977, is reproduced in Paul McNeil, *A Visual History of Type*, Lawrence King, London, 2017, p. 429.

Wim Crouwel
1. Graham Sturt, Dutch Design Heroes: Wim Crouwel: https://medium.com/dutch-design-heroes/dutch-design-heroes-wim-crouwel-871a902ea15d (accessed 13 December 2023).
2. In the 1990s Total Design changed strategy to become an organization focusing on identity development, corporate image and reputation

management. In 2000 the company changed its name to Total Identity in order to confirm its new intent. At the beginning of 2018 Total Identity merged with the agencies Total Active Media and Koeweiden Postma, and reverted to the original name Total Design once more.
3. For example: *Cybernetic Serendipity* at the ICA Gallery London, 1968, and *The Machine, as Seen at the End of the Mechanical Age*, Museum of Modern Art, New York, also 1968.
4. Max Bruinsma, 'Wim Crouwel interview', *Items* 5/6, 1997.
5. See http://davidquaydesign.com/foundry-architype-3 (accessed 13 December 2023).

Bram de Does

1. Matthieu Lommen, *Bram De Does*, Uitgeverij de Buitenkant, Amsterdam, 1999, p. 6.
2. Bram de Does, *Romanée en Trinité*, Aartswoud, Amsterdam, 1991, p. 7.
3. Sebastian Carter, 'The Spectatorpers: The Press of Bram de Does', *Parenthesis*, 14, Fine Press Book Association, 2008.
4. Jan Middendorp, *Dutch Type*, 010 Publishers, Rotterdam, 2004, p. 161. This is an extract from a much longer interview.
5. Ibid.
6. Progress in the digitization of the Enschedé library has been particularly slow, due in part to complications regarding copyright issues, but also to Noordzij's perfectionism. For example, *Romanée* was digitized by Noordzij and Fred Smeijers and a preliminary version was used by Martin Majoor in 1995 for a book to accompany an exhibition of Van Krimpen's work at the Museum of the Book in The Hague. However, the definitive version of *Romanée* is, apparently, still in preparation.

Margaret Calvert

1. Margaret Calvert in correspondence with the author, 19 August 2021.
2. In 1949 the Royal College, under Robin Darwin, established one of the earliest graphic design courses in the UK run by John Brinkley and John Lewis under the stewardship of Richard Guyatt.
3. Phil Baines, 'The Time of the Signs' (interview with Margaret Calvert), *Frieze* no. 77, 10 September 2003.
4. The number of hours required by full-time professors to attend the RCA was kept generously low in order to lure professional designers into academia. Hence, Kinneir was not only able to run the graphic design department at the RCA – as well as run his own design practice – but he also had time to teach part-time at Chelsea School of Art.
5. https://www.RCA.ac.uk/news-and-events/news/margaret-calvert/ (accessed 13 December 2023).
6. At a later stage, when Gatwick Airport was enlarged and updated, the colour scheme was changed to black on yellow to bring it line with all other British Airports Authority airports (beginning with Heathrow).
7. Dr Theodore W. Forbes was an American traffic engineer. Between 1945 and 1949 he designed a new signage alphabet to be used across all American highways. It consists of six fonts: 'A' (the narrowest), 'B', 'C', 'D', 'E', 'E(M)' (a modified version of 'E' with wider strokes), and 'F' (the widest). It has since been copied, sometimes with minor adjustments, by many countries. Tobias Frere-Jones designed *Interstate*, a digital typeface, during 1993–99, which was licensed by Font Bureau. The typeface is based on Style Type E of the FHWA (Federal Highway Administration) Series.
8. The origins of *DIN 1451 Engschrift* ('condensed face') date back to 1905, when the Prussian State Railways prescribed a standardized lettering style for use on all its rolling stock and later stations. Then, as a by-product of the 1920 consolidation of all German railway companies into the *Deutsche Reichsbahn*, *DIN 1451* became a *de facto* national standard. The DIN Committee of Typefaces was set up a few years later, headed by the Siemens engineer, Ludwig Goller (1884–1964). After minor refinements *DIN 1451* was released as an official standard in 1936 and used on the new German Autobahn system from 1938.
9. Ben Bos (editor), Margaret Calvert, 'Battle of the Serif', *AGI: Graphic Design since 1950*, Thames & Hudson, London and New York, 2007. The letter was dated 26 June 1958.
10. Ibid. Also, Ole Lund, *Typography Papers* 5, 2003, p. 104.
11. Ibid.
12. Nicolas Barker, *Stanley Morison*, MacMillan, London, 1972, p. 464.
13. Ole Lund, *Typography Papers* 5, 2003, p. 106. In March 1961, the BBC planned a debate between Jock Kinneir and David Kindersley in the 'Tonight' show, a popular early evening current affairs programme. However, the Ministry of Transport advised Kinneir not to participate, while also reassuring him that he had the committee's full support. Lund was quoting from a letter received by Kinneir from the Ministry of Transport, dated 24 March 1961.
14. In fact, there were two versions of the Kinneir Calvert *Transport* that were tested. The first was a lowercase with initial capitals – as already employed on the Preston Bypass – and the same letters again but in a smaller size and applied with additional interlinear space and wider margins.
15. The Underground Group was absorbed by the London Passenger Transport Board in 1933. www.thebeautyoftransport.com/2015/05/13/on-line-typeface-

rail-alphabet-typeface-uk (accessed 13 December 2023).
16. John L. Walters, 'Britain's Signature', *Eye*, no. 71, spring 1909.
17. Daniel Wright, *The Beauty of Transport*, www.thebeautyoftransport.com (accessed 13 December 2023).
18. Jock Kinneir, *Words and Buildings: The Art and Practice of Lettering*, Architectural Press, London, 1980, p. 8.
19. John L. Walters, quoting Henrik Kubel, 'Britain's Signature' *Eye*, no. 71, spring 1909.
20. Margaret Calvert in correspondence with the author, 19 August 2021.

PART FOUR: DIGITIZATION
Introduction
1. The mouse had been introduced with Lisa, Apple's previous computer. In fact, the Macintosh had much of the same technology and identical user-interface as Lisa.
2. The first LaserWriter had thirteen fonts: *Times, Helvetica, Courier* (each with four variations) and *Symbol*. *Zapf Chancery* (medium italic) was planned as part of this set, but the Type 1 version wasn't ready in time.
3. The development of a PostScript language began in 1976. John Warnock and Chuck Geschke founded Adobe Systems in December 1982 and then, with Doug Brotz, Ed Taft and Bill Paxton, finalized PostScript, which was released in 1984. Steve Jobs then asked them to adapt PostScript to be used as the language for driving Apple's LaserWriter desktop printer.
4. Steve Jobs, from his introduction to the Apple Macintosh, at its premiere at the Boston Computer Society General Meeting, 30 January 1984.
5. Emily King, *New Faces* (Chapter One: Technological and Industrial Change: Setting the Scene) Thesis, 1999: https://www.typotheque.com/articles/new-faces-introduction (accessed 13 December 2023).

Matthew Carter
1. John Dreyfus, 'The Dante Types', *Fine Print on Type*, Bedford Arts, San Francisco, 1989, p. 98.
2. *Dante* was cut by Charles Malin for exclusive use by Giovanni Mardersteig's Officina Bodoni. Monotype, at Stanley Morison's behest, arranged to issue *Dante* modified for machine composition but with additional weights; Carter was employed to cut some of the initial punches of the semi-bold. *Dante* was issued by Monotype in 1957.
3. Phyllis Hoffman, *Matthew Carter: Reflects on Type Design* (thesis), Rochester Institute of Technology, 1999, p. 17: https://scholarworks.rit.edu/theses/3850/ (accessed 13 December 2023).
4. In 1949, the Photon Corporation in Cambridge, Massachusetts, developed equipment based on the Lumitype phototypesetting invention of French engineers and inventors René Higonnet and Louis Moyroud. The Lumitype-Photon was first used to set a published book in 1953, and for newspaper work in 1954.
5. J. Abbott Miller, 'Matthew Carter', *Print* magazine, 1 September 1995: https://www.printmag.com/design-matters-with-debbie-millman/design-matters-at-15-matthew-carter/ (accessed 13 December 2023).
6. At that time Linotype machines had constraints on the number of characters in a font, so it was impossible to include the full character set Carter had designed. For example, he had designed versions of both the 'n' and 'm' with a flourish at the end. It was the same flourish, but there was only room for one, so the 'n' with a flourish was included but the 'm' was not.
7. Nick Sherman, 'Bell Centennial: Form and Function': https://nicksherman.com/articles/bellCentennial (accessed 13 December 2023).
8. Emigre digital type foundry, run by Rudy VanderLans and Zuzana Licko, began selling typefaces (independent of the manufacture of typesetting systems) from around 1985.
9. Phyllis Hoffman, 'Matthew Carter Reflects on Type Design', Thesis (Rochester Institute of Technology), 1999, p. 65: https://scholarworks.rit.edu/theses/3850/ (accessed 13 December 2023).
10. Matthew Carter, interviewed by Erik Speikermann, 'Reputations', *Eye*, no. 11, 1993.

Gerard Unger
1. John L. Walters, 'Reputations: Gerard Unger', *Eye*, no. 40, vol. 10, 2001.
2. Ibid.
3. *Kwadraatbladen* (Square Format) was a journal edited by Pieter Brattinga and published by the printing company Steendrukkerij de Jong in Hilversum for distribution primarily to designers.
4. Riccardo Olocco, 'The Inner Consistency of Gerard Unger', CAST, 18 May 2017: https://articles.c-a-s-t.com/the-inner-consistency-of-gerard-unger-7a42add9e900 (accessed 13 December 2023)
5. Ibid. Unger: 'I know that writing instruments, the broad-nib and pointed and flexible pen have left indelible traces, but calligraphy so often becomes expressionistic. When I was a student I liked that as it was new. Later I thought of it as over-expressive.'
6. John L. Walters, 'Reputations: Gerard Unger', *Eye*. no. 40, vol. 10, 2001.
7. The first digital typeface ever created was probably *Digi-Grotesk*, developed in Hell's design studio in 1968. The first generation of original type designs for the Digiset were

Marconi in 1973 followed by *Edison* (both by Hermann Zapf, *Marconi* is generally considered to be the first digital typeface). *Demos* and *Praxis*, by Gerard Unger, followed. *Napoleon* and *Monanti* were developed by Hell's in-house type department.

8. These would be 'Didot points', which are slightly larger than the US/UK point system of measurement: one US/UK point is .351mm, Didot is .376mm.
9. Gerard Unger, 'The Design of a Typeface', *Visible Language*, vol. 13, no. 2, 1979, p. 134.
10. Quoted by Jan Middendorp, *Dutch Type*, 010 Publishers, Rotterdam, 2004, p. 168.
11. Christopher Burke, *Gerard Unger: Life in Letters*, Uitgeverij de Buitenkant, Amsterdam, 2021, p. 100.
12. Linotype would be acquired by Monotype in 2006.
13. 'In Memoriam: Gerard Unger 1942–2018', typeroom, www.typeroom.eu/article/memoriam-gerard-unger-1942-2018 (accessed 13 December 2023).
14. Christopher Burke, *Gerard Unger: Life in Letters*, Uitgeverij de Buitenkant, Amsterdam, 2021, p. 205.
15. Ibid. p.218.

Erik Spiekermann

1. Erik Spiekermann in correspondence with the author, 7 June 2021.
2. Erik Spiekermann, 'Post Mortem, or how I once designed a typeface for Europe's biggest company', *Baseline*, 1987, p. 8. Alternatively, see: www.spiekermann.com/en/wp-content/uploads/2005/05/baseline0785_meta3.pdf (accessed 13 December 2023).
3. This is one of several suggestions offered to the Advisory Board at ITC, although it was headed 'My favourite idea'. The single-side document is reproduced in Johannes Erler, *Hello I am Erik*, Gestalten, Berlin, 2014, p. 114.
4. MetaDesign had already worked with Adobe in 1987 on a publishing pack titled 'Forms and Schedules' which held a disc containing three typefaces – Lucinda, News Gothic and Univers – plus an explanation by Spiekermann on the design and function of forms, with examples.
5. The reasons for Spiekermann leaving MetaDesign are described in grisly detail by Johannes Erler, *Hello I am Erik*, Gestalten, Berlin, 2014, p. 203.
6. For a fulsome account of P98a see: Ferdinand P. Ulrich, 'P98a', *Parenthesis* 34, Fine Press Book Association, 2018, p. 28.

Neville Brody

1. During 1968 Hornsey College was the scene of protests when students occupied the Crouch End Hill site in protest at the withdrawal of Student Union funds. During their six-week period of occupation they took over the administration of the college, and called for a major and consultative review of the art curriculum. Other art schools around the UK followed suit. The college was repossessed by local authorities at the beginning of the summer break. Hornsey College was amalgamated into Middlesex Polytechnic, which then became Middlesex University in 1992.
2. This is Brody's estimate.
3. Beatrice Warde, *The Pencil Draws a Vicious Circle: The Crystal Goblet*, Sylvan Press, London, 1955. Also, Nicholas Barker wrote: 'J.R. Riddell, when Head of Printing at the LCP, said "artists should be kept in their place", and he had all the technician's resentment when they (in the form of "typographical consultants") strayed into the printer's preserve'. Nicholas Barker, *Stanley Morison*, MacMillan, London, 1972, p. 232.
4. Brody interviewed by Marcus Fairs, 2009: www.dezeen.com/2014/11/21/neville-brody-dezeen-book-of-interviews (accessed 13 December 2023).
5. Ibid.
6. Alex McDowell moved permanently to Los Angeles in 1986, to work in the burgeoning music video and commercials industry in Hollywood before moving into the film industry.
7. Jon Wozencroft, *The Graphic Language of Neville Brody*, Thames & Hudson, London and New York, 1994, p. 9.
8. Paul Gorman, *The Story of The Face: The Magazine That Changed Culture*, Thames & Hudson, London and New York, 2017.
9. Neville Brody in correspondence with the author, July/August 2021.
10. Jon Wozencroft, *The Graphic Language of Neville Brody*, Thames & Hudson, London and New York, 1994, p. 10.
11. From the film, *Helvetica*, directed by Gary Hustwit, 2007.
12. Neville Brody in correspondence with the author, July/August 2021.
13. Ibid.
14. Ibid.
15. As with all these early digital type 'foundries/libraries', part of their service was to take the original drawings provided by the designer and redraw the characters – ensuring consistency was applied across the all characters, and to add any missing punctuation, accented letters, currency symbols etc. Creating additional weights and accompanying italics might also be part of the service.
16. David Berlow, *Neville Brody Joins Type Network*: https://typenetwork.com/articles/neville-brody-joins-type-network# (accessed 13 December 2023).
17. FSI was co-directed by Brody, Erik Spiekermann and his wife Joan Spiekermann, who had started it together.
18. Neville Brody in correspondence with the author, July/August 2021.
19. Rick Poyner, 'Reputations: Neville Brody', *Eye*, no. 6, 1992.

20. Prior to Brody's *Times Modern* in 2006, other adaptations of Morison's *Times New Roman* had been created, including: *Times Europa*, designed by Walter Tracy in 1972, *Times Millennium*, designed by Gunnlaugur S.E. Briem and Aurobind Patel in 1991, and *Times Classic* designed by Dave Farey and Richard Dawson, 2001.

Carol Twombly

1. Adobe licensed *Stone* to ITC in 1988. Stone left Adobe in late 1989 to set up his own type foundry in Palo Alto, California.
2. Tamye Riggs, 'The Adobe Originals Silver Anniversary Story', Adobe Typekit Blog, 2014: https://blog.typekit.com/2014/06/30/the-adobe-originals-silver-anniversary-story-expanding-the-originals (accessed 13 December 2023).
3. Adobe's Christopher Slye (who joined Adobe in 1997 and helped to expand the design and functionality of Adobe Originals typefaces, including *Myriad*) later said that he had been concerned that Robert Slimbach had damaged his health struggling to apply multiple master technology to *Adobe Jenson* in the late 1990s. See Tamye Riggs, 'The Adobe Originals Silver Anniversary Story', Adobe Typekit Blog, 2014: https://blog.typekit.com/2014/06/30/the-adobe-originals-silver-anniversary-story-expanding-the-originals (accessed 13 December 2023).

Martin Majoor

1. Donald Beekman and Liza Enebeis, *Interviewing Martin Majoor*, 4 April 2010: www.martinmajoor.com/9_lectures (accessed 13 December 2023).
2. *FF Balance* was released in PostScript form as part of FontShop's FontFont Library in 1993. Its long period of development was due in large part to fast-changing technology that preoccupied the 1980s.
3. The type specimen listing the five Dutch type designers and their fonts was the first FontFont to be released and was designed by Just van Rossum. It contained *Rosetta, Vortex, Network, Cutout* and *Scratch* by Max Kisman; *Newberlin* by Peter Verheul; *Brokenscript* and *Justlefthand* by Just van Rossum; *Erikrighthand* by Erik van Blokland; and *Scala* by Martin Majoor. The specimen came in three language versions: English, Dutch and German.
4. Martin Majoor, *The Story of FF Scala*, www.scalafont.com/story (accessed 13 December 2023).
5. Kinross, Robin, 'The Digital Wave', *Eye*, no. 7, 1992, p. 26.
6. 'Soft-edged modernism' is a term used by Emily King: 'The humanist sans serif, which has been a significant trend in post PostScript type design, might be seen as the outcome of a cultural sensibility that is particularly Dutch. Types of this kind could be said to combine a commitment to positive change with a respect for the past, effectively displaying a kind of soft-edged modernism.' From Emily King, 'New Faces: Scala', 1999: https://www.martinmajoor.com/1.2_scala_article_king.html (accessed 13 December 2023).
7. Martin Majoor, 'Nexus: A family of three "connected" typefaces', https://martinmajoor.com/4.2_nexus_article_overview_majoor.html (accessed 13 December 2023).
8. See www.fonts.com/font/fontfont/ff-nexus-typewriter/story (accessed 13 December 2023).
9. Robin Kinross 'Critical Spirit of a Telephone Book', *Eye*, Spring 1995.
10. Ibid.

Zuzana Licko

1. Rudy VanderLans, in correspondence with the author, 3 June 2021.
2. Rhonda Rubinstein, 'Eye Reputations', *Eye*, no. 43, 2001.
3. There were sixty-nine issues of *Emigre* in total, in a range of formats from roughly A3 down to paperback book, before closing in 2005.
4. 'Interpretation' is the term used by Rudy VanderLans in *Notes on Filosofia*, the specimen booklet for *Filosofia*, 1996.
5. Rudy VanderLans and Zuzana Licko in correspondence with the author, May 2021.
6. Stanley Morison, 'Memorandum on a Proposal to Revise the Typography of "The Time"', *Selected Essays on the History of Letter-Forms in Manuscript and Print*, David McKitterick, ed., Cambridge University Press, Cambridge, 1981, p. 307.
7. The exchange of correspondence was also included in the specimen booklet for *Filosofia*, 1996.

Jeremy Tankard

1. Jeremy Tankard in correspondence with the author, 30 May 2021. Also: 'I remember watching the first "Big Brother" Apple Mac advert and avidly writing a program using "MegaBasic" to make my Spectrum screen look like a Mac. By the time I had done it the computer had no memory left with which to do anything.'
2. The school merger with the Central School of Art and Design (previously the Central School of Arts and Crafts) to become Central St Martins School of Art and Design was established in 1989, although the graphic design course Tankard attended was already jointly run by Central School at Southampton Row and St Martins at Long Acre and Charing Cross Road, London.

3. Emily King, 'Compare and Contrast', *Eye*, no. 25, 1997. With a decline in interest in lettering during the 1980s (as with drawing), The Central Lettering Record might well have been forgotten but for the revival of interest in the resource among certain staff members, and in particular Phil Baines, and the emergence of a new source of funding for research in the Higher Education Funding Council in 1993.
4. Gillian Crampton Smith wrote (via correspondence with Richard Doust) that there was a computer course for graphic design at Coventry College before that of St Martins.
5. The work displayed by RCA students at their annual graduation exhibition fed back into art schools around the UK. Kitching caused letterpress not only to be reevaluated, but reborn, this time as a 'new' and innovative technology: more immediate, more versatile, more adaptable, cheaper and recyclable. All of this was particularly pertinent in the midst of what was heralded a 'digital revolution'.
6. Jeremy Tankard, quoted by Jack Yan, 'Jeremy Tankard: Idiosyncratic Type' (interview), *Cap Online Features*, published in association with DZ3, 1999: www.jyanet.com/cap/1999/0605fe0.htm (accessed 13 December 2023).
7. Bradbury Thompson first began developing his concept regarding a unicase alphabet in 1944, which culminated in 1950 with *Alphabet 26*. The idea was to use one symbol for each letter by combining the most distinct letters from both the capital and lowercase sets. As this approach rested on using existing letter shapes, there was no need to introduce new designs. However, inconsistent inter-character spacing, some poor character connections, and the lack of ascenders and descenders severely hindered the flow and readability of the text.
8. Jeremy Tankard, quoted by Jack Yan, 'Jeremy Tankard: Idiosyncratic Type' (interview), *Cap Online Features*, published in association with DZ3, 1999: www.jyanet.com/cap/1999/0605fe0.htm (accessed 13 December 2023).
9. Tankard taught typography at Colchester Institute, where the author was head of graphic design, working in its newly established letterpress workshop. When Tankard left, Kelvyn Smith took his place.
10. Jeremy Tankard, quoted by Jack Yan, 'Jeremy Tankard: Idiosyncratic Type' (interview), *Cap Online Features*, published in association with DZ3, 1999: www.jyanet.com/cap/1999/0605fe0.htm (accessed 13 December 2023).
11. Jeremy Tankard in correspondence with the author, 30 May 2021.
12. Ibid.
13. Chris Palmieri, 'Facetime2: Type Designer Jeremy Tankard on Bliss', 27 July 2007. For a description of the origins of 'English' typography see: James Mosley, 'English Vernacular: A Study in Traditional Letterforms', *Motif* no. 11, The Shenval Press, 1963–64, p. 3.
14. See Mark Ovenden, *Johnston & Gill*, Lund Humphries, London, 2016.
15. Jeremy Tankard: www.studiotype.com/originals/shire-types (accessed 13 December 2023).
16. Chris Palmieri, 'Facetime2: Type Designer Jeremy Tankard on Bliss', 27 July, 2007, https://www.aqworks.com/blog/facetime-2-type-designer-jeremy-tankard-on-bliss.
17. Jeremy Tankard, Enigma, www.studiotype.com/originals/enigma (accessed 13 December 2023). Hendrik van den Keere (c.1541–80) was a punchcutter and engraver who lived in Ghent, Belgium. From 1568 he worked almost exclusively for Christophe Plantin of Antwerp. Van den Keere's roman types would influence future Dutch types and in turn, those of England.
18. Ibid.

Tobias Frere-Jones
1. Tobias Frere-Jones in correspondence with the author, 29 May 2021.
2. Quoted by Rick Poyner (ed.), *Typography Now Two*, Booth Clibborn Editions, London, 2002, no page numbers.
3. Tobias Frere-Jones in correspondence with the author, 29 May 2021.
4. See https://typostitch.wordpress.com/2013/03/08/part-iv-523-tobias-frere-jones-interstate-1993-95/.
5. Tobias Frere-Jones and Doug Wilson, 'Designing Whitney', https://frerejones.com/blog/designing-whitney.
6. David Dunlap, 'Two Type Designers, Joining Forces and Faces', *The New York Times*, 19 October 2004.
7. Tobias Frere-Jones in correspondence with the author, 29 May 2021, and www.frerejones.com/families/retina (accessed 13 December 2023).
8. John Brownlee, *Hoefler & Frere-Jones: the final interview*, Fast Company, 25 February 2014, www.fastcompany.com/3028099/hoefler-frere-jones-the-final-interview (accessed 13 December 2023).
9. Tobias Frere-Jones, 'Mallory: Drawn out from Memory', https://frerejones.com/blog/mallory-drawn-out-from-memory, 18 June 2019.

Bibiliography

Journals
American Journal of Psychology
Architectural Review (The)
Arts et Métiers Graphiques Paris
Art Technique Now
Baseline
British Printer
Century Guild Hobby Horse (The)
Courrier Graphique (Le)
Emigre
Eye
Fine Print
Fleuron (The)
Frieze
FUSE
Glyphs
Icon
Imprint (The)
Inland Printer
Items
Kwadraatbladen
Les Divertissements Typographiques
Matrix
Monotype Recorder (The)
Neue Grafik
Parenthesis
Popular Science
Printing History
Printing Impressions
TypoGraphic
Typographica
Typographische Monatsblätter
Type & Press
Typography
Typography Papers
US Library of Congress Quarterly Journal
Visible Language
Woodcut (The)

Books
Adams, Marion, *The German Tradition: Aspects of Art and Culture in German-Speaking Countries*, Wiley, Chichester, 1971.
Annenberg, Maurice, *Type Foundries of America and their Catalogs*, Oak Knoll Press, Delaware, DE, 1994.
Anon. *Composition: Seven Shop Discussions*, The Boston Club of Printing House Craftsmen, Boston, MA, 1927.
Archer, Caroline, *The Kynoch Press*, British Library and Oak Knoll Press, London and Delaware, DE, 2000.
Avis, F. C., *Edward Philip Prince: Type Punchcutter*, Glenview Press, London, 1967.

Aynsley, Jeremy, *Graphic Design in Germany, 1890–1945*, Thames & Hudson, London and New York, 2000.

Barker, Nicolas, *Stanley Morison*, MacMillan, London, 1972.
Beckemeyer, Sylvia, *Object Lessons: Central Saint Martin's Art and Design Archive*, Lund Humphries, London, 1996.
Berra, Sandro, *A Story with Character: Ten Years of Tipoteca Italiana*, Tipoteca Italiana Antiga Edizioni, Treviso, 2006.
Berthold, Arthur B., *American Colonial Printing as Determined by Contemporary Cultural Forces*, Lennox Hill, New York, NY, 1967.
Bigelow, Charles (editor) *Fine Print on Type*, Bedford Arts, San Francisco, CA, 1989.
Blumenthal, Joseph, *The Printed Book in America*, The Scholar Press, London, 1977.
Boag, Andrew, 'Typographic Measurement: A Chronology', *Typography Papers*, 1, Department of Typography and Graphic Communication, University of Reading, 1996, p. 105.
Brooks, Chris, *The Gothic Revival*, Phaidon, Oxford, 1999.
Bos, Ben (ed.), *AGI: Graphic Design Since 1950*, Thames & Hudson, London and New York, 2007.
Burke, Christopher, *Active Literature: Jan Tschichold and New Typography*, Hyphen Press, London, 2008.
— *Gerard Unger: Life In Letters*, De Buitenkant, Uitgeverij, The Netherlands, 2021.
— *Paul Renner: The Art of Typography*, Hyphen Press, London, 1998.
Burlingham, Cynthia and Whiteman, Bruce, *The World From Here: Treasures of the Great Libraries of Los Angeles*, UCLA Grunwald, Center for the Graphic Arts, LA, 2001.

Carter, Harry, *A View of Early Typography up to About 1600*, Hyphen Press, London, 2002.
Carter, Sebastian, *Twentieth Century Type Designers*, Lund Humphries, London, 1987.
Cave, Roderick, *Fine Printing & Private Presses*, British Library, London, 2001.
— *The Private Press*, R.R. Bowker, Chatham, NI, 1983.
Chamaret, Sandra, Julien Gineste, Sébastien Morlighem, *Roger Excoffon at al Fonderie Olive*, Bibliothéque Typographique, Paris, 2010.
Chappell, Warren and Robert Bringhurst, *A Short History of the Printed Word*, Hartley & Marks (second edition), Vancouver, British Columbia, 1999.
Child, Heather and Justin Howes (eds.), *Lessons in Formal Writing*, Lund Humphries, London, 1986.
Clair, Colin, *A History of Printing in Britain*, Cassell & Company, London, 1965.
— *Christopher Plantin*, Cassell & Company, London, 1960.
Cockerell, S.C., *A Note by William Morris on His Aims in Founding the Kelmscott Press*, Kelmscott Press, London, 1898.
Connolly, Joseph, *Faber and Faber: Eighty Years of Book Cover Design*, Faber & Faber, London, 2009.
Consuegra, David, *American Type Design and Designers*, Allworth Press, New York, NY, 2004.

Cooper, Ozwald Bruce, *The Book of Oz*, Society of Typographic Arts, Chicago, IL, 1949.
Corrigan, A. J., *A Printer and his World*, Faber & Faber, London, 1945.
Cost, Patrica A., *The Bentons: How a Father and Son changed the Printing Industry*, Cary Graphics Arts Press, New York, 2011.

Day, Kenneth, *The Typography of Press Advertisements*, Ernest Benn, London and Tonbridge, 1956.
De Does, Bram, *Romanée en Trinité*, Aartswoud, Amsterdam, 1991.
De Vinne, Theodore Low, *The Practice of Typography: Title Pages*, The De Vinne Press, New York, NY, 1902.
— *The Printers' Price List: A Manual for the use of Clerks and Book-keepers in Job Printing Offices*, 1870.
— *The Practice of Typography: Correct Composition*, The New York Century Company, NY, 1902.
Deacon, Richard, *William Caxton*, Frederick Muller Ltd., London, 1976.
Dormer, Peter, *The Meanings of Modern Design*, Thames & Hudson, London and New York, 1990.
Dowding, Geoffrey, *An Introduction to the History of Printing Types*, British Library and Oak Knoll Press, London and Delaware, DE, 1998.
Dreyfuss, John, *Into Print*, British Library, London, 1994.
— *The Book as a Work of Art: The Cranach Press 1913 to 1931*, Triton Verlag, Vienna, 2005.
Dwiggins, William A., *Layout in Advertising* (revised edition, originally published 1928), Harper & Brothers, New York, NY, 1948.
Dyson, Anthony, *Pictures to Print, The Nineteenth-century Engraving Trade*, Farrand Press, London, 1984.
Duffy, Patrick, *The Skilled Compositor 1850–1914: An Aristocrat Among Working Men*, Ashgate, Farnham, 2000.

Eisenstein, Elizabeth L., *The Printing Revolution in Early Modern Europe*, Cambridge University Press (Canto Edition), 1993.
Erier, Johannes, *Hello I am Erik*, Gestalten, Berlin, 2014.
Evans, Eric J., *The Forging of the Modern State: Early Industrial Britain 1783–1870*, Longman Group, London, 1983.

Ferebee, Ann, *A History of Design from the Victorian Era to the Present Day*, Van Nostrand Reinhold, New York, NY, 1992.
Frayling, Christopher, *The Royal College of Art: One Hundred and Fifty Years of Art and Design*, Barrie & Jenkins, London, 1987.

Gehl, Paul F., *Chicago Modernism & the Ludlow Typograph: Douglas McMurtrie and Robert Hunter Middleton at Work*, Opifex, New South Wales, Australia, 2020.
Gill, Eric, *Autobiography*, Jonathan Cape, London, 1940.
Gorman, Paul, *The Story of The Face: The Magazine That Changed Culture*, Thames & Hudson, London and New York, 2017.
Goudy, Frederic W., *A Half Century of Type Design and Typography 1895–1945*, The Typophiles, New York, NY, 1946.
Gray, Nicolete, *Lettering on Buildings*, Architectural Press, London, 1960.
— *Nineteenth Century Ornamented Types and Title Pages*, Faber & Faber, London, 1938.
Gress, Edmund G., *The Art and Practice of Typography*, Oswald Publishing, New York, NY, 1917.
— *Fashions in American Typography, 1780 to 1930*, Harper & Brothers, New York, NY, 1931.

Haley, Allan, *Typographic Milestones*, Van Nostrand Reinhold, New York, NY, 1992.
Harling, Robert, *The letterforms and Type Designs of Eric Gill*, Eva Svensson, Kent, 1976.
Hartwell, R.M., *The Industrial Revolution and Economic Growth*, Methuen & Company, London, 1971.
Hefting, Paul, *PTT Art and Design*, Royal PTT Nederland, The Hague, 1990.
Hoffman, Phyllis, 'Matthew Carter: Reflects on Type Design', thesis, Rochester Institute of Technology, Rochester, NY, 1999.
Holiday, Peter, *Edward Johnston: Master Calligrapher*, British Library and Oak Knoll Press, London and Delaware, DE, 2007.
Hollis, Richard, *Swiss Graphic Design*, Laurence King, London, 2006.
Holtzberg-Call, Maggie, *The Lost World of the Craft Printer*, University of Illinois Press, Champaign, IL, 1992.
Hornung, Clarence P., *Will Bradley's Graphic Art*, Dover Publications, New York, NY, 2017.
Houghton, Thomas Shaw, *The Printer's Practical Every Day-Book*, Simpkin, Marshall & Company, London, 1841.
Howe, Ellic, *The Trade: Passages from the Literature of the Printing Craft, 1550–1935*, Printers' Pension Corporation, London, 1943.
Howes, Justin, *Johnston's Underground Type*, Capital Transport, London, 2000.
Hunter, Martin, *The Merrymount Press: An Exhibition on the Occasion of the 100th Anniversary of the Founding of the Press*, Harvard University Press, Cambridge, MA, 2005.
Hutt, Allen, *Fournier: The Compleat Typographer*, Rowman & Littlefield, Lanham, MD, 1972.

Isaac, Peter, and Barry McKay (eds), *The Mighty Engine: The Printing Press and its Impact*, Oak Knoll Press, Delaware, DE, 2000, p. 165.

Jacobi, Charles Thomas, *Some Notes on Books and Printing*, Charles Whittingham & Company, London, 1890.
Joyner, George, *Fine Printing: Its Inception, Development, and Practice*, Cooper & Budd, London, 1895.
Joachim, Leo H., *Production Yearbook*, Calton Press, New York, NY, 1948.
Jury, David (ed.), *TypoGraphic Writing*, International Society of Typographic Designers, London, 2001.
— *Graphic Design Before Graphic Designers; The Printer as Designer and Craftsman, 1700 to 1914*, Thames & Hudson, London and New York, 2012.
— *Reinventing Print: Technology and Craft in Typography*, Bloomsbury Publishing, London, 2018.
— *Mid-Century Type: Typography, Graphics, Designers*, Merrell Books, 2023.

Karolevitz, Robert F., *Newspapering in the Old West: A Pictorial History of Journalism and Printing on the Frontier*, Superior Publishing, Seattle, Washington, WA, 1965.
Kelly, Jerry, *100 Books Famous in Typography*, Grolier Club, New York, NY, 2021.
Kelly, Jerry and Beletsky, Misha, *The Noblest Roman: A history of the Centaur Types of Bruce Rogers*, David R. Godine, Boston, MA, 2016.
Kelly, Rob Roy, *American Wood Type: 1828–1900*, Van Nostrand Reinhold, New York, NY, 1969.
Kinneir, Jock, *Words and Buildings: The Art and Practice of Lettering*, Architectural Press, London, 1980.
Kinross, Robin, *Modern Typography*, Hyphen Press, London, 1992.
Knights, Charles C., *Print User's Year Book*, Print User's Year Book Ltd., London, 1934 and 1935.

Lambert, Julie Anne, *A Nation of Shopkeepers* (exhibition catalogue), Bodleian Library, Oxford, 2001.
Lambourne, Lionel, *The Aesthetic Movement*, Phaidon, London, 1996.
Larkin, H.W., *Compositor's Work in Printing*, Staples Printers, London, 1969.
Larson, Magali Sarfatti, *The Rise of Professionalism: A Social Analysis*, University of California Press, Berkeley, CA, 1979.
Last, Jay T., *The Color Explosion: Nineteenth Century Lithography*, Hillcrest Press, Santa Ana, CA, 2005.
Laver, James, *Victoriana*, Ward Lock & Company, London, 1966.
Lawson, Alexander, *The Compositor as Artist, Craftsman and Tradesman*, The Press of the Nightowl, Pittsburgh, PA, 1990.
Lewis, John, *Anatomy of Printing: The Influences of Art and History on its Design*, Faber & Faber, London, 1970.
— *Collecting Printed Ephemera*, Studio Vista, London, 1976.
— *Printed Ephemera*, Faber & Faber, London, 1969.
Lewis, John and Brinkley, John, *Graphic Design*, Routledge & Kegan Paul, London, 1954.
Loos, Adolf, *Ornament and Crime*, Ariadne Press, Riverside, CA, 1998.
Lommen, Matthieu, *Bram De Does*, Uitgeverij de Buitenkant, Amsterdam, 1999.
Loxley, Simon, *Emery Walker: Arts, Crafts, and a World in Motion*, Oak Knoll Press, Delaware, DE, 2019.
— *Printer's Devil: the life and work of Frederic Warde*, White Label, Woodbridge, 2010.
Lubelski, Charles, *Pride, Passion and Printing: The Life and Times of Percy Lund Humphries*, Croft Publications, Bradford, 2018.
Lucie-Smith, Edward, *The Story of Craft: The Craftsman's Role in Society*, Phaidon, Oxford, 1981.

MacCarthy, Fiona, *William Morris: a Life for Our Time*, Alfred A. Knopf, New York, NY, 1995.
MacGrew, Mac, *American Metal Typefaces of the Twentieth Century*, Oak Knoll Press, Delaware, DE, 1993.
McKitterick, David, *Stanley Morison & D. B. Updike: Selected Correspondence*, The Scholar Press, London, 1979.
McLean, Ruari, *Typographers on Type*, Lund Humphries, London, 1995.
— *Jan Tschichold: Typographer*, David R. Godine, Boston, MA, 1975.
McNeil, Paul, *A Visual History of Type*, Lawrence King, London, 2017.

Mardersteig, Giovanni, *The Officina Bodoni: an account of the work of the hand press 1923–77*, Officina Bodoni, Verona, 1980.
Marthens, John F., *Typographical Bibliography: A List of Books in the English Language on Printing and Its Accessories*, Bakewell & Marthens, Pittsburgh, PA, 1875.
Meggs, Philip B., *A History of Graphic Design*, Allen Lane, London, 1983.
Meynell, Francis, *My Lives*, The Bodley Head, London, 1971.
Meynell, Francis, and Herbert Simon, *Fleuron Anthology*, Ernest Benn, London and Tonbridge, 1973.
Middendorp, Jan, *Dutch Type*, 010 Publishers, Rotterdam, 2004.
Moran, James, *Printing Presses: History & Development from the 15th Century to Modern Times*, University of California Press, Berkeley, CA, 1978.
— *Stanley Morison: His Typographic Achievement*, Lund Humphries, London, 1971, p. 26.
Morison, Stanley, *A Tally of Types*, Cambridge University Press, Cambridge, 1973 (re-issued paperback edition 2011, with introduction by Mike Parker).
— *Printing the Times Since 1785*, Printing House Square, London, 1953.
— *Four Centuries of Fine Printing*, Ernest Benn, London and Tonbridge, 1924.
— *The Typographic Arts*, Sylvan Press, London, 1945.
Morris, May (ed.), *The Collected Works of William Morris*, vol. 15, Longmans, Green & Company, London, 1912.
Morris, William, *The Ideal Book; Essays and Lectures on the Arts of the Book*, University of California Press, Berkeley, CA, 1982.
Moxon, Joseph, *Mechanick Exercises*, The Typothetae of the City of New York, New York, NY, 1896.
Myers, Robin and Michael Harris (eds), *Spreading the Word: The Distribution Networks of Print 1550–1850*, St Paul's Biographies, Winchester, 1990.

Nathan, Paul, *Printing Business*, The Lotus Press, New York, NY, 1900.

Osterer, Heidrun, and Philipp Stamm, *Adrian Frutiger Typefaces: The Complete Works*, Birkhäuser, Basel, 2014.
Owen, L.T., *J.H. Mason, Scholar-Printer*, Frederick Muller Ltd., London, 1976.

Pepler, Hilary, *The Hand Press*, Ditchling, Ditchling Press, Sussex, 1952, p. 1.
Pizzitola, Louis, *Hearst Over Hollywood: Power, Passion, and Propaganda in the Movies*, Columbia University Press, New York, NY, 2013.
Poyner, Rick (ed.), *Typography Now Two*, Booth Clibborn Editions, London, 2002.

Raven, James, *Free Print and Non-Commercial Publishing since 1700*, Ashgate, Farnham, 2000.
Reed, David, *The Popular Magazine in Britain and the United States*, British Library, London, 1880–1960.
Rimmer, Jim, *Stern*, P22 Type Foundry, Buffalo, NY, 2008.
Rogers, Bruce, *The Centaur Types*, Purdue University Press, West Lafayette, IN, 1949.
Rogers, Bruce and James Hendrickson, *Paragraphs on Printing*, William

E. Rudge's Sons, Mount Vernon, NY, 1943.
Rosner, Charles, *Printer's Progress, 1851–1951*, Sylvan Press, London, 1951.

Schmoller, Hans, *Two Titans: Mardersteig and Tschichold*, The Typophiles, New York, NY, 1990.
Sennett, Richard, *The Craftsman*, Yale University Press, New Haven and London, 2008.
Sivulka, Juliann, *Soap, Sex, and Cigarettes: A Cultural History of Advertising in America*, Wadsworth Publishing Company, Belmont, CA, 1998.
Shipcott, Grant, *Typographical Periodicals between the Wars*, Oxford Polytechnic Press, Oxford, 1980.
Skingsley, T.A., 'Technical Training and Education in the English Printing Industry', *Journal of the Printing Historical Society* (printed in two parts), nos 13 and 14, 1978/79.
Silver, Rollo G., *Typefounding in America, 1787–1825*, University Press of Virginia, Charlottesville, VA, 1965.
Simon, Oliver, *Printer and Playground*, Faber & Faber, London, 1956.
Smeijers, Fred, *Type Now*, Hyphen Press, London, 2003.
Southall, Richard, *Printer's Type in the Twentieth Century. Manufacturing and Design Methods*, British Library and Oak Knoll Press, London and Delaware, DE, 2005.
Stauffacher, Jack, and Hermann Zapf, *Hunt Roman: The Birth of a Type*, Pittsburgh Bibliophiles, Pittsburgh, PA, 1965.
Steinberg, S.H., *Five Hundred Years of Printing* (new edition, revised by John Trevitt), British Library and Oak Knoll Press, London and Delaware, DE, 1996.

Tames, Richard, *The Printing Press: Turning Points in History*, Heinemann Library, Portsmouth, NH, 2001.
Thomas, Isiah, *History of Printing in America*, Gramercy, Bexley, OH, 1988.
Tracy, Walter, *Letters of Credit*, Gordon Fraser, Cambridge, 1986.
— *The Typographic Scene*, Gordon Fraser, Cambridge, 1988.
Tschichold, Jan, *The New Typography* (originally published 1928), University of California Press, Berkeley, CA, 1998.
Turner, E.S., *The Shocking History of Advertising*, Penguin Books, Harmondsworth, 1952.
Twyman, Michael, *Printing 1770–1970*, British Library, Oak Knoll Press & Reading University, 1998.

Updike, D. B., *Printing Types: Their History, Forms and Use*, 2 vols, Oxford University Press, Oxford, 1937 (second edition).

Volkov, Shulamit, *The Rise of Antimodernism in Germany: The Urban Master Artisans, 1873–1896*, Princeton University Press, Princeton NJ, 1978.

Wallis, Lawrence, *George W. Jones: Printer Laureate*, The Plough Press, Oxford, 2004.
— *Typomania, Selected Essays on Typesetting and Related Subjects*, Severnside Printers, Upton-upon-Severn, 1993.
Warde, Beatrice, *The Pencil Draws a Vicious Circle*, Sylvan Press, London, 1955.
Webb, Brian and Skipworth, Peyton, *Harold Curwen and Oliver Simon*, Antique Collectors' Club, Woodbridge, undated.
Weedon, Alexis, *Victorian Publishing*, Routledge, London, 2016.
Wlassikoff, Michel, *The Story of Graphic Design in France*, Gingko Press, Richmond, CA, 2005.
Wozencroft, Jon, *The Graphic Language of Neville Brody*, Thames & Hudson, London and New York, 1994.

Websites: typographers, designers, writers

Devroye, Luc, *Type Design, Typography, Typefaces and Fonts*: https://luc.devroye.org/fonts
Frere-Jones, Tobias, *Designing*: https://frerejones.com/blog
Heller, Steven, *The Daily Heller*: https://www.printmag.com/categories/daily-heller/
Lawson, Alexandre S., *The Composing Room*: https://alexanderslawsonarchive.com/bibliography/articles/composing-room
Majoor, Martin, *Majoor's Type Blog*: https://www.martin majoor.com/o_my_type_blog.html
Mosley, James, *Typefoundry*: https://typefoundry.blogspot.com/
Shaw, Paul, *Blue Pencil*: https://www.paulshawletterdesign.com/category/blue-pencil/
Reynolds, Dan, *Typeoff*: https://www.typeoff.de/
Tankard, Jeremy, *Studiotype*: https://studiotype.com/

Websites: general

Eye, London, UK. Print and online magazine about graphic design, typography and visual culture, published since 1990, with an archive of online articles: https://www.eyemagazine.com/
Lamont, Matt, *Design Reviewed*, Bradford, UK. A substantial digital collection of printed matter from the twentieth century, specializing in design magazines with a searchable online database: https://designreviewed.com/
Letterform Archive, San Francisco, US. A museum and archive dedicated to collecting materials relating to lettering, typography, printing and graphic design, with a searchable online database: https://letterformarchive.org/
MacMillan, David M., Wisconsin, US. *Circuitous Root: Studies in Antiquarian Technology and Other Matters*. Explores machines, tools and processes by which type was made before the digital era: https://circuitousroot.com/
St Bride Foundation, London, UK. Home to the world's largest print and publishing library, with a searchable online catalogue and digital collections: https://sbf.org.uk/

Picture Credits

Unless credited below, images are from the author's collection and the St Bride Library.

Allard Pierson Collection, University of Amsterdam: 285
Courtesy of Michael J. Babcock Jr: 53
Bodleian Library, MS. Laud Misc. 237, fol. 244r (above); Bodleian Library, MS. Canon. Misc. 378, fol 3v (below): 12
Bodleian Library, Kelmscott Press b.1: 32-33
Bodleian Library, 256 c.24: 42
Bodleian Library, Rec. d.538: 60
Bodleian Library, Rec. d.538: 64
Bodleian Library, Arch. C c.3 (v.1), p. 27: 75
Bodleian Library, 28854 d.3, pp 88-9: 79
Bodleian Library, Broxb. 51.10, v.1, pp 16-17: 82
Bodleian Library, M. adds 65 c.1, pp 4-5: 86
Bodleian Library, Arch. C c. 39, title page: 144
Bodleian Library, Chadwyck-Healey c.598, no 61-66, foldout facing p. 40: 209
Bodleian Library, OUP Type Specimens 282: 262
Bodleian Library, Ryder 798, p. 76: 268
Courtesy of Margaret Calvert: 292 – 301
Hugh Collier: 158, 163
Courtesy of Émigré Fonts: 356-63
Courtesy of Fontstand: 6
Courtesy of Tobias Frere-Jones: 374
Letterform Archive: 8, 62, 108, 116, 138, 216, 232, 238, 256, 260, 270
Courtesy of Lundgren +Lindqvist AB: 302-3

Martin Mahoor: 348-54
Newberry Library, Chicago: 190, 193, 194, 197
Courtesy of The Old School Press: 269
Riccardo Olocco: 10
Oxford University Press Archives: 36-37, 39, 40, 92-3, 242-3
Courtesy of Erik Spiekermann: 324-31
Courtesy of Jeremy Tankard: 364-73
Coll. Gerard Unger Archive, Allard Pierson, University of Amsterdam; taken from the book by Christopher Burke, *Gerard Unger: life in letters* (Amsterdam: Uitgeverij de Buitenkant, 2021): 316
Photo: Chris Vermaas: 318
Wikimedia Commons, https://commons.wikimedia.org/wiki/File:De_Aetna_1495.jpg: 9
Wikimedia Commons, https://en.wikipedia.org/wiki/File:A_Specimen_by_William_Caslon.jpg : 18
Wikimedia Commons, https://en.wikipedia.org/wiki/File:Granby_font_sample.jpg: 90
Wikimedia Commons, https://commons.wikimedia.org/wiki/File:James_Pryde,_cover_for_The_Poster,_February_1899.jpg : 128
Wikimedia Commons, https://commons.wikimedia.org/wiki/File:Sample_UK_Childs_Ration_Book_WW2.jpg : 147
Wolpe Archive, photographed by Prof. Phil Cleaver: 226–31

Acknowledgements

I am indebted to those who have provided photographs, comments and corrections in the making of this book: principally, Michael J. Babcock Jr., Margaret Calvert, Oliver Clark, James Clough, Hugh Collier, Phil Cleaver, Richard Doust, Tobias Frere-Jones, Nick Gill, Allan Haley, Steven Heller, Will Hill, Zuzana Licko, Simon Loxley, Martin Majoor, Riccardo Olocco, Martyn Ould, Andrew Schuller, Paul Shaw, Erik Spiekermann, Jeremy Tankard, Rudy VanderLans and Chris Wakeling.

I am also indebted to Martin Maw at the Oxford University Press Archive, Sandro Berra at Tipoteca Italiana, Cornuda, and especially the staff at St Bride Print Library, London.

I have collected and correlated the research and writing of so many type designers and historians (recorded in the bibliography), but none more than Sebastian Carter, whose book *Twentieth Century Type Designers* was included in *One Hundred Books Famous in Typography*, published by the Grolier Club in 2021.

Finally, I want to thank colleagues at the Bodleian, Samuel Fanous, Susie Foster, Janet Phillips, Leanda Shrimpton and Dot Little, and copy-editor Miranda Harrison.

Index

(Typefaces listed separately)

Adobe 255, 330, 344-7
Adobe Originals 306-7, 344-7, 368-9
advertising 24-5
Albion Press 28, 30, 173
Almeida, José Mendoza y 234, 239-41
American Institute of Graphic Arts 24
American Type Founders Company 21, 44, 47-8, 53-5, 63, 98, 100-107, 110, 129-30, 136, 161, 184, 191, 196
Apollinaire, Guillaume 217
Apple Corp. 23, 171, 307
Arden Press 34
Arena [magazine] 336-7
Arrighi, Ludovico degli 64-5
Art Deco 208
Arts and Crafts Exhibition Society 30, 69, 88-9
Arts and Crafts movement 41, 51, 77, 83, 142
Arts et Métiers Graphiques 210-211
Ashendene Press 34, 71-72
ATypI (Association Typographique Internationale) 235, 251, 350
Austin, Richard 95, 104
automation [of printing] 27-35

Ballantyne Press 76, 161
Barnhart Brothers & Spindler Foundry 56, 103, 129-31
Baskerville, John 13, 362
Bauer type foundry 121-5, 210, 227, 254
Bauhaus 44, 113-14, 119-23, 183-4, 207, 209, 216-21, 277, 349
Bayer, Herbert 114, 122, 219
Benton, Linn Boyd 47-8, 100-102
Benton, Morris Fuller 47-8, 100-107, 139, 161, 196, 240
Berthold [type foundry] 200, 253, 287, 295, 327
Bertsch, Fred 127-9 261
Bézier 250-51
Biddulph, Nicholas 365
Bigelow, Charles 343
Bill, Max 253, 273, 277
Birdsall, Derek 365
Bitstream Inc. 307, 313, 315, 350
blackletter 10, 77, 80, 87-8, 109-13, 118, 120, 169, 200, 203, 215, 225, 229, 264, 372-3
Bloemsma, Evert 349
Blokland, Frank 322-3
Bodoni, Giambattista 13-15, 16, 39, 64, 66, 105, 131, 184, 361
Bowden, William 31
Bowles, J. M. 51
Bradley, William 34, 43, 45, 127, 136, 160
Brattinga, Pieter 280, 319
Bridges, Robert 64
Brodovitch, Alexey 208
Brody, Neville 306, 329, 333-41, 357, 375-6
Brothers Beggarstaff 128-30
Bullen, Henry Lewis 63-4, 105
Butti, Alessandro 257-60, 267

Calvert, Margaret 293-301, 365
Cambridge University Press 57, 162, 163
Carson, David 359
Carter, Harry 286, 288, 309-10
Carter, Matthew 7, 230, 308-15, 355, 376-7
Caslon, William I 14, 20
Caslon, William IV 17, 20
Cassandre, A.M. 207-13, 277
casting [type] 10, 18, 31, 38-9, 48, 58, 61, 94-5, 101, 131, 184, 192, 204, 240, 244-5, 269, 312
Caxton, William 28-9, 31
Century Guild Hobby Horse, The 29-30
Century Magazine, The 104
Chermayeff, Ivan 107
Chiswick Press 29-30
Cleland, Thomas Maitland 134
Cleverdon, Douglas 146
Cloister Press 161-2
Cobden-Sanderson, T. J. 34, 72-77, 85-8, 142
Cockerell, Sidney 57, 69, 71
Colonial [USA] printing 20
Columbian Press 28
Continental Type Founders Association 49, 194, 208
Cooper, Oswald 127-31, 133, 195, 310
Cranach Press 74, 78, 80, 87-8, 160, 183
Crane, Walter 34, 123
Crouwel, Wim 274, 277-83, 317-18, 353-4
Curwen, Harold 89, 151-7

De Aetna 10, 187
De Praeparatio Evangelica 10
De Vinne, Theodore Low 103-6, 240
De Zilverdistel Press 74, 173-4
Deberny & Peignot [type foundry] 208-13, 233-5, 253, 271-3, 310-11
Design & Industries Association 90, 142
Detterer, Ernst F. 191-2
Didot, Firmin 13, 21, 104, 139, 169
Die Neue Typographie 217-18, 222
digital 23, 250-51, 255, 261, 268, 279-81, 290-91, 301, 303-7, 313-15, 319-23, 329-30, 336-40, 343-7, 349-50, 360-67, 375-8, 349, 350-51, 365-73
Dijck, Christoffel van 178
Display types 15, 220, 229, 236, 245, 249, 259-60, 265-8, 314, 337, 346, 351, 362, 370, 373, 375
Does, Bram de 285-91, 309
Dorfsman, Lou 310
Doust, Richard 366-7
Doves Press 72-7, 85-8, 118, 142, 146
Dreyfus, John 78, 180, 188-189
Drost, Henk 288, 318
dry-transfer ['rub-down'] lettering 261, 282, 296, 329
Dutch Type Library 24, 322-323
Dwiggins, William A 34, 45, 127, 133-9, 166, 195, 310, 373

Emigre 306, 337, 358-63
Estienne, Robert 13
Excoffon, Roger 213, 232-41, 311-12

Faber & Faber [publishers] 230-231
Face, The [magazine] 334-7, 339
Fanfare Press 65, 228
Fann Street Foundry 16, 31
Fella, Edward 359
Figgins, Vincent 17, 257
Fleischman, Joan Michael 20, 174
Fleuron, The 81, 113, 137, 156, 163-6, 178-9, 185
Fonderie Olive [foundry] 25, 203, 233-41, 272
Fontographer 306, 322, 337, 361
FontShop 307, 329-30, 339-40, 350, 367
Fournier, Pierre-Simon 13, 14, 20, 95, 105

Frutiger, Adrian 247-8, 254, 271-5, 311, 323, 346
FUSE 306, 333, 340, 376

Gage, Harry L 135-6
Gage-Cole, Harry 76-7
Garnett, Blake 17
Garnett, Porter 178
German Werkbund 117-18
Gibbings, Robert 144-5
Gill, Eric 83-5, 98, 109, 141-9, 151, 160, 164-6, 180, 295-6, 379
Golden Cockerel Press 34, 142-6, 149
Goudy, Frederic 10, 22, 34, 42-9, 97-8, 127, 130, 133-4, 192-3, 195, 310
Grabhorn Press 178
Granjon, Robert 14, 224, 312
gravure 30, 244, 265
Gray, Nicolette 365
Gregory, Eric (Peter) 223
Griffith, Chauncey H. 137-9, 167, 313-14, 322
Griffo, Francesco 10-14, 187, 260
Gutenberg, Johannes 10, 30, 38, 159, 175

Haas [foundry] 241, 253-5, 261, 273
Hague & Gill 148-9
Hammer, Victor 263
Harling, Robert 223
Hartz, Sem 177, 181, 287, 318
Hell, Rudolf 149, 250, 268, 280, 319-23
Hewitt, Graily 76, 83, 87, 90
Hoefler, Jonathan 377-9
Hoffmann, Eduard 253-5, 258, 273-4
Holme, Frank 44, 127, 133
Holmes, Kris 343-4
Hornby, St John 34, 71
Houghton, Mifflin & Company 51-2, 54
humanism 11-12, 117, 57, 136, 254, 328, 370, 416
Humphries, Eric 162-3

Ideal Book or Book Beautiful, The 85, 87
Ikarus [system] 250-51, 290, 321, 328, 349
Imprint, The 88-90, 159-60, 173-4
Ingham, Ernest 65, 228
Insel Verlag 77, 87, 109, 123, 143, 151, 159, 215
Inland Printer, The 101, 127

Jacno, Marcel 237-8
Jacobi, Charles T. 29, 160
Javal, Louis Émile 105-6, 240
Jenson, Nicolas 10, 13-14, 16, 31, 47, 51, 56-7, 71, 74
jobbing printing 16-17, 19, 24, 28, 80, 99, 152, 160, 211, 218, 229, 236, 259, 271, 285
Jobs, Steve 304, 306
Joh. Enschedé [Foundry] 20, 66, 103, 118, 174-81, 285-91, 309-10, 312, 318
Johnston, Edward 76-80, 82-91, 109, 114, 263, 141-7, 151, 191, 295, 297, 371

Keedy, Jeffery 359
Keller, Ernst 253, 273
Kelmscott Press 13, 28-35, 51, 57, 69-72, 76, 84
Kessler, Count Harry 77-81, 87-8, 91, 143, 159, 165
Kindersley, David 296-7, 379
Kinneir, Richard 'Jock' 293 -301
Kitching, Alan 365-6
Klingspor foundry 110-15, 122, 203, 227
Knopf, Alfred A. 135
Knuth, Donald 343

413

Koch, Paul 40, 227, 263
Koch, Rudolf, 34, 108–115, 146, 151, 195, 227–8, 263
Krimpen, Jan van 98, 166, 173–81, 286–7, 235–6, 286–7, 309, 317, 320, 350
Kubel, Henrik 301
Kynoch Press 161–2

Lardent, Victor 168–9, 255
Layout in Advertising 135–6
Le Bé [foundry] 20
Lethaby, W.R. 83–4, 90
lettercutting 38–9
Lettergieterij [foundry] 173, 203, 220
Lewis, Walter 57, 161–3
Licko, Zuzana 306, 337, 356–63
Limited Editions Club 113, 134, 135, 149, 156, 181, 188
Linofilm 247, 311
Linotype 22, 38, 58, 94–9, 135–9, 171, 205, 230, 311–15, 323, 339
Lissitzky, El 217
Lubalin, Herb 310
Ludlow Typograph 38, 99, 106, 191–7, 247
Lumitype Photon 246–8, 250, 271–3, 310–11
Lund Humphries [publishers] 161–3, 223

Macintosh, Apple 171, 251, 304–6, 313, 337, 350, 357–60, 366
Mackellar, Smiths & Jordan 21, 102
MacLean, Ruari 76, 223
McMurtrie, Douglas 192–5
Macy, George 113, 135, 149, 181
Majoor, Martin 149, 346, 349–55, 377
Malin, Charles 41, 164–6, 178–89
Mallmarmé, Stéphane 217
Mallon, Jean 211–13
Manutius, Aldus 10–14, 187, 260, 266
Mardersteig, Hans 66–7, 180, 183–9, 310
Martin, William 137–9
Mason, John H. 76–7, 83, 88, 90, 159–61
measurement [of type] 20–22, 388
Meier, Hans Eduard 328
Merrymount Press 52, 74, 133–4, 161, 178
Meynell, Francis 76, 81, 152, 223, 228, 223, 228, 309
Meynell, Gerard 88–9, 152–3, 159–63, 165
Microsoft 171
Middleton, Robert H. 191–7
Miedinger, Max 253–55, 258, 273
Mifflin, George H. 51–4
Miller & Richard [foundry] 76, 95, 120, 138
Modernism 90, 115, 194, 209, 213, 220–1, 277, 282–3, 283–5, 315, 339, 349, 351, 355, 360–61
Monotype Corporation 14–15, 22–4, 38, 49, 88, 95–9, 144–5, 159, 162–71, 178–81, 184–9, 228–30, 287, 307, 310
Monotype Drawing Office 67, 87–88, 98, 144–149, 165, 180–181, 286–287
Monotype Recorder, The 162, 228
Monotype typesetter 57–8, 61–6, 81, 94–9, 137, 192–3, 224, 247, 249, 260, 271, 273–4, 29 305, 307
Moran, James 168
Morisawa [foundry] 343–4
Morison, Stanley 14–15, 27–35, 38, 57, 63–6, 137–8, 144–8, 152, 156, 159–71, 177, 179–81, 184–9, 193, 223, 228, 230, 235, 255, 296, 309, 322, 363
Morris, William 13–14, 27–35, 43–7, 51, 56, 69–76, 81, 83, 109–10, 117, 127, 134, 142, 145, 151, 161, 173, 215
Müller-Brockmann, Josef 253, 277
Multiple Master 346–7, 369–70
Museum of Modern Art (MoMA) NY 211
Museum Press 54

Nebiolo [foundry] 25, 238, 257–61
New Traditionalism 223, 255
New Typography 194, 199–200, 209, 216–18, 221–2, 273
Newdigate, Bernard 34, 152, 160
Noordzij, Peter Matthias 290–91
Noverese, Aldo 257–61

Officina Bodoni 66, 184–9, 310
Olive, Marcel 233–41, 272
Oxford University Press 309, 320

Pannartz, Arnold 71–2, 88
pantograph 19, 39, 41, 48–9, 95–7, 101, 164, 177, 239
Parker, Mike 307, 311–15
Peignot, Charles 209–13, 234–8, 246, 271–3, 310–11
Pelican Press 152, 160–61
Penguin Books 215, 223–4
Penrose Annual 162–3, 223, 225, 245
Pepler, Hilary 143–4
Perry, Mike 366
Phinney, Joseph W. 53, 102, 106
phototypesetting 22, 38, 221–2, 235, 244–51, 260–61, 273, 287–9, 304–5, 310–11, 319, 327, 343
Pick, Frank 89–91, 153–4, 156, 159
Pickering, Charles 91
Pierpont, Frank H. 88, 146, 164, 168–9
Pleiade Press 181
Plumet, Charles 65
Pöschel & Trepte [printers] 215, 217
Postmodernism 283, 339
PostScript 23, 251, 255, 291, 305, 313, 337, 344
Prang, Louis 51
Prince, Edward 31, 41, 72, 74, 78, 80, 88
Princeton University Press 63–4
Print Revivalism 35, 46, 153, 162, 177–8, 296
Printer's Grammar 20
Printing Types: Their History, Forms and Use 15–16, 162
punchcutting 40–41, 70, 74, 76, 88, 95–6, 103–4, 164–6, 177, 178–89, 202, 264, 269, 309–10, 349

Quay, David 283, 300

Rädisch, Paul H. 41, 103, 176–7, 180
Reid, Jamie 333
Renner, Paul 114, 117–25, 136, 146, 199–202, 217, 221
Riverside Press [Cambridge, Mass.] 51–4
Riverside Press [Chicago] 193
Rodchenko, Alexander 208–9, 217, 335
Rogers, Bruce 34, 41, 47, 50–59, 61–7, 81, 89, 98, 160–61, 180, 191–2
Rollins, Carl 57
Roos, Sjoerd Hendrik de 173–4
Rosenberger, August 264–6
Rubeus, Jacobus 74
Ruder, Emil 274, 277
Rudge, William Edwin 58, 61–3
Ruskin, John 151

Sack, Freda 283, 300
St Dominic's Press 143–4
Schelter & Giesecke [foundry] 220
Schneidler, F.H. Ernst 199, 202
Schwartz, Christian 330–31
Simon, Herbert 161
Simon, Oliver 81, 156–7, 161–3, 223
Simons, Anna 83, 123, 173
Slimbach, Robert 307, 344–6, 346–7, 369
Smeijer, Fred 349
Smith, John 20
Specimen of Printing Types [Figgins] 16–17
Spiekermann, Erik 255, 325–31, 339–40, 350, 375
Stanhope [press] 27

Steltzer, Fritz 88, 146, 163–4, 168–9
Stempel type foundry 111, 122, 125, 203–5, 255, 261, 264–7, 269, 328
Stephenson Blake 19, 22, 27, 90–91
Stone, Reynolds 230, 296, 306–7, 313, 344–5, 379
Sweynheym, Konrad 71
Swiss (International) Style 253, 255, 273–5, 277

Tankard, Jeremy 364–73
Times, The 27, 89, 94, 159, 166–71, 180, 231, 296, 321, 341
Thompson, Bradbury 368
Thompson, J. Walter 24, 45
Thorne, Robert 17
Thorowgood, William 17
Tiemann, Walter 215
Tiffin, Percy 72, 74, 80
Torresani, Andrea 10
Tracy, Walter 149, 168–9, 235
Trajan [stone column] 91, 153, 155, 258, 345
Trump, Georg 198–205, 222
Tschichold, Jan 194, 199–200, 214–25, 235, 245
Tuscan [type style] 17
Twombly, Carol 307, 342–7, 369–70
Typographische Mitteilungen 194, 217

U&lc [magazine] 313
Uhertype 220–22, 245, 246–7
Unger, Gerard 250, 278, 282, 316–23, 343, 353
Updike, Daniel B. 15, 46, 51, 97, 133–4, 161–3, 178
Urbi & Orbi [design studio] 241, 311

VanderLans, Rudy 337, 357–63
Vignelli, Massimo 363
Village Press 22, 44–5, 48, 133
Vox, Maximilien 210, 234

Walker, Emery 30–35, 44, 56–7, 69–81, 83–8, 142–3, 165

Warde, Beatrice 61–5, 105, 166, 179, 333
Warde, Frederic 58, 60–67, 185–7
Weber [foundry] 200–205
Wells, Darius 19
Whittingham, Charles 29
Wiebking, Robert 45, 56–7, 191, 195
Writing & Illuminating & Lettering 83–4, 91, 109, 123, 143, 173, 263, 370
Wolpe, Berthold 227–31, 263–4
Wood [type] 18

Zapf, Hermann 7, 204–5, 236, 250, 263–9, 319, 321, 323, 343
Zwart, Piet 199, 217

Typefaces
*Illustrated

Akzidenz Grotesk 106*, 253–4, 274, 279, 295, 299
Albertus 227*–31*
Alchemy 372*
Aldus 265–6*
Alisal 315
Antique Olive 240*
Arbiter 261*
Argo 322
Armada 375*
Arrighi (original) 62*
Arrighi 60*, 64*, 65–7, 187
Augustea 258
Auriga 312

Balance 349
Banco 235*–6, 259
Barbou 249
Base 900 359*
Baskerville 14, 269, 362
Bell Centennial 312*–14
Bembo 10, 14*, 184
Bifur 207*–11
Big Caslon 315
Bliss 367*, 370–71
Blue Island 368*–9
Blur 336*
Bodoni 15*, 184, 361–2
Brunel 300
Bulmer 137, 139*

Caledonia 137, 138*–9
Calvert, 293*, 299–300
Calypso 239*, 240
Cascade 312
Caslon 14, 18*, 20, 43, 45, 52, 104–5, 144–6, 151, 162, 164, 248, 345
(Adobe) Caslon 307, 345*
Catalogue 281*, 283
Centaur 50, 54*–7, 66–7, 191
Century 103–7
Century Broad Face 103*
Century Expanded 103*, 105
Century Oldstyle 104*
Century Schoolbook 105*–6
Chadwick 340–41*
Chambord 213, 234*–6, 259
Chaparral 347*
Charlemagne 342*, 345
Chaucer 31–4*, 74
Cheltenham 105
Choc 232*, 237
City 198*–9, 222
Clearface 104*
Comenius 269
Cooper Black 126*, 128–31
Cooper Fullface 131*
Cranach Italic 79*, 87
Cranach Jenson 78–80*
Curwen Sans Serif 153*–5
CyberFuse 338*, 339
Cyclone 229

DB Type 331*
Dante 10, 182*, 188–9
Decorata 231
Delphin 203
Demos 250, 319*–21
DIN 294–5
Disturbance 364–6*
Dolores 375

Dome 340, 375
Doves Type 10, 53, 72–5*, 77*

Edison 250
Eldorado 139*
Electra 132*, 136–7, 166, 312
Elephant 315
Emigre 358*
Emperor 358*
Enigma 372–3*
Erbar 154, 218
Eurostile 256*, 257
Eusebius 191*–2

FHWA Series 294, 376–7
Fibonacci 376
Filosofia 361–3*
Folio 254, 273–4
Fontana 187*–8
Fortune 254
Forum 201*–3
Fournier 14
Franklin Gothic 107*, 195
Franklin Gothic no. 2 107*
Frutiger 274–5*, 346
Futura 105, 114, 120–25*, 136, 146, 154–5, 195–6, 200, 210, 220, 253, 257, 273, 275, 319, 210, 273

Galliard 311*–13
Garage Gothic 376
Garaldus 260–61*
Garamond 10, 14, 161, 224, 385*
Gilgengart 264*
Gill Sans 140*, 142*, 146–7, 148, 153*, 154, 221, 298–9, 370, 377
Globe Gothic 106*–7
Golden 29*, 31, 51, 74
Golden Cockerel Type 144*, 145–6
Gotham 378*–9
Gothic 375
Goudy Oldstyle 10, 20*, 22
Granby 90*, 91
Granjon 14
Gridnik 283
Griffo 185*, 187
Gulliver 323*

Haarlehammer 179
Hamlet Type 88–9
Harlem 339*, 375
Helvetica (see Neue Haas Grotesk)
Hollander 321*–2,
Hollandsche Mediaeval 174
Horseferry 340–41*
Hunt Roman 269*
Hyperion 227*

Imprint 87*
Industria 336*
Ingenieur 283*
Insignia 334*
Ionic 167*

Jacno 237–8
Janson 266–7*
Jenson 8*, 10*–14, 16, 30, 47, 51, 56–57, 74
Jessen 112*, 227

Kabel 108*, 114*, 218,

Lexicon 290–91*
Lithos 345

Ludlow Black 195
Lutetia 10, 175*–7

M.O.L. 318*
Mallory 379*
Mantinia 314*–15
Marconi 250, 269*
Markeur 318*
Maximilian 110*, 112
Melior 266–7*
Meta 326*–9
Metro 136
Microgramma (see Eurostile)
Microphone 376
Miller 315
Mirarae 343*–4
Mistral 233*, 236, 259
Mixage 261
Montaigne 41, 54, 56
Mrs Eaves 356*, 361–2
Myriad 345–6*

Neuland 112*
Neue Haas Grotesk 254–5, 299, 255*, 258, 273–5, 299, 327–9, 336, 351, 363, 377
New Alphabet 277*, 280*–3, 318
News Gothic 196, 377
Nexus 351*–2
Nobel 376
Nord 240*
Normal Grotesk 253–4*
Novarese 261*
Nuava 346–7*

Oakland 358*
Officina 328*
Ondine 272*
Optima 267*

Palatino 205, 263*, 265–6
Palomba 202
Panture 318
Pegasus 229*
Peignot 25*, 213
Perpetua 146, 159*, 164, 165*–6, 168
Phoebus 272
Plantin, 168*–9
Pop 339*
Praxis 250, 317*, 319*–321
Président 272
Prisma 115*

Quadraat 355

Rail Alphabet 298, 299*–300
Reactor 376
Record Gothic 196–7*
Recta 258
Redisturbed 365*
Ritmo 238, 258*
Riverside Caslon 51, 53*
Romanée 177*, 178–9, 285–9
Romulus 166, 176, 178*, 350

Sabon 224–5*, 249
Sachsenwald 229*
Saphir 266*
Saskia 219*
Satanick 110
Scala 346, 349*–52
Schadow 200*, 201–2
Scotch Roman 137–9
Semplicità 257*

Shaker 373*
Shelley 312
Shire Types 370*–72
Signum 202
Snell Roundhand 311*
Sophia 315*
Spartan 196
Spectrum 173*, 178–80
Stedelijk 283
Stellar 196
Stop 259–60*
Subiaco 71*–2
Swift 322*
Symbol 261
Syntax 328

Taylor Gothic 107
Telefont 352*, 353*–5
Tempest 228*
Tempo 195*, 196
Times Modern 340*–41
Times New Roman 10, 166–8*, 169–71, 219, 255, 322–3
Tokyo 340, 375
Trajan 344*, 345
Transito 218*, 220
Transport 294*, 295–6*
Trinité 288*, 289–90, 352
Troy 30*, 31, 74
Trump Deutsch 200*
Trump Mediaeval 202–4*, 205*
Typeface Four 375
Tyson 339*, 375

Ultra-Modern 193*, 195
Underground Alphabet 89–91*, 115, 231, 295
Unit 329*–30
Univers 241, 247, 254–5, 258, 260, 270*, 271–3*–5, 278*, 319, 328, 351
Universal [Bayer] 114, 219, 122*
Universal [Licko] 358*
Universal [Tschichold] 216*, 219

Van Dijck 178–9
Vendôme 203
Vicenza 65*–6
Vierkant 281*, 283
Virtuosa 266*
Viva 347*

Walker 315*
World 340

Zilvertype 174
Zeno 186*, 187
Zeus 219*–20

415

This book is dedicated to Rita, Rachael and Ben.

First published in 2025 by Bodleian Library Publishing,
Broad Street, Oxford OX1 3BG
www.bodleianshop.co.uk

ISBN: 978 1 85124 581 9

Text © David Jury, 2025

This edition © Bodleian Library Publishing,
University of Oxford, 2025

David Jury has asserted his right to be identified
as the author of this Work.

All rights reserved.

No part of this book may be reproduced, stored in a retrieval
system, or transmitted in any form or by any means, electronic,
mechanical, photocopying, recording, or otherwise, without
the written permission of the Bodleian Library, except for the
purpose of research or private study, or criticism or review.

Publisher: Samuel Fanous
Managing Editor: Susie Foster
Picture Editor: Leanda Shrimpton
Design: David Jury
Typesetting and production design: Dot Little
Text and headings set in Enigma, captions set in Shaker,
both designed by Jeremy Tankard.
Title and major headings set in Eurostile, designed by Aldo Novarese.
Printed and bound in China by C&C Offset Printing Co., Ltd. on 157gsm Chinese
Golden Sun Matt Art paper

British Library Catalogue in Publishing Data
A CIP record of this publication is available from
the British Library